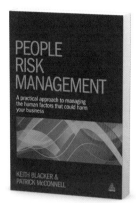

People Risk Management

A practical approach to managing the human factors that could harm your business

Keith Blacker and
Patrick McConnell

KoganPage

LONDON PHILADELPHIA NEW DELHI

First published in Great Britain and the United States in 2015 by Kogan Page Limited

2nd Floor, 45 Gee Street	1518 Walnut Street, Suite 1100	4737/23 Ansari Road
London EC1V 3RS	Philadelphia PA 19102	Daryaganj
United Kingdom	USA	New Delhi 110002
www.koganpage.com		India

© Keith Blacker and Patrick McConnell, 2015

The right of Keith Blacker and Patrick McConnell to be identified as the authors of this work has been asserted by them in accordance with the Copyright, Designs and Patents Act 1988.

ISBN   978 0 7494 7135 4
E-ISBN 978 0 7494 7136 1

British Library Cataloguing-in-Publication Data

A CIP record for this book is available from the British Library.

Library of Congress Cataloging-in-Publication Data

Blacker, Keith.
  People risk management : a practical approach to managing the human factors that could harm your business / Keith Blacker, Patrick McConnell. – 1st Edition.
    pages cm
  ISBN 978-0-7494-7135-4 (paperback) – ISBN 978-0-7494-7136-1 (ebk)   1. Personnel management.   2. Risk management.   3. Leadership.   I. McConnell, Patrick (Patrick J.)   II. Title.
  HF5549.B567 2015
  658.3–dc23

                                                                                                  2015000916

Typeset by Graphicraft Limited, Hong Kong
Print production managed by Jellyfish
Printed and bound by CPI Group (UK) Ltd, Croydon, CR0 4YY

CONTENTS

Best wishes Dom
Kilt
9/10/15,

FIGURES AND TABLES LIST

Thanks to Susan and Sue

People Risk in context

Men willingly believe what they wish. **ATTRIBUTED TO JULIUS CAESAR**

This book looks at why people, in particular business managers, sometimes make very bad decisions especially, as behavioural psychologists have found, decisions that involve taking risk. This chapter provides a brief introduction to the concepts covered in the book, its contents and its structure. It introduces the concept of People Risk, or the risk that people will sometimes make bad, even disastrous, decisions.

1.1 A quiet revolution in decision-making

The past 30 years has seen a *quiet revolution* in our understanding of how people make decisions and particularly those that involve taking risk. Far from being the cool, coherent, cerebral process described in management textbooks, psychologists and neuroscientists have shown, through novel experiments, that human decision-making is often chaotic – a mix of the rational and intuitive and sometimes downright irrational. When humans make decisions, we are often unaware of our own behavioural or *cognitive biases* and the *invisible* pressures in our environment that affect us. And having made a decision, humans are adept at rationalizing it in their own minds and will blithely begin to implement the decision with confidence. Having embarked on a particular course of action, people will then be loathed to backtrack.

Behavioural psychologists have found that even our most cherished personal traits, such as honesty, are malleable and can be manipulated by subtle cues in the environment. For example, in a novel experiment, a group of psychologists at an English university[1] tested their colleagues on their honesty. To measure the importance of visual cues in decision-making, the researchers placed a small notice over the 'honesty box' in their shared coffee room and, over a period of several weeks, monitored how much people contributed for their coffee. What they found was that if a picture of staring eyes was pinned to the notice the contributions went up. However, if a less threating picture of a bunch of flowers was displayed, contributions went down, by a factor of three! Even though none of the unwitting participants reported being aware of the visual cues, their decisions to contribute or not, and by how much, was decidedly affected by the cue.

Just as worrying is that psychologists have found that a decision-maker can be influenced not only by the pros and cons of a question being considered but by the way that the question is asked. In his bestselling book, *Thinking, Fast and Slow*,[2] Nobel Prize-winning psychologist Daniel Kahneman has described how people will make one choice when a question is asked one way, such as for example selecting measures for saving lives in a pandemic, but will choose the opposite option when asked in another way, even when none of the underlying information has been changed. This means that the way a question, such as whether to invest in a new venture or not, has been *framed* will affect a decision-maker's response and he/she will often be unaware of it. This is disturbing because senior decision-makers, however canny, can be manipulated to lean towards a particular option by the way that proposals are framed by proponents.

A decision-maker's physiology also plays a part in how he/she makes decisions. Using the latest functional Magnetic Resonance Imaging (fMRI) technology, neuroscientists have been able to monitor a person's brain activity when decisions, especially those related to risk, are being made. Behavioural scientists found that there is a positive physical reaction in the most primitive parts of a person's brain when an optimistic choice is being considered but much less so when an unpleasant option is presented.[3] In other words, researchers conjecture that humans are 'hardwired' to prefer optimistic alternatives. As Julius Caesar wrote, 'Men willingly believe what they wish' – we want to believe that the future will be rosy and will put aside doubts that it will not be. Neuroscientists, such as John Coates, have also studied the effect of hormones on decision-making and have found, for example, that an elevated level of the hormone testosterone causes some people to take more risk. However, with higher levels of the hormone and under stress people will become *risk averse* and then take much less risk. Findings such as these go some way to explaining the seemingly manic behaviour of financial traders in volatile markets.

Economic and business school orthodoxy holds that every business decision should be approached on its own merits with a clean sheet to consider the various alternatives available as regards potential benefits and risks. The 'rational' decision-maker is then supposed to make a choice based on the best alternative according to their pre-determined *appetite* for risk and reward. This is a spreadsheet view of the world that, of course, only holds in very limited circumstances where a decision-maker has all of the information and time needed to consider the alternatives thoroughly and objectively. In the real world of business, decision-makers rarely have that luxury and lacking information and time, resort to their experience and their intuition. In practice, experienced decision-makers use rules of thumb, or *heuristics*,[4] to fill in the information that they are missing. Most of the time this approach works, or at least nearly works, as business managers get better at decision-making as they gain more experience. But rules of thumb are not always appropriate to a particular business decision, especially if the conditions are novel, and, in some cases, a well-used heuristic may give the wrong answer.

This revolution in our understanding of how people actually make decisions and the invisible pressures that result in particular types of decisions is *quiet* because the full implications of these research findings have not yet been factored into day-to-day business practice. But that is not a unique situation as it often takes some time for theories developed from research to be incorporated into business best practice. However, senior managers should be aware of these emerging theories because if, as is believed, a decision-maker's choice can be impacted by invisible factors, such as undetected external cues, the way a question has been asked, their personal rules of thumb or even his/her hormonal makeup at the time, how many business decisions will turn out, in retrospect, to have been less than optimal or even *bad*? The risk that a decision-maker can make a bad decision is a called a *People Risk*, because this risk is related to the individual making the decision rather than any external factors over which he/she has no influence.

This book considers the uncomfortable truth that among the countless decisions made within a large organization each year, a number of them will be bad, that is they will be made without due consideration of all of the facts, or will be the result of invisible biases and inappropriate personality traits. A proportion of those bad decisions will be disastrous, seriously damaging or even destroying a firm. Furthermore, the individuals involved in a bad decision can be anywhere in a company from the bottom to the very top. And the higher in the organization that bad decisions are made, the more serious can be the potential consequences if/when they go wrong. For example, terrible decisions made by senior executives at Royal Bank of Scotland (RBS), Lehman Brothers, Tesco and JPMorgan, which we will return to in more depth in Chapter 4, have had catastrophic consequences for their firms' shareholders and in some cases the economy in general.

1.2 The Global Financial Crisis

There are numerous examples of people making bad business decisions, some of which are expanded upon in Chapter 4, but the Global Financial Crisis (GFC)[5] of 2007–2009 provides many such examples from the relatively minor to the catastrophic. Some of these decisions were fraudulent (in fact a very small percentage from the number of successful legal prosecutions) and by definition bad, because they involved breaking laws and opening individuals and firms to the possibility of legal sanctions. But many other decisions were bad because, although not fraudulent, were made without full consideration of their consequences. Many of these decisions were bad because the decision-makers were subject to cognitive biases, especially *overconfidence* or as Alan Greenspan, ex-head of the US Federal Reserve named it, 'irrational exuberance'.

The bad decisions were made throughout the whole of the financial industry from small town banks to global behemoths.[6] Homeowners, who overestimated their ability to repay their rising debts, were extended even more credit by local bankers, who underestimated the possibility that borrowers would fail to repay their excessive debts. However, thanks to financial innovation, these ballooning household debts were no longer held by local bankers but were packaged and sold on to investment banks as mortgage-backed securities. In their rush to sell these debts on to investors, such as insurance companies, the investment bankers did not do the necessary due diligence on what they had just bought but instead pooled the securities into ever more fantastical financial instruments, such as Collateralized Debt Obligations (CDOs). These CDOs were so complicated that few understood them, certainly not rating agencies, such as Moody's and Standard and Poor's (S&P), who rated many of them as being of triple A (AAA) quality. Optimistic ratings made these securities easier to sell to professional investors, who suspended their natural caution, blinded by the higher returns available in these magical new securities. In short, there was overconfidence and lack of sound decision-making throughout the mortgage supply chain – it was People Risk on an industry-wide scale.

The GFC was not caused by a natural event or even economic turmoil, save for a relatively minor downturn in US regional construction, but by the fact that thousands of people were caught up in the excitement of a new, seemingly profitable market opportunity. Bankers and brokers bent or broke the rules that they had dutifully followed for many years previously. Worries about the possible consequences of a 'housing bubble' were raised,[7] for example by the FBI, but concerns were buried in the euphoria. As the presidential inquiry into the GFC concluded, the crisis was caused by individuals not doing the due diligence they should have done, thus undermining the integrity of the global financial markets.

Economists and politicians have argued that the underlying cause of the GFC was greed and this may be so to a greater or lesser degree. But greed is an emotion that distorts the thinking of the greedy person, in that the anticipation of reward overwhelms the perception of the risks involved. This makes the decision a bad one, even if the person gets what they desire. In this book, when we refer to *good* or *bad* decisions, we are not referring to the morality of the outcomes but to the quality of the decision-making. A *good*, or well-made, decision might well have a morally dubious outcome, whereas on the other hand a *bad* decision might have a beneficial result – in other words, a lucky escape.

As a consequence of the GFC, several large international banks, such as Lehman Brothers, RBS, Merrill Lynch, Northern Rock, Halifax/Bank of Scotland, Washington Mutual and Anglo Irish Bank, failed or had to be bailed out by governments. One of the lessons that emerges from these and other failures is that *personality* played a key role. Several of the key figures such as Dick Fuld of Lehman, Fred Goodwin of RBS and Sean Fitzpatrick of Anglo Irish have been widely castigated in official reports and the media as being arrogant and overbearing. But despite their prominent positions as CEOs or Chairs of their firms, these men were only one (albeit very important) member of the board and management of their companies. Where were the other directors and executives and why did they not stand up to these powerful individuals?

In considering the causes and disastrous impact of the GFC on the UK banking system, a special Commission of the UK Parliament[8] held a series of public hearings finally producing recommendations for *Changing Banking for Good*. In damning the prevailing ethos of the UK banking system and echoing what had been said by other investigative commissions, the UK Commission concluded that:

> Too many bankers, especially at the most senior levels, have operated in an environment with insufficient personal responsibility. Top bankers dodged accountability for failings on their watch by claiming ignorance or hiding behind collective decision-making.

The Commission's primary recommendation was that there should be a new emphasis on 'making *individual responsibility* in banking a reality, especially at the most senior levels'. We as authors support these initiatives but also argue that the need for improved personal responsibility extends to all individuals in a firm, not just senior executives and not just in banks but also all large organizations who wish to manage their People Risks effectively.

Massive losses and failures do not only occur in the banking sector. Private sector companies such as RIMS, the Canadian maker of the popular Blackberry gadget, and Tesco plc, the second-largest retailer in the world, have also made very costly errors in their strategic decisions, because they were overconfident in their ability to handle any challenges thrown at them. This is often called *hubris* and, like pride, often comes before a fall. Huge private corporations such as Enron, the US energy giant, and WorldCom, the telecommunications company, failed because of over-confidence and corruption at the very highest level of the corporations. At the operational, rather than the strategic, level companies such as Eli Lilly, the US pharmaceutical giant, and BAE Systems, the UK defence contractor, have been fined for bribery and corrupt sales practices. These are examples of bad decision-making because, as with the GFC, the drive to succeed overcame the imperative to act lawfully and honourably and overwhelmed the fear of getting caught. While these cases are described in Chapter 4, it must be admitted that in this book there is an emphasis on banking not merely because that is where some of the largest losses have occurred but also for the very good reason that these cases have been the subject of intensive inquiries by governments, parliaments and regulatory bodies around the world. There is a wealth of research material to draw upon from these inquiries and the book gives copious references to these sources.

It must also be acknowledged that this book considers examples where decision-making was *bad* and hence a valid question might be 'are there no examples of *good* People Risk Management?' The examples in Chapter 4 are just a few of the many that relate to bad management of People Risk and there are more than enough instances to fill one book. But the authors' choice not to provide examples of good risk management is not capricious as it is very difficult to find such examples, simply because they are just not documented. Instead, many executives prefer to take personal credit for success rather than give credit to others who do the hard work of day-to-day risk management. An example of 'good risk management' that is often given is the takeover of NatWest Bank by the RBS in 2000, which thrust RBS into the forefront of UK banking.[9] The integration of NatWest into RBS was driven ruthlessly by Fred Goodwin, who became CEO in 2001 and was given, or assumed, much of the credit for the success of that integration. However, the management of people in the new bank has been much criticized,[10] as Goodwin was brutal and instead of looking to integrate existing executives into the new structure, cut them adrift. Was there no board or executive talent in NatWest worth keeping? How much this destruction paved the way for the Groupthink that later affected RBS in its take-over of ABN AMRO, as described in Chapter 4, is beyond this book other than to note that while a decision may look good at one point in time, its longer-term impact may not become apparent for many years.

1.3 Failure to challenge

The extensive research into cognitive biases in decision-making is interesting and has important implications for management practice but tends to be focused on individuals and how they actually make decisions. In business, however, individuals rarely make decisions in complete isolation, but are subject to review and detailed consideration by colleagues and management. This begs the question – why don't others pick up and challenge bad decisions? In most cases they do, but in some cases they don't. The truth is that decision-makers are human and like to be liked – it is much easier to conform and 'get with the programme' than to be seen as a 'squeaky wheel' who is always raising embarrassing questions. People like to be part of their *group* and will often suspend perfectly valid challenges to decisions in deference to their colleagues, resulting in what is called Groupthink, or as Irving Janis[11] describes, the tendency of a group to search for 'concurrence' rather than fully consider divergent opinions. A particularly striking example of Groupthink is that of the takeover of ABN AMRO bank by RBS.[12] The RBS board was initially inclined to pass on the takeover opportunity, but after a few months had all become convinced, with minimal new evidence, that it would be a good deal – which it decidedly was not! Overwhelmed by optimistic but unrealistic projections, the directors of RBS just did not do the amount of due diligence essential for such an important strategic decision and waved through the CEO's proposals.

But why do we not see things that are so obvious with hindsight? It turns out it may not always be incompetence, laziness or extreme optimism. It may be that it is because we are very good at what we do, albeit that what we do is very narrow and specific. Psychologists have discovered that we all at times suffer from what is called 'Inattentional Blindness' (IB), in other words when looking at something, we see what we are looking for and miss the unusual. This is commonly known as having a *blind spot*, and was demonstrated in a now-famous behavioural experiment[13] by Christopher Chabris and Daniel Simons, two US psychologists, who videoed a practice basketball session between two teams. Groups of volunteers (subjects) were then asked to watch the video and count the number of passes between members of the team in white shirts, which they did diligently. The subjects were then asked how many passes they had counted and whether they noticed the gorilla! Almost nobody, across many experiments, reported they had seen a gorilla but when the video was replayed, everyone immediately noticed someone in a gorilla suit walking slowly across the court, waving at them. While concentrating on counting the passes, the subject's brains had apparently blocked out the gorilla. This experiment, and others that are described in Chapter 3, show that all of us, including the senior management of large firms, suffer from a whole range of cognitive biases, including blind spots that distort our judgements.

In business, who could miss a gorilla? In the case of the GFC, the answer was almost everyone. Answering stiff questions from legislators during official inquiries into bank failures in the United States and UK, directors and executives all said that they did not see the crisis coming.[14] They were not lying and many lost personal fortunes as they bought up stock in their own firms that other investors were offloading as the GFC loomed. Believing their own spin, directors and executives were deluded – they had all missed the 'Invisible Gorilla' of a housing boom about to go bust.

1.4 What is People Risk?

People should do the right thing and follow the rules that are laid down for them, but sometimes they don't. On the other hand, people should not put themselves, their colleagues, their firm, its customers or the general public in any danger because of their reckless actions – but sometimes they do. Each day, there are countless mistakes, acts of thoughtlessness or even illegal actions made by people in organizations around the world, the vast majority of which have negligible consequences other than to increase the cost of doing business. However, some of these misdeeds and mistakes do cause damage and result in considerable financial loss to a firm. Some of these mistakes may even cause injury and death to innocent people. Every now and then, the misdemeanours and blunders add up to create a major disaster, which can result in many millions of dollars of losses to the firm involved and even loss of life. This is what is called People Risk or the risk that people, inside and outside of the firm, will make bad decisions that cause losses to the firm.

People make bad decisions for a host of reasons but mainly because they are human. Emotions get in the way of our ability to think rationally and objectively. People make some decisions even though they do not have enough information to make them but they rely on their experience and ability to dig them out of a hole if something goes wrong. But, sometimes the hole is too deep. People make some decisions even though they think the decisions may be wrong, but they decide go along with the group for an easier life, choosing the battles they want to fight. People sometimes make bad decisions because they desperately want a particular decision to be the right course of action, often as a vindication of previous decisions they have made (this is called a *confirmation bias*).

People are not machines that can be programmed to do the same thing every time and even the most trustworthy individuals sometimes get tired, sloppy, overconfident, over-trusting, suspicious, worried, frightened, angry, resentful, vindictive and a myriad of emotions in between. Some people make decisions that are illegal, causing losses to the firms in the form of theft and fraud; and others may indulge in unethical acts which can cause loss to the reputation of their firms and fines by regulators. These are all potential causes and examples of People Risk.

If we know that People Risks can cause losses, including even the failure of the firm, how should such risks be managed? The authors recognize that attempting to develop practical suggestions for managing People Risk across a wide spectrum of organizations would be fruitless, at least until some of the groundwork is done for large organizations. The types of people-related risks faced, for example, by a sole trader (such as a shopkeeper or a lawyer) are very different to those faced by a large firm (such as a bank or an oil company). This book therefore concentrates on the people-related risks faced by large commercial firms. The renowned expert on disasters, the late Professor Barry Turner,[15] argued that large organizations are more prone to large losses because of their complexity and size:

> Disasters, other than those arising from natural forces, are not created overnight. It is rare that an individual, by virtue of a single error, can create a disastrous outcome in an area believed to be relatively secure. To achieve such a transformation he or she needs the unwitting assistance offered by access to the resources... of large organizations, and time.

Turner's insights imply that large organizations are more prone to People Risk than other firms and that the senior management of these firms should take People Risk Management seriously, at least as seriously as they take other risks.

1.5 Structure of the book

The management of People Risk is not a completely new subject and two areas in particular, accidents and criminality, have been covered well by experts such as James Reason and James Coleman,[16] whose theories are described in Chapter 2. However, these very valid areas of research and practice tend to treat risk in isolation and focus on the outcomes of a particular risk, such as death/injury in the case of accidents and theft/fraud for criminality. To complement these very important strands of research, this book takes a step back and, from the perspective of individuals within organizations, considers the question of what is common across different types of *loss* related to People Risk, including human life, money and reputation.

Before going on to discuss how People Risk can be managed, Chapter 2 defines People Risk and describes some of the existing theories around specific People Risks such as Frauds and Accidents. The chapter also develops a new model of People Risk grounded in existing theories. Chapter 3 discusses the complex topic of the *human dimension* of risk and introduces current thinking around the topics of cognitive biases and heuristics. Chapter 4 illustrates through case studies a number of recent examples of the enormous negative consequences to firms, their shareholders and sometimes taxpayers of not properly managing People Risk.

Learning from these cases, Chapter 5 develops a new 'Framework' for the effective management of People Risk, and looks at how People Risks arise from the *interactions* between people inside and outside of the organization. One of the key lessons learned from the cases of People Risk described is that the *culture* of an organization is critical to managing people-related risk. The corporate board is central to changing any organizational culture but the board, because it is made up of humans, is itself also a source of People Risk. Chapter 6 discusses this problem and makes concrete suggestions as to how directors can address people-related risks in their own ranks. Like risk, culture is a very complex concept and Chapter 7 describes some of the theories and debates surrounding organizational culture and the difficulties of changing culture, especially in a large firm. Pulling together some of the lessons learned from the previous chapters, Chapter 8 focuses on the roles and responsibilities of those responsible for managing people-related risks and makes suggestions as to how these activities may be coordinated more effectively throughout the firm.

But People Risk cannot be managed by the board and executives alone. Without every individual in a company taking, and being rewarded for taking, individual responsibility, people-related risks just cannot be managed. Chapter 9 looks at improving individual decision-making, by recognizing potential biases through a structured decision process and Chapter 10 considers individual responsibilities and, in particular, improving conduct through Personalized Codes of Conduct. Finally, Chapter 11 summarizes some of the lessons learned and suggestions made in the book and discusses the growing importance of People Risk Management.

Risk Management has the reputation, sometimes warranted but often overstated, of being a mathematical discipline and, particularly in the financial field, descends very quickly into complex formulae and abstruse statistical theory. This book, however, does not contain any complex mathematical formulae or statistical theory, although a few high-level concepts on the statistics of operational losses will be introduced, as this is necessary to understand why People Risk is difficult to quantify and, in turn, manage.

1.6 Audience

This book is aimed at directors, senior executives, line managers and risk practitioners who are looking for practical suggestions as to how to manage the sometimes very significant losses attributable to people, inside and outside of their organizations. It is also aimed at departments that relate specifically to people inside the firm, such as Human Resources and Compliance, and also departments that deal with people outside the firm, such as Marketing/Sales, Legal and Procurement. The suggestions in the book are part of a general 'Framework' for the management of People Risk, described in Chapter 5, which must be tailored to the needs of the individual firm. While the book can be read cover to cover, it is hoped that it can also be used as a reference when managers have People Risk issues that they need to consider. Our aim is to provide practical, implementable advice to practising managers, but practice, if not informed by theory, is little more than experimentation. The book therefore contains a mix of the latest thinking in business management and risk management with practical suggestions informed by theory and analysis of relevant case studies. This book is about expanding the concept of People Risk into areas that are traditionally not considered part of business operations, such as, for example, the psychology of strategic decision-making, where directors make decisions that not only turn out to be bad in their outcomes but were bad decisions to start with.

Notes

1 The novel and insightful experiment into honesty is documented in Bateson, M, Nettle, D and Roberts, G (2006) Cues of being watched enhance cooperation in a real-world setting, *Biology Letters*, 22 September 2006 **2** (3) pp 412–14. The psychologist Dan Ariely has written several important books on cognitive biases and dishonesty, most notably Ariely (2013), which has the interesting sub-title *How we lie to everyone – especially ourselves.*

2 Daniel Kahneman is recognized as the founder of what is called Behavioural Finance for which he received a Nobel Prize in Economics in 2002. His work is summarized for business audiences in his best-selling and eminently readable book, Kahneman (2011).

3   The work on monitoring optimism in the human brain using fMRI is described in Sharot (2011).

4   The use of heuristics in individual decision-making is covered well by the leading expert Gerd Gigerenzer (2008, 2010 and 2014). At this point it should be noted that the concepts of cognitive biases and heuristics are still a matter of significant academic discussions as to how and where they interact and which is (or should be) given supremacy.

5   There is a mass of literature on the Global Financial Crisis, too voluminous to reference here but Schiller (2008) provides an excellent summary. For more detail, the reports produced by the congressional Financial Crisis Inquiry Commission (2011) provide copious detail and will be referenced in Chapter 4 in the section on the GFC.

6   A detailed discussion of the People Risks encountered in the GFC is given in McConnell, P and Blacker, K (2011) The Role of Systemic People Risk in the Global Financial Crisis, *Journal of Operational Risk*, 6 (3) Fall pp 65–123.

7   One of the few public thinkers who raised doubts about the US housing boom of the early 2000s was Nobel Prize-winning economist Robert Schiller who explained the phrase *Irrational Exuberance* in Schiller (2005).

8   The inquiry into the failures of several UK banks and recommendations for changing the systems can be found in the Parliamentary Commission on Banking Standards (2013).

9   In an echo of the later flawed decision to takeover ABN AMRO bank, Fraser (2014) describes the NatWest takeover as less a rational economic decision than one driven by a deep desire to beat RBS's old enemy – the Bank of Scotland (BOS).

10 See Fraser (2014) for a description of the cull of senior NatWest executives.

11 The definitive work on Groupthink was conducted by Irving Janis (1971) but has proved difficult to apply to wider instances because of lack of access to board-level information. A discussion of Groupthink and its benefits and limitations and the example of Northern Rock is provided in McConnell, P (2013) Northern Rock – The group that thinks together, sinks together, *Journal of Risk and Governance*, 2 (2), pp 105–33.

12 Detailed references for the RBS/ABN AMRO case are provided in Chapter 4. Ian Martin's excellent book on RBS (Martin, 2013) describes the internal tensions surrounding the deal and the personalities at play.

13 The Invisible Gorilla clip has become a world-wide phenomenon on YouTube, being downloaded millions of times. The rationale and results of the experiment are documented in Chabris and Simons (2010) showing how our brains deceive us, creating blind spots to prevent cognitive overload.

14 In testimony to various inquiries, such as the US Financial Crisis Inquiry Commission (2011) and the UK Parliamentary Commission on Banking Standards (2013), senior executives maintained that they did not see the risks emerging. These testimonies are archived on the various inquiry websites for detailed analysis.

15 The work of the late Professor Barry Turner is critical to understanding the evolution of large scale 'man-made disasters' and his seminal paper can be found in Turner (1976).

16 See Reason (1990, 2008) for excellent summaries of the causes and costs of industrial accidents and James Coleman (2001), one of the definitive books on White Collar Crime.

Definition and models of People Risk

02

> *Risk comes from not knowing what you're doing.*
>
> ATTRIBUTED TO WARREN BUFFETT

KEY MESSAGES

- Risk is uncomfortable for people – it is invisible, we cannot see or touch it.

- A 'Risk Event' has a Likelihood of occurring and Consequences if it does, but we are often uncertain as to the magnitude of either Likelihood or Consequences.

- Where we are uncertain about risk and, lacking information, we often have to make a subjective judgement as to the magnitude of a particular risk. This uncertainty gives rise to People Risk.

- People Risk is difficult to define, it covers a wide field of activities and impacts a diverse range of stakeholders.

- There are, however, several well-established 'models' of People Risk that may be used to improve People Risk Management.

2.1 Introduction – what is People Risk?

Risk is an *uncomfortable* topic for the vast majority of people. That is because risk is not physical. We can't see risk or touch it. Risk is *invisible*. Risk is an abstract concept, like freedom, but it is not personal to the individual, as a risk can exist whether an individual perceives it or not. And to make matters worse, the concept of risk is extremely hard to communicate. Professor David Spiegelhalter,[1] the Winton

Professor of the Public Understanding of Risk at Cambridge, co-author with Michael Blastland of the enlightening and highly entertaining *Norm Chronicles: Stories and numbers about danger*, which looks at the everyday risks of just living, writes that he has 'often reported people's communication of risk and found the communicators don't really know what they are communicating. Just when anxious people most want clarity, they find muddle. There is a reason for that. It is a *muddle*.'

In this chapter we will work through the example of hiring a new employee before deriving some lessons that help frame some of the subsequent discussions about People Risk in general. Although not often recognized, when recruiting, firms are actually introducing a potential source of People Risk into their business. This short detour will also introduce some of the concepts and terminology developed by the International Standards Organization (ISO) in its Guide 73,[2] which attempts to develop a new *Risk Management Vocabulary*. Nevertheless, it should be noted that, to add to the muddle, there is no universally agreed language for talking about risk. Before considering the example, a few basic concepts are described.

2.1.1 Likelihood, consequences and uncertainty

A *risk event* is a change in circumstances or an occurrence that leads to a *loss* (or alternatively a *gain*)[3] of some kind. For example, a member of staff might steal from a firm or its customers or a firm might lose money because of a bad management decision. For risk management two questions are important. Before the event happens, what is the *Likelihood* that such an event could occur? And when the event does happen, what are the *Consequences*? The concept of *risk* is often described as the combination of the likelihood of an event occurring and the consequences if it does. From this point on, the concept of risk starts to go downhill rapidly but it is worth teasing out some simple examples of the concepts of likelihood and consequences before considering the complexities of the real world.

The diagram in Figure 2.1 is called a *Risk Heat Map* or matrix on which Likelihood and Consequences are two axes, from Low to High and Small to Large. For example, if a particular risk event has a high likelihood of occurring and the consequences will be large then it will be placed in the top right, darkest quadrant (High/Large) which, following the so-called 'traffic lights' convention, is often coloured Red for 'danger'. On the other hand, an event that is unlikely to happen and will have negligible consequences will be placed in the lower left quadrant (usually coloured Green in the traffic lights convention).

Heat maps are used widely in business as a way of prioritizing risks to be managed since it is fairly obvious that those events in the top right quadrant should be tackled as a matter of priority as they are both likely to occur and would have serious or even catastrophic consequences if they did. But first there is a question that must be asked; what is high and what is low?[4] Unfortunately, the answer is often subjective, situation-dependent and changes over time. But sometimes the answer can be fairly straightforward.

For example, by tracking inventory and sales, companies can track losses due to what is euphemistically called 'shrinkage' or staff theft. For a large firm, such as a food retailer, there may be a high likelihood that theft will occur somewhere, but

FIGURE 2.1   Risk Heat Map

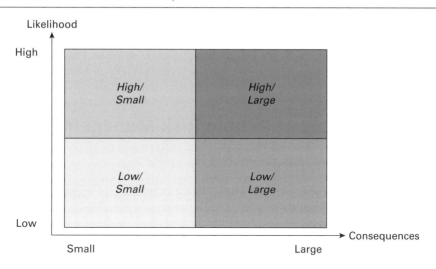

given the nature of the products, the consequences of each event (ie theft) will be small. The risk event then would in the top left quadrant of the map (High Likelihood/ Small Consequences). But what if the company is a technology or pharmaceutical company and a theft involves not food but Intellectual Property (IP) that has not yet been patented? The consequences of such a theft could be very large, even cata-strophic, if it were to give a competitor an edge. What is the likelihood that such a theft could occur? That is *uncertain* and depends on many unknowns such as the state of the industry, the ethics of competitors, the feelings of the staff towards the firm and the *control environment* set up by the organization. In most business situations, both Likelihood and Consequences will be uncertain and managers will have to estimate these two values, a problem that will be discussed in later chapters. Warren Buffet's definition of risk succinctly captures the problem of uncertainty: 'risk comes from not knowing what you are doing'. The more uncertain we are (ie the less we know) the more risk we are taking on, but unfortunately we don't know how much. As a result, risk can be extremely difficult to quantify precisely.

2.1.2 Risk events and causes

People only *experience* risk when an event happens. It can be an unexpected event, such as a fire in an office, or a run-of-the-mill event such as hiring a new employee, who unexpectedly turns out to be a thief. Most run-of-the-mill events are not con-sidered risky – not because there are no risks but because there are usually standard processes, procedures and rules for handling them. Though rarely stated explicitly, the objectives of standard operating procedures include *managing* the risks associated with a particular event.

Before providing an example, it is worth noting here that a particular risk may arise from multiple causes. For example, in the case of IP theft, a potential thief may need money to cover debts, or may wish to ingratiate him/herself with a new employer, or alternatively may feel aggrieved at being overlooked for promotion. On the other hand, the loss of IP may be a result of industrial espionage or theft by outsiders. The risk to the firm in both situations is that valuable IP will be lost and the process of identifying possible causes, especially those related to people, is part of the structured risk management processes described briefly in Chapter 5.

2.2 An example of People Risk Management

2.2.1 The hiring process

Taking the example of the hiring process, which is familiar to most managers, we look at how standard Human Resources (HR) processes actually include managing people-related risks. In risk terminology, hiring processes are designed at least in part to reduce the *likelihood* that someone unsuitable will be employed. All firms of any size will have a formal hiring process, usually run by the HR department, which will include a series of checks to ensure that:

  a the job for which the firm is hiring is well defined;

  b a suitable pool of candidates is identified and targeted through industry-specific channels;

  c potential candidates are identified through a process of matching credentials and experience against job requirements;

  d shortlists of candidates are prepared and candidates are screened using personality and competence tests and (often many) interviews;

  e suitable candidate(s) are selected, offers are made and backgrounds are checked;

  f if negotiations are successful, formal legally binding offers of employment are exchanged and plans are made for the successful candidate(s) to join the firm; and lastly

  g when the new employee joins the firm, final legal documentation is exchanged and there is normally some process of induction in which the employee is introduced to his/her new firm, role, colleagues and job.

This is a complicated, time-consuming process that involves many individuals: candidates, interviewers, managers, HR specialists, recruitment firms, etc. Each of these people has different objectives, biases and conflicts of interest and, if they don't do their jobs properly, can give rise to risks *after* the candidate is hired.

2.2.2 Risks in the hiring process

What is the likelihood that a large firm will find the perfect candidate for *every* job that it advertises? The likelihood is infinitesimally small, if only because the ideal candidate for any one particular job may not be looking for a new opportunity and be quite happy to stay with a competitor. So, despite the wording of many job advertisements, the hiring process is really about getting a '*good enough*' match between a particular job and those candidates that are both available and suitable.

What are the *consequences* if the match is not 'good enough'? For most firms, the hiring process does not end when a new employee starts work and there is often a probationary period in which a new employee has to show that they are indeed suitable for their new job and has been honest in their completion of their job application. Although the firm holds the upper hand with a new employee, who having left their old company is at risk of dismissal, the firm cannot be too capricious as hiring is an expensive undertaking. Increasingly, casual employment is used to evaluate a potential employee's job performance before a formal offer of permanent employment is made. Though rarely considered as such, such casual employment is actually a form of risk management as it reduces the uncertainty associated with understanding a candidate's abilities. In most cases, this complex process is designed to hire an individual whose *inherent risk* is in the bottom left quadrant of the Risk Heat Map shown in Figure 2.1, ie a Low Likelihood of hiring a completely unsuitable candidate with Low Consequences if one is in fact hired.[5]

The list of steps in the idealized hiring process above glosses over much of the boring detail that is designed to ensure that potential employees are who they say they are and can do what they claim. For many jobs, the hiring process is tortuous and time-consuming, frustrating for both potential employees and employers. There is a real risk that overly bureaucratic processes will turn off good candidates, further increasing the risk that less suitable individuals will be hired. Failure to attract the best candidates is not, however, the risk considered in this book. Instead, here we are looking at the risk that the firm hires an employee who is or *becomes* a significant risk in the future.

People Risk, in the hiring process, is not only about a firm hiring the wrong employee but also about an employee joining the wrong firm. If a firm oversells the company or a particular job opportunity then this creates a situation where, from day one, an employee may be dissatisfied and feel cheated or be 'out of their depth'. In such a situation, firms create People Risk, not least by creating the impression that it is acceptable to lie about the firm and its capabilities. Of course for 'good' candidates the tendency of HR and line managers will be to 'gild the lily' and to emphasize the positives, sometimes changing a role to suit a candidate rather than the other way around, in the process possibly reinforcing narcissistic predispositions in the new employee. As the cases in Chapter 4 will illustrate, narcissism is a common factor in many instances of People Risk.

2.2.3 Risks after the hiring process

But People Risk does not disappear when an employee is integrated into the firm. People change over time. A personality test applied to a potential recruit will say very little about the behaviour of the same person several years on in their mid-career. In his groundbreaking book, *Thinking, Fast and Slow*,[6] Daniel Kahneman tells the story of how during his national service he was assigned to perform aptitude tests for potential officers in the Israeli army. In characteristically honest fashion, Professor

Kahneman admits that after applying the tests he was very confident of his conclusions about the potential of different candidates. However, when feedback about performance in later tasks was received, he learned that he and his colleagues' ability to predict actual performance using the tests was negligible, in fact just better than random. So what did he and his colleagues do? They continued to apply the tests as it was 'the army after all and that is what we did', admits Kahneman. Likewise with administering personality tests during the hiring process, that is often what organizations do, because they have nothing better to use.

2.2.4 Risks in hiring senior employees

The standard hiring process is not, however, suitable for all levels of job in a firm, especially where the *consequences* of making the wrong or right choice can be significant, such as with the hiring of directors, CEOs, senior executives and so-called 'rainmakers', who are proven revenue generators. The process in these situations is often less hiring than poaching, persuading someone to jump ship. At senior levels, the emphasis is less on matching to a pre-existing job specification than creating a new job that fits both the firm and the candidate. This is an intricate negotiation process that is often outsourced to specialist executive search firms or 'head hunters'. If a good match is found the consequences can be extremely positive for both the firm and the new employee (the upside of People Risk) but a mismatch can be disastrous.

2.2.5 When hiring goes wrong

Chapter 4 will describe some of the situations where a mismatch was, at least in part, responsible for disaster. One of the most high-profile cases of such a mismatch is that of Andy Hornby,[7] the last CEO of the ill-fated Halifax/Bank of Scotland (HBOS) before it failed during the GFC and was forcibly acquired by Lloyds Bank at considerable cost to the British taxpayer. Mr Hornby was initially successful, increasing the bank's share of the retail mortgage market. However, he was not a banker nor, to his credit, did he claim to be. In 2004, the UK financial regulator, the Financial Services Authority (FSA), expressed serious concerns[8] about the bank's risk management capabilities and in particular that all was not well with risk management in the traditional business banking divisions of the bank. Unfortunately Hornby, who had a retail background, was not well acquainted with that particular side of the business and did not instigate the actions needed to get on top of the problems. In a report entitled 'An Accident Waiting to Happen',[9] the UK Parliamentary Commission on Banking Standards criticized the board and senior management of HBOS for 'insufficient banking expertise', recommending that among other things Mr Hornby 'should be prohibited from holding a position at any regulated entity in the financial sector'. Chapter 4 provides more detail on the HBOS failure but, in summary, Andy Hornby was the wrong man in the wrong place at the wrong time. In hindsight, although not solely responsible for the disaster, his was a disastrous hire, creating enormous People Risk for HBOS.[10]

2.2.6 Judgement calls

So why do firms take the (sometimes enormous) risk of hiring people? They have to, of course, otherwise their business will decline as people leave or retire. Ultimately, line and HR managers make a judgement call as to whether someone, whom they may only have met for a few short hours, is suitable for a particular job in the company. In the majority of cases, these judgements turn out to be at least satisfactory and sometimes very good (the upside of People Risk). However, in some situations the decision is erroneous and there is a disaster, or near disaster. Why do people make wrong, sometimes disastrous decisions?

Most of the information that managers use to make a decision on hiring an individual is uncertain. There will, of course, be some evidence exchanged as to a candidate's capabilities but save for exceptional jobs, such as airline pilots, spies or astronauts, the information will usually be fairly superficial. It is only when a new employee sits down with his/her colleagues that the interpersonal dynamics, so important to successful integration, will come into play. As in other processes, in the normal hiring process there are many sources of uncertainty, including:

a whether the job described to potential employees is actually the job that he/she is required to do (eg misunderstanding of requirements or inaccurate expectations);

b whether the candidate has correctly communicated his/her capabilities (eg overconfidence);

c whether the person will fit in to the group(s) with whom he/she has to work (eg personality conflicts especially with peers who had been overlooked for the role);

d whether the employee or the firm has emerging problems that were not discussed in the hiring process;

e whether the new employee will have regrets about leaving their previous employment, and so on.

While a good hiring process will endeavour to address some of these uncertainties, there will invariably be questions unasked or unanswered and information not disclosed or even concealed.

So how do we manage such risks? Business managers pride themselves on being adept at solving problems as they arise. If a new employee is unhappy but performing well, then a good manager will attempt to resolve issues by just sitting down and talking, but a bad manager might start to assign blame and make the situation worse. If, on the other hand, a new employee is happy but is not performing well, remedial action will have to be taken even to the extent of firing him/her. In most cases, however, where there is good hiring process, new employees will be reasonably happy and perform at least adequately. In risk management jargon, if we treat an offer to hire someone as a 'risk event', the actions taken beforehand to reduce risk, such as checking credentials, are called *preventive risk treatments*, while those taken after the event are called *reactive risk treatments*. Such treatments, which may include the imposition of new procedures, are needed since many of the uncertainties that arise are because we are dealing with human beings who misunderstand each other, misinterpret information, and even when well intentioned sometimes obfuscate and even dissemble. Nothing is ever certain with people, and hence there is always People Risk.

2.3 Definition of People Risk

2.3.1 The difficulties of defining People Risk

Before defining the concept of People Risk, it is worth noting the difficulties that such a definition may present. The definition of People Risk in this book will encompass actions that are both criminal, such as fraud, and non-criminal, such as misguided decisions that lead to losses. The criminal dimension in the companies discussed in this book is often referred to as *White Collar Crime*. But White Collar Crime remains an area that is not well defined. Although White Collar Crime has been discussed since the mid-1930s by respected criminologists such as Edwin Sutherland,[11] the discipline has been bedevilled by problems in defining the concept precisely. The debate focuses on whether the definition should be broad (covering almost any occupational misdemeanour) or narrow (highly specific and prosecutable). Both approaches to the definition have advantages and disadvantages. As might be expected, the FBI, as an enforcement agency, has a definition[12] that covers only those acts that are illegal but is, however, broad in its definition of types of illegal, non-violent activity. Even today there is no universally agreed definition, but the so-called 'modern' definition of White Collar Crime is very broad and covers a wide range of illegal and unethical conduct, including, as described by the noted academic criminologist Brian Payne,[13] not only criminal activity, but also:

- moral or ethical violations;
- violations of civil law;
- violations of trust;
- violation of regulations;
- social harm; and
- workplace deviance.

In 1996, a workshop of leading academic criminologists developed a so-called *consensus definition*[14] of White Collar Crime, which is very broad and covers many of the elements discussed in this book:

> Illegal or unethical acts that violate fiduciary responsibility or public trust, committed by an individual or organization, usually during the course of legitimate occupational activity, by persons of high or respectable social status for personal or organizational gain.

Note this consensus definition covers: illegal or unethical acts; individuals or organizations; legitimate occupational activity; and personal or organizational gain. In this book, no judgements are made as to 'social status' as reference to 'high status' was originally intended to narrow the definition for practical purposes by excluding minor misdemeanours, such as petty theft. Our view echoes those of criminologist Susan Shapiro[15] who argued for the need to see White Collar Crime as an abuse of trust:

Offenders clothed in very different wardrobes lie, steal, falsify, fabricate, exaggerate, omit, deceive, dissemble, shirk, embezzle, misappropriate, self-deal, and engage in corruption or incompliance by misusing their positions of trust.

This perspective is particularly true of those who are held in the highest confidence in corporations, specifically the board and senior management, who sometimes do abuse positions of trust, regardless of social status, as for example in the insider trading case of Raj Gupta, described in Chapter 4. If, despite many years of discussion, it has proved problematic to define White Collar Crime, it is naturally going to be difficult to define People Risk because it includes not only illegal acts, recognized as White Collar Crime, but also other acts that are not illegal, but are unethical or have unintended disastrous consequences.

2.3.2 Definition of People Risk

Like 'risk' itself, there is no universally agreed definition of 'People Risk' although a trawl of Google for definitions throws up many references to the so-called Basel Committee[16] definition of Operational Risk, which is 'the risk of loss resulting from inadequate or failed internal processes, people and systems'. In this definition, *people* is just one of four domains in which losses due to Operational Risk can occur and is not expanded beyond a number of examples, such as 'staff fraud'. In the Basel definition, losses are predominately financial and do not include difficult to measure 'soft' losses, such as reputation, nor hard losses such as death or injury.

Capgemini, a large European consultancy, criticizes the Basel definition as being too process-focused, providing an alternative as 'the risk to the firm caused by its people and the risk to the firm caused by what the firm does to its people'.[17] But the Basel definition does not differentiate between losses due to the decisions *of* or those *due* to the decisions *about* people and so encompasses the consultancy's definition. Nor is the Basel definition focused purely on 'its people', recognizing that losses can be caused by people outside a firm, such as with External Fraud. The Basel definition does, however, have a weakness in that it relates to what people do, not what people do not do (although the non-specific 'inadequate or failed' could be stretched to encompass 'non-decisions'). Losses occur not only because people do what they should not, but also because people fail to act when they see something wrong.

The definition of People Risk in this book explicates the Basel definition of Operational Risk specifically for the subset of People Risk as *the risk of loss due to the decisions and non-decisions of people, inside and outside of the organization.*

Note that in this definition, 'loss' is not just financial but also includes: loss of human capacity (eg death and injury); loss of corporate reputation; and loss of organizational capacity (eg inadequate decision-making leading to sub-optimal shareholder returns or loss of key personnel).

In this definition, *people* are not just individuals within an organization, such as employees, managers, directors, control functions (such as auditors, accountants, risk managers, etc.) and external experts hired by the organization (such as external auditors, consultants, interim managers, etc) but also a wide range of external parties that *interact* with the organization, including:

- customers: purchasers of products and services;
- suppliers: providers of products and services that the organization uses to add value;
- competitors: organizations that compete with the firm in its many markets;
- regulators: bodies that regulate markets and organizations;
- shareholders: beneficial owners of the organization;
- government agencies: which have an interest in the organization, such as Tax Authorities;
- general public: which may be affected by the organization's decisions;
- others, such as governments, education bodies (trainers of people), the press, local communities, charities (where donations are made).

The landscape for People Risk is therefore extremely broad, ranging from day-to-day decisions by frontline staff that may result in financial, human and reputation losses, such as fraud, accident misselling, discrimination lawsuits, etc, and decisions by senior management, such as market manipulation or misreporting to shareholders or regulators. It also includes decisions by a board, such as entering new markets without sufficient resources or inadequate due diligence before mergers or acquisitions. Because the landscape of People Risk is so wide-ranging it has traditionally been tackled by breaking down the problem into distinct specializations, such as Health and Safety (H&S), Compliance, Human Resources, Fraud, Financial Accounting, Procurement and Legal, which concentrate on managing the risks related to people from different technical perspectives.

In our view, what has been missing to date is a holistic view of People Risk and how it has the potential to cause losses for the organization, especially losses that can cause significant financial and reputational damage. Important too are the inter-dependencies between the groups of people inside and outside the organization that can create risk, such as collusion between suppliers and staff to defraud a company or social media smear campaigns that are designed to damage a company's image.

The different disciplines that manage People Risk within organizations tend to concentrate on the *outcomes* resulting from decisions of individuals. For example, H&S professionals focus on ensuring that employees' actions do not inadvertently cause accidents that injure or even kill fellow employees, customers or the general public. HR professionals attempt to reduce losses to the organization by ensuring that employees are being trained to the appropriate standards and by ensuring that staff are aware of the firm's policies covering inter-personal interactions such as bullying and discrimination. Likewise other disciplines, such as Procurement and Legal, concentrate on the interactions of staff with external parties, such as potential bribery.

However, just as important as decisions are *non-decisions* because deferring, deflecting or not making decisions, according to pre-defined rules, may also ultimately result in losses to the firm. This book considers not only the examples of People Risk Management already in place in organizations but also looks at the risks that fall through the gaps between various disciplines and the risks that arise from non-decisions.

2.3.3 Definition of People Risk Management

Employing the ISO vocabulary (Guide 73), People Risk Management (PRM) is here defined as 'coordinated activities to direct and control an organization with regard to risk (and in this context, People Risk)'. The key word here is *coordinated*; implying that People Risk Management is not itself a *directing* activity but one that assists others, especially the board and senior executive, to direct and control the organization's approach to People Risk. As noted above, the landscape of People Risk is so broad that coordination will itself be a major activity, involving specialist groups inside and outside of the firm. In order to be effective, this will require the active participation and demonstrated support of the highest levels of the organization. Before considering how People Risk may be managed, it is worth looking at existing models of people-related risk to assist in developing a suitable model for People Risk Management.

2.4 Models of People Risk

2.4.1 The Fraud Triangle

Fraud is one particular instance of the *consequences* of People Risk. In the early 1970s, the US sociologist and criminologist Donald Cressey,[18] described three elements of fraud in the form of what has become known as the Fraud Triangle, as seen in Figure 2.2:

- *Motivation*: or the *pressures* on a potential fraudster to commit a fraud;
- *Opportunity*: the *openings* provided to commit a fraud; and
- *Rationalization*: the *justifications* that a fraudster makes to him/herself and others for committing a fraud.

FIGURE 2.2   The Fraud Triangle (after Cressey)

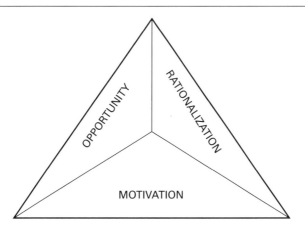

The classic Fraud is one where an employee, often under financial pressure, and using their knowledge of a firm's control systems, redirects funds or other resources for their own use. Often, the employee will not see this as theft but will *rationalize* or *neutralize* it by excuses such as 'I am only borrowing the money and will pay it back later' or 'I am due the money because the firm does not appreciate all the hard work I have put in'. A study[19] by the Australia Institute of Criminology (AIC), in 2003, summarized the characteristics of serious fraud offenders in Australia as being typically: male, aged in their mid-40s, Australian (rather than a temporary resident), having no prior criminal record, having a secondary education or professional qualification, being a director or accounting professional, and with relatively stable employment in the victim organization. In other words, the offender may be one of the firm's most trusted senior employees. The AIC study found that offenders tended to act alone in the commission of a fraud and were most often motivated by greed or gambling debts, but financial and personal stress also provided motivations.

Before moving on to consider how the Fraud Triangle could be expanded to consider outcomes other than fraud, it is worth noting that the three elements of Cressey's model are not wholly negative and can be used to identify positive consequences. For example, if an employee's *motivation* is to gain a promotion then he/she might choose to take the *opportunity* to work overtime with the *rationalization* that the overtime might help to win a contract for the firm and later help to gain promotion and its financial benefits. So Cressey's triangle provides a model not only of how to describe aberrant conduct but also its opposite – virtuous and desirable behaviour. It is because decent motivations have come to be expected and opportunities are assumed to be positive that firms sometimes forget the drivers of good behaviours, which need to be continually encouraged.

2.4.2 *White Collar Crime*

Similar findings to those in Australia have been reported by the US expert on White Collar Crime, James Coleman,[20] although he argues that for other kinds of White Collar Crime, such as market manipulation or bribery, the motivations and rationalizations are much more complicated than those described by Donald Cressey. Coleman found that the major *dispositional factors* for white collar criminals were: male, strong competitive drive, risk-seeking temperament; and impulsivity. He found that male white collar criminals tend to be driven by fear of failure and loss of status rather than greed. And such fears are more likely to occur in the later phases of a person's career when he has attained a degree of status but feels overlooked or undervalued by the organization and his colleagues, and managers have not yet noticed this. On the other hand, female white collar criminals (a much smaller group) appear to be motivated by family or emotional needs rather than status. The example of Ms Rajina Subramaniam illustrates Coleman's observations of female white collar criminals.

In 2012, Ms Subramaniam, an accountant with the Sydney office of the large Dutch bank ING, was found guilty of defrauding her employer of some AUD $40 million over a five-year period.[21] She was sentenced to 15 years' imprisonment but the term was reduced on appeal to a minimum of six years. Aside from being female, Ms Subramaniam matches many of the typical criteria of an Australian white collar criminal, being a trusted, long–serving employee in the bank's accounting division. She had a deep knowledge of the bank's control systems and was able to easily divert funds to her personal account for a considerable time before being detected. Because of her position, Ms Subramaniam had the *opportunity* to commit fraud on a grand scale but what were her *motivation* and her *rationalization*? Her motivation was not greed. In fact, although she went on lunchtime shopping sprees buying expensive jewellery and giving shop assistants huge tips, she did not use the items she bought, many being found not yet unpacked under her desk. She also bought several beach-front properties but did not occupy them.

In line with Coleman's insights, Ms Subramaniam was motivated not by greed nor by the need to purchase expensive objects but by a desire for revenge against a colleague with whom she had been having an allegedly abusive sexual relationship for a number of years. The judge at her trial noted that she also appeared to have an overwhelming need for positive affirmation.[22] Ms Subramaniam claimed that her supervisors were bullying her and her rationalization was to 'get back at the system' for the abuse and the bullying she was allegedly receiving.

This ING case illustrates the difficulties of detecting and managing People Risk. A major deception and fraud was committed by a competent and trusted employee who, presumably unnoticed by management, harboured a deep grudge about her treatment by supervisors and colleagues but continued, while in work, to behave with the utmost professionalism. Paradoxically it was her trusted position that was key to the fraud. Our biases suggest we ignore, or are 'wilfully blind' to, people we trust when looking for potential fraudsters.[23] But as the Subramaniam case illustrates, even the most trusted individual can go on to commit fraud and their motives might seem very strange indeed.

Before continuing, and to counteract possible charges of 'gender bias', it should be noted that the Subramaniam case is one of the very few cases of female white collar criminality encountered by the authors during their research and this is confirmed by Coleman. Most White Collar Crime is committed by men. However, because there is little evidence to support such a hypothesis, the authors do not assert that women are somehow more trustworthy than men in the business context. This may indeed be true but much more research needs to be done before such a hypothesis can be proved or not. In the meantime, it is assumed in this book that People Risk is not gender determined.

Of the three elements of the Fraud Triangle, management effort has traditionally been concentrated on the one element that they have most control over – *opportunity*. In particular, management has worked to reduce opportunities for fraud by increasing financial and operational controls to prevent and detect aberrant activities. Firms can, and do, attempt to manage motivation by introducing systems that recognize achievement and reduce workplace harassment but these are seen as good actions in themselves rather than as ways of mitigating People Risk. It is difficult, however, to affect *rationalization* as this is often driven by the culture of the firm. For example see the arrogant belief, which was engendered in Enron employees before its failure that, as described in Chapter 4, they were the 'smartest guys in the room'.[24]

In considering the concept of *Rationalization* in Cressey's Fraud Triangle, James Coleman identifies six common techniques used by people for rationalizing their behaviour:

1 *Temporary Use*: The person plans (or hopes) to reverse the situation before it is detected, for example, moving clients' money to cover trading losses.
2 *Victimless Crime*: the people hurt by the activities are remote and unknown to the white collar criminal, for example, consumers of defective products.
3 *Distrust of Law*: the white collar criminal considers the regulations and laws covering his/her activities to be not applicable or outdated.
4 *Economic Necessity*: the economic situation is thought to be so dire that illegal or unethical actions are considered to be necessary to survive.
5 *Ubiquity*: the illegal/unethical activities have become so widespread in the industry or the firm that they have come to be considered acceptable.
6 *Just Desserts*: the illegal/unethical activities are considered to be acceptable because of perceived deficiencies in other areas, such as non-recognition of hard work.

TABLE 2.1   Typical rationalizations of white collar criminals (after Coleman)

Rationalization	Example (from Chapter 4)
1. Temporary Use	Most rogue trading scandals
2. Victimless Crime	PPI (Payment Protection Insurance)
3. Distrust of Law	LIBOR Scandal
4. Economic Necessity	WorldCom
5. Ubiquity	LIBOR Scandal
6. Just Desserts	ING Fraud

Table 2.1 shows some example of these rationalizations, which are expanded further in Chapter 4.

It should be noted that rationalizations often exist well before an individual has the motivation to act. Typical white collar criminals do not suddenly take the opportunity to defraud their company. This happens over a prolonged period of soul searching and, over time, the person's rationalization melds into their motivation.

2.4.3 *White Collar Crime – red flags*

Agencies concerned with White Collar Crime, such as the FBI and the UK Serious Fraud Office (SFO), often produce 'laundry lists' of so-called *red flags* that can raise an alert that a problem may be about to occur. Some examples of these red flags are listed in Table 2.2. However, it should be remembered that these behaviours do not indicate that a misdemeanour will definitely be committed, so any attempt to

TABLE 2.2   Some red flags for potential People Risks

Type	Red Flags (examples – not comprehensive)
Individual	Domineering/controlling personality
	Significant personal debt, living beyond means
	Strong desire for personal gain
	Sudden and significant change in behaviour
	Significant use of alcohol/drugs
	Excessive overtime, failure to take holidays
	'Too good to be true' performance
	Does not take kindly to review or criticism
	'Beat the system' mentality, covering lack of confidence
	Implausible/creative responses to queries
	Over-familiarity with suppliers and/or customers
Organizational	Over-dependence on one individual, no/insufficient segregation of duties
	Documents altered or lost
	Mistrust of or antagonism to external authority, eg auditors and regulators
	Transactions taking place at odd times and/or with unusual counterparties
	Weak control environment identified in multiple audits and not resolved

discriminate against an individual on the basis of one, or even a few, red flags without more detailed investigation would be wrong, and might invite retaliation, such as litigation for constructive dismissal.

2.4.4 The Safety Triangle

In the 1960s the late Frank Bird,[25] an expert in industrial safety, undertook a massive study into some 1.75 million accidents in almost 300 US companies. Bird verified the observations made earlier by a number of other safety experts that for every accident resulting in a fatality there were some 600 *incidents* (or near misses) that were abnormal, and of those there were some 30 major accidents of which ten were serious. From this research Bird constructed a *Safety Triangle* as shown in Figure 2.3(a). From Bird's analysis and insights, the enormous costs of incidents and accidents, even if they are not fatal, can be seen and these insights gave rise to the new field of Health and Safety (H&S) management. The chart in Figure 2.3(b) is another way of

FIGURE 2.3(a)   The Safety Triangle

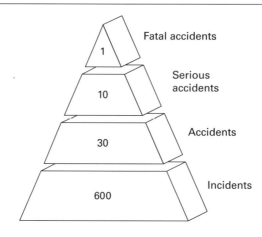

FIGURE 2.3(b)   Loss Distribution

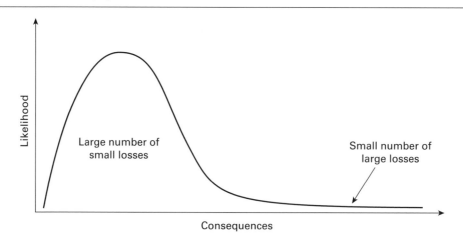

representing this phenomenon as a so-called *Loss Distribution*, which is a represen-tation of a statistical Probability Distribution Function (PDF).

Studies have found that Operational Losses in banks under Basel II regulations follow just such a distribution,[26] colloquially 'a large number of small losses, a small number of large losses and the occasional very large loss'. In searching for the largest potential losses related to People Risk, then, we are looking for very small needles in very large haystacks.

2.4.5 Analysis of disasters

Professor Barry Turner catalogued the events that led up to, and followed on from, some major disasters, such as the tragedy in which 116 children and 28 adults died of suffocation when a small school was engulfed by thousands of tons of colliery waste stored above the little village of Aberfan in South Wales. An official inquiry found that the tragedy was preventable and that there had been numerous warnings about the potential instability of the waste tip before the tragedy. Professor Turner found that ignoring prior warnings was one of a number of common themes that appeared in what he called the *Development of a Disaster*.

Professor Turner described what has become to be known as the 'stage model of a disaster' with *six* distinct stages:

1 Initial Beliefs and Norms prior to a disaster;

2 Incubation Period immediately prior to the disaster;

3 Precipitating Event that triggered the disaster;

4 Onset of the disaster;

5 Rescue and Salvage; and

6 Full Cultural Adjustment, after the disaster.

Turner identified features that appeared to be common to many 'man-made disasters' but he concentrated on the first two stages because he argued that it was *before* the onset of disasters that the significant organizational failures tended to occur. By considering the root causes in several disasters, Turner argued that disasters build up gradually over time and the signs *should be* apparent to management, but instead go unnoticed or ignored because of what he called 'cultural rigidity', which tends to manifest itself in erroneous assumptions about reality and reluctance to face unpalatable outcomes. These, of course, are the same as some of the cognitive biases that have been identified by behavioural scientists, and described in Chapter 3.

Turner found that in Stage 1 – Initial Beliefs and Norms – it was common that, although there were well-defined and well-communicated regulations, policies and procedures in place, in reality the organization failed to comply with these regulations. This was because, over time, management had come to feel that the rules were not relevant to them but no one had bothered to inform authorities that regulations were being ignored. This of course is an example of 'non-action', which in the cases studied by Turner was a contributing factor for a subsequent disaster. An example of such disregard of regulation (or 'Distrust of Law') is the LIBOR scandal, which is described in Chapter 4, where many in the banking industry just ignored the rules for setting LIBOR, a key interest rate benchmark, because the rules were considered to be out of date.

It was in the second stage – the Incubation Period – however, that the rot began to set in for most disasters. Turner identified seven *features* common to many disasters in this stage, although not all need to be present to create the potential for a disaster:

1 rigidities of belief;

2 decoy phenomena;

3 disregard of complaints from outsiders;

4 information difficulties and noise;

5 the involvement of strangers;

6 failure to comply with discredited or out-of-date regulations;

7 minimizing [ie underestimating] emergent danger.

TABLE 2.3   Features of a disaster and rationalizations (after Turner)

Feature of disaster	Rationalization – examples
Initial Norm – failure to comply with regulations	We know better, we are smarter
1. Rigidities of belief	We are convinced we are correct
2. Decoy phenomena	We cannot do X easily so let's do Y instead
3. Disregard of complaints from outsiders	We know better than outsiders
4. Information difficulties and noise	We are confident we have all the information we need
5. Involvement of strangers	We must pay attention to outsiders to get them off our backs
6. Failure to comply with discredited or out-of-date regulations	We know better than others how to run our business
7. Minimizing emergent danger	We know best, we are confident we can handle it

Most of these features are related to human behaviours, biases, motivations and rationalizations, as shown in Table 2.3. It should be noted that Turner's model deals with *collective* rather than *individual* decision failures, since it is accumulated biases at the organizational level that create situations where individuals may trigger a disaster.

2.4.6 The Risk Thermostat

In his book *Risk*, John Adams describes a so-called Risk Thermostat, which he argues people use to mediate their actions.[27] According to Adams, risk management is a balancing act that involves balancing rewards against risks. This Risk Thermostat is shown within the shaded box in Figure 2.4 and consists of four major drivers of our risk-taking behaviour, as described by Adams:

FIGURE 2.4   The People Risk Thermostat (adapted from Adams)

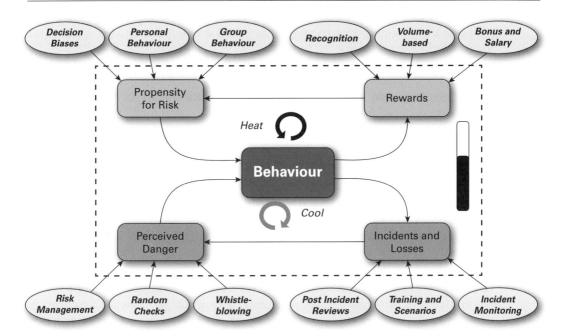

- Propensity for Risk: our personal attitude to risk-taking;
- Rewards: the positive consequences to us of our risk-taking behaviour;
- Incidents and Losses: events that bring the consequences of risk to our attention;
- Perceived Danger: our perception of unacceptable risk in our environment.

The first two of these drivers (Rewards and Propensity for Risk) cause us to increase, or heat up, our risk-taking behaviour, whereas the latter two (Incidents and Losses and Perceived Danger) cause us to reduce (or cool down) our risk-taking. Adams argues that we are constantly trying to balance these heating and cooling effects to arrive at our preferred level of risk-taking behaviour. Likewise, if management can manage these four drivers, they can help to maintain (but unfortunately not guarantee) an acceptable level of risk-taking behaviour among employees. In this diagram, we add a number of other risk-impacting sub-drivers, which contribute to the four main drivers identified by Adams: these are shown outside of the box. These sub-drivers and others are discussed further in Chapters 9 and 10.

2.4.7 Human error

In considering *human errors*, James Reason[28] identified that mistakes are shaped by a variety of behavioural biases, and particularly identified the problem of *under-specification*, where the mental processes necessary for correct performance are incorrectly specified. Though under-specification may take many forms, such as incomplete or ambiguous information, Reason notes that the mind's response is very predictable – it 'defaults to a response that is frequent, familiar and appropriate for the context'.[29]

The work of Bird, Cressey, Reason and others concentrates quite properly on the organization or system, more than the individual, and on improving the processes of the organization to reduce the number of adverse incidents or near misses. The primary mechanism that these experts advocate for improving the overall safety performance of a firm is *reporting* the number of incidents, ie counting near misses and analysing the *root causes* of incidents, however small. But in reporting incidents and near misses we run into a very human problem in that people don't like admitting mistakes, especially those where no damage has been done, such as in a safety near-miss. The old proverb, 'what you don't know doesn't harm you' is actually a so-called *heuristic* that can work well in tricky social situations but rarely in business.[30] If a firm has a *culture of blame* then people will not tend to admit to small mistakes. So in order to collect statistics about incidents and accidents, firms must create a culture where not only are mistakes reported but also prompt reporting is rewarded. To improve workplace safety, behavioural modification techniques are regularly employed. For example, posters that report the number of days since a major accident are displayed in prominent places in safety-conscious firms. These, as described in Chapter 3, are *anchors* that remind people of the importance of safety and that *frame* the issue in a positive way.

2.4.8 Causes and complexity

It should be noted that the Safety Triangle and Loss Distribution, represent the out-comes or *realized consequences* of events that have occurred. They do not represent the underlying causes of these events. Loss events can have one or many causes; for example a fatality can be due to insufficient training, equipment failure and/or insufficient on-site medical support. James Reason identified that there are multiple levels of causes of accidents, in particular: the *organization*, where the culture, processes and management decisions can lead to losses; the *workplace*, such as unsafe equipment and conditions; and the *person* who makes mistakes or violates rules. Reason distinguishes between two concepts that lead to accidents and losses: *active failure*, or unsafe actions by people who are in or have direct contact with the system in which an event occurs, eg pilots or doctors; and *latent conditions*, or 'resident pathogens', that exist all of the time in a system but when triggered in a certain way lead to failure or even catastrophe as, for example, the accident at the Fukushima Daiichi nuclear power plant in March 2011 as described in Chapter 4.[31] In this book we will be dealing mainly with *active failures* rather than *latent conditions* that are situation-specific and organizational.

Charles Perrow is an American sociologist who studies accidents in complex, high-technology systems, such as nuclear power stations.[32] Perrow identified that in such situations there is a combination of *interactive complexity*, or non-linear or unstable interactions between system components, and *tight coupling*, where failures can cascade in an unpredictable way because components are closely interlinked.

Such systems are *inherently risky* because of the uncertainty that any one incident may cause the system to run away very quickly and overwhelm the people who are controlling it. Perrow's 'paradox' notes that whereas complex systems require systematic diagnosis to identify the root cause of a new problem, on the other hand, tightly coupled systems require rapid action to prevent a new problem from cascading through the system. The disastrous fire on the BP Deep Water oil exploration platform, described in Chapter 4, illustrates Perrow's analysis in that a small mistake in pouring concrete spiralled out of control quickly causing death and destruction.

2.5 The People Risk Triangle

Donald Cressey's formulation of the Fraud Triangle provides a basis for considering the consequences of People Risks beyond fraud and addressing some of the shortcomings identified by Coleman and others. In Cressey's model, the *motivation* or pressure to defraud tends to be specific in that an individual tends to have an explicit and bounded need, such as the need for money to cover a debt. The *opportunity* typically arises because controls in an organization do not operate as intended and there are holes that the white collar criminal exploits. The *rationalization* tends to be individual in that it relates to the person who defrauds the company. However, Rajina Subramaniam's motivation was not specific but appears to have been an *ambiguous* need to punish somebody – anyone! Because Ms Subramaniam had an intimate knowledge of the bank's accounting systems she was able to take advantage of their *unintended* deficiencies. Her rationalization was *individual* in that she personally wanted to punish her tormentors, even though it must have been obvious to her that it was not them but her employer's shareholders who would suffer. There was nothing neat and tidy about her actions.

The model in Figure 2.5 expands on Cressey's Fraud Triangle by recognizing that its three elements can be expanded to describe more complex situations than Fraud. For example, fraud can usually be considered a result of a *specific* motivation (eg gambling debt), exploiting an *unintended* opportunity (eg accounting loopholes) with an *individual* rationalization (eg Just Desserts). On the other hand, a mistake can be considered as arising as a result of a specific motivation (eg to complete an assigned task) where an individual *intends* to follow procedures but makes a mistake because he/she is tired/bored/ill-trained (*rationalization*). Likewise, a salesperson might missell a product to a customer who is ineligible (*unintended opportunity*) for example to attain monthly sales targets (*collective rationalization*) designed to increase the company's share price (*ambiguous motivation*).

This *People Risk Triangle*[33] has the same three high-level elements as Cressey's Fraud Triangle, but each dimension has two sub-elements:

- *Motivation*: can be *Specific* (a reasonably definitive goal) or *Ambiguous* (vague and ill-defined, such as 'to improve customer perceptions');
- *Opportunity*: can be as *Intended* (as described by formal policies and procedures) or *Unintended* (contrary to the intention of the formal policies); and
- *Rationalization*: can be *Individual* (such as 'I personally am being overlooked') or *Collective* (such as 'for the good of the firm').

FIGURE 2.5   The People Risk Triangle

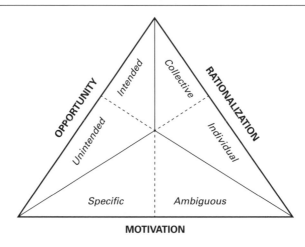

The situations where there are confused emotions, such as ambiguous motivations, unintended opportunities and collective rationalization will naturally give rise to the greatest risks because of the effect of uncertainty. If, as behavioural science suggests, our judgements are often biased, then uncertainty and ambiguity will increase the errors that are made.

The People Risk Triangle in Figure 2.5 gives rise to eight different combinations as identified in Table 2.4, with only one example of Consequences in each category. The examples are expanded upon in Chapter 4.

Cressey's Fraud Triangle is based on the assumption that an employee will take the opportunity to act against the company's wishes and, in the case of fraud against a company that is a perfectly reasonable perspective. But what if the company is itself

TABLE 2.4   The People Risk Triangle – consequences

Motivation	Opportunity	Rationalization	Consequence	Example
	Intended	*Individual*	Mistake	Minor errors
		Collective	Serious accident	BP Oil Disaster
Specific	Unintended	*Individual*	Fraud	Insider trading
		Collective	Market manipulation	LIBOR scandal
	Intended	*Individual*	Insider trading	Rajat Gupta
		Collective	Tax avoidance	NZ Banks
Ambiguous	Unintended	*Individual*	Rogue trading	UBS
		Collective	Product misselling	PPI

doing the wrong thing and the employee is following the company's directions? In some cases, fraud can still occur but in those cases it tends to be fraud or deception on customers, shareholders, suppliers and/or taxpayers rather than the company itself. A classic example of such a situation is misselling of financial products, such as Payment Protection Insurance (PPI), which is described in more detail in Chapter 4, using the People Risk Triangle introduced here.

The definitions, theoretical models and concepts introduced in this chapter are mainly concerned with the consequences of people making mistakes or behaving badly. But these theories do not deal with the underlying reasons why people make bad decisions, beyond those related to criminal activities. Existing theories do not describe the full gamut of People Risks, which requires an understanding of human psychology. Before describing real-life case studies of People Risk, the next chapter considers the human dimension of People Risk and the biases and conflicts of interest that give rise to People Risk.

Notes

1   See Blastland and Spiegelhalter (2013) for an interesting perspective on how people perceive risk and consistently misjudge risk probabilities.

2   *ISO Guide 73:2009 Risk Management Vocabulary* is a component of the *ISO 31000 – Risk Management Standard* as developed by International Standards Organization technical committee TC/262. The Guide is available for purchase from national standards organizations but an overview is available at Wikipedia, article *ISO 31000*.

3   The ISO 31000 standard, which is discussed further in Chapters 5 and 9, specifically recognizes that risk covers both losses and gains. However, for the reasons stated in Chapter 1 this book concentrates on the negative or downside of risk events, ie losses.

4   Note the heat map is shown as a 2 × 2 matrix but, in practice, organizations often use a matrix of 5 × 5 or more to have additional granularity in their analysis of risks.

5   As with all risks, 'low' does not mean zero! There is always *risk* and sometimes an event with a very low likelihood might indeed occur and the consequences could turn out to be grave.

6   See Kahneman, 2011.

7   The story of Andy Hornby's rise and fall at HBOS is told in Perman (2013). In 2012, Mr Hornby gave evidence to the Parliamentary Commission on Banking Standards (2013a), and the testimony is available in Volume 2 of the Commission's final report, http://www.parliament.uk/bankingstandards.

8   The failure of the FSA to act on its reservations about HBOS was disclosed in the report 'An Accident Waiting to Happen' published by the Parliamentary Commission on Banking Standards (2013a).

9   See the Parliamentary Commission on Banking Standards (2013a).

10 In terms of a Risk Heat Map, because Mr Hornby was hired into a very senior role, the risk would be in the bottom right quadrant, ie Low Likelihood (because of his prior record) but High Consequences (because of his position). Unwittingly, when he was promoted to CEO, his risk moved to the Top Right quadrant, because the Likelihood of a serious risk event occurring was heightened by his lack of banking experience. It was his promotion (by the board) rather than his hiring that created the major People Risk.

11 See Braithwaite, J (1985) White Collar Crime, *Annual Review of Sociology*, **11**, pp 1–25.

12 See Ball, R (2006) The Logic of White Collar Crime, *Kriminologija i socijalna integracija*, **14**, pp 23–32.

13 See Payne (2012).

14 For details on the *Consensus Definition* see Helmkamp, J, Ball, R and Townsend K (1996) *Definitional Dilemma: Can and should there be a universal definition of white collar crime?* Proceedings of the Academic Workshop 20–22 June, sponsored and co-hosted by National White Collar Crime Center and West Virginia University.

15 See Payne (2012).

16 The Basel Committee on Banking Standards (BCBS), which was set up by the Bank for International Settlements (BIS), is the body that sets the global banking standards known as Basel I, Basel II, etc. In 2004, the BCBS agreed a set of standards for *Operational Risk Management* in its Basel II standards, available from www.bis.org

17 See Cap Gemini Consulting (undated) *Your People Are Your Biggest Asset and Your Biggest Risk: How people risk management is an achievable top priority* [online] www.capgeminiconsulting.com

18 For an appreciation of the importance of Donald Cressey see Coleman (2001) and for background see the Wikipedia article *Donald Cressey*.

19 See Smith, R (2003) Serious Fraud in Australia and New Zealand, published jointly by Australian Institute of Criminology and PriceWaterhouseCoopers [online] www.aic.gov.au

20 See Coleman (2001).

21 The details of the Subramaniam case were covered in a rather lurid fashion by media in Australia and the UK such as by the Daily Mail: Female Accountant who stole £30m, spent millions in her lunch break and tipped shop assistant £900k, 10th February 2012 [online] www.dailymail.co.uk

22 See News.Com (2012) *Rajina Rita Subramaniam jailed for $45m luxury spree*, 10 February www.new.com.au

23 See Heffernan (2011) for examples of *wilful blindness*.

24 See McLean and Elkind (2004).

25 See Germain, G and Clark, M (2007) A Tribute to Frank E. Bird Jr. 1921–2007, *Professional Safety*, **52** (10) p 26, October.

26 See for example the 2012 report of the Operational Riskdata eXchange Association (ORX), an independent consortium that collects data on Operational Risk events, available at www.orx.org

27 See Adams (1995).

28 See Reason (1990, 2008).

29 As described in Chapter 3, when their thinking brain (System 2) becomes overloaded or cannot find an answer then people will, rather than persevere, revert to using their reactive brain (or System 1) and rely on their intuition and gut feel, which can be disastrous.

30 Heuristics are described in more detail in Chapter 3.

31 Detailed references for the Fukushima case are provided in Chapter 4.

32 See Perrow (1999) for a description of 'tightly coupled systems'.

33 The People Risk Triangle has been developed by the authors as a basis for classifying People Risks that go beyond Fraud.

The human dimension of People Risk

03

> *Humans are not a rational animal, but a rationalizing one.*
> **LEON FESTINGER**[1]

KEY MESSAGES

- Human decision-making is complex.

- In making decisions, people are often driven by biases of which they are unaware, such as overconfidence, or the influence of colleagues and conflicts of interest.

- People, especially experts, operate much of the time on intuition based on experience learned throughout their career, rather than deliberate analysis. This gives rise to the risk that in certain circumstances their intuition may not be correct.

- People are hardwired to be optimistic and take pleasure in considering an optimistic future, which can lead to overoptimistic decisions.

- One of the primary goals of People Risk Management is to make decision-makers aware of their own blind spots, *making the invisible visible to them*.

As described in Chapter 2, people find risk an uncomfortable concept that is difficult to define and describe. But even with an agreed definition, individuals still find it difficult to make risky decisions. This is because humans do not always approach problems completely objectively but bring with them considerable baggage: some good, such as the experiences they have gained over time; some less good, such as any ingrained biases they may have. The latest research into how individuals actually make decisions shows that people are much more emotional than we would like to think and thus sometimes may make bad, even disastrous, decisions. This chapter describes some of the latest theoretical and practical thinking in this fascinating area. As with all disciplines, Behavioural Science[2] has its own technical terminology, for example there are many different sub-types of so-called *behavioural* or *cognitive biases*, such as 'biases', 'effects', 'fallacies', 'illusions' and 'neglects'. However, for the purposes of this chapter these types will all be categorized as 'cognitive biases'.

3.1 Decision-making

The process of making a decision, even a relatively routine one, is not easy. When faced with a decision, decision-maker(s) must consider multiple *inputs* many of which are uncertain or ambiguous, but at least are *Visible*, usually in the form of documents gathered and presented to support the decision-making process. The major *visible* inputs are as shown in Figure 3.1:

- *Strategies* and *Tactical Goals* against which any decision will be evaluated;
- *Proposals* for a decision and *Options* available for execution;
- *Projections* of future changes that will affect the decision;

FIGURE 3.1   Visible and Invisible pressures on decision-makers

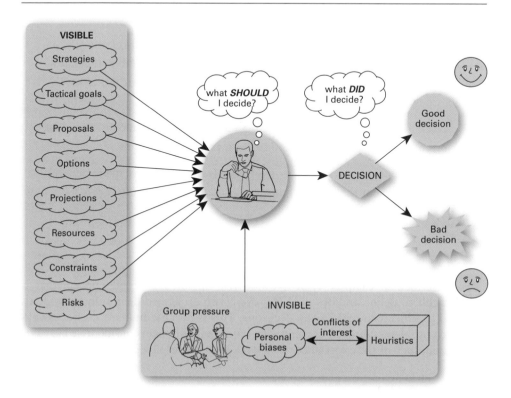

- *Resources* available to execute the decision, including capital, people and time;
- *Constraints* that must be considered, such as regulations and availability of resources;
- *Risks* that may affect any particular decision.

Here *visible* means that all inputs to the decision are available to other people who can evaluate and audit the decision-making process or potentially even independently remake the decision. In the public sphere, for example, some decisions may even, in the interests of public accountability, be evaluated by legislative bodies.

Management literature abounds on how to approach making business decisions and managers are routinely taught methods, such as the widely used *Business Case* approach,[3] for evaluating options and producing recommendations. But management literature assumes that, having followed the methods suggested the decision will be *good*. Here 'good' means that the decision-makers(s) will have: used all of the visible inputs in a rigorous, objective and transparent fashion; evaluated all of the options in an unbiased process; selected the 'best' option(s) according to pre-determined strategic objectives and tactical goals; created a watertight plan to execute the decision; gained agreement from all parties affected; allocated the resources necessary to execute the decision, including the resources to monitor its execution; and communicated the decision to all interested stakeholders in a manner that is well understood. This is a complex set of activities and thus are unfortunately prone to error and misunderstanding.

But even if decision-making is methodical, there is no guarantee that any particular decision will be *good*. For example, projections of the future may not be comprehensive *enough*, and any uncertainty in projections may not be integrated fully into the decision-making process. And even though a decision and its implications may be communicated *to* interested stakeholders, there is no guarantee that those listening will have correctly heard the message that was given. Failure to provide the environment in which a decision is executed properly also constitutes a *bad* decision. The problem is that, if a decision-maker does not consider all of the visible inputs in a rigorous fashion, this will not be detected, unless the thought process is fully documented. This is compounded by the increasing use of standardized spreadsheets, which force decisions into what may be an unsuitable model.

Another potential problem is that each decision-maker, depending on his/her experience, will prioritize the relative importance of each visible input differently, ie will give different inputs and different weightings when making a decision. For example, a decision-maker with a legal or regulatory background will tend to give more weight to a regulatory constraint, whereas an accountant might view financial projections as being more important. And where conclusions differ, especially for a major decision, there will be a tendency to reconcile the differing positions, possibly arriving at a decision that is sub-optimal for everyone and prone to risks that nobody fully understands.

Humans are not dispassionate automatons and beyond the *Visible* pressures there are also *Invisible* pressures in most decision-making processes. An obvious example of an invisible pressure is from the *Group(s)* of which the decision-maker is a functioning part. Since many decisions will require at least acceptance from a wider group, if not actual participation in the form of resources, there will invariably be pressures on a decision-maker to take into account the considerations of others in the group, potentially undermining the reliability of the decision that is actually made. In addition to external pressures, a decision-maker him/herself will have *Personal Biases* that will affect consideration of any decision. For example, it would be a rare decision-maker who would willingly jeopardize their own job and future well-being in making a decision that is adverse to them personally, even though such a course of action may the best one for the company. Furthermore, decision-makers do not always follow a rigorous process for making decisions but often short-circuit the process based on their experience and intuition and use 'rules of thumb', or *heuristics*.

In real life, decision-makers also face many *Conflicts of Interest* that must be *resolved* in order to make a decision. In some situations, resolution of a conflict is obvious but sometimes it is not. As Leon Festinger, warns 'humans are not a rational animal, but a rationalizing one'. That is, rather than make tough decisions, we work to justify to ourselves the decisions that we have already made. In their excellent book,[4] *Mistakes Were Made (But Not by Me)*, Carol Tavris and Elliot Aronson give many examples of decision-makers, especially politicians, but point out that the fault is in all of us:

> As fallible human beings, all of us share the impulse to justify ourselves and avoid taking responsibility for any actions that turn out to be harmful, immoral, or stupid.

Unfortunately, the difference between 'what should I decide?' and 'what did I decide?' is rarely visible, as only one decision is actually made. And running a second and independent decision-making process in parallel is rarely practised, except in situations such as 'war games' in the military. This means that it is rarely possible to distinguish between a *good* and a *bad* decision at the time it is made, unless the decision is so obviously 'bad' that its deficiencies stand out. At this point it must be remembered that the outcome of a particular decision is not relevant, since a very good decision may still result in a bad outcome because, for example, an unlikely 'risk event' actually occurs, as risk cannot be completely eliminated. On the other hand, sometimes 'bad' decisions may have good outcomes but that is mere luck, which of course will often be claimed as exceptional prescience by the decision-maker(s). The remainder of this chapter, considers some of the most important of such *Invisible* pressures on decision-makers.

3.2 Cognitive biases

3.2.1 Anchoring

A test that one of the authors administers to executives in all of his risk management courses is called 'What is the population of Turkey?' In the test,[5] which is based on a famous experiment undertaken by Daniel Kahneman and his colleague Amos

Tversky, each participant is handed a sheet of paper with two simple questions and asked to answer quickly. As the test is usually administered just before morning coffee there is an incentive to complete it speedily. Answers are collected and analysed on the spot. The two questions are as follows:

Q1 Is the population of Turkey greater than 100 million?   Yes / No

Q2 What is your best estimate of the population of Turkey?   ____ Million

In 2012, the correct answer to this question was just below 80 million. However, the correct answer is not relevant. When asked the follow-up question 'Do you actually know the population of Turkey?' most participants replied that they did not, but just gave a response anyway. When asked why they did that, it was mainly because they were asked (by someone in perceived authority) to give an answer, so they did.

But there is a twist to this test. Half of the students were given a sheet that for Q1 asked if the population was greater than 100 million, while the other half were given a sheet where the question asked if the population was greater than 35 million. The distribution of test sheets was random so no one was likely to pick up the slight difference in questions. When analysed, the difference in the answers to the two sets of questions was significant and on average those who were asked whether the population was greater than 100 million answered higher than those who were shown the lower figure. Why should this be? Because the sheet that each student received gave a clue (100 or 35) that became an *anchor* around which they made their guesses. This is called *anchoring bias* and is particularly insidious form of bad decision-making. For example, anchoring on a competitor's rate of growth might cause an executive to pursue particularly risky opportunities, even though the competitor's growth rate is not relevant to their own business situation.

In his book *Predictably Irrational*,[6] Dan Ariely describes experiments that demonstrate our tendency to anchoring, even when we don't know it. In one experiment, participants were asked to write the last two digits of their Social Security Number[7] (SSN) at the top of their answer sheets and then to estimate the prices of a number of items ranging from a bottle of rare French wine to a box of chocolates. Before estimating the price of each item the participants were asked to again write the last two digits of their SSN against each item and then to estimate the price. Bearing in mind that the last two digits of anyone's SSN will be random, what happened? In test after test, the participants with the higher SSN numbers made the higher estimates. As the price of an item should in no way be related to a random SSN number this should make no difference to the price but it does – because we are human. In practice, people don't solve every problem by starting with a clean sheet; we all come with baggage and while some of that baggage may be completely irrelevant to the decision in hand, it sometimes does affect the outcome, simply because it is in the forefront of our minds at that moment in time.

Examples of anchoring in business abound. For example, salespeople know purchasers better than we know ourselves. Techniques such as displaying the Manufacturer's Suggested Retail Price (MSRP) on a product and also advertising a discount is a pretty blatant way of anchoring the higher MSRP amount in a buyer's head, making the discounted price seem a bargain. While the MSRP is not quite random it is pretty irrelevant to a purchase decision as few sellers actually use the higher price. It gets more bizarre. Joseph Hallinan, in his book, *Errornomics*,[8] describes the phenomenon whereby when stores place some (arbitrary) limitation on a purchase, such as 'Limit – six per customer,' sales will go up and moreover will go up even more as the limit is increased (until sales tail off at a nonsensical limit). This is not rational, but people are fixated by numbers and so tend to anchor on to them when making decisions, *whether relevant or not*. The risk is that individuals will, rather than look objectively at risks, be moved to make bad decisions by irrelevant anchors. And in business an anchor need not be financial but, for example, salespersons may pressure customers to close a deal by a certain date, which is often arbitrary, for example tied to their sale departments' rather than customers' deadlines.

3.2.2 Framing

Anchoring is related to another insidious human bias known as *framing*. Simply put, humans will often give a different, sometimes contradictory, answer if a question is reworded or reframed. Joseph Hallinan even goes so far as to say that 'a great many day-to-day [decision-making] errors come about because we frame, or look at, an issue in the wrong way'. Hallinan gives an example of an experiment in the wine section of a grocery store when at various times French or German music was played. Researchers found that when German music was played, sales of German wine went up, even though shoppers generally expressed a preference for French wines. When asked why they had chosen a particular wine, only 14 per cent pointed to the music as a trigger. Frames are so powerful, Hallinan says, precisely because we don't know they are there.

Many of the insights into the power of framing come from the work of Kahneman and Tversky, who studied how people make different decisions when a problem is restated in a different way.[9] In a series of experiments that helped Kahneman win the Nobel Prize for Economics, they showed that people make different decisions depending on the way that a question is asked or a situation framed. For example, when considering possible outbreaks of deadly disease, experiments showed that people would choose a solution where some lives will be 'saved' *for sure* as opposed to a solution that will possibly 'lose' the remainder. Preferring certainty to risk is known as *risk aversion*.[10] When the problem is reframed as the first option being stated as lives 'lost' rather than 'saved' and the second option is stated as the possibility of lives saved rather than lost, people tend to switch their choice, *even though the statistical outcomes are identical*. This shows that people turn from being *risk averse* when faced with gains (here lives saved) to *risk seeking* when facing losses (here lives lost). We will return later to discuss the implications of how people's risk behaviour changes depending on their winning/losing state, as it goes some way to explaining why rogue traders desperately double their bets when trying to cover up losses. For the moment, Box 3.1 illustrates an example of *framing* in the business world.[11]

Box 3.1   Example of framing – Entremed

Surely seasoned business and investment managers would not fall for such a transparent switching of questions or information?

Joseph Hallinan tells the story of Entremed, a small US biotech company that published mildly positive results of trials of its new anti-cancer drug in the scientific journal *Nature* in 1998. The *New York Times* subsequently printed a short technical summary of the research findings on an inside page. Some five months later, on what must have been a slow news day, the *New York Times* recycled the story on its front page with a headline that employed upbeat words, such as 'hope', 'awe' and 'eradicate', but crucially added no new information. It was an old story but with different framing.

The share price of Entremed went ballistic, increasing by a factor of seven during trading before falling back to a 300 per cent increase at the end of the day. This is still one of the greatest single-day increases in US stock market history. But then reality kicked in and over time it became apparent that other companies were finding it difficult to recreate the initial trial results. The stock price of Entremed plummeted. Note that in mid-2014, Entremed[12] was still trading and still testing its drug with some minor victories but its stock is only 5 per cent of what it was at the peak.

Entremed itself was not to blame for the euphoria; investment managers believed the headline hype and the re-framing of the proposition by the newspaper.

Similar stories of so-called *irrational exuberance* have been repeated throughout history from the Dutch Tulip Mania of 1637[13] to the US housing bubble of the early 2000s[14] that helped to create the Global Financial Crisis.

3.2.3 Groupthink

In one of the most influential studies in the behavioural sciences, Irving Janis considered the question of why a group of intelligent, thoughtful, professional decision-makers can sometimes make decisions that, in retrospect, are deeply flawed.[15] In particular, Janis studied several examples of flawed decisions made by the US government, such as the Bay of Pigs invasion, the failure to prepare for the attack on Pearl Harbor and the escalation of the Vietnam War. He concluded that the individual decision-makers were victims of a type of behavioural bias that he called *Groupthink*, and which he described as:

> The mode of thinking that persons engage in when <u>concurrence seeking</u> [original emphasis] becomes so dominant in a cohesive group that it tends to override realistic appraisals of alternative courses of action [and] refers to a deterioration in mental efficiency, reality testing and moral judgements as a result of group pressures.

In other words, when seeking to make a decision, decision-maker(s) are sometimes overly influenced by the thinking of their colleagues and search for consensus rather than optimal outcomes. Janis describes 'self-censorship' by decision-makers in the context of Groupthink as the 'voluntary censorship of one's own opinions when they deviate from the apparent group consensus'. The Groupthink phenomenon is in fact very difficult to demonstrate in practice unless all information about a flawed decision is available, which is rare. But inquiries into major disasters, such as the space shuttle Challenger calamity[16] and the lemming-like rush to lend to the construction industry by Irish banks before the GFC,[17] highlight the influence of Groupthink and so-called *herding* behaviour. But not only bankers were subject to Groupthink. An analysis by sociologists[18] (note not economists) at the University Of California, Berkeley, of the minutes of the Federal Open Markets Committee (FOMC), the body that sets interest rates for the United States (and arguably the world) found that the members of the Federal Reserve Board 'whose job it is to make sense of the direction of the economy were more or less blinded by their assumptions about how reality works'. The world's leading economists could not see the Invisible Gorilla of the impending crisis in their own backyard.

Groupthink is insidious because the pressure on dissenters becomes over-whelming, gradually wearing them down in the face of growing (if actually misplaced) unanimity as described in Box 3.2, which provides an example of Groupthink in the case of RBS and its acquisition of ABN-AMRO bank.[19]

Box 3.2   Example of Groupthink – Royal Bank of Scotland

In describing the ill-fated decision to acquire a large part of the ABN AMRO bank by the board of Royal Bank of Scotland (RBS), Iain Martin in his book, *Making it Happen*, documents the change of heart of RBS directors toward the acquisition first proposed by the CEO, Sir Fred Goodwin. Initially the board were lukewarm to the idea of a takeover of even part of ABN AMRO as they had recently committed to an 'organic growth' strategy. But over a period of only six months, and a small number of full board meetings, directors came around to the idea, mainly motivated by the fact that the acquisition meant that, after the acquisition, RBS would be 'Bigger than Barclays'.

Although the directors had previously agreed an organic growth strategy, at crucial board meetings, no one spoke against the proposal, even though the structure of the deal, and hence RBS's risk, was continually changing as other parties joined or left the takeover consortium. Furthermore, insufficient due-diligence was done by RBS on the target, because the ABN AMRO board considered RBS's approach to be unwelcomed.

Nonetheless, the consensus of the board focused on 'how the deal should be done' rather than 'whether it should be done'. As described in Chapter 4, this misplaced harmony proved disastrous for RBS.

To counteract Groupthink, Janis recommends that for every major decision that a firm takes, a 'devil's advocate' should be appointed, from internal or external sources, to challenge each major point. The rationale is that by getting counter-arguments onto the table, secret dissenters would be emboldened to express their doubts. This suggestion is discussed later in Chapter 9.

3.2.4 Denominator neglect

Managers often claim that they work to the bottom line, ie profit, but in fact are most often addicted to the top line, ie income/revenue, when looking at performance numbers. Paul Slovic,[20] a distinguished expert in psychology and risk, describes what he calls *denominator neglect*, where individuals look at the 'headline figure' and tend to ignore the context. Slovic cites an example of an experiment where people judged a disease that 'kills 1,286 people out of every 10,000' to be more dangerous than a disease that 'kills 24.4 out of 100'. The ratios are, of course, the opposite since 12.86 per 100 in the first case is less rather than more dangerous, because the preference for the higher figure ignores the denominator. Gerd Gigerenzer, a leading expert in the field, believes that people are not good at interpreting statistics and prefer data presented as 'frequencies' to the same denominator.[21] In this case, a directly comparable frequency (12.86 out of 100 versus 24.4) would have better communicated the true risk.

In business, performance is often measured by numbers such as asset growth or the number of new customers. But such measures are 'numerators' neglecting important denominators such as 'asset risk growth' or 'cost per new customer'. Chapter 4 documents a number of firms that fell into the trap of chasing top-line growth without considering underlying risks (the denominator) but Box 3.3 describes the example of Egg plc[22] which illustrates a chase for inappropriate performance figures, in their case new customers.

Box 3.3   Example of denominator neglect – Egg

At the height of the dot-com boom of the late 1990s, there was a corporate fashion for giving new companies unusual names that were supposed to resonate with Gen X and Gen Y, under-thirty, technology-literate customers. In 1998, following in the footsteps of Apple and Next, the rather staid UK insurer Prudential[23] named its new internet banking venture Egg. Egg was not burdened by the costs of a branch network as customers interacted with its staff via call centres and the internet, and these platforms were to be used to 'cross-sell' the company's insurance and investment products into a new, younger market. The first few years of Egg's life were spectacularly successful as their goal of increasing customer numbers each year was met. From a standing start in 1998, the company had already acquired over 2 million customers by the end of 2002 and was listed on the prestigious London Stock Exchange (LSE).

At that point, Prudential announced its intention to sell off the company to investors, presumably at a sizeable profit. But acquiring new customers is one thing – acquiring profitable new customers is quite another. Egg had been issuing millions of credit cards to its youthful Gen X/Y customers but, in hindsight, this was not a stable or profitable market and credit defaults were beginning to rise. In fact, Egg had never been profitable due to the financial drag of the huge investment needed in new technology to get started.

By 2006, Prudential was forced to buy Egg back and to de-list it from the Exchange. In a classic 'death spiral', a wave of cost–cutting and redundancies followed and, in 2007, Egg was sold to Citigroup. Blinded by the potential of the internet, the board and management of Egg had pursued customer growth at the expense of prudent banking. The numerator in their performance measure was 'number of new customers per year'. The denominator should have been something like 'who were good credit risks', but wasn't, as the firm only chased the top-line growth in new customers, regardless of their risk profiles.

But Egg was not unique. Other firms, such as HBOS, Tesco and Washington Mutual, were making the same mistakes at the same time but, as described in Chapter 4, on a much larger scale.

3.2.5 Optimism and overconfidence

When making decisions, humans appear to be prone to numerous cognitive biases including anchoring, framing and Groupthink as described above, but one bias in particular is important in business, and that is *overconfidence*. Humans are optimists. In her book, *The Optimism Bias*,[24] neuroscientist Tali Sharot describes how humans are 'hardwired' for optimism and to be perennially optimistic is part of our basic make-up. Using a functional Magnetic Resonance Imaging (fMRI) scanner, Dr Sharot and her team recorded brain activity in volunteers as they were asked to imagine specific events that might occur to them in the future. For pleasant events, the volunteers' brain scans showed a strong reaction by lighting up certain parts of the brain, but not so when asked to consider unpleasant events. Dr Sharot traced these feelings to one of the most primitive regions of the brain, the amygdala, which regulates the production of positive feelings. She concluded that people are hardwired to be optimistic and, furthermore, take pleasure in considering an optimistic future.

Optimism is generally considered to be good. It helps people to be resilient in the face of adversity and somewhat paradoxically it helps people to learn from their mistakes, as the future will be, or at least feel, better if they do learn. Without optimism, many business ventures would not get off the ground, as the desire to have a better future drives many personal and business ventures. Tali Sharot and her colleagues have found that optimism actually makes us feel good in a physical sense. Even if the optimistic future is illusory, optimism makes us feel better in the moment, which is not to be dismissed as, for example, a study into cancer survival described by Sharot found that optimists did actually survive a little longer than pessimists.

But optimism, if it is misplaced, can be dangerous, making people make bad decisions because they have a good feeling about the potential outcomes, even if the outcomes are unlikely. People are often *overconfident* in their ability to predict the future. Daniel Kahneman notes that optimism is also 'widespread, stubborn and costly' to shareholders. In particular, research showed that 'highly confident CEOs took excessive risks' and were 'more likely than others to overpay for target companies and undertake value-destroying mergers'. The takeover of ABN AMRO by Royal Bank of Scotland, as described in Box 3.2, was certainly value-destroying, driven by the supreme overconfidence of the RBS board and its CEO, Sir Fred Goodwin. In an object lesson in optimism, they were prepared to buy the company even though there was insufficient time to do proper due diligence. If they had not been so confident, the disastrous takeover of ABN AMRO may not have happened.

As far back as 1977, pioneering behavioural experiments by, among others, Baruch Fischoff and Sarah Liechtenstein, found that as a general rule, people tend to be overconfident in their assessments of risks,[25] that is they exaggerate the extent to which what they know is correct. They also found that some people displayed *extreme overconfidence* and for those people 'answers to which extremely high odds had been assigned were frequently wrong'. In other words, such extreme optimists often overestimated their ability to succeed in very high-risk ventures. Optimism coupled with extreme overconfidence in one's own judgement is a toxic cocktail, which can result in potentially reckless decisions being made. In his groundbreaking book on Strategic Risk, *The Upside*, Adrian Slywotzky[26] documents typical failure rates for specific business initiatives, such as the likely failure of a new pharmaceutical product being over 90 per cent, and warns, 'when you overestimate the odds, you will underestimate the investment needed to win'. Optimists perennially overestimate the odds of success and thus may set the firm/project on a course towards failure.

3.2.6 Inattentional Blindness

Chapter 1 introduced the amusing Invisible Gorilla experiment. Surely such a fun experiment would not work with real professionals in real life? Trafton Drew[27] and his colleagues at Harvard Medical School devised an insightful experiment into so-called Inattentional Blindness (IB) or 'blind spots' in professionals. Box 3.4 gives an example of missing an Invisible Gorilla.

Box 3.4   Example of blind spots

The Harvard experimenters presented a series of five Computed Tomography (CT) scans of patients' lung cavities to a group of trained radiologists and expert examiners asking them to identify possible cancer tumour nodules in the scans. A control group of novices without medical training were also shown the pictures. Hidden in the group of pictures was one scan with a small but discernible picture of a gorilla inserted.

Surely the experts could see the gorilla? The researchers found not – in fact over 80 per cent of the experts did not report seeing a gorilla even though the inserted picture was many times the size of the cancerous nodules that they were looking for. None of the non-experts spotted the gorilla.

However, all of the experts and non-experts found the gorilla when they were presented with the scans again and specifically asked to find it.

The researchers characterized the results of their experiment as an example of a phenomenon known as *satisfaction of search*, in which 'detection of one stimulus interferes with detection of subsequent stimuli'. In other words, we are so pleased that we are doing our job well that we sometimes miss the unusual but obvious. These experiments, and others that are discussed above, show that all of us, including the senior management of large firms, suffer from a whole range of cognitive biases that distort our judgements, including *'blind spots'*. Daniel Kahneman notes that the Invisible Gorilla study highlights two important facts about our thinking: even experts can be blind to the obvious, but, probably more important, we can be blind to our own blindness.[28] One of the goals of People Risk Management is to help make people become aware of their own blind spots, *making the invisible visible to them*.

3.2.7 Common cognitive biases

There have been numerous studies into cognitive biases that have thrown up many examples that have been classified by different names by different researchers. There is no definitive list of all cognitive biases[29] nor definitive definitions of the most commonly used ones, but the biases in Table 3.1 appear most often in the literature. These biases are particularly applicable to business decision-making and are referenced throughout the book.

TABLE 3.1 Common cognitive biases

Cognitive biases	Informal definitions
Overconfidence	The tendency to overestimate the likelihood that outcomes will be positive and/or to underestimate the risks in new venture.
Loss aversion	The tendency to weigh losses greater than equivalent gains, often resulting in a willingness to take unnecessary risks to recover or avoid losses.
Groupthink	The tendency to conform to group beliefs, also called Herding or the Bandwagon effect.
Anchoring bias	The tendency to rely too heavily on one piece of information (the anchor) rather than search for other, more relevant, information.
Confirmation bias	The tendency to search for information that supports existing beliefs.
Illusion of control	The tendency to overestimate one's ability to control future events especially those out of one's control.
Planning fallacy	The tendency to underestimate the difficulties of implementing a decision, often in the mistaken belief that the decision is somehow novel and unique, sometimes justified as 'this time it is different'.
Sunk cost fallacy	The tendency to stick with a decision because the loss incurred in reversing it is unpalatable, though that is the best thing to do.[30]
Availability bias	The tendency to give undue prominence to information available at the time of making a decision. Similar to 'recency bias' and is exacerbated when the new information is repeated by others to make it appear even more important – 'recency illusion'.
Attentional bias	The tendency to concentrate on certain alternatives that are emotionally prevalent or recurring in one's thinking.
Ambiguity bias	The tendency to dismiss alternatives where information is unavailable in favour of those where information is available.
Action bias	The tendency to prefer action rather than continuing to analyse a problem, colloquially 'Just Do It'.

TABLE 3.1 *continued*

Cognitive biases	Informal definitions
Halo effect	The tendency to uncritically extrapolate someone's success in one area to another.
Denominator neglect/bias	The tendency to misinterpret statistics that are specified with different denominators, sometimes called 'Base Rate Neglect'.
Illusion of skill	The tendency to attribute outcomes that are outside of one's control to skill rather than 'luck'.
Status quo bias	The tendency to prefer that things stay the same, making necessary changes harder to justify.

Before considering their dangers, it is worth noting that cognitive biases are definitely not personality defects. Biases come into play in specific situations and an individual might be subject to a particular bias in one situation but not in another. For example, even a normally pessimistic individual might, in the heat of the moment, succumb to a burst of overconfidence and agree to a course of action that later they are loath to reverse. Over millennia, humans have developed practices to counter biases, such as 'sleep on it' to counter the so-called 'availability' bias in which recent information is given undue prominence because it has just come to our 'attention'. And the wise old saying, 'don't throw good money after bad' is an attempt to counter the so-called 'sunk cost fallacy'.[30]

3.2.8 Dangers of cognitive biases

Cognitive biases can be dangerous in business. Most experiments into cognitive biases tend to focus on one specific bias, such as overconfidence or loss aversion. That it is because it is methodologically difficult to separate the effects of multiple interacting biases when considering the outcomes of any one decision. Multiple biases appear to reinforce one another. It is not difficult to envisage a situation where an executive is supremely confident (even overconfident) in his/her own judgement and ability, and primed by advocates for a particular view with a prediction that a particular venture will be a great success (framing) will produce a particular return for shareholders (anchoring). In such a situation, it would be natural for an executive to champion such a venture, even though that may be a bad decision, because risks have not been properly evaluated.

But what about board members? With even less information than executives and with executives framing a proposal in ever more glowing terms, directors, unless they are very strong, might be prepared to let a decision go through 'on the nod'. Chapter 4 will show that that is exactly the situation that led to the strategic blunders that eventually sank companies such as Lehman Brothers and Royal Bank of

Scotland. In considering the systemic failure of Irish banks during the GFC, Michael Dowling and Brain Lucey identified that boards and senior management had failed their shareholders:[31]

> Lax risk management, aided by poor board oversight and behavioural biases among senior executives, is now viewed as one of the primary causes of the over-lending during the 'Celtic Tiger' years which fuelled the excessive growth in credit and subsequent banking implosion, eventually resulting in all Irish banks ending in state ownership.

3.3 Heuristics

Over the past quarter of a century behavioural scientists have identified that people do not always think and behave as might be expected when solving a business problem. Experts such as Daniel Kahneman, Paul Slovic, Baruch Fischoff and Gerd Gigerenzer have found that people do not analyse most problems they face in great detail before coming to a judgement but instead make use of rules of thumb or *heuristics*, which have been learned from experience. The Nobel Prize winner Herbert Simon,[32] one of the fathers of organizational theory, believed that people have to rely on heuristics because their *rationality* is *bounded* or limited by:

a the amount of information that they have;

b the time they have to make a decision; and

c the cognitive limitations of their minds.

Knowing this, managers must be constantly aware that there may be something important that they do not know and must continue to search for it, even if they are moving forward with a particular course of action.

Humans are heuristics machines.[33] In many situations, we operate almost as if we are on autopilot. Certainly for mundane tasks such as crossing the road we do not perform complex calculations on the relative speeds of approaching cars but (in most cases) we nevertheless navigate a crossing successfully using our experience and intuition. However, sometimes we trust our intuition too much. In the United States the National Highway Traffic Safety Administration (NHTSA) reports[34] that pedestrian accidents increase in evenings in autumn and winter (because darkness reduces the visual information we have to make a good decision). Accidents also increase as a pedestrian's blood alcohol level rises (ie we have diminished cognitive capabilities). Our heuristics, learned over many years, can sometimes let us down, often because we become overconfident in our 'gut feel'. Intuition can of course be right most of the time, which only goes to reinforce our belief in using it in most instances. But other invisible pressures, such as conflicts of interest, also come into play.

3.4 Conflicts of interest

Conflicts of interest exist throughout business. In fact, the basic profit motive that drives firms is based on the conflict between maximizing profits as against non-financial considerations, some ethical and some practical.[35] For example, the decision to push staff to their physical limits by over-working them may generate profits in the short term but may also burn out employees. Some conflicts of interest produce situations where individuals make decisions that are illegal, as in the case described in Chapter 4 of Rajat Gupta, a director of Goldman Sachs,[36] who was jailed for *insider trading* for passing information gained in board meetings to a friend. Directors are routinely warned of the conflicts of interest between their personal and fiduciary roles, but sometimes prioritize one interest (in the Gupta case, friendship) over another (Gupta's fiduciary duty).

Other conflicts of interest are not so easy to identify. For example, rogue traders, as described in Chapter 4, do not 'steal' money but attempt to gain time to recover their trading losses by misrepresenting their dire situation. They resolve the inherent conflict of interest between making profits for the firm as against accurate reporting to shareholders, by prioritizing the firm (and, in the process, themselves) over shareholders. Note that in most rogue trading incidents, the tactic used to misrepresent the situation had been used multiple times, with success, before it failed. In other words, the 'culture' of the firm and its deficient control environment provided the opportunity for, and may even have encouraged, traders to resolve conflicts of interest, using unethical and potentially illegal means.

Conflicts of interest are *invisible* because, unless specifically raised by a decision-maker, it will not be obvious to an observer that such a conflict exists. Chapter 10 discusses the concept of company Codes of Conduct/Ethics, which almost always prohibit conflicts of interest but mainly in the context of personal as against company advantage, not intra-company conflicts, such as misselling products to customers to increase revenue.

3.5 Systems of human decision-making

Recent advances in understanding human behaviour, especially using brain-scanning equipment, have led to new models of human decision-making. When faced with a stimulus, humans appear to have two quite different modes or *systems of thinking*: one which is instinctive and intuitive, and the other, which is deliberative and reflective. The originators of the dual systems concept, Keith Stanovich and Richard West,[37] described the two *systems* thus: System 1 thinking is automatic, largely unconscious, and relatively undemanding of computational capacity; whereas System 2 comprises various characteristics that have been viewed as typifying controlled processing and the processes of analytic intelligence. In his bestselling book, *Thinking, Fast and Slow*, Daniel Kahneman portrays these two systems as 'characters' that he describes as: System 1, which operates automatically and quickly, with little or no effort and no sense of voluntary control; and System 2, which allocates attention to the mental activities that demand it, including complex computations. For example, when we cross the road we are using System 1 thinking whereas when we add up a column of numbers we are thinking in System 2.

The concept of dual systems thinking goes some way to bridging the gap between the traditional perception of deliberative decision-making that is subject to 'bias' and the notion of heuristics that are evolutionary and often find a satisfactory solution much faster than deliberation. The analytical System 2 is traditionally considered superior to System 1 as a mode of thinking, because it encourages a more complete consideration of the benefits, costs and risks involved. In business and in business education, the analytical System 2 is promoted as *the* method of thinking and philosophers and scientists are esteemed for their rigorous logical approach, even though we, *and the philosophers*, spend most of our time in System 1 mode. As we become more expert at our jobs we come to rely on and use our intuitive system more as we capture and embed our experience in our practice. Experts don't have to consider each new problem from scratch; their experience tells them that they can rule out a whole class of possible answers with only a minimum of information. For example, bankers can tell a lot about the financial health of a company looking to borrow by some simple financial figures, such as cash flow and inventory turnover. However, such figures may be meaningless for a new technology start-up and may cause a banker to miss out on a great opportunity, if constrained by simple numbers and lack of familiarity with new technology.

The two thinking systems are not mutually exclusive. For example our *attention* is shared by both systems; our initial reaction to a stimulus, such as a loud noise, will be involuntary with System 1 unconsciously searching for the source and System 2 analysing the causes once we have *decided* that we do not have to flee the scene.[38] But the converse sometimes happens. For example, when a person is *cognitively busy* with a System 2 activity such as adding up columns of figures, they will often react to a new stimulus with an immediate System 1, rather than a thoughtful System 2, response. From a business perspective, this is a warning that getting too involved in the detail may cause us to miss warning signs. This appears to have been the case with Sir Fred Goodwin, the last CEO of RBS before its collapse, who was characterized in official inquiries as a control freak who meddled constantly in decisions about minutiae, such as furniture costs,[39] and missed the looming credit crisis. The convenient accounting heuristic 'take care of the pennies and the pounds will take of themselves' did not appear to work in the RBS case.

In this book we will be looking at the problems that arise in both systems of thinking, particularly at situations where our intuition causes us to do something that is wrong because we haven't recognized it as a new problem, and also situations where our deliberation gives us the wrong answer, because for example we are overly confident in some of our assumptions. Before that, we consider a (somewhat) hypothetical example.

3.6 A hypothetical example

Box 3.5 shows a (*hypothetical*) proposal being made by a CEO of a successful UK company to expand into France. It is part of the CEO's report to a (*hypothetical*) board meeting.

Box 3.5   Example of a hypothetical CEO proposal

Board agenda item: CEO presentation

As the preliminary financials show, we have had another spectacular year, exceeding our guidance to the Stock Exchange by increasing our customer base *yet again* by over 40 per cent, mostly in our target demographic of 19–40 year olds, the tech-savvy generation in need of our banking and insurance products and not well served by our competitors. We expect this success at home to continue to grow but as a management team and board we are always on the lookout for new opportunities. We believe that as an internet-based organization, we can go anywhere and France may be just the first step in our global journey.

France, our closest neighbour, has a population that is almost identical to the UK (some 63 million) and a median age that is about the same (40 vs. 39.7 years). Paris is the famed city of light, a world-class capital of culture, fine wine, amazing food and 'joie de vivre', or joy of life. Using the CEO's discretionary R&D budget, the CFO has already acquired a small office in the middle of Paris as a convenient base to look into the French market as one that may be ready for our products. She has already concluded that French financial institutions are just as staid as in Britain and our target market is not well served. But first impressions are not enough, so the CFO has already contacted a local marketing consultancy and engaged a hip internet developer to do a mock-up of what our site might look like for our French demographic. Our marketing director will give a quick demo of this new site after this board meeting.

As CEO I have suggested, and the Chairman has readily agreed, that we hold our next board meeting as an away-day in Paris to discuss our strategy and other opportunities for international growth. By that point, our Head of Strategic Planning and the CFO will have pulled together the necessary financials and marketing information to allow a decision to be made on whether or not to grasp this opportunity. The initial modelling looks 'trés bon'.

I would like your initial feedback on this concept. On a scale of 1–9 how do you feel about it? Where 1 means 'I don't like it, we should stick to what we are used to' and 9 is 'Yes, excited to be part of this new phase in our company's development'.

The reader might at this point reflect on their own feelings about this hypothetical opportunity as presented to the board and make a mental note as to their feelings on the suggested 1–9 scale.

This example is not completely hypothetical but is based on a strategic decision by the board of Egg plc to enter into the French market in 2002, after four years of spectacular growth in the UK. This venture turned out, however, to be the peak of the firm's ambition. In mid-2004, Egg was forced to retreat from their disastrous foray into France, because as the board of the parent company, Prudential, admitted, they just did not have the money to continue.

This example is, of necessity, simplistic and we do not imply that it represents the actual arguments made by the then head of Egg, Paul Gratton,[40] a ferociously hard-working CEO who was nominated by Businessweek in mid-2002 as 'one of the most innovative financial-services executives in Europe'. The fictitious pitch made by the CEO was designed to illustrate some of the biases described in this chapter. The narrative is *confident* and resolutely upbeat using words such as 'amazing', 'new opportunities' and 'excited' that are designed to make the reader feel good. The argument is *framed* in the positive, stressing the upside and downplaying the risks (except for the throwaway 'first impressions are not enough'). There are lots of *anchors*, '40 per cent', '63 million', 'aged 40' but these are all irrelevant to the strategy being described. There is also a hint of Groupthink in that the Chairman, CEO and CFO are already on board and anyone who does not agree that is a great opportunity is being backward. The story plays on good feelings about Paris and its attractions, and is designed to engender positive feelings in the reader.

The tone of this proposal is deliberately confident but no more so than the actual words[41] used by Egg's board when describing the initial few months of the new venture:

> We have had 28,000 card accepts in the first month and early indicators suggest that we are attracting a higher quality of applications than expected. The average salary of our card customers is €50,000, which is 30 per cent higher than the French average and is indicative that our brand is appealing to a more up-market base consistent with our experience in the UK.

This official statement by the board of Egg to the market is brimming with confidence (eg 'consistent with our experience in the UK'), largely irrelevant anchors (eg '€50,000') and positive framing (eg 'more up-market base'). The confidence of the board, however, proved to be illusory.

The vehicle used by Egg to initially enter this new market was its acquisition of Zebank, an online finance subsidiary of the large French luxury goods conglomerate Groupe Arnault. But Zebank was already loss-making when it was purchased and Egg was unable to turn it around. This begs the question 'why would Egg, an inexperienced UK company, be able to turn around a French company when it could not be done by acknowledged marketing experts such as those who owned Dior and Dom Perignon?' This is an example of the so-called *planning fallacy* or the unwillingness to look elsewhere for examples of contra viewpoints or projections when considering a new project, which is often tied to overconfidence and confirmation biases. In the grip of the planning fallacy, Daniel Kahneman warns that executives make decisions based on 'delusional optimism rather than on a rational weighting of gains, losses, and probabilities. They overestimate benefits and underestimate costs.' As history has shown, the 'delusional optimism' of Egg's management and board was misplaced. But they are not the only managers to suffer from this particular bias, as the example of Tesco in Chapter 4 will illustrate.

This chapter looked at the surprisingly wide variety of biases and illusions, such as overconfidence and Groupthink, that we all are subject to and which, as behavioural psychologists have found, can cause us to make bad, sometimes disastrous, decisions. But before moving onto describe examples of cognitive biases in real-life business situations, as authors we must address the issues of whether we too have biases. The answer, of course, is yes. In fact, writing a book is an exercise in searching for examples that support the hypotheses being put forward, which is, of course, a *confirmation* bias. We are very aware of the confirmation biases that we may be subject to but endeavour to view the information as dispassionately as we can. For example, we are aware that the Fukushima disaster was caused not by individuals per se but by a catastrophic natural event; however, the deficiencies in the preparations to handle the consequences of such a disaster were enormous, as identified by the official inquiry. Better People Risk Management, such as improved training and more effective challenge to perceived wisdom would *not* have stopped the tsunami from wreaking havoc, but *might* have made the reaction more effective. Unfortunately, we will never know.

Notes

1   Leon Festinger (1957) was the developer of the theory of Cognitive Dissonance where conflicting attitudes, beliefs or behaviours produce a feeling of discomfort leading to an alteration in one of the attitudes, beliefs or behaviours in order to reduce the discomfort.

2   When used in economics the terms Behavioural Economics and Behavioural Finance are often used.

3   The problems with evaluating Business Cases for risky projects have been known for many years, for example see Hodder, J and Riggs, H (1985) Pitfalls in Evaluating Risky Projects, *Harvard Business Review*, 1 January 1985, www.hbr.org

4   See Tavris and Aronson (2008).

5   See Watchorn, E (2007) Applying a structured approach to operational risk scenario analysis in Australia, *Australian Prudential Regulation Authority*, www.apra.gov.au

6   Ariely, D (2008) *Predictably Irrational: The hidden forces that shape our decisions*, HarperCollins.

7   In the United States, a Social Security Number (SSN) is issued to all permanent and temporary residents for Social Security (and Tax) purposes. It is a 9-digit number assigned randomly.

8   Hallinan (2009).

9   Described in Kahneman (2011).

10   See Kahneman (2011) for a description of Loss Aversion and its part in Prospect Theory for which Kahneman jointly won the Nobel Prize for Economics.

11   See Hallinan (2009) for discussion of the Entremed case.

12   In mid-2014, Entremed changed its name to Casi Pharmaceuticals, see http://www.casipharmaceuticals.com

13   For a discussion of Dutch Tulip Mania see the Wikipedia article *Tulip Mania*.

14   For a good discussion of the causes and impact of the US housing bubble of the early 2000s see Nobel Prize winner Robert Schiller (2005 and 2008).

15 See Janis (1971).

16 See Heffernan (2011) and see Wikipedia article *Space Shuttle Challenger.*

17 See Nyberg (2011) and Lucey *et al* (2012).

18 For a discussion of professional blind spots see, Fligstein, N, Brundage, J and Schultz, M (2014) Why the Federal Reserve failed to see the financial crisis of 2008, Department of Sociology, University of California Berkeley, http://sociology.berkeley.edu

19 See Martin (2103) for a discussion of the RBS/ABN AMRO takeover.

20 For an introduction to the concept of denominator neglect and Paul Slovic, see Kahneman (2011) and Kahneman *et al* (1982).

21 See Gigerenzer (2008, 2010 and 2014).

22 For a history of Egg see Osborne, A (2011) The History of Egg: A shattering experience: How Britain's first internet bank left insurer Prudential with plenty of Egg on its face, *Daily Telegraph*, 1 March, www.telegraph.co.uk

23 Although its existing banking subsidiary was staid, concentrating on basic banking products, Prudential did have advanced and profitable insurance operations around the world.

24 See Sharot (2011).

25 For a discussion on the importance of Overconfidence see Kahneman (2011) and also Lichtenstein, S, Fischoff, B and Phillips, L (1982) Calibration of Probabilities: The state of the art to 1980 in Kahenman *et al* (1982). See also Sutherland (2013) for a description of Fischoff's groundbreaking research on overconfidence.

26 See Slywotzky (2007).

27 Drew, T, Ho, M and Wolfe, J (2013) The Invisible Gorilla strikes again: sustained inattentional blindness in expert observers, *Psychological Science,* published online at http://pss.sagepub.com/content/24/9/1848

28 See Heffernan (2011).

29 See Lloyds (2010) *Behaviour: bear, bull or lemming?* Lloyds Emerging Risk Report, www.lloyds.com. There is also a very long list of biases in the Wikipedia article *List of Cognitive Biases*, which also points out some of the definitional pitfalls.

30 This is not to suggest that 'sunk costs' should be ignored, only that they should be considered in the light of options that provide a better alternative, having taking into account writing off the sunk costs. In some situations, such as the need to meet real, as opposed to self-imposed, deadlines, continuing the current course of action may be the best (or only) option available.

31 See Dowling, M and Lucey, B (2014) From hubris to nemesis: Irish banks, behavioural biases, and the crisis, *Journal of Risk Management in Financial Institutions*, 7 (2).

32 Herbert Simon is the father of Decision Sciences and won a Nobel Prize in Economics for describing how managers in organizations actually make decisions. See Kahneman (2011) for a description of his influence and the Wikipedia article *Herbert A. Simon*.

33 See Neth, H, Meder, B, Kothiyal, A and Gigerenzer, G (2014) Homo Heuristicus in the financial world: from risk management to managing uncertainty, *Journal of Risk Management in Financial Institutions*, 7 (2).

34 See National Highway Traffic Safety Administration (2008) National Pedestrian Crash Reports, http://www-nrd.nhtsa.dot.gov/

35 In Classical Economics, conflicts of interest between shareholders and management are described by what is called Agency Theory, see for example Kahneman (2011) in the context of 'sunk costs'. Agency Theory assumes that managers will act 'rationally' and behave in the best interests of the firm and furthermore that shareholders can ensure that managers do not make adverse judgements against them by use of judicious compensation strategies. As the case studies in this book show, however, managers are driven by more than compensation and sometimes succumb to personal conflicts of interest not covered by Agency Theory.

36 See McCool, G and Basil Katz B (2012) Ex-Business Titan Gupta Guilty of Insider Trading, *Reuters*, 15 June.

37 See Kahneman (2011).

38 System 1 controls the so-called 'flee or fight' response that has evolved in most animals in reaction to perceived dangers.

39 See Fraser (2014) for details of Goodwin's obsession with furnishings.

40 See *BusinessWeek* (2002) Paul Grattan, 16 June.

41 See Egg (2002) *UK business on track to deliver further growth in quarterly profits, Egg France launches successfully*, Egg plc Pre-Close Trading Statement 12 Dec 2002.

Case studies in People Risk

04

> *A few lucky gambles can crown a reckless leader with a halo of prescience and boldness.* **DANIEL KAHNEMAN**[1]

KEY MESSAGES

- People Risk events occur within organizations at multiple levels with varying likelihood of occurrence and unpredictable consequences when they do.

- People Risk events occur because of bad decisions arising from individual and group biases and conflicts of interest.

- People Risks are apparent at every level from a simple incident/accident to a whole industry.

- People use common rationalizations to explain their actions and mistakes.

4.1 Summary of cases

The cases described in this chapter are many but nonetheless are only a fraction of those that could be covered in this book. These cases were chosen because they cut across industries, countries and organizational types, although all involve large corporations. The losses run from the almost risible, such as the reputational damage in the HBOS statement case, to untold misery following the Global Financial Crisis. But they have one thing in common – they were caused by people, *not* natural events. They occurred on the frontline, such as in the BP Gulf of Mexico oil spill, and in the boardroom, such as the failure of RBS or the disastrous business strategies of Tesco and Lehman Brothers.

The cases also illustrate the fickleness of human nature, as corporate heroes are showered with praise one day only to be castigated as fools the next. But as Professor Barry Turner[2] noted perceptively, disasters are rarely caused by one person no matter how senior, but instead are caused by the biases and inaction of many, *who should have known and done better*. The failure of one firm at one time may be passed off as merely due to bad management or, if generous, bad luck. However, massive losses in or even the collapse of so many hitherto successful organizations must raise the question, are there common factors in these cases and if so what are they? The answers lie deep within each one of us, particularly in our inability to see ourselves as being less than perfect. Humility not hubris is the key to averting such disasters.

Table 4.1 summarizes the cases discussed in this chapter using the 4Is Model described in section 4.1 below. It summarizes the losses incurred and describes the main *rationalizations* discussed in Chapter 3.

TABLE 4.1 People Risk – summary of case studies

Case	Description	Losses	Rationalizations
INCIDENTS			
HBOS – mistaken bank statement	Delivery of 75,000 statements	Reputation – embarrassment	Mistake – unknown operator
Air New Zealand – Flight 901	Fatal air crash	257 deaths	Miscommunication and lack of situational awareness
Medical fatality – Elaine Bromiley	Medical emergency	One death	Experts' blind spots, and lack of situational awareness
INDIVIDUALS			
Bank fraud – Ms Rajina Subramaniam	Fraud	AUD $40 million	Just Desserts – revenge for perceived abuse
Rogue trading – Barings, AIB, etc	Fraud	Various	Temporary Use – covering up for losses
Medical fatalities – Dr Harold Shipman	Patient murders	> 215 deaths	Unknown – possible addictive personality
Fraud – JPMorgan and Bernie Madoff	Failure to report fraud	US $2 billion fine	Distrust of Law
HBOS – banking fraud	Fraud	Unknown > £35 million	Economic Necessity, Just Desserts
Insider trading – Goldman Sachs	Fraud	£118 million	Distrust of Law and Victimless Crime

TABLE 4.1 *continued*

Case	Description	Losses	Rationalizations
INSTITUTIONS			
Royal Bank of Scotland	Strategic overreach	Acquired by UK Government	Ubiquity, Distrust of Law
Enron	Fraud – corporate	Bankruptcy	Distrust of Law, Victimless Crime
WorldCom	Fraud – corporate	Bankruptcy	Temporary Use, Distrust of Law
Washington Mutual	Bad lending	Bankruptcy	Ubiquity, Distrust of Law
HBOS	Bad lending	Acquired by Lloyds Bank	Ubiquity, Economic Necessity
Co-operative Bank	Strategic overreach	Acquired by Private Investors	Economic Necessity
JPMorgan – The Whale	Trading losses	US $6 billion	Economic Necessity, Distrust of Law
HSBC	Money laundering	US $1.9 billion fine	Ubiquity, Distrust of Law
Eli Lilly	Misselling drugs	US $1.4 billion fine	Distrust of Law, Victimless Crime
BAE Systems	Bribery	£280 million fine	Distrust of Law
Siemens AG	Bribery	US $1.3 billion fine	Distrust of Law
NHS – Mid Staffordshire	Excess deaths (unknown number)	Forced administration	Economic Necessity, Distrust of Law
RIM – Blackberry	Strategic overreach	Forced acquisition	Economic Necessity
Tesco plc	Strategic overreach	> £1 billion	Economic Necessity
Lehman Brothers	Strategic overreach	Bankruptcy	Economic Necessity, Ubiquity
BP – Gulf of Mexico oil spill	Death and pollution	US $4 billion ++	Economic Necessity, Ubiquity, Distrust of Law
Fukushima nuclear plant	Nuclear accident	Unknown	Economic Necessity, Distrust of Law

TABLE 4.1 *continued*

Case	Description	Losses	Rationalizations
INDUSTRY			
Big Tobacco	Unsuitable products	Unknown	Ubiquity and Distrust of Law
New Zealand tax	Tax avoidance	NZ $2.5 billion	Ubiquity, Distrust of Law, Victimless Crime
PPI	Misselling products	£18 billion	Ubiquity, Distrust of Law, Victimless Crime
IRHP	Misselling products	£2.5 billion	Ubiquity Distrust of Law, Victimless Crime
Auto parts	Price fixing	US $2.5 billion fines	Ubiquity, Economic Necessity, Victimless Crime
LIBOR	Market manipulation	> US $4 billion fines	Ubiquity, Distrust of Law, Victimless Crime
Global Financial Crisis (GFC)	Misselling	US $6–14 trillion	Ubiquity, Distrust of Law, Victimless Crime

4.2 The 4Is Model

In considering fraud or errors, especially those that lead to serious losses, researchers tend to look to the organization or the system as the primary cause for disasters. It is not that they ignore the role of the individual but argue that on their own it is difficult for one individual or even a small group of individuals to cause a major loss or create a major disaster. While difficult, it is not, however, impossible and the higher and more entrenched an individual or small group of individuals are in an organization the greater the potential damage can be. It is true that there have to be pre-existing *latent conditions*[3] that provide the opportunity for creating large losses. But in order to create a significant disaster it takes the power of thousands of individuals in multiple organizations or institutions across an industry. Figure 4.1 shows the 4Is model[4] that juxtaposes the *likelihood* of losses occurring against the *consequences* if they do, at four different levels:

- *Incident*: in every business situation there will be many incidents that, as Frank Bird and others showed, are mainly 'near-misses' but can sometimes produce losses, including fatalities.
- *Individual*: in every business there may be many individuals who may perpetrate a fraud or make a serious error, but in general, management and financial controls in an organization/system and follow-up prosecution will tend to minimize but, unfortunately, not eliminate resulting losses.

FIGURE 4.1 The 4Is Model

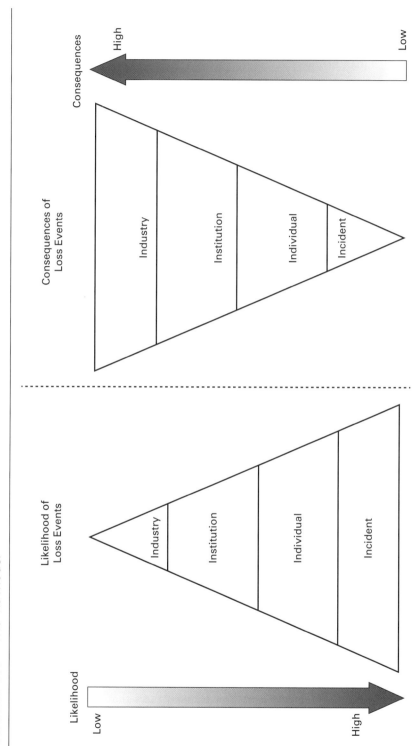

- *Institution*: most institutions/firms will make losses from time to time but every now and then an institution will fail with disastrous consequence for shareholders, as with Enron, and even for the global economy as in the case of Lehman Brothers.
- *Industry*: it is at the level of an industry that the consequences of People Risk can be greatest, such as, for example, the costs to the shareholders of banks as a result of the PPI scandal in the UK.

In the 4Is model, it is at the level of an *Industry* that the greatest losses do occur. For example, US economists Tim Curry and Lynn Shibut,[5] have estimated that the Savings and Loan (S&L) crisis of the 1980s cost the US taxpayer at least $150 billion. The term S&L refers to the many thousands of small banks that provided basic lending and savings services to local customers and dominated the US banking system until massive consolidation of the system in the 1990s as a result of this S&L crisis. Before and just after the Second World War, S&Ls were an integral part of life in the United States as typified by the fictitious Bailey Building and Loan Association in the classic film[6] It's a Wonderful Life, which showed what could happen if such a trusted institution were to fail. The S&L crisis was precipitated by changes in the late 1970s in the laws that deregulated the so-called 'thrift' industry, in effect giving S&Ls the same privileges as banks *but without* the same levels of regulation.

In terms of Turner's model, introduced in Chapter 2, the 'Precipitating Event' for the S&L disaster was a series of interest rate rises engineered by the US Federal Reserve to dampen inflation in the US economy. These rises meant that S&Ls, which tended to give out fixed rate mortgages, were suddenly faced with increased funding requirements. In effect, like several banks that failed in the GFC, their assets did not match their liabilities and many S&Ls failed. But the losses were compounded by the fact that, freed by the new regulations, the boards of several large S&Ls had been lending recklessly, chasing profits and, for some, personal gain whereas previously they had sought safety and security. In some S&Ls there had also been rampant fraud, particularly *control frauds* where creative accounting was used by individuals to deceive shareholders into believing that an S&L was solvent when, in fact, it wasn't.

In the same way that Bird, Cressey, Perrow and Turner argued, as described in Chapter 2, that one must look beyond individuals to organizations as the source of mistakes, errors and frauds, one must also look beyond *Institutions* to the *Industry* as the source of potentially even larger losses. This chapter is organized in line with the 4Is model and describes case studies of loss events at each level starting from the bottom – *Incidents*. Many, but not all of the cases are taken from the financial services industry, which is the one in which major financial losses have occurred in the last decade. Importantly, unlike other private corporations, firms in the financial services industry are highly regulated and therefore exceptional events tend to be the subject of intensive inquiry, analysis and opportunities for learning. It should also be noted that within each section the cases are organized from the simplest, usually a specific case to illustrate a point, to more complicated cases that illustrate the complexity and ambiguity of People Risk.

A number of cases of risk events that relate to the UK-based, but internationally active, Halifax/Bank of Scotland (HBOS) at various times and various levels are explicitly covered. This is NOT to suggest that HBOS was especially negligent, fraudulent or corrupt, but that in any large firm there will be many opportunities to commit fraud, make mistakes and have lapses of corporate judgement. A similar set of risk-related cases could easily be developed for other so-called Systemically Important Financial Institutions[7] (SIFIs), such as JPMorgan. The cases described here, however, form an unbroken thread from the bottom to the very top of the HBOS organization that shows that people at any level can sometimes precipitate losses.

4.3 Incidents

4.3.1 HBOS – mistaken bank statements

One evening after work in January 2007, a young woman from Aberdeen in Scotland arrived home to find five large packages of post left on her doorstep. Ms Stephanie McLaughlan had requested a bank statement from her bank, HBOS, but was surprised when she found the statements of 75,000 other HBOS customers in the packages.[8] While at first sight such a mistake might seem amusing to someone not involved, the delivery of such sensitive information was a serious breach of customer privacy and, in the wrong hands, could have led to 'identity theft'. The Scottish Information Commissioner Office (ICO) investigated the breach with HBOS management. No details of regulatory actions or fines were published but the bank's reputation suffered, as it was seen as incompetent. Unfortunately, HBOS did not learn the lesson, as the ICO fined them £75,000 in 2013 for breaches of customer confidentiality over several years. On those occasions the bank sent sensitive information on fax machines to wrong numbers. With these incidents there is no suggestion of individual wrongdoing, merely that mistakes were made, probably as a result of inexperience, lack of training or lack of care. In terms of the People Risk Triangle, introduced in Chapter 2, the *motivation* was specific (to send a statement by post or fax), the *opportunity* was clearly unintended (probably caused by a computer entry error or incorrect details stored on file), while the *rationalization* was collective and benign (eg to meet efficiency/customer service targets).

4.3.2 Air New Zealand – crash of Flight 901

Not all incidents, however, are so amusing to the outsider or relatively innocuous, and incidents that turn into accidents can have deadly consequences. One example of a tragic incident/accident[9] is the 1979 crash of Air New Zealand Flight 901 into Mount Erebus, an active volcano of over 12,000 feet on Ross Island in Antarctica. The DC-10 plane was on a regular 13-hour sightseeing round trip from Auckland to Antarctica planning not to land but to fly low over the Polar icecap. The immediate cause of the accident, in which 257 passengers and crew died instantly, was a relatively minor correction to computerized flight path coordinates that was not relayed to the crew. The change in flight plan took the plane directly over, rather than parallel to, the mountain. As bad luck would have it, as the plane approached the volcano there was a meteorological phenomenon known as a 'sector whiteout' that distorted the horizon, making the pilots visually unaware of the fast-approaching mountain. This is an example of what is called *lack of situational awareness*, or not being aware of the dangers around one. The plane's systems did eventually warn of the on-rushing proximity of the ground but unfortunately without sufficient time for the pilots to take evasive action.

As might be expected there were several inquiries into the accident, at the time the world's fourth-worst plane crash, but controversy ensued when one inquiry blamed the pilots whereas a subsequent Royal Commission absolved them, instead blaming the disaster on the miscommunication of the flight path changes. The crash was a horrible accident caused by a simple slip-up that was not picked up. James Reason notes[10] that the Mahon Report of the Royal Commission was a milestone in accident reporting as it shifted the thinking away from a culture of blame (ie the original pilot fault hypothesis) to one where an organizational malfunction (ie miscommunication) was the underlying cause. In terms of the People Risk Triangle, the *motivation* in the crash was specific (to descend to 6,000 feet to view the icepack); the *opportunity* was clearly unintended (caused by changes to coordinates stored on the flight computer and compounded by meteorological conditions), while the *rationalization* was collective and benign (to see the formidable sights of Antarctica up close). The People Risk was simply the failure of proper communication between people in the organization, in that the flight controllers did not discuss the possible implications of changing the flight plan with the pilots, making the pilots unaware of the new risks they were running.

4.3.3 *Medical fatality – Mrs Elaine Bromiley*

The death of anyone in a preventable incident is tragic but the pain is somewhat ameliorated if lessons are learned and lives are later saved. One such case is that of Elaine Bromiley, a 37-year-old mother of two children, who in 2006 was admitted to a private clinic near London for a routine operation to clear chronically blocked sinuses. The case is well documented[11] but, in summary, while being anaesthetized Mrs Bromiley suffered a sudden and unexpected blockage of her airways that unfortunately cut off the oxygen supply to her brain (hypoxia). The experienced clinicians involved in the operation and senior specialists called in on the emergency were unable to force (intubate) the supply of oxygen and after some 20 minutes of trying to resuscitate they decided to abandon the operation, wake Mrs Bromiley up and transfer her to a recovery ward. Unfortunately, in the recovery ward, the patient's condition deteriorated and she was transferred to an Intensive Care Unit (ICU) but did not recover and her life support was turned off 13 days later.

However, the incident did not end with Mrs Bromiley's death. Her husband, Martin, was an airline pilot and is very familiar with the post-incident reviews taken as a matter of course after air accidents, such as Air New Zealand Flight 901. He was dismayed to find that no review had taken place into the circumstances leading to his wife's death and was shocked to discover that such reviews were rare in the UK National Health Service (NHS). With admirable negotiating skills, Mr Bromiley persuaded the clinic to commission an independent review into the incident by a well-respected professor of anaesthetics and intensive care medicine, Michael Harmer.

Crucially, the review was not trying to apportion blame but to discover if lessons could be learned from the unfortunate incident. Professor Harmer concluded that the clinicians and hospital were of high standard and had provided the appropriate levels of care and equipment up until the emergency occurred and continued to conduct themselves professionally afterwards. But the emergency was not handled well in that the clinicians became engrossed in trying to solve the breathing problem and (in hindsight) let valuable time go by. This is another example of *lack of situational awareness*, which the UK Health and Safety Executive (HSE)[12] notes is a major cause of accidents especially in construction. Humans become so engrossed in detail that sometimes we lose sight of dangers elsewhere. It is also another example of the Inattentional Blindness that we encountered in the Invisible Gorilla experiments described in Chapter 3.

To his credit, Martin Bromiley has turned the tragedy of his wife's death to good, setting up a charity and working, with some success, with the NHS to introduce the concepts of Human Factors and Safety Science into UK clinical practice.[13] In this, he appears to be pushing on an open door, as after generations of doctors being trained in a hierarchical profession with the consultant at the top and never to be argued with, there was a growing realization in the NHS that mistakes, many of which are preventable, can kill patients. The best way to prevent these unnecessary deaths is to be more open and collaborative about potentially deadly actions – in other words to recognize potential People Risk. In hospitals around the world today simple risk mitigation procedures, such as referring to standard checklists similar to those used by pilots, are routinely saving lives.[14] The traditional hierarchical culture of the medical profession is changing, albeit slowly, to a more open and questioning one.

4.3.4 Summary – Incidents

The cases above are relatively simple, but representative of many such *Incidents* caused by people. These incidents were caused by individuals doing the wrong thing, such as a data input or computer programming error, in the case of the flood of statements at HBOS or the trivial but fatal data mistake that caused the accident to Flight 901. In the case of the death of Mrs Bromiley, a number of very experienced individuals became so tied up in solving the immediate problems facing them that they took fatally wrong decisions. People make mistakes because they are human, they cannot be pre-programmed to be right all of the time. As a result of incidents such as Flight 901, in the airline industry, and the death of Mrs Bromiley in the health sector, much work has been done to change the culture of those industries and replace the prevailing culture of blaming the individuals involved with a culture that promotes openness, constructive criticism and, most importantly, preventative actions. Business in general can learn from the aviation and medical professions about how to make such a change in culture.

Incidents and accidents are not aberrations but a natural part of what businesses do as they are constantly forced to adapt to external changes. Business managers therefore must accept the fact that incidents and accidents will *definitely* happen and these may be caused by individuals, ie People Risk. The trick is to ensure that even if a minor incident occurs without losses, lessons are learned and actions taken to reduce the likelihood that such an incident will happen again. People need to be constantly reminded of the risks that they are taking on behalf of their firms. Of course, no one can guarantee that expensive mistakes will not happen but we must work towards that ideal. The costs and disruptions caused by accidents can be huge, and authors such as James Reason have written extensively on the impact of accidents. What has not been covered so well, however, are the upper levels of the 4Is model (Individual, Institution and Industry) where really significant losses have occurred.

4.4 Individuals

4.4.1 Bank fraud – Ms Rajina Subramaniam

A classic case of a lone *Individual* causing a major loss due to People Risk was that of Ms Rajina Subramaniam, who was introduced in Chapter 2, and was found guilty of defrauding her employer, ING, of over AUD $40 million. Chapter 2 describes Donald Cressey's Fraud Triangle, with three dimensions – motivation, opportunity and rationalization – that are used to identify People Risks in the cases throughout this chapter. Ms Subramaniam's *motivation* was not greed but a desire for revenge against a colleague with whom she had been having an allegedly abusive sexual relationship for a number of years. Her *opportunity* to commit fraud was her position as a trusted employee in charge of accounting and her *rationalization* was revenge, to get back at the system for the abuse and bullying she was allegedly receiving.

4.4.2 Rogue trading – Barings

Another rich area of Individual People Risk is so-called *rogue trading*. The term *rogue trader* was first used to describe Nick Leeson, who was convicted of defrauding the venerable UK bank, Barings, of some $1.4 billion.[15] Leeson served three years of a six-and-a-half-year prison sentence in Singapore where the offence took place. As a result of these losses, Barings was bankrupted and was acquired by ING Bank for the miserly sum of £1. But Leeson's 'fraud' was quite unlike that of Rajina Subramaniam or other individuals described in the Fraud Triangle in Chapter 2. Leeson was found guilty of falsifying records, *not* stealing or diverting money.

The Barings case is well documented but can be summarized as follows. Nick Leeson, a manager and futures trader for Barings on the Singapore International Monetary Exchange (SIMEX), took a routine bet on the value of the Nikkei 225 Index of top Japanese stocks. Unfortunately, the calamitous Kobe earthquake of 17 January 1995 caused the index to fall precipitously, also causing Leeson's bet to lose a lot of money. In fact Leeson, because he was *writing* (ie selling) options, was like the bookmaker for his bet and the further the index fell the more he lost. Rather than take his losses, however, Leeson doubled his bet, but lost even more and then turned to subterfuges to cover his losses until he could find a way to recover. He never did recover the losses and Barings, London's oldest investment bank, went bust. This behaviour is an example of 'risk aversion' as described by Daniel Kahneman, in so-called Prospect Theory; that is the somewhat paradoxical tendency of many people to take *more*, rather than *less*, risk when in a losing situation to try to reverse it.[16]

4.4.3 Rogue trading – other cases

The Nick Leeson case was the model for several other rogue traders who followed, for example:

- John Rusnak, an employee of Allied Irish Bank[17] (AIB) who concealed US $691 million in losses at Allfirst, an AIB subsidiary in Baltimore, United States;
- Jerome Kerviel,[18] a derivatives trader at the large French bank Société Générale who reputedly lost a monumental US $7 billion; and
- Kweku Adoboli,[19] a derivatives trader at the London branch of the giant Union Bank of Switzerland (UBS), who was found guilty of causing a loss of some US $2 billion.

In none of these cases did the Rogue Trader divert the money that the bank eventually lost, but, as predicted by Coleman's description of *White Collar Criminals*, were instead motivated by the need to preserve their jobs and their entitlements to quite substantial bonuses. For example, Mr Adoboli admitted in court that he had large gambling debts and was dependent on his expected bonus to stay solvent. In sentencing Adoboli, the judge noted that he was guilty as charged and provided an assessment[20] of his overconfident and reckless character (which incidentally fits other rogue traders):

> The fact is that you are profoundly unselfconscious of your own failings. There is the strong streak of the gambler in you, borne out by your personal trading. You were arrogant enough to think that the bank's rules for traders did not apply to you. And you denied that you were a rogue trader, claiming that at all times you were acting in the bank's interests, while conveniently ignoring that the real characteristic of the rogue trader is that he ignores the rules designed to manage risk.

The *motivation* then for Adoboli (and other Rogue Traders) was specific (ie to maintain the firm's profits and hence their bonuses), the *opportunity* was unintended, making use of the fact that all of these rogue traders were extremely knowledgeable about the control environment in which they were trading and could easily circumvent the controls. The *rationalization* in these cases was Temporary Use as they all used illicit methods to cover up losses for the firm until they could recoup them. This common rationalization was typified by Kweku Adoboli in his tear-filled testimony at his trial: 'UBS was my family and every single thing I did, every single bit of effort I put into that organization, was for the benefit of the bank.'

The causes of these rogue trading cases were not merely confined to specific Individuals, but they also involved breakdowns of basic *control processes* in the Institution, as was brought out in the official inquiries that followed the discoveries of the losses. In *all* of these cases, and others not documented here, senior management was criticized for a lack of good governance and risk management, in particular not monitoring trading risks. These inquiries found that senior management often did not understand the risks that were being taken by traders on their bank's behalf but let them take the risks anyway; a clear case of People Risk. The Barings case particularly highlights management dysfunction in that the official Bank of England inquiry could find no one in the bank who admitted to being Nick Leeson's direct boss or anyone who really understood how the Singapore business was making so much money.[21] And in the AIB case, the rogue trader John Rusnak made use of the fact that there was organizational infighting between US and Irish executives. In all of these cases, some senior managers were fired for their failures but escaped judicial sanctions.

4.4.4 Rogue trading – National Australia Bank

In the context of the 4Is model, 'Individual' does not refer only to a single person working alone but one or more individuals who have a common purpose and collectively make a mistake or collude to commit a fraud. It is as if the group is acting with one mind. The term Groupthink is often used to describe such a situation but that term is better used when discussing decisions at the highest level of an organization. Here, a group of individuals are working outside, rather than within, the norms of the overall organization. We call this phenomenon *Teamthink*, to distinguish from Groupthink, as it is related to a very small group, which is often at odds with the stated goals of the organization, and thus has slightly different characteristics.

A case of such Teamthink is the small group of Foreign Exchange (FX) traders working for National Australia Bank (NAB)[22] in Melbourne, Australia. In a situation similar to that of Barings and AIB, the FX team, led by aggressive head trader Luke Duffy, had made losses selling financial options, betting on the relative strength of the US and Australian dollars. Their bets had gone wrong, so, like Leeson and Rusnak, they doubled up, trying to claw back their losses, and covering their tracks with false trades. But this was a losing battle and, in January 2004, losses of some AUD $360 million were brought to light. It should be noted that the losses were uncovered not through existing controls but by a whistleblower new to the team. As is customary in these cases, senior management including the CEO and Chairman resigned or were sacked, and the rogue traders were charged with fraud and sent to prison for various periods. Regulators investigated the incident and discovered that unauthorized trading had been going on for some time, undetected by management, and that there was a culture of blame and suppressing 'bad news' in the organization. People were just not doing their job, turning a blind eye to obvious misdemeanours or, especially in the case of the Board Risk Committee who, overloaded with information, were guilty of Inattentional Blindness, completely missing the fraud.

4.4.5 Rogue trading – Goldman Sachs

A particularly interesting case of People Risk is that of the rogue trader Matthew Taylor[23] a former Goldman Sachs employee, who pleaded guilty to a single count of 'wire fraud' in December 2013. Taylor was sentenced to nine months in prison for covering up a US $8.3 billion unauthorized trading position he had accumulated in 2007 in futures contracts tied to the Standard & Poor's 500 stock index. He was also ordered to repay Goldman some US $118 million losses that the firm had incurred in unwinding the losing position. As in other rogue trading cases, Taylor was losing money on his trading positions and, to claw back the losses, he made some big bets that lost even more money. He covered up the losses by entering false trades into Goldman's trading systems and lying to risk managers. Mr Taylor told the court that he 'accumulated this [losing] trading position and concealed it for the purpose of augmenting my reputation at Goldman and increasing my performance-based compensation – I am truly sorry'. The *rationalization* again was one of Temporary Use, attempting to claw back losses.

While the Taylor case is similar to other cases, such as Jerome Kerviel at UBS, it has important differences that caused the trial judge to comment that the case was 'a paradigm of everything that is wrong with Wall Street and the regulators charged with protecting the public'. As required, Goldman Sachs had reported the misdemeanour but did so in a low-key statutory filing to one of its regulators. This report was put on the back burner at the time, in the run-up to the GFC, only to be brought to court some six years later. In the meantime, Goldman had fired Taylor but watched as he was hired shortly afterwards by Morgan Stanley, where he continued to work for several more years. Even though Goldman had lost US $118 million, through its own risk management failures, they appeared quite willing to bury the bad news. Goldman's message to its employees appears to be not 'don't do wrong' but 'don't get caught doing wrong, but if you do keep it quiet'. This is at odds with Goldman's new Code of Conduct which, as described in Chapter 10, states that 'the Goldman Sachs Code of Business Conduct and Ethics embodies the firm's commitment to conduct our business in accordance with the highest ethical standards and in compliance with all applicable laws, rules and regulations'. In this case, executives were not living up to their ethical aspirations – a clear case of People Risk.

Another common aspect of rogue trading cases is the conflicts of interest that are involved. Financial traders are driven by the need to make profits for their firms – it is their primary raison d'etre and they do little else. It is hardly surprising then that other responsibilities such as the protection of shareholder value are sometimes if not ignored, then downplayed. If a position is losing money, trying to retrieve the losses becomes of overriding concern, and in addition personal concerns such as loss of income or job also become intertwined with the conflicted objective. It would be a brave and probably foolhardy trader who made a loss and immediately reported it to management before trying to recoup the loss.

In the cases described, although on the surface the rogue traders had quite different personalities, there were several behavioural traits that they had in common. Traders are by nature optimistic and resilient.[24] They have to be confident that their 'bets' on market direction will go well and be able to bounce back quickly when some bets go badly. But these particular traders, doubtless like many others whose losses did not overwhelm their banks, were *overconfident* in their ability to turn a losing situation around. This overconfidence was engendered by the fact that the huge losses occurred not on the first time that bad bets were made but instead after similar tactics had been employed over a number of years, and in those earlier instances smaller losses had been recouped. Losing bets had been made many times before the 'big one' and had not been detected by control functions or management. Aside from Jerome Kerviel, who was considered to be a quiet introvert, the other rogue traders were reported to be flamboyant and narcissistic, outwardly flaunting their success, while at the same time suppressing the anguish that their mounting losses must have engendered. In these cases, this narcissism was frequently manifested in bullying of juniors, often to get them to break rules for the rogue trader's benefit.[25] The cases of NAB, AIB and UBS also showed that bullying extended not only to juniors but also control staff and even other companies who were giving warnings of problems.

4.4.6 Medical fatalities – Dr Harold Shipman

The examples of People Risk above and frauds and accidents studied by Frank Bird, Donald Cressey and James Reason tend to be fairly instantaneous events, occurring over a period of days or weeks, even though the underlying causes may have emerged over several years. But a People Risk event can occur over a much longer period, as the disturbing case of Dr Harold Shipman illustrates.[26] Although doctors are no longer required to swear an oath of 'first, do no harm', the sentiment is nonetheless one of the core principles of medical ethics. The so-called Hippocratic Oath certainly precludes administration of poison to end a person's life. Such a proscription would certainly have applied to Dr Harold Shipman, a doctor who lived and practised for over 20 years in the North West of England. In 1998, Dr Shipman was unmasked as a serial killer who had, over his career, probably murdered over 200 patients, mostly female, elderly and defenceless.

The official inquiry[27] into the case by Dame (Justice) Janet Smith found that Shipman was hard working, highly regarded by his professional colleagues and his patients and considered by some of his victims to be the best doctor in the area. However, Dame Janet's report identified at least 215 patients whom Shipman appeared to have murdered over his career, usually through the 'administration of a lethal dose of an opiate'. Although at the time of his arrest Dr Shipman was working as the sole doctor in his single-handed practice in Manchester, for several years prior to moving there he had worked in practices with multiple doctors. Yet, the some-times-suspicious deaths of his patients went unnoticed until 1998 when a doctor in a nearby practice, Dr Linda Reynolds, concerned by the number of cremation certificates requested by Dr Shipman, took her concerns to the local coroner who initiated a police inquiry. After a preliminary inquiry that found no cause for con-cern, a second, better-resourced investigation was started after a further death, which uncovered multiple murders. Dr Reynolds's intervention as a whistleblower was critical to uncovering these crimes, which went undetected for many years by official controls, such as coroners' inquests and independent death certification.

Why did Shipman murder so many people? In prison, Dr Shipman refused to undergo any form of psychiatric assessment so the Smith inquiry had to piece together the murderer's motivations from expert analysis of his actions. Save for one case of forging a will, which was ultimately to prove his downfall, Shipman was not, the experts found, motivated by monetary gain (although there was some evidence that Shipman had taken and secreted some of his victims' personal possessions). Surprisingly, Justice Smith concluded that Shipman's crimes were without motive. The Smith report noted that 'Shipman was encouraging and sympathetic but at times he was cold, brusque and offhand. Often, he seemed unable to empathize with the bereaved.' The report also noted 'other well-marked traits of Shipman's personality were aggression, conceit, arrogance and contempt for those whom he considered to be his intellectual inferiors ... He appeared arrogant and conceited, even during his trial.' On the other hand, Shipman was a family man with an outwardly happy marriage and two children. His wife continued to maintain his innocence even after his suicide in prison.[28] The inquiry's expert psychiatrists postulated that Shipman's admitted addiction to pethidine, a prescription painkiller, may have been indicative of an 'addictive personality' and even that he may have 'become addicted to killing'. Experts suggested to the Smith inquiry that:

> [Shipman's] arrogance and over-confidence are almost certainly a mask for poor self-esteem [and ...] for most of his adult life, he was probably angry, deeply unhappy and chronically depressed [and ...] that he has a deep seated need to control people and events. Once he fears that he cannot control events, he feels threatened and reacts so as to take or regain control.

In terms of the People Risk Triangle, Shipman's *motivations* were ambiguous, other than the potential to gain illicit access to prescription drugs, and the *opportunity* was clearly unintended as he had almost unlimited access to his murder victims. His *rationalization* is individual but unclear and appears to have been the result of a deep-seated personality defect. The important point here, however, is that Shipman was a serial killer who went unnoticed for many years. The NHS is a huge organization, with thousands of well-educated, highly professional, caring employees and the ability of one man to create such damage illustrates that trusted individuals can go unnoticed in any organization. Dr Shipman was clearly 'hiding in plain sight',[29] and his actions were not seen by others who should have been watching for errant behaviour. But his colleagues were just not looking closely. This again illustrates a conflict of interest, in this case between the well-being of patients and the profession itself. In its response to the Shipman case, the overall regulating body of UK doctors, the General Medical Council (GMC),[30] identified that medical professionals have an overriding duty of care to patients to raise concerns about the practices of their colleagues.

Unfortunately, Harold Shipman was not the only example of a well-respected criminal 'hiding in plain sight' within the NHS. In reporting the investigation[31] into the widespread abuse of juveniles in the care of the NHS over many years by the UK TV personality Jimmy Savile, the police officer in charge of the investigation used the memorable phrase – Savile was *hiding in plain sight*. But he was not only hiding in the NHS, he also went undetected by his bosses and colleagues in the British Broadcasting Corporation (BBC), who were warned several times about Savile's aberrant behaviour.[32] This is typical of many of the situations described in this book. The people involved are 'one of us'. We trust them. And when wrongdoing is detected, we are shocked that we did not see it before. Why people have such blind spots is hard, with hindsight, to understand but probably arises from a combination of the biases and conflicts of interests described throughout this book. Most of us are confident in our ability to 'read people', especially professional colleagues, and if others in our group/profession appear to be equally sure, then we push nagging doubts to the back of our minds.

4.4.7 Fraud – JPMorgan and Bernie Madoff

In 2009, Bernard (Bernie) Madoff, a highly-respected US investment adviser, pleaded guilty to running a massive Ponzi[33] scheme for over 20 years that had defrauded thousands of investors of billions of dollars. At the time this was the biggest ever case of investor fraud in the United States and Madoff was sentenced to some 150 years in prison. Although the Madoff case is fascinating (and an example of People Risk) it is well documented elsewhere and is not the subject of interest here, but the actions of one of his bankers is.

In January 2014, JPMorgan was fined over US $2 billion for breaking the long-standing US Bank Secrecy Act which requires banks to alert authorities to suspicious financial activity.[34] JPMorgan had been Madoff's primary bank for two decades and facilitated the numerous transfers of money between the myriad of US and overseas bank accounts that Madoff used to cover his tracks. Madoff's firm was one of the biggest clients of JPMorgan's Private Clients division and thus was subject to so-called Anti-Money Laundering (AML) monitoring.[35] In fact, on several occasions, the bank's AML systems did raise red flags on the types of transactions being executed by Madoff's firms, but these flags were discounted by JPMorgan staff. This is an example of the Distrust of Law rationalization, here ignoring both internal and regulatory prohibitions.

In considering the Madoff case, the US Department of Justice did not accuse any JPMorgan staff of collusion with Madoff to commit fraud, only that bank staff had valid concerns that were not acted upon. In fact, in the mid-1990s, another large bank discontinued its relationship with Madoff because it suspected fraud and in fact communicated this to JPMorgan. Furthermore, the UK office of JPMorgan did alert[36] local AML regulators to the fact that Madoff's investment returns were 'so consistently and significantly ahead of his peers' that the results 'appear too good to be true'. However, in contravention of the US Bank Secrecy Act, JPMorgan staff did not inform US authorities. In a clear case of People Risk, many individuals in JPMorgan did not do the job expected of them, as was admitted by the bank in that it 'could have done a better job pulling together various pieces of information and concerns about Madoff'. As described in Chapter 8, JPMorgan, acting as a stake-holder (in this case a supplier) was a 'line of defence' in monitoring potentially fraud-ulent AML transactions in the banking system but, in an example of People Risk, individuals within the bank failed to act appropriately.

The case also illustrates an example of a conflict of interest in that JPMorgan staff were faced with two conflicting priorities; making profits for the bank and reporting possible misconduct. Madoff's accounts were profitable for the bank as it appears that in moving large sums of money between linked accounts on an almost daily basis, JPMorgan made considerable income on the interest charged. If an employee were to make an accusation against Madoff, JPMorgan would almost certainly lose this lucrative business, whether the accusation was shown to be true or not. Without overwhelming information, it is somewhat understandable that, although wrong, someone might take the easy option and decide to 'let sleeping dogs lie'. Some senior executives appear to have compounded the People Risk by not promoting open dis-cussions about potential customer misconduct, even though they are legally required to do so.

4.4.8 HBOS – distressed assets

Before considering People Risks at the next level, the Institution, it is worth considering another case of a group of individuals conspiring to defraud a company, but with most of the group *outside* rather than inside of the firm. This case is an example of People Risk where there are internal and external individuals involved and again uses the example of the accident-prone HBOS. It is a long-running criminal investigation[37] that at the time of writing is still working its way very slowly through the UK judicial system. And it is a case that without the intense scrutiny following the failure of HBOS might have never seen the light of day. In 'Operation Hornet', the UK National Crime Agency and the Thames Valley Police force are investigating allegations against two former senior managers in the corporate division of HBOS and eight other individuals.[38] The HBOS employees are accused of transferring fraudulent business loans through a so-called 'turnaround consultancy' in exchange for gifts over a period of seven years from 2003 and 2010. The alleged fraud involved the HBOS bankers handing over 'distressed' or 'impaired' loans, ie those in arrears and likely to default, to a specialist consultancy – Quayside Corporate Services. To date, the bankers, their wives, the directors of the consultancy and other parties have been charged with conspiracy to corrupt, fraudulent trading and money laundering, all serious charges that may, if proven, result in long prison sentences.

The alleged fraud happened because of the massive losses that HBOS was experiencing in the bank's corporate division in the mid-2000s and the bankers were seeking ways to get the assets off their books, even at a substantial loss.[39] The ownership of over £1 billion of distressed assets was transferred to the consultancy in return for personal gifts and the consultancy was able to profit by restructuring and recovering some of the loan assets. This is collusion between people inside and outside an organization to defraud it. The *motivation* was specific (greed – to acquire assets at below value), the *opportunity* was clearly unintended (the assets should have been sold at proper market value), while the *rationalization* was both individual (eg to profit from HBOS' troubles) and collective (eg to reduce HBOS' portfolio of distressed assets). This is an example of People Risk because the perpetrators were clearly fraudulent but the controls (rules) failed to take account of the situation that HBOS would ever have to sell distressed loans in such numbers. HBOS executives had just not considered that unlikely possibility, whilst the perpetrators appear to have exploited it, a clear People Risk.

4.4.9 Insider trading – Goldman Sachs

In October 2012, Rajat Gupta[40] a former Goldman Sachs director was sentenced to two years in prison and ordered to pay a US $5 million fine for 'insider trading'. The details of the case are well documented but in summary, Mr Gupta was found guilty of passing sensitive market information to a friend and former colleague, Raj Rajaratnam, billionaire founder of the Galleon Group, one of the largest hedge fund companies in the world. Mr Rajaratnam was also found guilty of insider trading,[41] for this and other instances, and jailed for 11 years and fined US $150 million.

While at first glance this may appear to be a run-of-the-mill case of insider trading, which is fraudulent in most western jurisdictions, the people involved make the case interesting from the perspective of People Risk. As a director of Goldman Sachs, Mr Gupta was at the peak of his profession, well respected and wealthy. From a relatively poor upbringing in Kolkata, India, Gupta, through diligence and hard work, rose to become the first non-American CEO of the prestigious business consultancy, McKinsey. Mr Gupta also held directorships with a number of high-profile corporations such as Procter & Gamble. He was also a noted philanthropist, founding the Indian School of Business and serving on the boards and advisory councils of prestigious universities, including schools at Yale and Harvard.

Why would such a business luminary get involved in what is clearly an illegal activity? Mr Gupta argued that he did nothing wrong but merely discussed business with Mr Rajaratnam, such as the confidential and highly sensitive information that Warren Buffet was considering investing in Goldman during the GFC. Nonetheless, based on wire taps of telephone conversations, a jury found him guilty of insider trading. What was Gupta's motivation? Unusually it appears to be friendship, which is rarely recognized as a motivation in White Collar Crime, and the *motivation* was not specific but ambiguous, as there is no evidence that Mr Gupta benefitted personally from the information passed. The *opportunity* was Mr Gupta's elevated position and insider knowledge of the deliberations of Goldman's board and the outcome was clearly *unintended*, by the Goldman board at least. In his disregard of the conventions of, and laws governing, board conduct, Mr Gupta's *rationalization* appears to be Distrust of Law and Victimless Crime. The case is interesting because it is not simple; the motivations and rationalizations of all those involved are murky. These are extremely rich, powerful people who seem to treat the rules under which they operate as discretionary rather than as binding obligations that they have. The lack of watertight proscriptions on disclosing information, even if not for nefarious purposes, is an example of People Risk at the board level of Goldman, as discussed later in Chapter 6.

4.4.10 Scapegoats

In considering the cases above of Incidents and Individual People Risk, it is always possible to identify fairly precisely the individuals or groups involved. And although there is a tendency today to look beyond personal blame towards organizational factors, it is nonetheless relatively easy to tie a particular case up neatly as being localized to a few individuals. This appears to satisfy the human need to have a 'scapegoat' when things go wrong.

The concept of a scapegoat is ancient, referenced in the Old Testament and pre-Christian Greek law. It is well established in human consciousness as providing a way in which our misdemeanours/sins can be diverted to someone/something else who will take any punishment due and thus allows everyone to move on with a clean slate.[42] Finding someone other than ourselves onto whom we can place guilt appears to be a common human need. It protects our self-image by allowing us to not dwell too much on past mistakes. Scapegoating is all too easy and by assigning fault to someone else we can somehow convince ourselves that, with the scapegoat punished, the event will not happen again. This is a sort of *confirmation bias* convincing ourselves that we are good, unlike the scapegoat. But scapegoating means that we don't learn from our mistakes.

An example of not learning from mistakes is that of the NAB case described earlier. When the official report of the John Rusnak fraud at AIB/Allfirst was published in 2002, the board of NAB quite appropriately asked its own internal audit function if 'a similar event could happen here?'. The auditors gave them assurance by reporting that 'there were no issues of concern for NAB' and a senior executive reportedly stated, 'It is extremely unlikely that a material fraud... would go undetected for any length of time'. In a rare tongue-in-cheek aside, the Australian Prudential Regulation Authority (APRA)[43] noted that 'in hindsight, [the AIB] report warranted a deeper, more detailed assessment' than that given to it by NAB's board and management. Because a perpetrator had been caught and punished, albeit on the other side of the world, NAB directors assumed that the punishment meted out would be sufficient to deter others. What they failed to notice was that the underlying problems of corporate governance at AIB that were fully documented in the report were also present in NAB. With hindsight, it is interesting to hypothesize that if much more severe punishments had been meted out to AIB directors and senior executives in 2002 it might have concentred the minds of the NAB board and CEO on their own governance problems that they were blind to. A thoughtful analysis of the AIB case might have discovered that NAB had similar governance problems. But hindsight is not history and the NAB board did not learn the lessons of AIB.

4.4.11 Summary – Individuals

The cases in this section are just a few of the many that could be used to illustrate People Risk at the Individual level. The cases show a continuum from a lone individual operating with ill-intent, such as Rajina Subramaniam and Harold Shipman, through 'rogue traders', alone or in a small group who, trying to recover from a losing situation, resort to accounting frauds to cover up their mistakes, such as in the case of Nick Leeson or Kweku Adoboli. The case of the fraudulent loan transfers at HBOS are an example of a small group of individuals, inside and outside of the bank, colluding to defraud it. These cases all, more or less, fit into the concept of the Fraud Triangle developed by Donald Cressey, but what is not reflected in that analysis is that, in all these cases, people whose role was to prevent individuals doing wrong just did not do their job. The cases illustrate that People Risk is about recognizing not only that people make wrong, sometimes fraudulent, decisions, but also there is the need for others to act on the knowledge that some individuals are not doing what they should. But having discovered that they have been deceived or have not acted in the way that they should, people try to shift the blame from themselves to others, ie scapegoats. In the next section we will consider People Risks at the firm or Institutional level where identifying risks and individual scapegoats is much more difficult.

4.5 Institutions

In this section, we are looking at well-documented cases where People Risk played a – possibly *the* – major part. Even then there are far too many cases for one book and those selected are designed to illustrate the behavioural problems and cognitive biases of the individuals and groups involved. As noted above, in the wake of institutional failures or disastrous losses, there is an inevitable but sometimes unsavoury race to find a culprit or at least a scapegoat, as if one person acting alone could wreak such havoc. CEOs, such as Richard Fuld of Lehman, Fred Goodwin of RBS, Andy Hornby of HBOS, Kerry Killinger of Washington Mutual, Sean Fitzpatrick of Anglo Irish Bank, and several others, have been hounded unmercifully by the press and their reputations trashed. While we personally believe that these figures deserve serious criticism for some of their decisions, in many cases the journalists shredding their reputations, often for irrelevant reasons such as the cost of refurbishing their offices, were the same people who were praising them for their superior management skills not long before. In the lynch mob search for scapegoats, public memories become very short, and more importantly the real causes of the underlying problems are glossed over.

4.5.1 *Royal Bank of Scotland*

A good example of this phenomenon is (ex-Sir) Fred Goodwin, whose story from relatively humble beginnings to becoming the CEO of what was at one time the largest bank in the world is compellingly told in two books by Iain Martin and Ian Fraser.[44] These books agree that Mr Goodwin, whose nickname was Fred the Shred because of his relentless drive to reduce costs, certainly had some unpleasant behavioural traits, not least the bullying of staff who did not come up to his standards. Ian Fraser even went so far as to describe Goodwin as a 'sociopathic bully whose achievements had been massively over-hyped'. But Goodwin has become the 'whipping boy' of British banking upon whom it appears any insult can be dumped, mainly because RBS failed as a result of an ultimately disastrous takeover of significant parts of ABN AMRO bank in October 2007. The takeover had been hurried, with insufficient time for full due diligence, and as a result the risks were underestimated. As Sir Tom McKillop, Chairman of the RBS board, admitted to questioning members of parliament,[45] in retrospect we bought ABN AMRO at the top of the market, so anything we paid was an error'.

But Goodwin was not a 'lone wolf', in fact he was handpicked, guided and mentored by one of the intellectual (if not physical) giants of UK banking, Sir (wee) George Mathewson, CEO prior to Goodwin's appointment and Chairman for most of his tenure. Fred Goodwin was reported to be a control freak with a cutting tongue who made colossal mistakes but he was also surrounded by some of the toughest and most seasoned bankers in the UK, who did little to avert the on-rushing catastrophe. As Ian Martin wrote:

> It suits many people at or near the scene of the disaster to make the British end of the financial crisis all about Fred Goodwin. Astonishingly, many who were most intimately involved have barely featured in the coverage of the crisis, or have been mentioned only fleetingly and gone on to continue their careers quietly. But Fred Goodwin at RBS did not operate alone, like some deluded young rogue City trader trying to make his first millions. Although his monumental management errors and dud decisions produced an end result that was catastrophic both for the bank he ran and for the rest of us, others shared his ambitions and collaborated each and every step of the way.

Why were so many people convinced that Fred Goodwin was correct in aggressively promoting the takeover of ABN AMRO? To his credit, Goodwin had an enviable record of acquisitions to that point, having led the takeover of a number of banks during his career. But that may only illustrate Daniel Kahneman's insight at the top of this chapter that 'a few lucky gambles can crown a reckless leader with a halo of prescience and boldness'. But why do heroes, such as Goodwin, fall from grace?

In ancient Rome, it was customary to grant a particularly successful general a 'triumph' in recognition of his great victories. But the Romans, who were astute students of human nature, sometimes placed a slave or companion with the general in his chariot to remind him of his mortality, as a 'Memento Mori'. In other words, 'enjoy this adulation while it lasts because success is fleeting'. Contrast this with successful businessmen who are lauded as heroes and showered with honours only to be roundly castigated when things go wrong later. In research into the collapse of a leading Irish financial institution,[46] researchers found that during the tenure of the CEO, who was in position just before the collapse, his hubris and narcissism grew year on year as he began to believe his own publicity. As time went on, he demonstrated 'extreme hubris' and 'more than half of the good news was attributed to the CEO [directly] and all the bad news was attributed externally'.

Before the GFC, Richard (Dick) Fuld[47] of Lehman Brothers was one of the longest-serving investment bank CEOs on Wall Street, a member of the New York Federal Reserve and in 2006 was named by the influential magazine, *Institutional Investor*, as the 'top CEO in the private sector'. In 2006, Oliver Wyman, one of the world's largest consultancies, anointed Anglo Irish Bank, headed by its charismatic Chairman Sean Fitzpatrick,[48] as the world's 'best bank'. And Andy Hornby, the last CEO of HBOS, was lauded by the UK business press as a retail marketing genius.[49] All are now business pariahs. But they were only one executive among many in their organizations. Of course they deserve their share of the opprobrium but the culpability goes much wider, to the directors and executives who 'got with the programme' and failed to act as the general's slave would have done, reminding heroes not to take themselves too seriously.

4.5.2 Enron

One particular case of 'fallen heroes' and institutional 'hubris' stands out – Enron Corporation. Before it collapsed in 2001, Enron was one of the world's largest energy services companies, which had expanded and diversified under the leadership of its dynamic CEO, Kenneth Lay, from operating gas pipelines into paper making, communications, information technology and commodities trading. The title of the book by journalists Bethany McLean and Peter Elkind, *Enron: The smartest guys in the room*,[50] gives a clue into the ethos of the company and its belief that it could do anything it wanted and would be successful doing it. The media agreed and *Fortune* magazine voted Enron as 'America's most innovative company' for six years in a row. But Enron was a sham. The firm's much-vaunted run of profits were, in fact, illusory, built upon complex financial engineering through so-called Special Purpose Entities (SPEs) where liabilities were taken off Enron's balance sheet into SPE shell companies. Enron really was a 'shell game'.

When the main architects of the scheme, Chairman Ken Lay, CEO Jeffrey Skilling and CFO Andrew Fastow were put under pressure by Bethany McLean, a journalist for *Fortune* magazine, to explain Enron's financial structure and sources of profitability they tried to bully Ms McLean into backing off. However, she persevered and after publishing her concerns the Enron house of cards came tumbling down. Jeffrey Skilling was subsequently convicted of securities fraud, making false statements to auditors and insider trading and was sentenced to 24 years in prison, reduced on appeal to 14 years in 2012. Andy Fastow, Enron's CFO and architect of the SPE strategy, entered into a plea bargain with prosecutors in return for helping in other prosecutions and served six years in a low security prison.[51] Ken Lay[52] was found guilty of fraud and conspiracy and was facing the prospect of spending the rest of his life in prison when he died during his appeal against conviction. In sentencing Lay, the judge elucidated for the jury that the concept[53] of 'wilful [as opposed to inattentional] blindness', which means that having a 'blind spot', is no defence in a criminal trial: 'you are responsible if you could have known, and should have known, something which instead you strove not to see.'

Of the three main protagonists, Ken Lay was seen as a sort of 'southern gentleman', courteous and philanthropic, although it was apparent in hindsight that this facade masked a win-at-all-costs business ethic. Despite Lay's outwardly genteel demeanour he, and four other senior executives, were found to have sold most of their Enron stock[54] before the collapse while at the same time encouraging Enron employees to buy stock for their pension plans, which of course became worthless after the company's bankruptcy. This is a clear conflict of interest in which Lay chose his personal benefit over that of Enron's employees and shareholders. Note only two other Enron executives out of some 20,000 employees were sentenced to short prison terms for their part in issuing deceitful accounts to regulators and two others paid fines for their illegal behaviour.

Enron was a huge company, with offices around the world and revenues of US $101 billion in 2000. Could no one see the house of cards for what it was? Apparently not, as it took a journalist to ask the hard questions that eventually unravelled the fraud. The so-called Enron whistleblower,[55] Ms Sherron Watkins, did eventually warn Ken Lay just before the collapse that the company would 'implode in a wave of accounting scandals' but of course Lay was intimately involved in the accounting frauds and the memo was not published until after Enron collapsed.

But why did no one else inside or outside of the company blow the whistle? The reason may be that the business culture of Enron was corrupt (based on an accounting fiction of endless growth in profits) and corrupting as, although its employees were highly rewarded, there was also a culture of firing employees for mediocre performance that created an overly aggressive culture. An example of the corrupting culture was illustrated well in the documentary film[56] of the McLean and Elkind book in which traders in the firm's electricity division deliberately engineered the shut-down of power plants in California to drive up prices on the newly deregulated Californian electricity market, impacting businesses and putting consumers in danger. The Enron energy traders cared for little other than the opportunity to make a profit and, because they could not envisage the damage to unknown consumers and businesses that would result, this was in their eyes a 'Victimless Crime'.

In terms of the People Risk Triangle, the *motivation* for Enron executives was undoubtedly greed, but not, as Cressey suggested, to resolve an 'unshareable' problem, since the fraudulent schemes were openly discussed by senior management, who were extremely well remunerated, powerful and, in the case of Ken Lay, very well connected politically. The *opportunity* to commit fraud was the stock market boom of the early 2000s, where company share prices were skyrocketing. Enron CFO Andy Fastow was able to create financial structures in specially constructed SPEs that appeared profitable but were extremely difficult to understand. His personal greed was evidenced by the fact that he acquired beneficial interests for himself in the sham SPEs. The *rationalization* of fraud on such a massive scale was provided by the firm's Distrust of Law, as securities regulations and accounting practice had not kept up with the complexity of modern derivatives markets and were difficult to police. Collectively, the senior executives of Enron resolved the conflict of interest arising from their personal greed as against the need to report accurately the financial condition of the firm to shareholders, by choosing to cover up the parlous state of the firm.

The main protagonist in the Enron collapse, Ken Lay,[57] was a fascinating character. The son of a southern Baptist minister, he had an outstanding academic career, earning a PhD in Economics and teaching at university before joining the oil industry with Exxon, after a period of service in the Navy. He spent some time in Washington working in the Nixon administration before joining a company that was the predecessor of Enron. Bethany McLean, the author of the definitive book on Enron, and Finnish academic Matti Rantanen[58] both point to a decisive weakness in Lay's character: he was a smart, charming man strong on interpersonal skills but he avoided tough decisions that could create conflict. In tough situations he was happy to delegate and defer to his subordinates and signed off on decisions that he subsequently disavowed when things went wrong. This is in line with Daniel Kahneman's observation that one of the downsides of optimism is that an 'optimistic style involves taking credit for successes but little blame for failure'. Matti Rantanen suggests that Lay's religious background made him 'hold on' to or remain steadfast in a particular position even when contra action was needed. When the situation for Enron started to go wrong, this conflict made him blind to the eventual disaster. So Lay's individual *rationalization* was to hold on in the hope that the situation would turn around. It didn't. This is a type of Temporary Use coupled with a Distrust of Law and regulation in general.

But if Lay was hiding the truth and scale of the impending disaster, maybe even to himself, what of the thousands of highly educated, well-paid staff that Enron employed? Only one appears to have had the courage to 'blow the whistle' and she was too late.[59] And what about outsiders, especially those who were supposed to protect shareholders? Before its collapse Enron's external auditor was Arthur Andersen LLP,[60] an accounting firm founded in 1885 and one of the so-called 'Big Five' firms that dominated auditing for large companies around the world at the time. The firm was severely criticized by the Enron liquidators for failing to fulfil its professional responsibilities in connection with its audits of Enron's financial statements, and for missing the importance of Enron's SPEs, which were after all merely accounting devices to move assets off the firm's balance sheet. The auditing firm was also found guilty of obstructing justice by shredding documents, a verdict that was later overturned but by that stage the reputation of Andersen was destroyed and it was wound up. In other words, bodies, such as corporate auditors, who do not fulfil their fiduciary duties constitute a People Risk. The failure of external auditors to pick up warning signs of disasters is a recurring theme that appears in a number of other cases.

4.5.3 WorldCom

But Enron was not the only corporation that was in reality a shadow of what it was reported to be. In 2002, WorldCom Inc. filed for Chapter 11 bankruptcy[61] after a relatively short but tumultuous rise from a small telephone company in 1985 to become, through acquisition, the second-largest telecommunications company in the United States in the late 1990s. But 2000 was the peak of the company's fortunes as its proposed merger with a large rival, Sprint, to become the biggest telecom company in the world, was knocked back by regulators. As a result, WorldCom's share price went into a sharp decline and with it the personal (paper) fortunes of its executives, in particular the long-time CEO Bernard (Bernie) Ebbers, who was forced to resign in 2002. But WorldCom's success in the late 1990s was not all that it was claimed to be and in fact from 1999 the company's accounts were being manipulated to disguise its falling earnings, for example by inflating revenues and understating costs.

The heroes of this tale are three internal auditors who uncovered the massive deception and blew the whistle.[62] This resulted in an investigation by securities regulators following which the company was fined some US $2.5 billion and declared bankrupt before being resurrected in 2005 as MCI. Also in 2005, Bernie Ebbers, who directed the deception, was sentenced to 25 years in prison. Five other executives, including the Chief Financial Officer, pleaded guilty of charges of fraud and conspiracy and were fined and jailed for shorter periods.[63] The executives had resolved the conflict of interest involved in protecting their own wealth as against their duty to report accurately to shareholders, by covering up the losses that were occurring. The *motivation* for the WorldCom fraud was clearly greed but its *rationalization* was, unusually, Temporary Use as Ebbers was trying to force the share price to move upwards because he was being pressured to cover margin calls on money he had borrowed to purchase the company's shares. Like Ken Lay, Bernie Ebbers was from a relatively humble background and was an overtly religious man who had, over a relatively short period of time, amassed a huge fortune that was based on his ownership of WorldCom shares. It is also interesting that Arthur Andersen, the accounting firm that was destroyed for its involvement in the Enron scandal, was also the external auditor for WorldCom. While not suggesting that any auditors from Andersen were involved in fraud at either company, these and other cases point to, at the very least, a lax attitude to auditing practice at large corporations, raising the questions, have some firms become 'too big to audit', and have large auditing firms learned the lessons of these major failures?

4.5.4 Washington Mutual

The collapses of Enron and WorldCom were clearly caused by people and their fraudulent activities. Enron was in reality little more than a Ponzi scheme that relied on getting into new businesses to continue to generate (largely illusory) profits. WorldCom on the other hand was not a Ponzi scheme but had overstretched its capabilities in its bid to become the largest telecommunications carrier in the United States. But there are other firms that have collapsed not by fraud but by a blind search for unlimited growth. This so-called 'Beanstalk Syndrome'[64] relates to firms whose management believe they have discovered a 'golden goose' that will provide never-ending growth and profits and where executives continue to climb the 'magic beanstalk' until they are eventually caught out and fall down.

One example of the Beanstalk Syndrome was Washington Mutual (WAMU),[65] whose snappy slogan the 'Power of Yes' is described well in Kirsten Grind's book, *The Lost Bank*. WAMU, a long-established mutual bank headquartered in Seattle, Washington became the largest bank failure in US history in September 2008. Under its Chairman and CEO Kerry Killinger, WAMU had grown in the previous two decades by acquiring dozens of smaller banks to become the sixth-largest bank holding company in the United States. During the US housing bubble of the early 2000s and with the 'Power of Yes', WAMU began to lend enormous sums of money in subprime mortgages, ie loans that are more likely than average to default. However, WAMU salespersons said 'Yes' too many times and when the US housing market bubble burst in 2007, WAMU was bankrupted by the rising tide of mortgage defaults. In his evidence to the US Congress,[66] Killinger testified that the firm's so-called 'High-Risk Lending Strategy' (HLS) was a deliberate business strategy that was signed off by the board and was recognized as being particularly risky. But rather than actively manage that risk, Killinger and the board got rid of the firm's Chief Risk Officer (CRO), James Vanasek,[67] who was issuing warnings about the unsustainable risk. Vanasek was replaced by Ronald Cathcart, who not only kept issuing the warnings but, after not being heeded, he too blew the whistle to the bank's regulator, the Office of Thrift Supervision (OTS). For this action, Cathcart was fired and the bank continued plummeting to its final bankruptcy and forced acquisition by JP Morgan. The WAMU case is an example of People Risk in that the board and executives were completely confident in their ability to succeed in what they admitted was a highly risky strategy but did little to manage those risks; in other words, they did not do what they should have done.

4.5.5 Behavioural defects of key executives

Enron and Washington Mutual were as far away from each other in business strategy as could be: Enron the energy giant constantly searching for new horizons in business; WAMU, a staid regional bank that became expert at acquiring other staid banks and incorporating them quickly into the WAMU way of doing things. But there were similarities between their leaders. From the Mid-West, Kerry Killinger joined Washington Mutual soon after university and in over 30 years rose through the ranks to become Chairman and CEO. Like Ken Lay, Killinger was known for his intelligence and easy charm but was more diffident and was not as flamboyant as Lay, eschewing political glad-handing and the trappings of high office. Killinger was earnest and hard working – one ad agency nicknaming him the 'Energizer Banker'. He was also successful, buying 18 banks in just seven years and as Kirsten Grind noted[68] 'not one of them was a lemon'. WAMU was his life. But like Lay, Killinger created a monster that got out of control, being described by one of his former senior executives as being 'like a sweet old lady who owns a giant Rottweiler'. Although brilliant and perpetually optimistic, Killinger, like Lay, did not relish conflict and avoided hard decisions, as senior colleagues told a McKinsey review[69] requested by the board sometime before the collapse. As problems grew, Killinger acknowledged problems in the US economy but he did not – *or could not* – take the hard decisions necessary to save the company. On the contrary, he reverted to type by proposing new takeovers. His former colleagues told McKinsey consultants that despite the fact that the writing was on the wall, Killinger was upbeat and believed that the risks could be managed; this is a so-called 'Illusion of Control', or overconfidence in one's ability to manage a situation come what may.

It is interesting to note at this point that although Fred Goodwin, ex-CEO of RBS, was known for lacerating executives in meetings, he, like Lay and Killinger, also tended to shy away from face-to-face conflict. For example, Goodwin often got others to fire people rather than do it himself.[70] An optimistic, driven, overly controlling chief executive who shies away from conflict appears to be a real source of People Risk, because if the company gets into trouble he/she may not be capable of taking the necessary avoiding action until it is too late. However, this is not a unique marker for potential disaster, as Dick Fuld, last CEO of Lehman Brothers, was also brilliant and driven but, in fact, did relish conflict. Fuld's nickname in Lehman was Gorilla because of his combative nature.[71] However, until the very end, like the other CEOs described here, Fuld was optimistic and kept maintaining that he could solve Lehman Brother's problems if only given time. The parlous state of the firm's accounts at the time of the bankruptcy showed that he was delusional about the firm's troubles.

4.5.6 Halifax/Bank of Scotland – HBOS

In 2001, the Bank of Scotland (BOS), founded in 1695, was merged with the Halifax, a 150-year-old building society recently converted to a bank, to become HBOS (Halifax/Bank of Scotland).[72] The merger of these two long-established and success-ful banks created a 'new force' in UK banking with combined assets already greater than Lloyds TSB, the smallest of the so-called 'Big Four' banks. Although BOS was the larger bank at the time, the Chairman of the merged bank (Lord Stevenson of Coddenham) and its CEO (James Crosby) came from the smaller Halifax. The merger of complementary skills appeared to make sound business sense, with Halifax being large and successful in retail mortgage lending and BOS successful, not only in mortgage lending but also in corporate lending and Treasury. However, in just seven years, the new firm collapsed spectacularly, eventually requiring an injection of over £20 billion from the UK taxpayer to support its government-organized takeover by Lloyds TSB bank in 2009. The collapse of HBOS has been well documented else-where, not least in the excellent book by Ray Perman, *Hubris: How HBOS wrecked the best bank in Britain*. But why did the merged firm with over 450 years of solid banking experience blow up so suddenly and spectacularly?

In its first few years, the new HBOS was extremely successful, with double-digit increases in profits each year based on a huge increase in lending. While ex-Halifax executives dominated the board, it was in the ex-BOS Corporate division that business was growing fastest. The Corporate division, headed by Peter Cummings, a local lad who joined the bank from school as a trainee and worked his way to the board through hard work and diligence, was the money-making engine of the Bank of Scotland. The 'Old Bank' as BOS was known, prided itself on continuing to lend to its loyal customers through good and bad economic times and had survived many banking crises in its illustrious history.[73] In mid-2008, as the housing bubble was beginning to burst, Cummings was unapologetic and characteristically confident: 'some people look as though they are losing their nerve – beginning to panic even – in today's testing real estate environment. Not us.'

Just a few months later, however, the firm collapsed and was forcibly acquired[74] by Lloyds TSB, which promptly announced a statutory loss of £10 billion before tax, of which £7 billion was impaired loans in the HBOS Corporate division. In short, HBOS had loaned too much and too recklessly to the commercial construction sector, which collapsed when the property bubble was pricked. Cummings was the 'whipping boy' for the collapse of HBOS. In 2012, he was fined £500,000 by the banking regulator, the FSA, and banned from working in the banking industry and is the only person to date officially censured for the collapse of HBOS.[75] The UK Parliamentary Commission on Banking Standards (PCBS) had some sympathy with Mr Cummings' assertion that he was being made a scapegoat[76] and that there was People Risk evident throughout the bank:

> The analysis that we have undertaken of the circumstances of the downfall of HBOS leaves no doubt that that downfall cannot be laid solely at the feet of Peter Cummings... Losses were incurred across several divisions. The losses were caused by a flawed strategy, inappropriate culture and inadequate controls. These are matters for which successive Chief Executives and particularly the Chairman and the board as a whole bear responsibility.

So why did the board of HBOS not pick up the impending disaster? The problem, as the bank's regulator noted, was that there was *culture of optimism* in the senior ranks of the bank that made them ignore warnings both from inside (HBOS fired one of their senior risk managers for giving bad news) and from outside (their regulators). In fact as early as 2004, the bank's regulator (the FSA) had told management that HBOS was an 'accident waiting to happen', but the warnings were ignored. This rejection of outside warnings is a symptom of Groupthink (in particular group insulation) and indicative of what Professor Turner called 'disregard of complaints from outside'. The inward-looking behaviour of the board was compounded by the fact that, as official inquiries found, several key executives and board members had no formal qualifications in banking. In other words, if the board had wanted to find problems they wouldn't have known where to look. The Parliamentary Commission[77] called the bank's lending strategy 'incompetent and reckless' and its execution a 'manual of bad banking which should be read alongside accounts of previous bank failures for the future leaders of banks, and their future regulators, who think they know better or that next time it will be different'. HBOS is a classic case of People Risk at the Institution level – the wrong people were at the wrong level, in the wrong company, at the wrong time.

4.5.7 Co-operative Bank

The takeover of HBOS by Lloyds did not just affect those two banks, but ultimately precipitated the near-collapse of another long-established UK financial institution – the Co-operative Bank.[78] The Co-operative Bank is a financial services subsidiary of the Co-operative Group, known colloquially as the 'Co-op'. The Co-op, a mutual organization owned and run by its members, is most well known as a food retailer but operates a wide range of retail businesses. The banking services of the Co-op was split off as a separate company in 1876 and as a full member of the UK Clearing System continues to provide banking services to over 8 million Co-op members.

In 2009, the Co-operative Bank announced a merger[79] with the Britannia Building Society (BBS), the second-largest building society in the UK at the time, with over 250 branches. The original plan for the merger was to re-brand all Britannia branches as Co-op by 2013 and to operate, after rationalization of the combined group, some 600 banking branches across the UK. In an echo of the merger of Halifax and Bank of Scotland, the CEO of the Britannia, Mr Neville Richardson – a non-banker – became CEO of the merged group.

Prior to the merger, Britannia was in trouble.[80] Like Northern Rock and other building societies, the BBS was heavily dependent on wholesale, rather than member, funding and had a not-insignificant exposure to sub-prime loans. And like others, the bank's funding strategy came under severe pressure during the GFC. The so-called Kelly Report,[81] authored by Sir Christopher Kelly, into the collapse of the Co-operative Bank reported that the UK regulator, the FSA, had already placed Britannia on a watch list and later concluded that 'Britannia would have failed had it not been for the Co-op'. But, in an example of Groupthink, overconfidence and lack of 'situational awareness', Kelly found 'no evidence that either Britannia management or its board was aware that the organization was on a watch list or thought it was in need of rescue'. Nor were the Britannia alone in underestimating the direness of their situation. Kelly reports that:

> There is no evidence that the [Co-op] board gave any serious consideration to the possibility of delay or walking away while it waited to see how the markets developed. At the very least, it might have been expected to ensure that great care was taken over due diligence, with a particular focus on commercial real estate.

Both parties saw benefits in a merger. The Co-operative Bank saw the opportunity the merger gave to significantly increase 'scale' at what appeared to be little cost and Britannia saw the opportunity to acquire current account and internet banking capabilities that it had decided that it was impractical to develop themselves. As noted in the Kelly report, the management of the respective firms, especially Mr Richardson, saw the opportunity to run much larger institutions with commensurate increases in their own status and remuneration.

At this point it should be noted that, even without significant impairment problems, the merger of two large financial institutions is not a trivial matter, requiring large-scale integration of computer systems and operating procedures and rationalization of two very different corporate cultures. Kelly notes that while Mr Richardson was a very experienced executive, he was not an expert in banking, a problem compounded when he 'brought with him a number of ex-Britannia executives, including the new Director of Integration and Change to lead a complex integration and IT replatforming programme'. The complexity of this 'IT replatforming' project was made even more difficult by the fact that the Co-operative bank had been in the middle of an earlier replatforming project that was prematurely cancelled after the merger in favour of a new vendor. The bank had decided to change IT horses in mid-stream. However, the subsequent failure to deliver this new 'Transformation Programme', which was crucial to the success of the merger, is not the issue considered here, other than to note that the bank's IT systems were in turmoil and not a suitable base for further expansion.

Following the takeover in 2009 of HBOS by Lloyds TSB, to become Lloyds Banking Group (LBG), the European Commission required, as a condition of approving aid from the UK government, that the newly-formed LBG should divest a substantial part of its business. To preserve competition in the UK banking sector, LBG was required to divest itself of 632 retail branches to create a new retail banking organization with projected assets of some £53 billion. This spin-off became known as Project Verde,[82] with the hope that this nascent retail bank would be acquired as a viable going concern by a third party. However, given that existing large banks would not qualify for purchasing Verde, for competition reasons, it was recognized that there were few possible bidders.

When initially approached by an investment bank with the idea of being a bidder for Project Verde, the board of the Co-operative Bank was lukewarm, because of the problems it was already experiencing in its various integration and IT programmes.[83] However, there were attractions, not least being that, after acquiring Verde, the Co-operative would become a major 'challenger bank' to the Big Four, with some 10 per cent of banking branches across the UK. The CEO was reported as describing the acquisition as being 'approximately 15 years' worth of organic growth in one transaction'. At this point the ownership of the Co-operative Bank came into play as the bank was wholly owned by the Co-operative Group, whose CEO, Peter Marks, was very supportive of increasing the whole Group's scale and scope.[84] Kelly notes that the Group CEO's 'relative lack of banking expertise and his commitment to finding a way of making the transaction succeed, made a dangerous combination'. Though not averse to such a transaction, the management of the Co-op Bank was wary of the risks involved in such an expansion, given the problems it was already facing in its earlier integration programme. Kelly reports that, in July 2011, the Co-op Group made a bid for Verde of some £1.75 billion but insiders believed that the Group board 'was not expecting anything to come of it'. Although the term was later denied the bid was reportedly described to the board as a 'punt'. It should be noted that only one other firm, NBNK,[85] an investment vehicle created specifically for the purpose by ex-bankers, made a bid for Verde.

For the next year, negotiations on the exact form of a final transaction took place, with the regulator (FSA) placing quite severe restrictions on the capital that could be injected into the deal by the Co-op Group and requiring detailed plans on how the IT systems could be integrated without significant operational risk. To make the deal more attractive, LBG also reduced the size of the transaction in terms of quantity and quality of assets to be transferred. In July 2012, both the boards of the Co-op Group and the Co-operative Bank agreed the terms of the purchase, though not without reservations by some directors.[86] However, before the purchase was completed the deal began to fall apart.

In July 2012, the FSA had placed the Co-operative Bank on its watch list[87] over concerns about its deteriorating capital position and had asked for more detailed plans on how the integration of the not-inconsiderable Verde would be accomplished. Almost immediately the bank's business position began to deteriorate due to increasing loan impairments, resulting in demands from the FSA to maintain extra capital. As its full costs became apparent, the acquisition became increasingly unattractive and in April 2013 the Co-operative Group formally withdrew from the transaction. Kelly notes that almost until the end, despite warnings of the risks in the acquisition from the firms' advisers, the momentum for the transaction inside the bank did not waiver, especially from the Co-op Group CEO, Peter Marks.

What was obvious in hindsight, and indeed widely canvassed at the time, was that the Co-operative Bank was in no position to undertake such a strategically important project. As a number of commissioned and external reports[88] concluded, the bank was 'overstretched' already and just did not have capital nor personnel capabilities to manage the acquisition. While it is likely that the Co-operative Bank's capital shortfall would have emerged in any case, the proposed Verde acquisition brought the bank's capital problems into the limelight. Almost from the Britannia acquisition, the combined bank's capital position had been deteriorating as a result of: (a) increasing regulatory capital demands following the GFC; (b) loan defaults due to a contracting economy; (c) additional provisions for PPI misselling; and (d) write-downs of now abandoned IT expenditure. In reality, the Co-op was in no position to acquire Verde. By June 2103, with increasing provisions for loan impairments, the bank's capital fell below some of its regulatory minimums, prompting Moody's to significantly downgrade its ratings and its auditor to cast doubt on the Bank's ability to continue as a 'going concern'.

The usual bloodletting followed, with the Chair and senior management of the Bank being replaced and a parliamentary inquiry was instigated.[89] The customary 'find the culprit' investigations turned up several unsavoury incidents, not least concerning the ex-Chair, the Rev. Paul Flowers.[90] The more thoughtful analysis by Sir Christopher Kelly concluded that, although by no means the only cause the Britannia acquisition was a 'significant one' and that 'some of the wounds were self-inflicted and could have been avoided with better management and leadership'. Kelly noted the board and management seem to have 'over-optimistically expected an economic upturn which would improve its profitability and get it out of trouble'.

The Kelly report concluded that the 'culture of the Bank contributed to the debacle in a number of ways', and in particular as regards board-level governance:

- the pursuit of too many initiatives, given limited management capability;
- a tendency not to welcome challenge;
- a willingness to accept certain key assertions without subjecting them to proper scrutiny;
- a tendency to promote good news and to delay bad news;
- a tendency towards being inward-looking;

- a failure to take seriously enough the warnings given by the Regulator or the (not always consistent) advice they received at different times from a series of professional advisers;

- a willingness to take opportunities to shift problems into the future when it would be more prudent to address them earlier;

- less than complete transparency;

- unwarranted optimism that an economic recovery would raise low levels of profitability and lift the value of property assets; and

- a board and Executive who allowed themselves to be carried along by events, rather than stepping back at appropriate points and taking stock.

These, of course, are all examples of some of the biases and People Risks identified in Chapter 3, including: unwarranted Optimism and Overconfidence; Illusion of Control; Groupthink; Disregard of Warnings; and Planning Fallacy. These People Risks caused the board and management to 'overreach' in their acquisition strategy. In terms of the People Risk model, the *motivation* for the takeover of Britannia and the proposed acquisition of Verde was to increase profitability for the Co-op's members, the *opportunity* was clearly intended by the bank as they refused to consider abandoning plans until finally forced to do so, and the *rationalization* was Economic Necessity as the board and executives considered that the firm needed to up-scale to survive.

4.5.8 JPMorgan – The Whale

As one of the largest international banks, JPMorgan is more likely than others to suffer recurring losses due to People Risks at all levels, from Individuals (such as its connection to Bernie Madoff as described above) to LIBOR manipulation (described in section 4.6.5). This section will describe the so-called Whale case,[91] in which JPMorgan executives admitted to losing over US $6 billion. This case is a salutary lesson that even the most trusted employees can incur significant losses as a consequence not of fraud but by bad decisions.

In 2012, the JPMorgan board decided that the bank should, in order to meet new regulatory capital requirements, reduce its risk across the bank and they set targets for each business line to do so. One of the business divisions required to reduce its risk was the Central Investment Office (CIO), which was responsible for managing the bank's own funds. The events that followed are well described in the report of an inquiry by the US Senate Permanent Subcommittee on Investigations (PSI).[92] In summary, the CIO considered various options for reducing risks as required by the board, but each of the alternatives considered gave rise to losses and importantly other risks as the strategy was being executed. Instead of going back to the board and senior management to thoroughly discuss the pros and cons of the various options available, the managers and traders in the CIO, some of the most experienced, respected and well-paid individuals in the firm, took a decision to execute a strategy to reduce overall risk by paradoxically taking on 'hedging' risk. The full details of this highly complex and intricate strategy were known only to a few but it was accepted by all senior executives within the CIO.

To compound the problem, the senior managers of the CIO decided at the same time to implement a new mathematical model for estimating the risks in their various portfolios. At this point it should be noted that these portfolios contained some very complex derivatives securities, known as Credit Default Swaps (CDS), which are in effect bets on whether companies will fail or not. There had been a long-standing belief among CIO management and traders that existing models had been overly penalizing the CIO for investing in such complex securities and when a new model, commissioned by the CIO, appeared to show this, management accepted and implemented it immediately, circumventing the bank's rules on model development.[93]

However, the complicated strategy devised by the CIO traders and management proved difficult to execute in practice, not least because, when the CIO traders began to invest heavily in supposedly risk-reducing securities, competitors became aware of what was planned and began to bet against JPMorgan. After only a few weeks, the strategy was failing and the bank was bleeding money but CIO management and traders kept up the momentum, trying to claw back their losses, much as rogue traders did in other cases. By the time the bank called a halt on the strategy, after only a few months, losses were estimated at around US $6 billion.[94]

While the new model had the effect of hiding the growing losses for a time, until the model was pulled out because of some serious errors that were detected in it, there were a multitude of other alarm bells ringing all over JPMorgan. In a classic case of Teamthink, the small group of CIO executives kept rejecting the warnings of other JPMorgan executives until the losses became too large to ignore. In an echo of rogue trader cases, the traders in CIO tried to cover up the extent of the losses using fairly transparent accounting trickery but did not attempt to enter false trades. Nonetheless this is technically a 'wire fraud' under US law and two relatively junior individuals have been charged for misleading investors.[95]

The Whale case, so called because of the sheer size of the risks taken by JPMorgan, illustrates People Risk in that a small group of individuals in the CIO believed that they could pull off a very complex and highly risky strategy without incurring any losses to the firm. This displayed extreme overconfidence in their own abilities, bordering on hubris. Like Fred Goodwin, they had been very successful throughout their careers and had little doubt that they could be the heroes again. They were wrong and the bank's shareholders suffered massively as a consequence. The case also illustrates an instance of CIO executives failing to satisfactorily resolve a very complex conflict of interest between following (vague) orders to reduce risk and (equally vague) pressures not to make losses. Their decision to try to walk the fine line between these two pressures proved inappropriate.

4.5.9 HSBC – money laundering

Banking losses can occur for reasons other than bad lending or liquidity management. In December 2012, one of the world's largest banks, HSBC (the Hong Kong and Shanghai Banking Corporation), entered into a settlement[96] with US regulatory authorities and paid fines totalling some US $1.9 billion in respect of criminal charges for allowing itself to be used as a money laundering conduit by, among others, Mexican drug cartels. The settlement arose from an investigation[97] by the Homeland

Security Committee of the US Congress which documented billions of dollars' worth of transactions handled by HSBC subsidiaries that not only violated Anti-Money Laundering (AML) laws but in some instances were deliberately disguised from US law enforcement agencies. The lack of a good compliance culture in its AML functions was cited as a major weakness that regulators demanded that HSBC fix. Commenting on the settlement,[98] the Group CEO, Stuart Gulliver said 'We accept responsibility for our past mistakes. We have said we are profoundly sorry for them, and we do so again. The HSBC of today is a fundamentally different organization from the one that made those mistakes.'

It is interesting, however, that, although the law breaking and associated compliance failures had been going on for many years, no senior executive or board member was prepared to take personal responsibility for these governance failures. The *motivation* for the scandal was maintaining bank profitability, the clearly very profitable *opportunity* was intended by the bank but unintended in the sense that they did not wish to break the law, which implies that the *rationalization* was Distrust of Law and Victimless Crime. This says much for the 'tone at the top' of HSBC and is an example of People Risk throughout the board and senior management, who proved unable to resolve the conflict of interest between making profits for the firm and obeying laws. HSBC's board and management clearly thought that they could get away with treading this fine line, and they did so for many years.

4.5.10 Eli Lilly – pharmaceutical misselling

HSBC was not the only major corporation that felt that somehow the law did not apply to them. Eli Lilly and Company is one of the world's great pharmaceutical companies, with a proud history of selling 'ethical drugs' for over 140 years. In 2009, Eli Lilly agreed to plead guilty to criminal charges laid by the US Department of Justice[99] and to pay the largest criminal fine at the time of some US $1.4 billion for promoting a drug for uses not approved by the Food and Drug Administration (FDA), the regulatory body for approving pharmaceutical drugs in the United States. The FDA had approved the company's anti-psychotic drug Zyprexa for specific uses and it is illegal for a company to sell approved drugs for other so-called 'off-label', unapproved purposes. In a deliberate and authorized marketing programme, Lilly's salespeople sought to convince doctors to prescribe Zyprexa for a range of off-label conditions such as Alzheimer's, depression, anxiety, and sleep problems. This programme lasted from the late 1990s to 2005 and involved training staff to disregard the law when marketing the product. The *rationalizations* here were a Distrust of Law, ie ignoring the process for approving drugs, but also Victimless Crime, as the patients to whom the drugs would be administered would *probably* not be harmed. The obvious conflict of interest between generating profit and behaving ethically was resolved by promoting profit-generating behaviour within the business.

The Eli Lilly case is a particularly egregious example of People Risk in that the legal restrictions on prescribing off-label medicines were well known to salespersons, sales trainers, marketers, managers, senior executives and directors in Eli Lilly and throughout the industry. But no one blew the whistle for many years, as breaking the rules had become 'business as usual'. Even more worrying is that physicians, who were equally aware of the prohibitions, appeared not to push back on the blatantly illegal sales tactics or, if they did so, did not go on to raise it to a higher level. It is interesting to note that investigations were only started after one of the company's employees eventually blew the whistle.

4.5.11 Bribery – BAE and Siemens

Another area where firms have sometimes skirted the law is in bribing foreign officials to win lucrative contracts. One such example is the huge defence and aerospace company, BAE Systems (previously British Aerospace), which in 2010 entered into a plea bargain[100] with the UK Serious Fraud Office (SFO) and the US Department of Justice (DOJ) in respect of charges of corruption and bribery of officials in several small countries. A fine of some £280 million was agreed although BAE did not admit liability. At around the same time, a long-running legal dispute between BAE and the SFO concerning bribery of Saudi officials in an enormous defence contract[101] was dropped to 'safeguard national and international security'. Clearly Distrust of Law does sometimes work for some large companies.

Nor is BAE alone in being charged with bribery of foreign officials; it is almost seen in some circles as a cost of doing business in international markets. For example in 2008, Siemens AG, the German industrial giant, paid fines of over US $1.3 billion to settle a case with US and German authorities concerning bribery of overseas officials.[102] Prosecutors claimed that bribery was deeply ingrained in Siemens' 'business model'. However, Siemens' response was exemplary and, in only a period of a few years, some 80 per cent of its top-tier executives were replaced in an effort to change the company's culture.[103] Few firms have been as brave and resolute in tackling People Risk as Siemens.

4.5.12 Mid Staffordshire Trust – medical fatalities

We will now turn our attention to an example from the public sector, in particular tracing a thread in medicine in the UK, from Elaine Bromiley through to Dr Harold Shipman to the Mid Staffordshire NHS Trust which, as an organization, was severely criticized for its failure to prevent patient deaths in the Accident & Emergency (A&E) facilities in one of its major hospitals. The NHS in England and Wales is organized into some 530 'Trusts', of various types and sizes, which have responsibility for managing medical services in their local areas. Some of these trusts are huge businesses, such as Bart's Health Trust, which provides health services to over 2.5 million residents of East London, employs some 15,000 staff, operates six major hospitals and had a financial turnover of £1.25 billion.[104] On the other hand the Mid Staffordshire (known as Mid Staffs) NHS Foundation Trust was relatively small with about 3,000 staff in two hospitals servicing a population of over 320,000 in Staffordshire in the English Midlands. Following concerns raised by the relatives of patients who had died, the body responsible for monitoring and improving NHS standards, the Healthcare Commission,[105] began in 2008 to investigate 'apparently high mortality rates in patients admitted as emergencies' to the main Stafford hospital. After an extensive investigation, the Commission severely criticized the Trust's management for the appalling conditions and inadequacies at the hospital that led to patient deaths. Although the Commission's report did not provide statistics, press reports estimated that there had been between 400 and 1,200 'excess deaths' at the hospital due to substandard A&E care between 2005 and 2008.[106]

The Commission's report noted that the Trust was small and was trying to provide a range of services that they did not have the resources to handle. For example, the Trust did not have the systems to monitor patient outcomes, such as 'excess deaths'. When pressed on their unacceptable mortality statistics the Trust's management did not address the issue directly but instead blamed 'data quality'. The Commission's report was highly critical of the Trust's management: 'The Trust's board and senior leaders did not develop an open, learning culture, inform themselves sufficiently about the quality of care, or appear willing to challenge themselves in the light of adverse information'. These were serious failings at the highest level of the organization as the board had created a 'closed culture' that permeated the Trust and also the local Strategic Health Authority responsible for regional trusts. The board did not see the problems, because they weren't looking for them. Professor Turner[107] talked about the distraction of a 'decoy phenomenon' in disasters, which in the Mid Staffs case was about the need for the Trust to meet financial targets, as the report concluded:

> In the Trust's drive to become a foundation trust, it appears to have lost sight of its real priorities. The Trust was galvanized into radical action by the imperative to save money and did not properly consider the effect of reductions in staff on the quality of care. It took a decision to significantly reduce staff without adequately assessing the consequences. Its strategic focus was on financial and business matters at a time when the quality of care of its patients admitted as emergencies was well below acceptable standards.

The Mid Staffordshire case is an example of People Risk because board directors and senior executives were not giving the correct degree of focus to their primary roles, which was to provide healthcare for their patients – they were not doing what they should have been doing. Collectively the management of the Trust did not resolve the conflict of interest between operating efficiency and duty of care to patients. In the inquiry into the failures, there was absolutely no suggestion that the individuals had been fraudulent or even negligent, just that, *overloaded by work*, their attention was elsewhere, on finances rather than medical operations. The Healthcare Commission's report made many recommendations for improvements which focused on managerial rather than clinical changes, including: creating a 'learning' culture; collecting and reporting incidents; identifying and managing risks; producing post-incident audit reports; and involving as many people as possible in diagnosing and solving problems. Openness was to be the catchword. However, the financial and health sectors are not the only examples of People Risk, and some other cases of problems occurring in non-financial institutions are now described.

4.5.13 Blackberry – strategic overreach

In the early 2000s, the must-have gadget for corporate warriors around the world was the Blackberry,[108] a sleek and elegant handheld device that allows executives to keep in touch with their company's email systems anywhere in the world where there is a mobile/cell phone connection. The spectacularly popular device, created by the small Canadian company RIM (Research in Motion), was owned not only by business people but also by pop stars, politicians and even royalty. The history of the Blackberry is short: sweet at first but sour at the end, as by 2010 the Blackberry was in deep trouble. The Blackberry, which grew out of RIM's two-way paging technology, was first released in 1998, giving users unprecedented access to their company's emails, even when out of the office. It was an instant success.

RIM was a survivor of the dot com crash of the early 2000s, bucking the global technology downturn and managing to hit the magic mark of 1 million email customers by 2004. In 2004, RIM added a telephone capability to its email and the Blackberry (now nicknamed the Crackberry because of its addictive qualities) really took off, with sales rising to over 6 million customers by the end of 2006. At that point, the Blackberry was the undisputed leader in the 'personal digital assistant' (PDA) market with almost 50 per cent market share, having seen off the Palm Pilot, its main competitor. But as management gurus Michael Porter and Victor Millar[109] warned as far back as 1985, technology leadership can be fleeting and illusory – new competitors can rise (and fall) very quickly. By 2012, there were some 80 million Blackberry subscribers around the world, but as the case of Egg showed in Chapter 3, increasing the number of customers is one thing, increasing the number of profitable customers is quite another.

In 2006, RIM had announced the Pearl, a new Blackberry 'smartphone' with an integrated MP3 player and digital camera, which was aimed at the consumer rather than the corporate market. By October 2007, RIMS announced its 10 millionth customer and very briefly became Canada's largest company by market capitalization. But early in 2007 Steve Jobs, charismatic CEO of Apple, announced a brand new product, the now legendary iPhone. Mike Lazaridis RIM's co-founder and co-CEO was suddenly faced with a new type of competitor, but he and his co-CEO, Jim Balsille, did not appear *outwardly* to be worried about Apple. In 2010, a former employee reported[110] that inside RIM, however, there was panic after Apple's announcement, when, following a series of emergency meetings, technicians convinced management that the iPhone couldn't or wouldn't work as intended. The technical experts believed that the product could not do all of the things Apple claimed because its battery was too small. When RIM later bought an iPhone after its launch and opened it up they were dismayed to find that it was really little more than a big battery with a tiny chip attached. The board, management and technical experts in RIM had convinced themselves that the Blackberry was so far ahead of the competition that it could not be overtaken.

This hubris was misplaced. By the end of 2007, the iPhone had already steamed past Blackberry in the total number of smartphones sold and the market became very crowded soon afterwards with the entry of technology giants such as Samsung and Google. The market for smartphones grew exponentially and RIM's shipment of its next generation of Blackberry also grew. However, the growth was not fast enough as the firm's market share plummeted and RIM went into the now-familiar death spiral; senior management were fired, inventory was written down, RIM's share price plummeted and in 2103 RIM was acquired by one of its investors to be broken up.[111] Blinded by its initial success RIM was just too slow to see the looming changes in the market that they once dominated. Brilliant technicians that they were, RIM's board and management had 'over-reached', and, overly confident in their existing, highly successful product, they did not ask the hard questions about their product's future. When they did move, it was too late and the directors chose to move into the path of their bigger competitors, who ran them over. People Risk, in the form of hubris and overconfidence by the management team, had triumphed over the prudent management of the risks to RIM's strategy.

4.5.14 Tesco – strategic overreach

RIM is a classic case study of an institution that did everything right but the directors were overly optimistic about the capabilities of their product and did not see the next technology wave coming *because they were not looking for it*. But they are not alone in taking such a rosy, overconfident view of the future and their ability to shape it. Tesco plc is one of the world's leading retailers, second in profitability to Wal-Mart and third in revenues to Wal-Mart and the French giant Carrefour. Although Tesco has, over the past two decades, expanded from its traditional base in the UK and Ireland, mainly into the former Eastern Bloc countries, it does not have the global reach of, for example, Carrefour. Given its dominance of the local market, it would be natural for Tesco's board to actively seek out international ventures.

In 2007, the Tesco Annual report[112] described the firm's long-term strategy as being four-pronged: (a) grow in the UK; (b) become a successful international retailer; (c) be as strong in non-food as in food; (d) develop retailing 'services', such as personal finance and the internet. At face value, this appears to be a sound diversified growth strategy based on a solid history of growth in group profits and dividend distributions. In 2007, the company also announced that it had set up a new chain of medium-sized grocery stores, named Fresh & Easy, in southern California as its bridgehead for expanding into the vast US market. With hindsight it is difficult to see how much expertise Tesco, headquartered half a world away, could bring to such a totally different market. A confidential report[113] by the global investment bank Credit Suisse reportedly concluded, at the time, that 'it may be Fresh but it won't be Easy', referring to the fact that food buying patterns in the USA were very different to the UK. Where, they asked, was Tesco going to differentiate itself? But the question is moot, as the venture was, if not set up in the wrong place, certainly started at the wrong time. Almost immediately, California was hit by the GFC, particularly affecting the middle-class neighbourhoods serviced by Fresh & Easy. The venture was in trouble from the start. But what did the Tesco board do? In a classic example of *Illusion of Control*, they decided to tough it out.

In 2008, at the height of the GFC, the firm's Annual Report was upbeat about its US venture. Stores were opening on schedule, sales were ahead of target, the main distribution centre was ramping up for increased business, and trading losses were some £62 million but still less than the £100 million projected. In a Q&A section in the next Annual Report in 2009, the CEO Sir Terry Leahy was optimistic: 'there's lots to be pleased about... the operation is very good and it's strong. We are expanding the business at a good rate and morale is high', but losses at £142 million were higher than expected. The firm chose to attribute these losses, however, to foreign exchange fluctuations, rather than operational losses. The 2010 Annual Report was slightly more circumspect, not pessimistic but less gung-ho. Nonetheless it claimed good progress for the venture, which had lost some £165 million for the year, but the report was confident that this loss was the expected peak. In a bizarre glass-half-full statement, the CEO claimed that in fact the GFC property crisis was good news for Fresh & Easy, as the cost of acquiring new sites would be lowered.

However, in the 2011 report, Tesco announced that Sir Terry Leahy had retired to be replaced by Philip Clarke. Mr Clarke's news was not good, as the US operation's losses, far from peaking, now stood at some £186 million. Nonetheless, he claimed that future was optimistic with 'strong growth in customer numbers driving steady sales improvement in each store'. In the next year, 2012, Philip Clarke announced that the US venture had turned the corner, 'delivering reduced losses [of £153 million] for the first time'. The CEO expressed confidence 'about the outlook for the business, although clearly much remains to be done'. The number of new Fresh & Easy stores was increasing and sales were expanding at over 20 per cent per year. Clearly this has an echo of Egg, where gaining customers is one thing but gaining profitable customers is quite another. But Mr Clarke did not get the chance to turn the corner. In 2013, after a strategic review, the Tesco board announced that it was abandoning the US venture, booking an overall loss of some £1.2 billion because the US business 'simply did not offer the prospect of acceptable returns in an appropriate time frame'.

Who is to blame for the failure of the Fresh & Easy venture? Clearly as ex-CEO, Sir Terry Leahy was a candidate for the scapegoat role and was duly anointed as such by Lord MacLaurin, the man who as Chairman had appointed Leahy as CEO. The ex-Chairman had clearly forgotten that in 2004 he had boasted that the selection of Leahy was one of his most important management decisions in his almost 40 years in the company.[114] There was clearly a lack of good corporate governance at the board level in Tesco whenever a strategic decision was made by the board but the risk management of that strategic decision was not followed through properly. The strategy to enter the US market in the manner chosen by Tesco may have been correct at the time and in the right circumstances may have generated huge profits, but the board did not put in place the necessary risk management of the 'strategic execution', and lost more money than if they had exited quicker.

This is a form of People Risk in that the board and senior management were unwilling to take the losses that would result from pulling out of their new venture. The Tesco board appeared to be suffering from what is known as a *loss aversion bias* where people hold on to losses longer than they should.[115] It should be noted that while with hindsight the decision was proved wrong, that was because of an unexpected event, the GFC. The board cannot be criticized for the strategy, but can be criticized for not recognizing that their initial assumptions had been shown to be incorrect and for not taking evasive action earlier. On a personal level, Sir Terry Leahy, who had joined Tesco straight after university, was known as a hard working if somewhat dour executive who, like Fred Goodwin of RBS, was obsessive about detail. Maybe that attention to detail blinded Leahy to the 'Invisible Gorilla' – that Los Angeles was not London.

4.5.15 Lehman Brothers – strategic overreach

The failure to manage the risks in their Fresh & Easy strategy was *relatively* inexpensive for Tesco, compared to the costs of the failure of Lehman Brothers to manage their particular growth strategy.[116] In 2006, Lehman CEO Dick Fuld explained to staff 'a new move toward an aggressive growth strategy, including greater risk and more leverage', describing the change, as a 'shift from a "moving" or securitization business to a "storage" business, in which Lehman would make and hold longer-term investments'. Lehman's board fully endorsed this new strategy and was made aware of the additional risks that such a 'holding strategy' would imply. As a result of the change in strategy, Lehman's mortgage-related assets almost doubled to some US $111 billion over the next year, with the firm regularly increasing and then exceeding its own internal risk limits. The company was still buying and holding mortgage assets into 2008, long after the US housing market had peaked and property prices were falling. Lehman's bankruptcy examiner[117] noted that the growth strategy was 'flawed' because the board and executives did not properly manage the risks inherent in it.

The history is now well known: the US housing bubble burst around 2007, housing prices fell, mortgage holders started to default, and firms such as Lehman were unable to fund their huge balance sheets. In September 2008, Lehman filed for Chapter 11 bankruptcy, the biggest US corporate default at the time, triggering a crisis that raced around the world. Dick Fuld, a hero inside Lehman for his tireless and successful efforts to save Lehman after the firm lost its offices in the 9/11 terrorist attack,[118] was known to be single minded, combative and supremely confident, insisting to the very end that the firm would survive if only given support by the US Federal Reserve. Fuld's failure to recognize the seriousness of the problems facing Lehman illustrates, among others things, a type of cognitive bias called *Illusion of Control*, which is a People Risk. Whether the GFC would have been as disastrous had Lehman's board properly curbed Fuld's overconfidence, *as they should have done*, will remain one of the great unanswerable questions in business.

4.5.16 BP – Gulf of Mexico oil spill

BP, once called British Petroleum, is one of the world's great innovative companies, leading the oil industry in new ways of extracting the vital energy that the world needs. BP is an exemplary company that takes Health and Safety (H&S) very seriously, not least because its workforce operates in some of the coldest, hottest, deepest and most dangerous places in the world. But even with an exemplary H&S focus, BP's board and management were found to be at fault for one of the world's greatest ecological disasters, the Gulf of Mexico oil spill of 2010.[119] On 20 April 2010, there was a blowout of methane gas on the Deep Water Horizon oil rig in the Macondo area off Louisiana in the Gulf of Mexico. The methane gas caught fire causing the Deep Water platform to explode and sink, killing 11 workers. After the explosion, there was an escape of crude oil from beneath the platform, which went uncapped because of the difficulty of capping a leak at such depths. For some 87 days, crude oil poured into the (fairly) pristine water of the northern Gulf of

Mexico, polluting the local fishing grounds and the tourist beaches of Alabama and Florida. Estimates of the oil spill range from some 2.5 million barrels (BP's estimate) to over 4 million barrels (US government estimates), but regardless of whichever estimate is agreed, there will be multi-billion dollar claims for damages caused to the Gulf Coast economies.

The details of the disaster are well documented not least in the official US government report by the National Commission, *Deep Water: The Gulf oil disaster and the future of off-shore drilling*. The aptly named Deep Water platform was an engineering marvel designed to drill at previously unreachable depths and at Macondo, BP was drilling an exploratory well of around 35,000 feet at 5,000 feet below the surface of the water. This was a complex task that earned the nickname 'the well from hell' because of the depth of the drilling and the geological complexity encountered. The immediate cause of the gas release and the subsequent explosion was a defect in a cement casing being constructed around the drill head deep under the water. Much of the subsequent discussion on the cause of the catastrophe has been around how thoroughly the pressure tests on the cement casing had been conducted and interpreted. A subsequent indictment[120] against three BP drilling supervisors by the US Department of Justice alleges that they were guilty of 'involuntary manslaughter' of the 11 dead oil workers through negligence in supervising the testing of the cement casings and seals.

So this was an incident/accident in which 11 men died that is at least partly attributable (it is alleged) to individual negligence by a few supervisors. However, the National Commission that was tasked by the US President with inquiring into the disaster was clear in its conclusions that the problem involved more than a few individuals, notably 'the explosive loss of the Macondo well could have been prevented' and crucially:

> The immediate causes of the Macondo well blowout can be traced to a series of identifiable mistakes made by BP [and subcontractors], Halliburton, and Transocean that reveal such systematic failures in risk management that they place in doubt the safety culture of the entire industry.

The Commission then went on to detail problems with the design of the well and the processes within BP and the industry for designing such wells, which are at the limits of human engineering. They also criticized an attitude of cutting corners to meet highly aggressive project schedules and for lack of open communication between the many people in multiple companies that were involved in such projects. The Commission found that the industry and its regulators had become complacent and overconfident in their ability to stretch the limits of oil exploration. Echoing Charles Perrow from Chapter 2 they noted 'complex systems almost always fail in complex ways'.

In November 2012, BP, under new management and following intense pressure by national and state governments, pleaded guilty to criminal charges over the deaths of the 11 workers.[121] The company paid a US \$4.5 billion fine in the first of many cases that are expected to run for several years and involve further settlements that are likely to exceed US \$10 billion. But the Deep Water tragedy was a wake-up call not only to BP but also to the whole of the oil industry on the need to be better at People Risk Management in such a sensitive ecological environment. People Risk was evident in the overconfidence of BP management and staff in drilling in highly risky conditions without really understanding the magnitude of the risks the firm was taking. The Presidential Commission wrote:

> The private oil and gas industry is the lead actor in exploration and production of Gulf energy resources. In the wake of the BP Deep Water Horizon disaster – a crisis that was unanticipated, and on a scale for which companies had not prepared to respond – changes in safety and environmental practices, safety training, drilling technology, containment and clean-up technology, preparedness, corporate culture and management behaviour will be required if Deep Water energy operations are to be pursued in the Gulf – or elsewhere. Maintaining the public trust and earning the privilege of drilling on the outer continental shelf requires no less.

4.5.17 Fukushima – nuclear accident

The so-called Great East Japan (or Tokohu) Earthquake[122] of 11 March 2011 was the largest earthquake ever to hit Japan (magnitude 9.0). It created a giant tsunami that reached a height of over 40 metres, devastating provinces along the Northeast coast of the main Japanese island of Honshu. National agencies estimated the number of deaths due to the tsunami to be over 16,000 people. But one event above all others is retained in people's memory of this horrendous natural disaster – the partial meltdown of two of the reactors in the Fukushima Daiichi nuclear power plant, which had been inundated by the tsunami. Pictures of smoking reactors and news headlines warning of nuclear armageddon flashed around the world with horrific TV pictures of death and destruction, which were in fact caused by the tsunami not by the nuclear accident. But the reality is much more prosaic. While there were thousands of deaths as a result of drowning due to the tsunami in the prefecture, only three people are counted as dying in the Fukushima accident itself, two drowning in the tsunami and one suffering a heart attack while working on restoring power to the plant.[123] Many press articles, however, implied that thousands had died in the Fukushima accident. Long-term damage has been lessened by largely successful work to contain toxic emissions and groundwater contamination from the plant. But it will take many years to clean up the site and major risks to health will remain until it is done. This is not to understate the magnitude of the problems encountered during the Fukushima incident nor the difficulties of managing complex systems such as nuclear power plants, but to put the accident into perspective.

The timeline of the accident is well documented[124] but in summary: the three reactors that were online at the plant at the time of the earthquake were shut down correctly prior to the tsunami that hit the plant. However, the tidal wave overwhelmed the electrical power running the reactor and also the electricity grid servicing the whole region. Crucially, the emergency electricity generators that were designed to cool the active and spent fuel rods in the event of power failure were located in a low-lying building that was overwhelmed by the tsunami. Battery backup generators kicked in but they were designed to only run for a short time until grid power was restored and they too stopped some 24 hours later. In other words, four levels of defence had been knocked out in quick succession. Without power, it was impossible to cool the fuel rods in the reactors and the risk was that the water in the reactors would boil off, leaving the rods exposed and triggering a partial or complete meltdown of the reactors. Over the few days following the tsunami, the plant staff worked to cool the rods by spraying them with seawater but steam built up in four of the reactors, causing explosions that ripped off the reactor roofs, releasing some radiation into the atmosphere. This caused panic in the population, media and government and evacuation of the surrounding areas began. Over the next few weeks the plant's operators, the Tokyo Electric Power Company (TEPCO), with the help of fire trucks, worked to cool the fuel rods and restore power. Cooling of the fuel rods was successful but that in turn left many millions of litres of contaminated water that has to be removed, a problem that will take many years to fix.

In June 2012, a specially convened Independent Commission of the Japanese Diet (Parliament) released a report[125] that was unequivocal in placing the blame on management failures at TEPCO and its regulators:

> The Earthquake and Tsunami of 11 March, 2011 were natural disasters of a magnitude that shocked the entire world. Although triggered by these cataclysmic events, the subsequent accident at the Fukushima Daiichi nuclear power plant cannot be regarded as a natural disaster. It was a profoundly manmade disaster that could and should have been foreseen and prevented. And its effects could have been mitigated by a more effective human response... Our report catalogues a multitude of errors and wilful negligence that left the Fukushima plant unprepared for the events of 11 March. And it examines serious deficiencies in the response to the accident by TEPCO, regulators and the government.

With admirable honesty, the Commission pointed out the deep cultural problems and biases that they believed first led to crisis and then the inability to solve it quickly:

> What must be admitted – very painfully – is that this was a disaster 'Made in Japan'. Its fundamental causes are to be found in the ingrained conventions of Japanese culture: our reflexive obedience; our reluctance to question authority; our devotion to 'sticking with the programme'; our groupism; and our insularity. Had other Japanese been in the shoes of those who bear responsibility for this accident, the result may well have been the same... This conceit was reinforced by the collective mindset of Japanese bureaucracy, by which the first duty of any individual bureaucrat is to defend the interests of his organization. Carried to an extreme, this led bureaucrats to put organizational interests ahead of their paramount duty to protect public safety.

In considering the case, however, it should also be noted that three other nuclear power stations were inundated by the tsunami, one of which was much closer to the epicentre than Fukushima Daiichi, but they were able to be closed down safely and so an across-the-board condemnation of Japanese safety culture may not be completely warranted.

The Commission was especially critical of organizational problems within TEPCO, concluding 'had there been a higher level of knowledge, training, and equipment inspection related to severe accidents, and had there been specific instructions given to the on-site workers concerning the state of emergency within the necessary time frame, a more effective accident response would have been possible.' It should be noted that the failure of management to ensure that staff are properly trained is a clear example of People Risk. To help to solve similar problems in the future, the

Commission made seven very far-reaching recommendations for reforming TEPCO and the regulatory bureaucracy, in particular recommending that TEPCO should:

> undergo fundamental corporate changes, including strengthening its governance, working towards building an organizational culture which prioritizes safety, changing its stance on information disclosure, and establishing a system which prioritizes the site.

A full discussion of the Fukushima accident, its causes and implications, not least for the future of the nuclear industry, are beyond this book other than to note that, as the commission stated, it was a *'man-made disaster'*. The *rationalizations* of the operators of the Fukushima plant that led to the escape of deadly radiation were Economic Necessity and Distrust of Law in that TEPCO had not worked with regulators to improve safety as a matter of priority. The cases of BP and Fukushima are wake-up calls to the vast energy industry that have echoes elsewhere, particularly in the financial and medical industries. These two cases show that within any organization, even a safety conscious one, anyone, anywhere can make a disastrous mistake and insidiously, because it is invisible, training and education of key individuals can fall below the levels needed to undertake risky and mission-critical tasks.

4.5.18 Summary – Institutions

In discussing the cases in this section, generally the Institutions are referred to in impersonal language, as the 'bank', 'firm' or 'corporation'. But corporations do not make bad decisions, *individuals do*. For example, Tesco did not make the decision to enter the US food retail market; the board and senior management of Tesco made that decision, but failed to follow up by managing the resulting risks. By using detached terms, such as 'Tesco', responsibilities are somehow obscured, implying everyone but no one was to blame. Furthermore, by selecting a scapegoat, such as Sir Terry Leahy, ex-CEO of Tesco, it diverts attention from other, arguably more responsible, individuals in the boardroom. CEOs must carry the can when something goes wrong but it is juvenile to believe that one individual leaving a company, to be replaced by someone, often with less experience, will make everything right. Others must also take *personal responsibility* for their actions and non-actions, otherwise bad decisions will continue to be made.

The common factor in the cases above is that major decisions taken by the senior management of the firms involved were wrong, from the disastrous take-over of ABN AMRO by RBS, through the failed growth strategies of Washington Mutual and HBOS, to the strategic overreach of Tesco, RIMS (Blackberry), Lehman Brothers and BP. A trend in these cases was excessive optimism and overconfidence by senior executives in their own abilities, bordering sometimes on the delusional. And board members appeared to sit by and watch the disasters happen. While the deceptive practices and frauds of Eli Lilly and BAE could not be traced back directly to the highest echelon of these firms it is nonetheless apparent that the practices were not overtly discouraged by senior management, which they should have been. Enron and WorldCom are examples of companies where fraud was being perpetrated at the highest level but no one blew the whistle, until after considerable damage had been done. In the case of the Fukushima disaster and the deaths at Mid-Staffordshire, specific individuals cannot be blamed, merely there existed a culture, in two different parts of the world, where not facing up to problems, or covering them up, was a way of life.

To reiterate, individuals in these institutions took, or failed to take, decisions that resulted in sometimes disastrous financial losses and even deaths. However, unlike the Incident and Individual levels there are not many prescriptions as to how to address this problem (which in part is the rationale for this book). There is much academic work in the areas of Corporate Culture and Governance, but 'culture' too is an impersonal misunderstood concept, as if the imposition of a culture, albeit very important, will make individuals take personal responsibility for their decisions. Coherence of culture is very valuable, but it must be remembered that Enron and BP had very strong coherent cultures that nonetheless encouraged rather than discouraged the very behaviours that precipitated significant losses.

4.6 Industry

Why people and firms become involved in financial booms and busts has been a question that has puzzled historians and economists for centuries, from the Dutch Tulip Mania of 1633 to the excesses of the Global Financial Crisis in the early 2000s. We do not claim to have the definitive answer but we can give examples of cases that may point towards how similar examples of 'irrational exuberance' across entire *Industries* may be tackled in future.

4.6.1 Big Tobacco – selling unsuitable products

The classic case of an entire industry behaving badly is the tobacco industry, and not for nothing are the companies involved called 'Big Tobacco', for their ability to influence events and politics to their advantage. In 1996, Philip Hilts, a prizewinning science journalist and author of *Smokescreen*,[126] brought to light the fact that, despite protestations to the contrary by the largest tobacco companies, the management of these firms had been aware of the addictive and deadly nature of tobacco smoking for many years. This was most evident in a US congressional hearing in which the CEOs of the seven largest tobacco companies each testified under oath that they did not believe smoking was addictive, even though their internal research had proven addiction to be the case many years before. The Oscar nominated film The Insider[127] portrayed this famous scene, and the fight of its hero to blow the whistle. However, some 30 years later the tobacco industry is still fighting a rear-guard action against national and state governments who are chasing them for compensation for the long-term harm caused by lung cancer now irrefutably linked to smoking. The costs to the tobacco companies have been enormous, but so too have been the profits (and incidentally taxes) that are generated from smokers. For many years a cat-and-mouse game has been played in courtrooms around the world as tobacco companies drag out what appears to be the inevitable collapse of their business. In documenting White Collar Crime in industries such as automobiles and pharmaceuticals, James Coleman[128] reserves his opprobrium for the tobacco industry: 'nothing comes close to the tobacco companies in the competition for the world's most deadly killers'.

The US Center for Disease Control (CDC) reports[129] that cigarette smoking is the leading cause of preventable death in the United States, accounting for more than 450,000 deaths and costing almost US $200 billion in the United States each year. These are lonely, sad deaths that do not individually register in the public consciousness even though the figure is over ten times the number of workplace-related deaths. In looking at the People Risk Triangle, the *motivation* for Big Tobacco is clearly greed, as tobacco is very profitable and the companies persist despite the damage to smokers' health. Although the *opportunity* is clearly intended by the industry its devastating consequences are clearly unintended by health agencies but Big Tobacco are experts at pushing the boundaries of the law to maintain their profitability. On the other hand, the *rationalization* is collective and uses the Ubiquity argument that 'everyone is doing it', and the Distrust of Law neutralization in claiming that laws restricting smoking may impinge on people's freedoms.

As we will see in other cases, Big Tobacco is a template for the motivations of other industries. The *motivation* in such cases is fairly specific, usually profit and often greed as easy profits become irresistible. The *opportunity* is intended by the industry players often pushing the limits of the law. Ubiquity and Distrust of the Law are frequently the *rationalizations* articulated by the perpetrators. Of these, Distrust of Law is extremely powerful because there is often a philosophical dimension to this rationalization. For example, although smoking is known to kill many of its users, there is a strong libertarian argument that people should be free to make the choice to smoke or not. This provides a convenient argument for industries to work to delay changes to legislation that may adversely impact them. Although we have strong views on such a stance, we do not argue from a moral perspective but point out that boards and the shareholders of large firms must actively manage the risk that the competitiveness of a whole industry might be compromised by reckless risk-taking by all or even a few major players in the industry. Further examples of 'reckless behaviour' by large companies across a whole industry are expanded on in the next sections.

4.6.2 New Zealand – tax avoidance

To paraphrase Benjamin Franklin, 'Nothing is certain but death and tax avoidance.' Where there is taxation, there will inevitably be some individuals who do not want to pay it. Some will choose illegal means, so-called 'tax evasion', whereas others will try legal means, or so-called 'tax avoidance' which usually involves testing the limits of the law. It is not always easy to distinguish between the two situations and the very fine line between them was characterized by Denis Healey, an ex-UK Chancellor of the Exchequer, as being 'the thickness of a prison wall'. Large firms spend millions each year on highly-priced tax advisers to minimize the amount of tax that they have to pay within the law. But what if the tax advisers are wrong and their advice ends up losing the firm money? This is a People Risk related to mistaken decisions made by individuals at the very top of the firms concerned. The risk is illustrated in the case of the so-called 'Big Four' banks in Australia who were found culpable of tax avoidance[130] by the New Zealand High Court and were required to pay back-taxes of a combined NZ $2.2 billion.

The New Zealand tax case involved all of the four major Australian banks operating through their wholly owned New Zealand (NZ) subsidiaries.[131] These four banks dominate the banking industry in Australia and New Zealand and are widely lauded for having successfully navigated the Global Financial Crisis. As might be expected for a case that took several years to wend its way through the NZ legal system, the details are convoluted, involving a highly complex web of onshore and offshore financial transactions. The NZ High Court finally determined that these transactions were in fact 'tax avoidance arrangements entered into for a purpose of avoiding tax'. A judicial finding against just one bank in one test case forced the other banks to settle taxation claims on all similar transactions with the NZ Inland Revenue Department (IRD). The tax transactions are too complex to describe here[132] but involved a spider's web of international payments and cross guarantees that magically turned taxable profits into non-taxable expenses. Nor is the morality of the transactions considered here but merely the fact that the boards of the four banks, consisting of some of the most experienced directors in Australasia, kept insisting in their annual reports over several years that they had no case to answer. Only towards the end of the litigation did the banks consider setting aside provisions for a settlement with the authorities. Their head-in-the-sand attitude cost their shareholders millions in legal costs and tax settlements.

The real question that relates to the management of People Risk is, how did four supposedly autonomous banks arrive at precisely the same situation where they were being pursued by a national tax authority at exactly the same time? One might assume that the boards of these banks had done their own due diligence and had independently reached the same view that the same types of financial transactions would have the same tax impact. Of course, that is rarely how business works. What actually happened is that, around 1995, the tax experts in one of the banks worked with an external tax adviser to create a transaction that they hoped would reduce the bank's overall tax bill. That transaction was given the green light by the IRD and then the floodgates opened with all of the other banks copying the model and simultaneously starting to reduce their tax bills. This was a frightening prospect for the NZ government as the four banks are among the largest firms in New Zealand and a major source of the country's tax revenue. The IRD then revisited these transactions and in 2003 found that subsequent transactions did not follow the original narrow format that had been approved but had expanded into much larger transactions whose sole purpose, according to the IRD, was avoiding tax.

At this point, the four banks could have reconsidered their positions, stopped doing the transactions and settled with the tax authorities, but instead, overconfident in their position, they decided to fight their case. In the years preceding the expensive settlement, all banks disclosed in their annual reports that they were in dispute with the IRD, disclosing a potential liability but stating, in terms similar to one of the key defendants, Westpac, that they were 'confident that the tax treatment applied in each case was correct and that the likelihood of ultimately being required to pay additional tax is low'. The banks were to continue to take this dismissive approach up to the final settlement, except that in the annual reports published just prior to the settlement, the banks made accounting provisions in their balance sheets for the settlement rather than just a note in their accounts.

But why were the banks so confident that the likelihood of them having to concede was low? As it turns out their optimism can be traced back to a single legal opinion given by a local NZ tax adviser to one of the banks that 'the risk of losing the case was small'. This statement was repeated and reinforced by the very small number of tax advisers and auditors active in the New Zealand market until it became 'accepted fact' rather than merely an opinion. But this original legal opinion was wrong and so were the later assumptions and assertions made by the banks. This is an example of a type of Groupthink, which we call *Systemsthink*, where caution is discarded and optimism, reinforced by shared belief, wins the day across a whole industry. This has also been called 'herding',[133] where the boards of large firms decide to move into the same markets in the same way.

In terms of the People Risk Triangle, the *motivation* was specific in making profits, in this case so excessive that it might be considered bordering on greed. The *opportunity* was the difficulty any national agency would have in tracing complex international transactions. The *rationalization* was Ubiquity, since all other banks are doing it, and Distrust of Law in that the banks disliked the prevailing taxation laws and held the tax authorities in low esteem. The banks believed that jointly they were somehow above the law and as an industry they could get away with tax avoidance. In particular, the banks had come to believe that they were 'too big to prosecute'.

4.6.3 PPI – misselling products

Another example of a whole banking industry doing the wrong thing occurred in the UK banking sector in the so-called Payment Protection Insurance (PPI) Scandal.[134] This scandal is estimated to have cost the major UK banks in the region of £18 billion, with, for example, Lloyds Banking Group (LBG), the new owner of HBOS, alone setting aside over £7 billion to reimburse customers for having sold them insurance policies that either they did not need or which were misleading. This example of People Risk at the Industry level was not an attempt to work around the law, as was the NZ tax scandal, but an attempt to sell a financial product that was in fact a useful product to some people, some of the time.

As the name suggests the PPI product was designed to provide insurance against a purchaser being unable to make payments on a loan taken to purchase a product, such as a washing machine. PPI grew out of similar insurance products that were designed to assist homeowners to continue to pay their mortgages if they became ill, had an accident or were made unemployed. In the right hands, with buyers who understood their benefits and limitations, such products provide very useful protection to borrowers. Unfortunately, because these products were designed to be very profitable, PPI became popular and easy to replicate. So, without considering the potential limitations of the product, every major bank in the UK jumped on the bandwagon at the same time and began selling similar products to a much wider audience. Unfortunately, not everyone needed or understood the PPI policies that were being sold by banks and complaints about the banks not providing the promised protection began to rise. In the late 1990s consumer champions such as *Which?* magazine began to question the products' usefulness. When sales of PPI products were analysed by official bodies, including the Office of Fair Trading (OFT) and the

UK Competition Commission,[135] they concluded that in many instances the PPI products had been *missold*.

As in the NZ tax case, the UK's major banks fought a fierce rear-guard action over several years but following a High Court judicial review that went against them in 2011 they were forced to capitulate and set up a reimbursement scheme and make provisions for billions of pounds in financial compensation. The whole industry appeared to have lost the caution normally associated with bankers and in a race for fast profits did the wrong thing. The outcry against the major banks that followed the revelations of PPI misselling scandal was undoubtedly made worse by the fact that the same banks had been forced to recompense many customers in an earlier scandal involving personal pension products. The banks appeared not to have learned the lesson of the earlier pension misselling scandal.

In terms of the People Risk Triangle, the *motivation* of the industry was again a search for profit, but in an ambiguous rather than a specific sense; in fact many bankers still contend that PPI products were not only profitable for them but also of great benefit to customers. And, PPI was indeed of benefit to some but not all customers. The *opportunity* was unintended, as the banks certainly did not set out to break any laws on product suitability. The *rationalization* was collective and based on Ubiquity, that is all other banks are doing it so it must be good. The PPI case is an example of People Risk in that individuals in boards and senior management positions throughout the UK banking industry just did not give full consideration to the possible side-effects and risks involved in selling what seemed to them to be a perfectly sensible product. There was a lack of imagination in assuming what was obvious to them would also be obvious to customers. This was coupled with a focus on setting and trying to attain sales targets based on, like Egg, volume rather than quality. Individuals were being set wrong performance targets by senior management, who did not analyse the risks in their products properly.

4.6.4 IHRP – unsuitable products

The PPI scandal was the responsibility, in the main, of the retail divisions of the major UK banks, ie those dealing with non-commercial customers. But these banks have also been found to have been misselling so-called Interest Rate Hedging products[136] (IRHP) to their small- to medium-sized business customers, who are often supported by separate business or corporate banking divisions. IRHP products are 'derivatives', or complex financial instruments, which are designed to provide protection to borrowers against sharp changes in interest rates. But as the Barings and NAB cases illustrate, derivatives are difficult enough for experts to understand and almost impossible for non-financial business people to comprehend. Many thousands of small businesses in the UK were sold expensive protection that they didn't understand and often didn't need. After complaints to the UK banking regulator, an investigation into misselling of IRHP products was instigated.[137] The regulator's investigation found that, like the PPI scandal, the banks' sales practices were poor and they had sold inappropriate and overly complex products to 'non-sophisticated' customers.

Having learned their lesson with PPI, the major banks immediately conceded that there were indeed problems and began a 'review and redress' process on all of the sales. By the end of 2013, the four major UK banks had set aside some £2 billion in provisions to cover the costs and losses incurred and it was likely that this figure will rise as more sales are reviewed. To date, no executives or board directors have been held to account for this IHRP misselling scandal. As with PPI, the *rationalization* was collective and based on Ubiquity, as it was a product that everyone was selling even though customers often did not understand it. The rationalization was also an example of a Victimless Crime in that although purchasers could be identified easily, it was extremely difficult to identify specific cases where the protection was inappropriate until consumer advocates opened the floodgate of complaints.

At no point during the PPI and IRHP scandals was it ever suggested that the major banks somehow got together to sell unsuitable products to naïve customers. In fact, while it may seem surprising, there was just no need to collude. Financial products, because they are not physical, are not subject to patent or copyright law and can be copied or re-engineered easily. Good ideas race around the financial industry quickly not least because it is a *small world*, consisting of a few thousand, sometimes only a hundred or so, experts in a particular field. And these experts move between financial institutions, often attracted with large bonuses, and replicate their knowledge for their new firms. Such movement between firms is not immoral – it is just the way the industry works. There is therefore little need for collusion between banks but such a situation creates People Risk in that individuals will often face a conflict of interest when dealing with their ex-colleagues on behalf of their current employer.

4.6.5 LIBOR – market manipulation

An example of collusion on an Industry, and in fact industrial, scale is that of the LIBOR manipulation scandal. The case involves financial traders in several large international banks and brokers colluding to fix the price of the most widely used benchmark for setting interest rates for borrowers – the so-called London Inter-Bank Offering Rate or LIBOR.[138] From its inception in the mid-1980s, LIBOR has become the most heavily referenced benchmark in global finance, being used as the basis for over US $300 trillion of derivatives contracts, such as interest rate swaps, which coincidently were sold improperly in the IRHP scandal. Investigations by regulators,[139] especially the US Commodity Futures Trading Commission (CFTC) and the UK Financial Services Authority (FSA) found that the traders responsible for estimating LIBOR rates, so-called submitters, far from giving their own independent expert opinions on borrowing rates, were influenced, even coerced, by traders and managers in their own banks and more surprisingly traders in other banks and supposedly independent brokers, to provide rates that benefited the banks themselves rather than their customers. To date some of the largest banks in the world, UBS, Barclays, RBS, JPMorgan and Deutsche bank, have been fined over US $4 billion for market manipulation. Investigations are continuing into collusive behaviour by other banks and criminal proceedings have begun against several traders and brokers.

The LIBOR scandal was widespread and long running as corrupt manipulation became 'business as usual' in the global financial markets. It was also corrupting, sucking each new generation of bank employees into illicit activities.[140] Senior executives and their employees ignored their personal responsibilities to customers in pursuit of easy profits. Paradoxically because manipulation of LIBOR was so embedded in the global banking culture it was very difficult to detect and only came to light as a result of investigations into banking standards after the GFC. It is an indictment of boards and senior executives throughout the industry that they did not detect what are, in hindsight, so obviously illegal activities. For the industry, the *motivation* was greed, as normal trading without manipulation was highly profitable; the *opportunity* was intended with illicit rate-setting by the traders involved for profit but unintended by the British Bankers' Association (BBA) the self-regulatory body responsible for overseeing LIBOR. The *rationalization* was, as in other cases, Ubiquity and Distrust of Law, but LIBOR was also an example of Victimless Crime as it was almost impossible to identify precisely who would suffer and how much they would suffer from a specific instance of manipulation. The LIBOR case is an example of People Risk as, even though some of their own senior executives were on industry monitoring committees, management just did not enforce the LIBOR submission rules in their own firms, so much so that breaking rules became business as usual. As Professor Turner[141] predicted, regulation, in this case the rules governing LIBOR, became out of date and rather than fix the rules, banks persevered with the obsolete rules in order to gain a financial advantage.

4.6.6 Auto parts – price fixing

Collusion between firms against customers exists in industries other than banking; one example is price fixing of auto parts in the automobile industry. For a number of years before 2012, the US Department of Justice (DOJ) had been undertaking an extensive investigation[142] into price fixing by Japanese auto parts manufacturers targeting US (and other) automobile manufacturers. Auto manufacturers, such as General Motors, do not make all of the components in their vehicles but source many smaller parts, such as seat belts, from specialist companies. Many of these parts are standard and are incorporated into many different models by different manufacturers. In the DOJ investigation, it was found that executives in some of the largest parts manufacturers met with competitors to fix prices, rig bids and allocate the supply of parts to the benefit of parts manufacturers, rather than customers.

By late 2013, over US $1.5 billion had already been paid in fines by 20 parts manufacturers and 17 American and Japanese executives had been sentenced to prison terms under US antitrust legislation. This particular case had been called one of the largest and longest-running international cartels uncovered by US criminal authorities. As regards the People Risk Triangle, the *motivation* was ambiguous, aiming to maintain margins on parts across the industry, the *opportunity* was intended, to fix prices, and the *rationalizations* were Economic Necessity, ie to preserve the company, and Ubiquity, as 'all suppliers are doing it'.

4.6.7 The Global Financial Crisis

The Global Financial Crisis (GFC) is the largest and certainly the most costly example of People Risk in recent times. The Financial Crisis Inquiry Commission (FCIC)[143] was set up by President Obama and the US Congress in 2009 with the aim of examining 'the causes, domestic and global, of the current financial and economic crisis in the United States'. The Commission held many open sessions questioning senior figures in the US banking industry and in their final report they were unequivocal in their condemnation of the whole financial industry and the corporate governance at major financial institutions. The Commission concluded with a stinging indictment of individual, institutional and industry behaviour:

> This financial crisis was avoidable... *The crisis was the result of human action and inaction*, not of Mother Nature or computer models gone haywire... We conclude dramatic failures of corporate governance and risk management at many systemically important financial institutions were a key cause of this crisis... Too many of these institutions acted recklessly, taking on too much risk, with too little capital, and with too much dependence on short-term funding.

The full impact of the Global Financial Crisis is still playing out as this book is being written, not only in the United States but also in countries such as Ireland, Spain, Greece and Iceland where local economies have been devastated by the collapse of their local banking systems in the wake of the crisis. In July 2013, economists at the Federal Reserve Bank of Dallas conservatively estimated[144] that as a result of the recession following the GFC the US economy suffered losses of between some 40 and 90 per cent of one year's economic output, or between US $6 trillion and $14 trillion. Such losses to economic value dwarf all other cases of People Risk.

The GFC cannot, however, be attributed to one single cause, although the US housing bubble of the early 2000s was pivotal to what subsequently occurred. In fact there are multiple instances of risk events and losses in the GFC at each of the four levels of the 4Is model:

- *Incident*: official inquiries found countless specific instances of mortgage fraud where unsophisticated customers were provided with fraudulent mortgages.[145]
- *Individual*: the various inquiries into the GFC found cases where individuals just did not do their job well, as for example Dick Fuld of Lehman and Kerry Killinger of WAMU.
- *Institution*: the inquiries found numerous examples of institutions that had a culture of excessive risk-taking and inappropriate behaviour. For example, credit rating agencies, such as Standard & Poor's, were widely castigated for compromising the quality of their ratings to maintain market share, ie the Economic Necessity rationalization.[146]
- *Industry*: not only did the banking industry lend injudiciously but also many firms embarked on a mad spree of asset securitization flooding the market with ultimately dud subprime securities. The industry was creating new types of financial instruments that few bankers understood but they sold them anyway to unsuspecting customers.

People were the cause of the GFC and people were also its victims. Not only did the man in the street get involved in a property craze that was as foolish as the Dutch Tulip Mania, bankers who should have known better convinced themselves, as several testified to inquiries, that a US-wide housing downturn never had, and never would, happen. If, however unlikely, a downturn did happen, highly paid executives were confident that they could, as in the past, cope with it. The boards of major banks convinced themselves that their ballooning balance sheets and the vast profits flowing from them were a result of their own prescience and skill. And banking regulators and investors foolishly believed that bankers knew what they were doing. While bean counters were totalling up the profits and auditors were ticking off the figures, everyone missed the 'Invisible Gorilla' of the housing bubble. People who should have known better were blind to the risks they were taking.

4.6.8 Summary – Industry

Why does a whole industry lose its way? The cases in this section show how seductive a bandwagon can be. If every other firm in an industry is doing something, even if it is on the borderline of being unethical or illegal, then there is pressure to join in – we are all in the same boat and we will all sink or swim together. The examples of massive misselling of PPI and IHRP products by all the major UK banks show that once a seemingly successful and highly profitable product takes off, everyone wants a piece of the action. In the subprime crisis that led to the GFC, banks around the United States and across the world all decided to create and sell products which the vast majority of individuals, customers and bankers, just did not understand. This phenomenon is a form of Groupthink, which we call *Systemsthink*. The case of the four major Australian banks in the New Zealand Tax scandal is another example of Systemsthink that can be traced back to an incorrect assumption about tax law by a single 'expert' that was adopted and promoted by the boards of the offending banks, because it was very profitable. The directors, as a group across the industry, just did not do their fiduciary due diligence.

The cases of the fixing of auto parts prices, and the manipulation of the LIBOR benchmark, show that people across these industries were prepared to bend and break rules to further their own business ends. So much so that breaking rules became the norm rather than the exception. Likewise the directors of Big Tobacco companies were engaged in deception or at least self-deception as to the medical dangers of their products. Because these People Risks arise in many firms at the same time, they are sometimes called Systemic People Risk, or the risk that the accumulation of risks in many corporations pose a risk to the whole system.

At the level of an enormous industry, such as banking, aerospace or health, the concept of individual decision-making and personal responsibility appears very remote and unimportant. If 'everyone is doing it', it takes a brave individual to swim against the tide. A principled individual might refuse to sell a deadly product or to give a bribe, but the chances are that such a decision would be career-limiting at the very least. But nonetheless the losses due to misconduct are related to the decisions and non-decisions of people (ie People Risk) albeit that the individuals are too numerous to identify. At the level of the Industry then, the effective solution has to be one where an individual can communicate their concerns to an Industry regulator, ie there has to be an effective systems-wide whistleblowing system, as we will discuss in Chapter 5.

4.7 Lessons to be learned from the cases studied

The remainder of the book considers the cases in this chapter when discussing how such risk events could possibly be managed in future. But before going on to consider practical actions, the cognitive biases and rationalizations of some of the cases are summarized in the tables below.

4.7.1 People Risk – cognitive biases

Traditionally, an analyst would categorize the cases in this chapter by their *outcomes*, such as fraud, health and safety, medical fatalities, bribery, product defects, engineering failures/accidents, market manipulation, legal and regulatory fines, business losses, bankruptcy and so on. This is an acceptable categorization of the cases as it helps point to potential solutions based on legal remedy. And importantly it is necessary in order to take the actions needed to minimize the sometimes catastrophic consequences of the risk events.

But such a categorization does not address the *causes* of the losses, deaths and failures so any remedy based on the types of outcomes will have only at best the secondary effect, of minimizing the Consequences not the Likelihood of a People Risk event. For example, a heavier fine or a longer term in prison is often assumed to be a deterrent to others in future. But the rationalizations that people give to themselves often preclude the possibility of sanctions; for example, if 'everyone is doing it' (ie Ubiquity) then 'I am unlikely to be the one who is caught'.[147] And in the cases of rogue trading for example, the individuals are trying to recover a losing situation which will have a much more serious and immediate impact than any future possible sanction, ie the immediate loss of one's livelihood.

Table 4.2 considers some the cognitive biases that were apparent in these cases and contributed to their causes. We believe that if individuals are able to recognize that they and their colleagues may be subject to such biases and take concrete steps to minimize the biases then losses such as those described in this chapter may be reduced. It should be noted that losses will still occur for other reasons not addressed in this book, such as for example as a result of an external event, such as terrorist attacks.

Table 4.2 shows that, in the cases described, overconfidence in their individual and group abilities is a major contributing factor. Where *Overconfidence* is coupled with *Groupthink* and *Illusion of Control*, it is a heady mix where decision-makers make bad decisions and then ignore others, who are more objective, when they raise concerns. Overconfidence also leads to other biases, such as the 'Planning Fallacy' where decision makers do not search for external examples of the course of action that they are taking and also 'Confirmation Bias' where decision-makers only search for positive, confirmatory information. Loss Aversion, as described by Kahneman and Tversky, is dangerous because its turns a normally conservative risk-avoider into a risk-seeker, mainly because they fear that the losses they are experiencing will diminish their authority, status and wealth. If colleagues do not notice this change, losses will get hidden until they are finally forced to the surface. Chapter 9 will suggest mechanisms for addressing such cognitive biases.

TABLE 4.2　Case studies – some cognitive biases

Cognitive biases	Examples of cases in which biases identified
Overconfidence (including stubbornness and unwillingness to change course)	RBS, Enron, WorldCom, HBOS, Co-operative Bank, rogue trading, RIM (Blackberry), Tesco, Lehman, BP, LIBOR, New Zealand tax, PPI, GFC, JPMorgan – Whale, Egg
Loss Aversion (including Sunk Cost Fallacy)	Rogue Trading, RIM, Tesco, Lehman, JPMorgan – Whale
Groupthink (including Teamthink and Systemsthink)	Harold Shipman, Enron, Washington Mutual, Co-operative Bank, Eli Lilly, Fukushima, Big Tobacco, New Zealand tax, PPI, IRHP, Auto parts price fixing, LIBOR, Egg
Confirmation Bias	RBS, Washington Mutual, RIM, Tesco, New Zealand tax, JPMorgan – Whale, Egg
Illusion of Control	HBOS fraud, rogue trading, HSBC, New Zealand tax, JPMorgan – Whale
Planning Fallacy	RBS, Co-operative Bank, RIM, Tesco, Lehman, BP, Egg
Availability (including blind spots)	Flight 901, Elaine Bromiley, JPMorgan – Whale, Enron
Action Bias	RBS, Co-operative Bank, Washington Mutual, Tesco, Lehman, BP, LIBOR, Enron, rogue trading

4.7.2 People Risk – rationalizations

In order to manage People Risks it is essential not only to manage the opportunities for risk events to occur but also to counteract the most common rationalizations used by individuals. Table 4.3 provides an analysis of some of the cases by selected rationalizations.

Of these rationalizations, two are predominantly Individual, ie Temporary Use and Just Desserts, while the remainder are collective, ie Victimless Crime, Distrust of Law and Ubiquity. On the other hand, Economic Necessity can be used by an individual, eg to repay debts, or by a collective, for example, to maintain the viability of a firm or an industry. The 'treatment' or risk management of these different types of rationalization will need to be approached differently.

Individual rationalizations, such as Just Desserts, relate to individuals, or small groups, who are at odds with the organization. If a person is dissatisfied because, for example, they feel under-appreciated, there is little an organization can do other than work to detect such dissatisfaction and then use HR techniques to address them but

TABLE 4.3   Case studies – common rationalizations

Rationalization	Some cases in which rationalization was employed
1. Temporary Use	*Rogue Trading, WorldCom*
2. Victimless Crime	*Goldman Sachs – insider trading, LIBOR, New Zealand Tax, PPI, GFC*
3. Distrust of Law	*New Zealand tax, LIBOR, Big Tobacco, GFC*
4. Economic Necessity	*Co-operative Bank, auto parts price fixing, Tesco*
5. Ubiquity	*Co-operative Bank, New Zealand tax, LIBOR, Big Tobacco, auto parts price fixing, GFC*
6. Just Desserts	*ING Fraud, HBOS*

in the interim they have to be closely managed. Likewise, if an individual rationalizes his/her illicit actions by Economic Necessity, this relates to situations outside of work that again can only be detected and managed by HR techniques, such as whistle-blowing. On the other hand, the rationalization of Temporary Use, such as 'borrowing' money or writing options in rogue trading cases, are not HR issues but relate to in-effective control processes. As noted in the Risk Thermostat, these must be addressed by increasing the 'Perceived Danger' or chances of detection, such as by random checks or whistleblowing as described in Chapter 9.

Collective rationalizations, however, relate to groups that are at odds with the stated or *espoused* culture of the organization. Note that the actual culture of an organization, as Enron demonstrated, may be very different to that officially espoused by its board and senior executives. What we do may be very different to what we say we do, and actions do speak much louder than words. For example, boards will maintain that they adhere to all relevant laws and regulations but, as shown in the case of HSBC and LIBOR, they are quite prepared to ignore specific rules when it suits them, ie Distrust of Law. Likewise, boards will often espouse a culture of independence and competition but will sometimes jump unthinkingly into a business just because competitors are perceived to be successful in it.

4.7.3 People Risk – conflicts of interest

Many of the cases here describe instances of conflicts of interest, where individuals were faced with multiple conflicting objectives and priorities and had to choose between them. In the majority of these cases the conflicts do not involve choosing between a personal and a business benefit, such as occurs for example in cases of 'insider trading'. The cases involve conflicts of interest that are *created* by the man-agement of the firms involved such as choosing profit over customer well-being, for

TABLE 4.4   Case studies – conflicts of interest

Conflicts of interest	Some cases in which conflicts occurred
Individual	*Rogue Trading, Harold Shipman, JPMorgan – Madoff, Goldman Sachs – insider trading, Enron*
Collective	*Enron, WorldCom, HSBC, rogue trading, Eli Lilly, BAE and Siemens, JPMorgan – Whale, Mid Staffordshire, Tesco, Lehman, BP, Fukushima, Big Tobacco, LIBOR, New Zealand tax, PPI, GFC*

example in cases of product misselling. The conflict of interest can be: (a) individual, in that a single person makes or is forced to make a decision between two conflicting priorities, such as in rogue trading cases; or (b) collective, where the conflict is part of what is expected as part of doing business, such as misselling. Table 4.4 analyses the cases between these two types.

In modern business it is *inevitable* that for many decisions, individuals will be faced with a conflict of interest and such conflicts can occur at any level of a firm. For example, while disclosure of information is a keystone of modern corporate governance, directors and senior executives are aware that negative information can have an inordinately large impact on company share prices, and hence have to tread a fine line between how much and when information is released. Examples of this conflict include WorldCom, Lehman and JPMorgan where management believed that given time they could turn things around and hence downplayed the problems they were facing. As shown in the case of Enron, this conflict not only engaged management collectively but also individually as senior executives offloaded stock while encouraging staff to buy shares in the failing company.

Conflicts of interest are insidious. They are often, if not invisible, then very difficult to detect. For example, when PPI products were first introduced, the banks selling them considered them to be useful to the customers who bought them – a win-win situation. But as the pressure grew to sell more and even more of these products, the care and attention to customers' needs became secondary to meeting sales targets. Over time the sales *rationalization* became not that 'we will sell a product that is good for the customer and the bank' but 'we will sell a product that is good for the bank and may be good for the customer', a subtle change in emphasis that cost the firms dearly.

The chapters that follow introduce models as to how the common factors of these cases can be viewed and make suggestions as to how People Risks may be identified and better managed using those models.

Notes

1 See Kahneman (2011).

2 See Turner (1976) and the description of his Six Stage Model of Disaster in Chapter 2.

3 See Reason (1990).

4 The 4Is (Incidents, Individuals, Institutions and Industry) model was developed first in McConnell, P (2008) People Risk: where are the boundaries?, *Journal of Risk Management in Financial Institutions*, **1** (4), September pp 370–81.

5 See Curry, T and Shibut, L (2000) The cost of the savings and loan crisis: truth and consequences, , *FDIC Banking Review*, **13** (2).

6 It's a Wonderful Life (1947 Liberty Films) is one of the most successful films ever made and describes the consequences of the near-failure of a small town S&L in the mythical Bedford Falls.

7 See Financial Stability Board (2012) *Update of group of global systemically important banks (G-SIBs)*, November, for a description of the classification of systemically important financial institutions. http://www.financialstabilityboard.org/

8 References to this case have been removed from the HBOS website (following the takeover by Lloyds). Newspaper archives include: BBC News, (30 Jan 2007) Woman gets 75,000 bank statements, *BBC News North East*, http://news.bbc.co.uk/2/hi/uk_news/scotland/north_east/6310633.stm. Similar cases can be reviewed at the Scottish Information Commissioner Office at http://www.itspublicknowledge.info/home/ScottishInformationCommissioner.aspx

9 Air New Zealand – Crash of Flight 901: A detailed summary of this case is given in Reason (2008). The archived report of the Royal Commission is maintained by the New Zealand Air Line Pilots' Association at www.erebus.co.nz/Investigation/MahonReport.aspx and in the New Zealand Government archives. A comprehensive discussion of the controversy is available in the Wikipedia article *Air New Zealand Flight 901*.

10 See Reason (1990, 2008).

11 After his wife's death Martin Bromiley helped to create an organization called the Clinical Human Factors Group which has published an anonymous version of the coroner's report and Professor Harmer's report under the article *Elaine Bromiley* at www.chfg.org

12 See statistics on fatal injuries in the workplace 2012/13, *Health and Safety Executive*, www.hse.gov.uk

13 See for example Implementing Human Factors in Healthcare, *Patient Safety First*, www.patientsafetyfirst.nhs.uk

14 See Gigerenzer (2014) and Gawande (2010) for examples of checklists saving lives in aviation and medicine.

15 For Nick Leeson's perspective on the scandal, see Leeson and Whitely (1996). A more objective analysis is provided in Rawnsley (1995). Much of the formal documentation has been lost or moved over the years but there is a Barings archive at the UK Government archives at www.gov.uk which contains a copy of the Report of the Board of Banking Supervision inquiry into the circumstances of the collapse of Barings.

16 In Kahneman (2011) one of the original papers on Prospect Theory that eventually lead to him winning the Nobel Prize is reproduced.

17 The so-called Ludwig report into the AIB/Allfirst rogue trader case was published by AIB plc: Ludwig, E (2002) *Report to the Board of Directors of Allied Irish Banks, plc… concerning currency trading losses*, Promontory Financial Group. An archive version is available at www.sba.muohio.edu/brunarkr/allfirst.pdf

18 The internal report of Société Générale (2008) *Progress report of the Special Committee of the Board of Directors of Société Générale* (mainly in French) is somewhat of a whitewash of the firm and its management. Kerviel's perspective is reported in Associated Press (2008) *Excerpts of police testimony from alleged rogue trader*, 29 January, and in the Wikipedia article *Jérôme Kerviel*.

19 For an official description of the Kweku Adoboli case see the fine imposed on UBS at Financial Services Authority (2012) *Final Notice – UBS*. http://www.fsa.gov.uk

20 See Justice Keith (2012) *R vs Kweku Adoboli*, Southwark Crown Court 20 November, http://www.judiciary.gov.uk

21 See the *Report of the Board of Banking Supervision inquiry into the circumstances of the collapse of Barings* referenced above.

22 For the official report into the NAB case, see Australian Prudential Regulatory Authority (2004) *Report into irregular currency options trading at the National Australia Bank*, Australian Prudential Regulatory Authority, 24 March, www.apra.gov.au

23 See for example, Fox News (2013) *Judge hits Goldman Sachs for its 'silence' as rogue trader gets jail time*, 8 December, www.foxnews.com. See Chapter 10 for a description of Goldman Sachs' Code of Conduct.

24 See Coates (2012) for insights into the psychology of traders.

25 See for example, in the NAB case, APRA (2004) above.

26 A timeline of the Harold Shipman case is available at the UK National Archives, http://webarchive.nationalarchives.gov.uk/. See also the Wikipedia article *Harold Shipman*.

27 See Smith, J (2002) *The Shipman Inquiry Vols.1 & 2*, Her Majesty's Stationary Office, Norwich.

28 See Heffernan (2011) for a discussion of the scale of denial or *'wilful blindness'* that Primrose Shipman needed to survive such an ordeal.

29 The term *hiding in plain sight* was used to describe the crimes of Jimmy Savile, who was found to have committed over 500 cases of sexual abuse in NHS facilities over 40 years. See Gray and Watt (2013).

30 See General Medical Council (2013) *Good Medical Practice* and the Shipman Archive, both at http://www.gmc-uk.org

31 See Gray and Watt (2013).

32 See BBC News (2014) *Jimmy Savile NHS abuse victims aged five to 75*, 26 June, www.bbc.com

33 Named after Charles Ponzi, a notorious fraudster in the early 20th century, a Ponzi scheme is one where investors get paid dividends out of their own money invested in the scheme rather than from income, with the scheme relying on attracting more and more new customers to survive.

34 See JPMorgan agreement at US Department of Justice (2014) *JPMorgan Chase Bank, N.A. – Deferred Prosecution Agreement*, United States Attorney, Southern District / New York, 6 January, www.justice.gov

35 See Wikipedia article *Money Laundering*.

36 See *Reuters* (2014) Decades-long ties to Madoff cost JPMorgan $2.6 billion, 7 January, www.reuters.com

37 See *Sunday Herald* (2012) Revealed: the hornet and the sting which are stopping us learning the truth about the collapse of HBOS, 28 February. See also the blog of journalist and author Ian Fraser, www.ianfraser.org

38 See *Herald Scotland* (2012) Corruption allegations, major fraud inquiries, a senate probe into deals with drug-running gangsters in Mexico … and a luxury yacht. Welcome to the world of banking, 22 July.

39 See Perman (2013).

40 See *Reuters* (2012) Ex-business titan Gupta guilty of insider trading, 15 June.

41 See *Bloomberg* (2011) Rajaratnam was told by Gupta that Goldman Sachs considered buying Wachovia, AIG, 16 March, www.bloomberg.com. See also the Wikipedia article *Raj Rajaratnam/Galleon Group, Anil Kumar, and Rajat Gupta insider trading cases.*

42 A similar concept of the 'whipping boy' was employed in medieval courts as someone, such as a tutor, who would take the punishment meant for a royal prince, who could not be chastised by commoners.

43 See Australian Prudential Regulatory Authority (2004) above.

44 See Martin (2013), Fraser (2014) and Financial Services Authority (2011) The failure of the Royal Bank of Scotland, www.fsa.gov.uk

45 See questioning of Sir Tom McKillop in *Examination of Witnesses (Questions 1660– 1679)* Uncorrected Proceedings of the Treasury Select Committee – Banking Crisis, UK Parliament, www.parliament.uk

46 See Brennan, N and Conroy, J (2013) Executive hubris: the case of a bank CEO, *Accounting, Auditing and Accountability*, **26** (2), pp 172–95.

47 See Tibman (2009).

48 See Carswell (2011), Nyberg (2011) and Lucey (2012). At the time of writing in early 2014, Sean Fitzpatrick is still embroiled in legal proceedings in Ireland.

49 See Wikipedia article *Andy Hornby.*

50 See McLean and Elkind (2004).

51 See *Financial News* (2011) The Enron cast: Where are they now? 1 December, www.efinancialnews.com

52 See Ken Lay's obituary in the *New York Times* (2006) Kenneth L. Lay, 64, Enron Founder and Symbol of Corporate Excess, Dies, 6 July.

53 See Heffernan (2011).

54 See Swartz and Watkins (2003).

55 See Swartz and Watkins (2003).

56 McLean and Elkind (2004) was turned into the film 'Enron: The Smartest Guys in the Room' (2005, Jigsaw).

57 For an overview of Ken Lay's career and political influence see Wikipedia article *Kenneth Lay.*

58 See Rantanen, M (2007) *Reasons of Systemic Collapse in Enron*, in Raimo, P Hämäläinen and E Saarinen (eds) (2007) *Systems Intelligence in Leadership and Everyday Life*, Systems Analysis Laboratory, Helsinki University of Technology, Espoo.

59 See Swartz and Watkins (2003).

60 For the rise and demise of Arthur Andersen, see Wikipedia article *Arthur Andersen*.

61 For details of the WorldCom Bankruptcy see Wikipedia article *MCI Inc.*

62 See *Wall Street Journal* (2002) How three unlikely sleuths exposed fraud at WorldCom 30 October, www.online.wsj.com

63 See *The Associated Press* (2009) Former WorldCom Exec Gets Prison, 11 February, www.ap.org

64 See McConnell, P (2013) Strategic risk management: the beanstalk syndrome, *Journal of Risk Management in Financial Institutions*, **6** (3).

65 For a history of Washington Mutual see Grind (2013).

66 Washington Mutual was used as a case study of bad lending practice in the investigation *Wall Street and The Financial Crisis: Anatomy of a financial collapse* by the US Senate Permanent Subcommittee on Investigations (2011). It is also called the *Levin-Coburn Report.*

67 See Permanent Subcommittee on Investigations (2011) for background on Jim Vanasek and Ronald Cathcart and their roles in trying to avert the firm's collapse.

68 See Grind (2013).

69 See Grind (2013).

70 See Martin (2013).

71 See Tibman (2009).

72 See Perman (2013), the Parliamentary Commission on Banking Standards (2013a) and also Fraser (2010) The Worst Bank in the World? HBOS's calamitous seven year life, which gives a timeline of the HBOS case, www.ianfraser.org

73 See Perman (2013) for a history of the Bank of Scotland.

74 See Perman (2013).

75 See the *Guardian* (2012) Peter Cummings statement on FSA lifetime ban and fine for HBOS crisis, 12 September, www.theguardian.com

76 See Parliamentary Commission on Banking Standards (2013a).

77 See Parliamentary Commission on Banking Standards (2013a).

78 For information about the Co-Operative group and the bank see *Our History* at the Co-operative Bank website, http://www.co-operative.coop

79 For a history of the Co-op case see the Kelly Review, Kelly, C (2014) *Failings in Management and Governance: report of the independent review into the events leading to the Co-operative Bank's capital shortfall*, published at the request of the Co-op Group and the Co-op Bank, 30 April, www.thekellyreview.co.uk

80 See Kelly (2014) above.

81 See Kelly (2014).

82 In 2013, the UK Parliament Treasury Select Committee set up an inquiry into Project Verde (which has still not reported in mid-2014). Much evidence has been presented to the committee and is available on their website at www.parliament.uk

83 See Kelly (2014).

84 As the Co-op was a 'mutually held' rather than a shareholder company, there was less pressure on the board to consult widely. This shows, however, that, contrary to what might be predicted by Agency Theory, lack of shareholder pressure appears to have the much the same effect as shareholder pressure when bad decisions are being made by senior managers.

85 See evidence to the Project Verde Inquiry on NBNK's submission to the Lloyds Bank board entitled *Risks to the Co-op and Verde transaction*, www.publications.parliament.uk

86 See Kelly (2014).

87 See Kelly (2014).

88 See Kelly (2014) the Project Verde Inquiry and the Myners Review (2014) into corporate governance at the Co-op by ex-director and politician Lord Myners: *Report of the Independent Governance Review* Commissioned by the board of the Co-operative Group Limited, 7 May, http://www.co-operative.coop/MynersReview/

89 See Project Verde Inquiry above.

90 See the *Guardian* (2014) Co-op bank considered Paul Flowers to be a 'perfect choice' as chairman, 7 March.

91 The case is known as the Whale because of the sheer size of the trading involved in the scandal. For details see the internal report from JPMorgan (2013) *Report of JPMorgan Chase & Co. Management Task Force Regarding 2012 CIO Losses*, 13 January, www.jpmorganchase.com. See also McConnell, P (2014) Dissecting the JPMorgan Whale: a post-mortem, *Journal of Operational Risk* (2), pp 1–42.

92 See Permanent Subcommittee on Investigations (2013).

93 This, of course, is an example of *Confirmation Bias*.

94 This is an example of *Illusion of Control*.

95 See *Bloomberg* (2013) Ex-JPMorgan employees indicted over $6.2 billion loss, 17 September.

96 See Permanent Subcommittee on Investigations (2012) for the background to the HSBC settlement.

97 See Permanent Subcommittee on Investigations (2012).

98 See the *Daily Telegraph* (2012) HSBC's 'money-laundering' apology, 12 July, www.telegraph.co.uk

99 For a background on the Eli Lilly fines, see *New York Times* (2010) Side effects may include lawsuit, 2 October, www.nytimes.com

100 See for example *Daily Mail* (2010) Campaigners' fury at £286m deal to end corruption probe after BAE Systems admits using cash to win contracts, 6 February, www.dailymail.co.uk

101 See Wikipedia article *Al-Yamamah arms deal*.

102 See *Bloomberg BusinessWeek* (2008) Siemens settlement relief: but is it all over? www.businessweek.com

103 See the *Guardian* (2013) Siemens and the battle against bribery and corruption, 18 September.

104 Note in 2013, Bart's was forced to call in specialist financial staff to avoid being placed into administration. See *BBC News* (2013) Barts Health NHS Trust calls in finance help squad, 17 July.

105 See Healthcare Commission (2009) *Investigation into Mid Staffordshire NHS Foundation Trust*, March. Note the Healthcare Commission was renamed as the Care Quality Commission, www.cqc.org.uk

106 See Wikipedia article *Stafford Hospital Scandal*.

107 See Turner (1976).

108 See Liyuan F, Fuyun, L, Siew Hui, S and Jiangtao X (2012) IEL / ETM Case Study Series Research In Motion (Rim) – Blackberry, National University of Singapore, http://www.eng.nus.edu.sg/etm/research/publications/iel1210.pdf. For a timeline of the rise and fall of RIM see *Telegraph* (2012) BlackBerry timeline: from RIM to RIP? 12 August, www.telegraph.co.uk

109 See Porter, M and Millar, V (1985) How Information Gives You the Competitive Advantage, *Harvard Business Review*, July–August, Reprint 85415.

110 See *Electronista* (2013) RIM thought iPhone was impossible in 2007, 27 December. www.electronista.com

111 See *Bloomberg* (2013) BlackBerry executives leave as CEO rebuilds management, 25 November.

112 See Tesco plc Annual Reports at www.tescoplc.com under *Investors*.

113 See reference to confidential Credit Suisse report in Lowe, M and Wrigley N (2010) Tesco: From domestic operator to multinational giant, Informal Class Case Study, University of Southampton. Available at www.esrc.ac.uk

114 The *Guardian* (2004) How Tesco took the lead, 20 October.

115 This is also called the *sunk cost fallacy* where managers are loath to recognize and terminate past investments that are no longer viable.

116 The definitive investigation of the Lehman case is the nine-volume, 2,000 page report by the official Bankruptcy Examiner, Anton Valukas (2010). This report is archived by, among others, the RepoWatch organization at http://repowatch.org/2010/03/11/the-valukas-report-2200-pages-about-lehman-and-repos. An insider's view of the collapse is given in Tibman, J (2009) and McDonald and Robinson (2009). Detailed examination of Lehman executives, including Dick Fuld, is reported in the official proceedings of the US Senate Permanent Subcommittee On Investigations in its report *Wall Street and the financial crisis: anatomy of a financial collapse*, published in April 2011 and available at www.hsgac.senate.gov. A description of Lehman's failed strategy is provided in McConnell, P (2012) Lehman: a case of strategic risk, *Journal of Financial Transformation*, **34**, pp 52–61.

117 See Valukas (2010).

118 See Tibman (2009).

119 See National Commission on the BP Deepwater Horizon Oil Spill and Offshore Drilling (2011) *Deep Water: The Gulf Oil Disaster and the future of offshore drilling – Report to the President*, January, www.gpo.gov

120 See *Reuters* (2014) Ex-BP well managers must face Gulf spill criminal charges, 28 January.

121 See *New York Times* (2012) *BP* will plead guilty and pay over $4 billion, 15 November.

122 What is often called the Great East Japan Earthquake, the largest earthquakes ever to hit Japan, is described Wikipedia article *2011 Tōhoku earthquake and tsunami*.

123 See *LA Times* (2011) Two workers bodies recovered at Fukushima nuclear plant, 3 April, www.latimes.com

124 See Fukushima Nuclear Accident Independent Investigation Commission (2012) *The official report of The Fukushima Nuclear Accident Independent Investigation Commission*, The National Diet of Japan, www.nirs.org

125 See Independent Investigation Commission (2012) report above.

126 See Hilts (1996).

127 The Insider (1999, Touchstone) describes the efforts of Dr Jeffery Wigand to blow the whistle on his employer B&W Tobacco.

128 See Coleman (2001).

129 See Center for Disease Control (2014) *Adult cigarette smoking in the United States: current estimates*, www.cdc.gov

130 High Court Justice Harrison handed down his verdict in the case Harrison, J (2009) *Westpac Banking Corp. and the Commissioner of Inland Revenue – Judgment*, 7 October, High Court of New Zealand, Wellington, archived at http://www.nzlii.org

131 The banks involved are the Commonwealth, ANZ, Westpac and National Australia banks.

132 See McConnell, P (2012) Systemic operational risk: smoke and mirrors, *Journal of Operational Risk*, 7 (3), pp 119–64.

133 See Nyberg (2011).

134 See McConnell, P and Blacker, K (2012) Systemic operational risk the UK payment protection insurance scandal, *Journal of Operational Risk*, 7 (1) Spring, pp 1–60.

135 For an overview of the scandal, see McConnell, P and Blacker, K (2012) as above. For the customers' perspective see *Which?* magazine (2011), Payment Protection Insurance, www.which.co.uk. For a regulatory perspective, see Financial Services Authority (2006) *The sale of payment protection insurance: results of follow-up thematic work*, www.fsa.gov.uk

136 See *Telegraph* (2013) Banks face £10bn bill over swaps mis-selling scandal, 1 February, www.telegraph.co.uk

137 See Financial Conduct Authority (2013) *Interest rate hedging products*, www.fca.org.uk

138 See McConnell, P (2013) Systemic operational risk: the LIBOR manipulation scandal, *Journal of Operational Risk*, 8 (3) pp 59–99.

139 See Wheatley, M (2012) *The Wheatley Review of LIBOR – Final Report*, HM Treasury, London. See also the UK official inquiry at Treasury Committee (2012), *Fixing LIBOR: some preliminary findings, Second Report of Session 2012–13 Volume I: Report, together with formal minutes*, and *Volume II: Oral and Written Evidence'*, 9 August, House of Commons, London, www.publications.parliament.uk

140 For an insider's view of the corrupting influence of LIBOR practices at Barclays see The *Independent* (2012) Whistleblower: 'The culture ultimately comes from the top', 7 July, www.independent.co.uk

141 See Turner (1976).

142 See among others, *New York Times* (2013) Companies admit that they fixed prices of car parts, 26 September and *Bloomberg* (2013) GM suppliers in Japan guilty in $5 billion cartel case, 28 September.

143 The major inquiry into the GFC was conducted by the Financial Crisis Inquiry Commission (2011). See also Ashby, S (2010) *The 2007–09 Financial Crisis: learning the risk management lessons* Financial Services Research Forum, Nottingham University, www.nottingham.ac.uk

144 See Atkinson, T, Luttrell, D and Rosenblum, H (2013) *How bad was it? The costs and consequences of the 2007–09 Financial Crisis*, Federal Reserve Bank of Dallas, https://dallasfed.org

145   It should be noted, however, that many economists, including three dissenting voices on the FCIC, argue that the people who recklessly borrowed money during the property boom were primarily to blame for the crisis. While the 'irrational exuberance' shown by many borrowers undoubtedly contributed to the crisis – there is blame enough to go around – the misbehaviour of downstream banks and rating agencies undoubtedly amplified these mistakes into an economic crisis.

146   See the Financial Crisis Inquiry Commission (2011) report for examples.

147   This rationalization is not without merit as only a handful of individuals have been convicted of illegal activities during the GFC.

People Risk Management Framework

05

> *It is the framework which changes with each new technology and not just the picture within the frame.* MARSHALL MCLUHAN

KEY MESSAGES

- Good models for risk management do exist and provide templates for firms to manage People Risks.

- Managing People Risks is about recognizing the Visible and Invisible pressures on decision-makers.

- Inappropriate interactions between individuals inside and outside of a firm give rise to People Risk.

- People Risks can be identified and managed using techniques, such as People Maps, to identify appropriate and inappropriate interactions.

- To manage People Risks, boards must put in place robust escalation processes including complaints handling and whistleblowing hot lines.

The first few chapters of this book defined People Risk, provided examples of human biases and, in Chapter 4, described cases in which People Risk played a significant role. The obvious question is how should People Risk be managed? This is not an easy question to answer as it requires consideration of the full gamut of human behaviours in a firm. At this point it should be noted that the book is concerned with how *individuals* behave in their working (not their personal) lives. It should be remembered, however, that people are unlikely to behave differently in their private and corporate lives. For example, a confident person is likely to be confident in both working and personal situations. But only in rare circumstances is it appropriate for behaviour in private life to be taken into consideration when evaluating an individual's suitability for employment and competence in their work role. Exceptions might include situations where someone has been convicted of theft or fraud and would be deemed unsuitable for employment in a fiduciary position.

Before providing suggestions as to how People Risk may be managed, it is necessary to create a 'framework' or 'map' of how different types of risk fit together. This chapter develops such a People Risk Framework.

5.1 Risk management

So what do boards and managers have to do to manage risks in general and People Risks in particular? First, and most important, directors and executives have to recognize that People Risks exist and must not be frightened of tackling the issue head-on. It is not a reflection on any one individual to recognize that, somewhere in their organization, someone might have the opportunity to cause significant losses to the firm. In fact, many people, even in the boardroom, will have such opportunities but only a few will succumb to temptation or inadvertently make a loss-making mistake. Despite the realization that even the most trusted employee could cause potentially catastrophic losses to the firm, it also must be recognized that any draconian overreaction will almost certainly be counterproductive. What is needed is a thoughtful, measured approach to the problem.

In taking such an approach, the board and senior management of a firm will have to look for a comprehensive *framework*, or mode of operating, that will ensure that their objectives for managing risks (not just people-related risks) are embedded throughout the firm. Experts recommend the use of a well-considered Risk Management Framework (RMF), such as one based on the agreed international standard *ISO 31000*. It should be noted that other such frameworks have been proposed, not least the COSO[1] framework, developed by the Committee of Sponsoring Organizations of the Treadway Commission (COSO), a privately funded body of peak US accounting and auditing organizations. The non-profit think tank, the Open Compliance and Ethics Group[2] (OCEG) has also developed an over-arching framework for Governance, Risk and Compliance (GRC), which brings together core governance topics under one umbrella. However, not least because it is emerging as a global standard, the use of ISO 31000 is recommended here as its suggested methods can be used in other frameworks – since the problem is the same, only the approaches differ.

5.1.1 ISO 31000 – risk management standard

In 2005, the International Standards Organization (ISO), set up a committee with the express purpose of harmonizing risk management standards around the world. After a prolonged period of consultation and discussion the new standard[3] was issued in 2009, through ISO's member bodies, as *ISO 31000:2009 – Risk Management: Guidelines on principles and implementation of risk management*. The new standard articulates 11 *Principles of Risk Management*, in three major categories:

1 *Corporate Governance*: how the firm considers risk, such as 'Risk management creates and protects value'.

2 *Risk Governance*: how risk is addressed throughout the firm, such as 'Risk management is part of decision-making'.

3 *Risk Process*: how the firm actually manages risk, such as 'Risk management is based on the best available information'.

While hard to argue with, because they are so general, these ISO 31000 principles are difficult to bring into effect, because they have to be embedded throughout the *culture* of the firm. The ISO 31000 standard also describes a generic *Risk Management Framework* (RMF) which is clear that the responsibility for setting up and maintaining a robust and comprehensive risk management framework is placed on the board and senior management of the company:

> The introduction of risk management and ensuring its ongoing effectiveness requires strong and sustained commitment by the management of the organization as well as strategic and rigorous planning.

In other words, risk management is not only part of day-to-day operations but is also part of strategic management. In the ISO 31000 framework, the board and senior management have specific responsibility for the so-called 'Mandate and Commitment' component. That is, they have to *mandate* that risk is being managed properly and *commit* to ensuring that sufficient resources (money, people and time) are devoted to it. This is a critical step and an absolute prerequisite for successfully managing any type of risk in a firm, including People Risk.

In the ISO 31000 framework, senior management, with the approval and oversight of the board and supported by the Chief Risk Officer (CRO), has responsibility for the four major components/processes to create the framework, ie its Design, Implementation, Monitoring and Continual Improvement. In practice, development and monitoring of these processes will be overseen by the Risk Management Department (RMD), usually headed by the CRO, in much the same way as the Internal Audit function monitors and gives assurance to the board on the operations and financial health of a firm.[4] It is obvious that the design of a framework must be tailored to the unique circumstances of each particular firm, but that is a topic beyond the scope of this book, other than where it deals explicitly with People Risk.

5.1.2 Role of the board in relation to the Risk Management Framework

Whichever basis for a framework is agreed, the board and management need to address some key issues to create a framework and the internal functions needed to make the framework operational. In ISO 31000 terms, this is termed 'Mandate and Commit' and consists of the following critical activities:

- articulate and endorse the risk management policy;
- determine risk management performance indicators that align with organizational performance indicators;

- ensure alignment of risk management objectives with the objectives and strategies of the organization;
- ensure legal and regulatory compliance;
- assign management accountabilities and responsibilities at appropriate levels within the organization;
- ensure that the necessary resources are allocated to risk management;
- communicate the benefits of risk management to all stakeholders; and
- ensure that the framework for managing risk continues to remain appropriate.

The purpose of the Mandate and Commit phase is, in fact, to make the *Invisible* (the risk management that is taken for granted as part of day-to-day activities), *Visible* (with a set of policies, objectives, organizations and responsibilities that are communicated to the whole firm). It is beyond the scope of this book to provide full details of all of the many processes and organizational activities needed to implement a robust Risk Management Framework, such as ISO 31000. However, a moment's consideration will show that this is a non-trivial set of activities that will demand the expenditure of significant time and effort by the board and senior management and a serious commitment to create and to maintain the agreed risk framework. So, in order to make the not-inconsiderable commitment of resources worthwhile, the leadership of the firm need to take *personal responsibility* for the development and maintenance of their firm's Risk Management Framework.

5.2 People and other Risks

Before discussing how to manage People Risks, it is worth addressing the questions, what is included in 'People Risk' and how does People Risk relate to other types of risks? In Chapter 2, People Risk was defined as 'the risk of loss due to the decisions and non-decisions of people inside and outside of the organization' and we discussed its relationship to White Collar Crime.[5] To begin with, illegal activities and inappropriate conduct are a distinct subset of People Risk, for example fraud, bribery, incorrect reporting and discrimination. But People Risk is wider. It encompasses non-decisions such as a failure to inquire into inappropriate conduct, for example, turning a blind eye to unethical activity. People Risk also covers issues that are about competence and capabilities, such as making decisions without due consideration or with biases. Figure 5.1 shows a hierarchy of risks:

1 **Illegal Activity**: actions liable to criminal sanctions. Note, as demonstrated in the case of LIBOR manipulation, actions that may not be specifically prohibited by regulations may nevertheless be considered criminal in law.

2 **Proscribed Conduct**: actions that include the *illegal* but are also prohibited or tightly controlled by corporate policies and/or regulations, such as bullying.

3 **People Risks**: decisions or non-decisions related to people that cause losses to a firm including illegal and proscribed activities as outlined above. Note, as

discussed later the concept of 'Conduct Risk' lies mainly within People Risk but also has, depending on the definition used, other Operational Risks associated with it.

4 Operational Risks: actions or non-actions related to operational factors, other than people, such as Process Risks.

5 Business Risks: in addition to People Risks, the full gamut of risks faced by a firm, such as Credit and Market Risks.

FIGURE 5.1   Hierarchy of Risks (illustrated subset)

From an *organizational* perspective, People Risk should be managed within an overall Operational Risk Management (ORM) department but as a distinct function within ORM with well-defined responsibilities and skill sets as described, for example, by Tony Blundell and John Thirlwell in their book, *Mastering Operational Risk.*[6] For the remainder of this book, however, People Risk Management (PRM) will be treated as a standalone discipline which should be incorporated as appropriate into an overall framework for managing what is often called Business or 'Enterprise' Risk.

5.3 People Risks in the Risk Management Framework

People Risks arise as a result of decisions made, or not made, by individuals and/or groups of individuals, which are somehow at odds with the goals/objectives of the firm and may cause losses. When people make a decision they may not take into consideration the full impact of their choices on their firm. But why?

Contrary to business folklore and teaching in business schools, making decisions is a complex, messy activity. In an ivory tower, a perfect decision is made by: collecting all the information necessary to make the decision; identifying and analysing various options; selecting the option that best supports the firm's strategic goals; and making a detailed plan to implement the option that is selected. In real life, decisions are rarely made like that. In real business situations complete information is rarely available, options are rarely obvious (and even if so some may be often unpalatable), and plans are often unrealistic (again because of lack of information).

In practice, most decision-makers try to do the best they can and, as described by Herbert Simon, a Nobel Prize winner for his work in Decision Theory, they develop a solution that '*satisfices*' or gets 'close enough'. But sometimes 'satisficing' is not good enough or decision-makers do not do enough work to find a solution that satisfices and they short-circuit the decision-making process prematurely. That is, they make a *bad* decision. The danger of course is that having made a bad decision, people convince themselves that they can make the decision work (ie overconfidence) and then refuse to recognize the consequences when a decision starts to go wrong (eg blind spots).

Why is making a decision so difficult? Because decision-makers are faced with a number of *pressures*, as illustrated in Figure 5.2 and discussed in Chapter 3:

1 *Visible*: the pressures normally associated with making any decision, such profitability/return versus risk, time to complete, resources available, etc.

FIGURE 5.2   Visible and Invisible pressures on a decision-maker

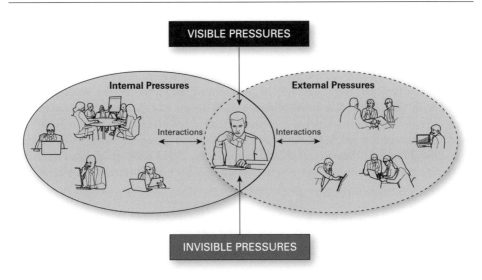

   2 *Invisible*: those pressures that in theory should not influence a decision, such
   as group pressure, biases, conflicts of interest and even personal ambition, but
   may do so even if inadvertently.

   3 *Internal*: pressures from within the firm, such as to meet target deadlines or
   to support other management initiatives, which may sometimes conflict with
   the Visible objectives.

   4 *External*: pressures from outside the firm, such as from competitors (eg to
   reduce prices), or regulators to meet new standards, or customers to deliver
   better products and so on. Again these external pressures may conflict with
   Visible and Invisible pressures.

A simple example might give a clue as to the messy nature of many business decisions
and the competing, conflicting pressures on decision-makers. Suppose that a large
competitor has cut the price of a product that is similar to a 'premium' product provided by your firm and your customers are beginning to move away. Senior management has, because the product is considered the firm's brand leader, just authorized,
and work has started on, a new computer system to support increased sales of this
particular product and you, as the decision-maker, have just been promoted to run
this major initiative. While in the long run the project investment will probably, but
not certainly, reduce the overall cost of the product, it will take some years to break
even. You suspect, but cannot prove, that the competitor may be using their competing
product as a loss leader to eliminate competition. What should you as the decision-
maker do? In such a decision, there are many Visible pressures (such as to meet sales
targets), but also there are Invisible pressures. In an ivory tower, a 'rational' decision-
maker should halt the project, assess the five-year return versus cost of producing the
product, and almost certainly recommend discontinuing the product. But that is not
the way business really works.

   In the real world, many decision-makers would put their head in the sand and
carry on regardless; that is they would take no action, hoping for the best. In Chapter 4,
the case of Blackberry illustrated this tendency to denial. But in this book, we are not
particularly interested in what the decision should be – that is for management textbooks – only that the actual decision may turn out to be disastrous. Imagine the
difference there would be if, rather than shoot the messenger, senior management
were to praise the decision-maker for in this instance having the courage to deliver
'bad news', especially if the decision-maker were to do so providing a plan that allows
senior management to take the fight back to the competitor.

   The purpose of People Risk Management then is to manage this complex set of
Visible, Invisible, Internal and External pressures upon the decision-maker. This
book will not deal explicitly with Visible pressures as they are covered well already
by existing management textbooks. Chapter 10 deals with handling some of the
Invisible pressures on individuals and the remainder of this chapter will address
the Internal and External pressures that create People Risks for all individuals in
the firm.

5.4 Internal and External People Risks

Figure 5.3 illustrates various types of '*interactions*' within a firm (ie *internal interactions*) and between the firm and three key external groups (ie *external interactions*):

1 *Internal*: risks, such as bullying, associated with individuals interacting *within* the organization;

2 *Customers*: risks, such as misselling, associated with people to whom the organization provides goods and services;

3 *Suppliers*: risks, such as bribery, associated with people and organizations from whom the organization receives goods and services;

4 *Regulators*: risks, such as incorrect financial reporting, associated with people and organizations that regulate an organization.

FIGURE 5.3   People interactions and the firm

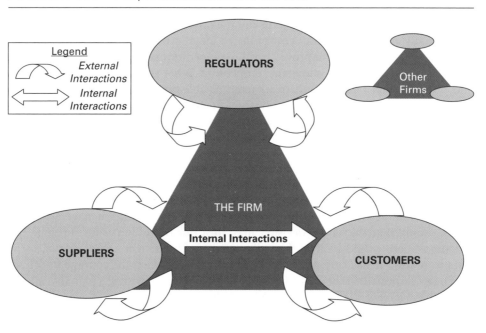

Each of these *interactions* gives rise to risks, and in this context, to People Risks. For example, a bank may lend money to a customer which gives rise to Credit Risk, but the sales interaction also gives rise to, for example, the risk that the loan documentation is not checked sufficiently or, alternatively, that a customer provides fraudulent documentation.

5.4.1 *Internal interactions that give rise to People Risk*

Figure 5.4 illustrates the *generic* interactions that take place within a firm, between employees, executives and directors. These interactions are multi-faceted and multi-directional, such as between a manager and an employee or an executive and the board. Interactions can be formal, such as between a manager and his/her staff, or informal, such as between colleagues. In the context of People Risk, informal interactions are important as they can lead to pressure on people to do the wrong thing. For example, the pressure that John Rusnak, the rogue trader at Allied Irish Bank, put on IT staff to change computer programs for his advantage, although he had no formal responsibilities in IT.[7]

The interactions in Figure 5.4 are merely representative of the many thousands of possible contacts that take place within firms on a daily basis. Many of these interactions will be formalized, such as in the relationship between an employee and his/her management as regards, for example, performance expectations. Others will be formal but negotiated, such as the precise interaction between a business line employee and an Assurance function such as Risk Management or Audit. Many, and maybe most, interactions, however, will be informal, such as those between colleagues. Colleagues in the same department/function will interact according to often unwritten rules that have evolved over time and have been reinforced by constant practice, in other words the actual, as opposed to the espoused, *culture*. Colleagues in different departments will usually interact on a semi-formal, negotiated basis, using standard procedures and agreed mechanisms to communicate information, actions and outcomes but also relying on interpersonal relationships to get the job done. Artefacts, such as meeting notes and semi-formal communication, such as emails, are also used to 'moderate' these interactions.

FIGURE 5.4   Examples of internal people interactions

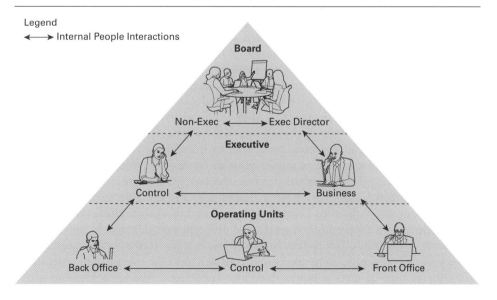

In any modern firm, face-to-face, telephone or electronic interactions are ubiquitous and good interpersonal communication is a key factor for every successful company. Many companies go out of their way to create so-called 'collegial' working environments, where respectful and friendly interpersonal interactions are encouraged. But, while extremely important, interpersonal interactions introduce risks. For example, in many interactions there will be a *power imbalance*, with one of those involved being more senior in corporate terms, more experienced in job experience, better remunerated, better educated, more forceful, or more persuasive than the other(s). In such a situation, personal attributes and agendas come into play. In many of the cases described in Chapter 4, people who were overly aggressive and volatile were reputed to be bullies whose aggression helped to propel them to senior positions, such as with Fred Goodwin of RBS and Dick Fuld of Lehman. And, when they reached the most senior positions, they created a situation in which others were unprepared, because of their reputations, to debate or argue with them.

But bullying is not the only way that an individual can convince others to do something that they should not. Appealing to common goals and shared experiences and using flattery is often effective too. In the LIBOR scandal[8] described in Chapter 4, traders requested LIBOR submitters to enter incorrect rates by appealing to camaraderie and shared goals, for example in making that year's profits. Such an approach is very seductive because it is much easier to be accepted into a team, especially a successful one, than to be an outsider. In fact, some of those who create the greatest People Risks and are the most difficult to detect are adept at *both* flattery and bullying, such as Dr Harold Shipman and the UBS trader at the centre of the LIBOR manipulation in Japan.

Internal interactions between people in the workplace are multifaceted. They are a multi-layered mix of the formal and informal, ambiguous and certain, simple and complex, honest and dishonest, contradictory and rational. They are not easy to classify because they are so personal and situation-dependent. And they also change when, for example, an individual comes under pressure and begins to change his/her attitude to others. But here, although important, we are not considering the full extent of these interactions but instead concentrating on those that give rise to *most risk*. It is of course the responsibility of the board and senior management, supported by Human Resources, to set the behavioural standards across a firm which describe acceptable/unacceptable behaviour when these interactions are taking place, and also of management trainers to ensure that messages are learned. Here we are interested in those behaviours that give rise to People Risk.

In every *internal interaction* there will be (at least) two parties with matching or competing objectives. Some of these objectives will be visible, such as discussing actions to complete a shared task. Some will be invisible, such as whenever parties have competing interests. For example, when discussing a project, an executive and project manager might discuss the actions and costs needed to complete the next phase of the project. Here they have a shared goal and are able to discuss various options openly and equitably. Everything appears to be visible. However, inevitably the participants will have hidden goals and different agendas which they may not share with one another. The project manager might wish to complete the next phase of the project without burning out his/her staff, whereas the executive might wish to hurry the project to meet a bonus deadline. These are invisible, competing goals.

In addition, the old adage 'information is power' sometimes comes into play, when one party has information that is not disclosed because it is detrimental to that individual's agenda.

How do we square this circle? There are no easy answers. However, there are ways to improve the situation so that at least some of the interactions are made more visible. In effect, this means identifying important interactions, their key components and the risks that they create. As described in more detail in Chapter 10, this means that having identified an ongoing interaction between individuals, for example an executive and a project manager, the rules and the risks of that *specific* interaction, including having competing goals, would be fleshed out. If the risk actually turns into a real risk event or issue then at least there is a basis for discussion and, if necessary, mediation between the parties. The key to success of course is making the articulation of these agreements not overly bureaucratic but something which is a natural process when two people are discussing the matter in hand.

5.4.2 *External interactions that give rise to People Risk*

Figure 5.5 illustrates the number and complexity of some of the most important interactions *external* to a firm.

The diagram shows *nine* of the most important interactions with the external groups identified:

1 *Customers*: which consists of three main groupings: (a) Customers to whom goods and services are supplied; (b) Brokers though whom individuals in the firm may approach and engage customers; and (c) Competitors, other firms that may interact with the same Customers and Brokers and the firm itself, for example through industry bodies.

2 *Suppliers*: which also consists of three main groupings: (a) Suppliers, who supply goods and services usually on a transactional basis; (b) Servicers, who provide services that are not provided internally, such as IT outsourcers (ie surrogate employees); and (c) Quality, specialist firms that provide independent quality assurance services, such as mortgage documentation appraisers.

3 *Regulators*: which consists of three main groupings: (a) Regulators that develop and enforce rules for an industry, such as competition regulators; (b) Governments, which develop and enforce the legal frameworks in which a firm operates; and (c) Shareholders, or their representatives such as investment firms, which own the company and hence must be engaged to a degree in monitoring its performance.

A large firm may interact with millions of Customers, thousands of Suppliers, hundreds of Brokers, Competitors and Shareholders (or their representatives), dozens of Servicers, Regulators and, in the case of an international firm, several Governments. It should come as no surprise then that some of these interactions do not always operate as desired. In fact, given the complexity of this multitude of interactions it would be more surprising if they did work perfectly. It is the sheer number and complexity of these interactions that gives rise to some of the most complex People Risks

FIGURE 5.5 Internal and external interactions

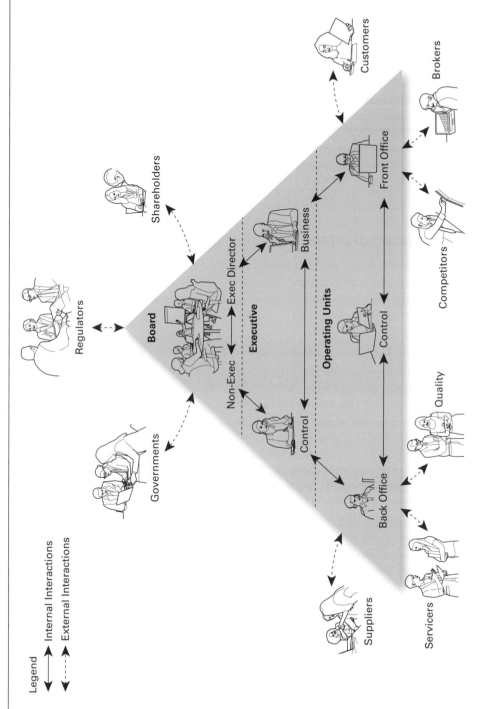

Legend

→ Internal Interactions

⇢ External Interactions

that subsequently lead to losses. Some of these losses will be small, such as customer theft, but some will be very large, such as the regulatory fines, described in Chapter 4, that were imposed on HSBC for money laundering offences.

Before proceeding it should be noted that the numbers and types of interaction will be different for different types of firms. For example, a legal or consulting firm will have few external interactions and those will be mainly concentrated in the area of Customers and, especially if a partnership, may not have many internal interactions. Most companies will have interactions with Suppliers and Regulatory bodies, especially when producing financial statements.

5.4.3 Example of interactions that give rise to People Risk

Figure 5.6 shows an example of the complexity of, and the People Risks that arise from, internal and external interaction. It shows a *part* of the interactions that took place during the LIBOR manipulation scandal described in Chapter 4.[9] In this case, regulatory inquiries found that many of the interactions were sometimes *Inappropriate* (such as collusion to manipulate rates between LIBOR submitters and Brokers) or were *Incomplete* (such as the failure of Control functions to manage conflicts of interest).

In this example, the central character is the 'LIBOR Submitter' whose role is to provide expert and independent estimates of interest rates to the marketplace. However, as various regulatory inquiries found, a number of submitters illegally provided rates that benefited their own firms to the detriment of their customers.[10] This illicit activity was not, however, restricted to submitters, but also came from colleagues and senior executives inside the firm who put *Inappropriate* pressure on submitters to enter bogus rates. In turn, some submitters and their trading colleagues colluded with external brokers and even their competitors to illegally manipulate rates. With hindsight, there were clear conflicts of interest in these interactions that were just not addressed fully by Control functions, executives and ultimately the board. Furthermore, there were *Incomplete* interactions by Assurance staff, such as risk managers and compliance officers, which allowed the manipulation to flourish by, for example, not creating a fire-proof Chinese Wall,[11] or information barrier, between functions. In other words, the rules for these important interactions were not enforced because, for a large part, the rules were not made explicit.

The inappropriate and incomplete interactions shown in Figure 5.6 took place in some of the largest financial institutions in the world, all of which had well developed Codes of Conduct. But, as discussed in Chapter 10, these codes were, and generally remain, remote and otherworldly, high on motivation and ambition but low on practical advice as to what to do in a particular business situation. Faced with direct orders from senior management or threats or inducements from more senior, more successful, better remunerated colleagues, what should a submitter do?

From an ivory tower, the advice would be to blow the whistle. But if the illegal request is seen to be 'business as usual' and 'everyone's doing it', it has to be admitted that such threats and entreaties would be very hard to resist. The person on the sharp end would have to have good support from management to resist such inappropriate pressures. Furthermore, people who are not involved but maybe should be (such as

FIGURE 5.6 Inappropriate interactions – example of LIBOR manipulation

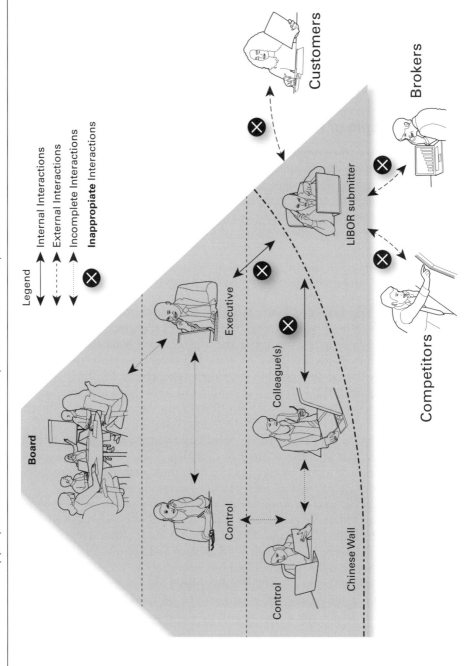

risk managers) must be given support to speak up and to insert themselves into discussions from which they have been intentionally or unintentionally excluded. Pious words appear not to be enough and practical guidance must be given when it is needed, not merely relying on employees remembering one of many messages given to them in induction material when they joined the firm.

5.5 People Risk and Conduct Risk

'Conduct' was the word of the year in banking circles in 2013. Following the Global Financial Crisis, the cases of misselling of financial products, such as PPI, and the illegal activity seen in the LIBOR manipulation, new regulators were set up in the UK and United States to regulate the conduct of banks. In the UK, the Financial Conduct Authority (FCA) was created to, among other objectives, 'promote innovation and healthy competition between financial services firms... [and] help them keep to the rules and maintain high conduct standards'. In the United States, the Consumer Financial Protection Bureau (CFPB) was created with a similar remit, but did not address the specific issue of 'business conduct', choosing instead to provide detailed guidance on specific consumer products. The phrase *Conduct Risk* was also used by regulators, particularly in the UK, but unfortunately neither the term nor its scope is well defined.

The Financial Services Authority (FSA), the pre-cursor of the FCA, provided as part of its so-called 'Treating Customers Fairly' (TCF) initiative,[12] a definition of 'Conduct Risk' as 'the risk that firm behaviour will result in poor outcomes for customers'. It can be seen that this definition is a true *subset* of our definition People Risk as illustrated within the Customer interactions in Figure 5.5. When the FCA emerged as a separate regulator from the FSA in 2013, the regulators chose not to develop a new definition of the term Conduct Risk but rather developed[13] a set of risks that they categorized as 'Conduct Risks', such as misselling. This approach has been categorized as *Conduct Risk – you will know it when you see it* and is not unreasonable in what has been called a focus on 'regulatory outcomes' rather than 'regulatory principles'.

The FCA did, however, identify a number of *drivers* of Conduct Risk, in three main categories:

1 *Inherent*: which includes 'Biases and Heuristics', 'Inadequate Financial Capabilities' and 'Information Asymmetries'. Note these are a subset of our *Invisible* pressures.

2 *Structures and behaviours*: which include 'Conflicts of Interest', 'Cultures and Incentives' and 'Ineffective Competition' which again are a subset of our *Invisible* pressures, except where some 'incentives', such as salaries, are *Visible*.

3 *Environmental*: which include 'Regulatory and Policy Changes', 'Technological Development' and 'Economic and Market Trends', which are a subset of our *Visible* pressures.

While these drivers are a subset of the People Risk Pressures, identified in Figure 5.2, the FCA also identifies a number of breakdowns in processes that give rise to Conduct Risk, such as poor governance over new product design and development. While one could argue that this example is indeed a wholly People Risk issue ('poor govern-ance'), there is obviously a process dimension that must be taken into account. So Conduct Risk, at least as defined by the FCA, has an additional but not significant Operational Risk component. But since the process component is not large, Conduct Risk will be considered as a subset of People Risk in the segment covering Customer interactions.

5.6 People Mapping

Figures 5.1–5.6 represent what is termed *People Maps* that show some of the very many interactions or linkages between various people and groups within an organization.[14] Figure 5.7 shows a sample People Map for one hypothetical individual employee (or rather one of a number of individuals who perform *exactly* the same role).

In this particular People Map, an individual is shown with a range of possible internal interactions, such as with colleagues, executives and control staff, as dis-cussed above, and a range of possible external interactions (dashed lines). It should be noted that the diagram shows the *complete range* of possible interactions for this particular individual and it is unlikely that a single individual will be involved in all or even most of these interactions. However, as described in more detail in Chapter 10, it is important to lay out the superset because, while an individual may not interact with a particular party as a matter of course, the actions to be taken when an in-appropriate interaction is initiated should be anticipated and clearly articulated.

For example, a salesperson will have a two-way interaction with a customer, which may give rise to, among others, the risk that the salesperson may try to sell the customer an inappropriate product. As described in Figure 5.6, LIBOR submitters and traders would have a wider range of interactions, with Customers, Brokers and Competitors in their markets. Alternatively, an individual in an Accounting depart-ment would most likely not have interactions with customers or suppliers but would be the source of information for Regulators and Shareholders (usually through the board and executives). He/she would be responsible for producing reports and data that are supplied to a variety of sources, inside and, after aggregation, outside of the company. Here the information provided to an external party, such as a shareholders, would be Visible but the information produced internally by the individual would be Invisible to its final recipients, creating the opportunity for deliberate or inadvertent misinformation.

This raises the question, does an individual have personal responsibility for the dissemination of information if it is subsequently manipulated by others? This was the dilemma faced by the Audit department of WorldCom, as described in Chapter 4. The audit professionals saw the information that was being provided by the board to shareholders and concluded that it did not accord with their understanding of the firm's true financial situation. In secret, a small number of auditing professionals

FIGURE 5.7 People Map for an individual – example

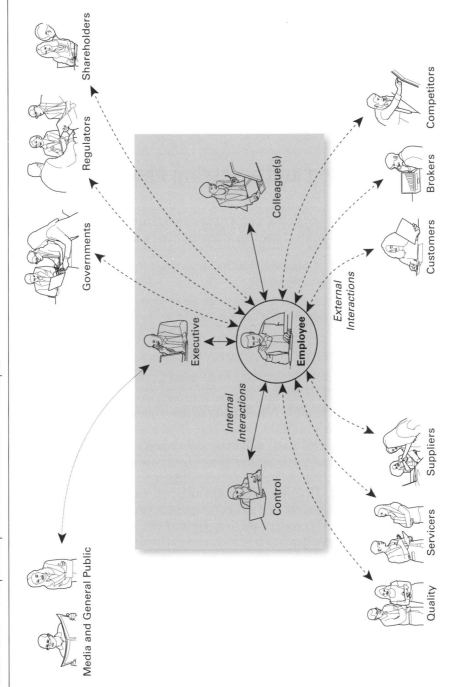

decided to re-analyse the data and in doing so uncovered a vast fraud that eventually resulted in the CEO, Bernie Ebbers, going to jail. In this case, the auditors took *personal responsibility* to make the invisible (fraudulent accounts), visible (evidence of fraud). A similar situation occurred at Washington Mutual where the Chief Risk Officer Ron Cathcart[15] took it upon himself to go to the bank's regulators when incorrect risk numbers were reported. Unfortunately, such situations appear to be rare as often those who are accountable for a particular interaction do not take responsibility when information is manipulated to deceive the receivers. Of course, in many situations that would be difficult for an individual to detect as information is often aggregated and changed as it is disseminated.

5.7 Identifying and assessing People Risks

Having identified the *interactions* that are a part of a particular individual's role, it is then necessary to consider each interaction and identify possible People Risks in those interactions. Examples of People Risks include, between:

- Individual <=> Colleague(s): which can give rise to Discrimination, Bullying, Health & Safety problems, etc.
- Individual <=> Executive(s): which can give rise to Discrimination, Bullying, Conflicts of Interest, Insider Trading, etc.
- Individual <=> Supplier(s): which can give rise to Bribery, Illicit Entertainment, Intellectual Property Theft, etc.
- Individual <=> Broker(s): which can give rise to Illicit Entertainment, Collusion, Insider Trading, etc.

Having *identified* the possible People Risks in these interactions it is then necessary to *assess* them for each individual/role. Not all interactions between a particular individual and an external party will carry the same level of risk. For example, the head of a Procurement function and their close subordinates will have a much greater risk of bribery when dealing with a supplier than say a clerk in the goods receiving department. That does not mean that the receiving clerk is not subject to the risk of bribery, merely that the consequences would be likely to be smaller, unless they are involved in wider collusion. The end result of this assessment exercise would be a list of People Risks that pertain to a particular employee/role ordered by 'level of risk'.

5.7.1 Risk Self-Assessment

An important question at this point is – who performs the identification and assessment of People Risks? The key to successful management of such risks is for the people involved to do the risk identification and assessment themselves. So-called *Risk Self-Assessment* (RSA)[16] is one of the standard methods used to identify Operational Risks, of which People Risk is a subset. The rationale for using self-assessment is important – only those closest to a particular risk can best identify it and fully gauge the potential consequences. RSA also has the distinct advantage that, having identified and assessed risks, the people who take part in the self-assessment exercise have the sense of ownership necessary to ensure that individuals take personal responsibility for subsequently managing the risks that they have identified.

Of course, while the individuals involved are the key players in any Risk Self-Assessment exercise, they are not the only participants. First, RSA is not an individual exercise, it is usually undertaken in a team that typically includes: a number of the individuals involved to promote questioning and a degree of objectivity; risk management experts to organize the exercise and to ensure that all issues that are raised are fully and properly considered; subject matter experts, who may or may not be affected by the risks, such as HR and Legal professionals; ideally independent reviewers, such as from a similar department, to ensure a fuller coverage of issues from their experience; and *provided that they do not dominate or skew debate on the issues*, management of the risk assessors, eg department heads. Even external parties, such as regulators or key shareholders, could be included if such an intervention was appropriate.

For example, an RSA exercise in a Procurement department would identify the possible opportunities for bribery, fraud, excess gifts and entertainment, theft, collusion, etc. with their particular set of suppliers. Possible conflicts of interest, such as trading off costs against quality, would be identified and assessed. At this stage, a particular supplier's ability to identify and manage conflicts of interest within their own operations would be assessed. An RSA is *NOT* a decision-making exercise. It should not choose between suppliers but merely identify the risks identified with existing suppliers or whenever a new supplier is added to a 'preferred supplier' list.

Figure 5.8 shows an example of an analysis of a hypothetical senior manager in a Procurement function, such as IT procurement, where bribery would be an ever-present danger. This theoretical analysis does *NOT* imply that the particular manager

FIGURE 5.8 Assessment of individual People Risks

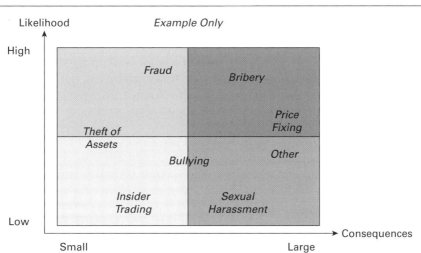

is likely to succumb to bribery only that for someone in his/her position the risk of bribery has serious consequences and needs to be addressed.

5.7.2 Risk treatments

Having identified and assessed a list of People Risks for a particular individual or group of individuals, management must make decisions as to how to '*treat*' or mitigate the most important of these risks. Management could, of course, say something like 'don't do it' but that is not sufficient because it is difficult to monitor compliance and does not give responsibility to the individuals most impacted. There are a number of common '*treatments*' for People Risk. These treatments and their rationales are organized in the example in Table 5.1 using the concept of John Adams' Risk Thermostat, as described in Chapter 2 alongside four drivers of risk behaviour:

- **Incidents and Losses**: events that bring the consequences of risk to our attention;
- **Perceived Danger**: our perception of unacceptable dangers in our environment;
- **Rewards**: the positive consequences to us of our risk-taking behaviour; and
- **Propensity for Risk**: our personal attitude to risk-taking.

The first two of these drivers (Incidents and Losses and Perceived Danger) cause us to reduce (or cool down) our risk-taking. On the other hand, the latter two of these drivers (Rewards and Propensity for Risk) cause us to increase our risk-taking behaviour. For all of these drivers, however, treatments must work to bring to the attention of individuals the impact of their risk-taking actions, ie making the invisible visible. Table 5.1 shows examples of generic treatments for People Risk.

The generic treatments above are designed to address an individual's risk-taking behaviours by reinforcing 'good' behaviour and making 'bad' behaviour more visible, using the concepts of behavioural psychology to address human biases. For example, the use of Risk Self-Assessment techniques and the development of a 'personalized code of conduct', as described in Chapter 10, can bring to people's *attention* their personal responsibilities. If individuals are encouraged to refer to such documents on a regular basis, for example taking their personalized codes of conduct to important meetings, they can be referred to when under pressure or when possible conflicts of interest arise.[17] In addition, material on People Risks can be sent out with contracts of employment for new employees (including reference to personalized codes of conduct) so that the message is reinforced about what constitutes acceptable and non-acceptable behaviour.

In some situations, treatments such as 'random checks' not only provide a confirmation that individuals are behaving as they should but also provide valuable lessons in what is working and what is not. For example, retrieving an input document at random from a day's work and following it though all of the processes and systems in which it was handled will show how people and processes are working in practice, not as in a semi-theoretical procedures manual. Although such 'walk through tests' are used in auditing, here they should be part of standard operations processes.

TABLE 5.1   Generic People Risk treatments – examples

Risk treatment	Actions/Rationale
Incidents and Losses	
Complaint Recording	A formal and published process for recording, analysing and reporting complaints from internal and external parties.
Recording Incidents	A formal system for recording incidents and 'near misses'.
Post-Incident Reviews	Convening a formal review of any incident that caused, or nearly caused, losses.
Case Studies	Development of a library of real and hypothetical 'case studies' with 'lessons learned'.
Group Behaviour	Analysis of group behaviour in an incident or 'near miss'.
Perceived Danger	
Procedures and Templates	Written rules as to how particular interactions are to be handled.
Checklists	Reminders as to how particular interactions are to be handled.
Controls	Special procedures to ensure that the procedural rules are being adhered to.
Attestation/Affirmation	Insisting that employees formally attest or affirm their compliance with rules, procedures and controls and that they have undertaken the necessary education.
Recording Interactions	Formal mechanisms for recording interactions, such as meeting notes and diaries.
Escalation Processes	Formal mechanisms for independent reporting and escalation of concerns, with a 'no-retribution' policy.
Random Checks	Independent mechanisms for randomly checking transactions, including documentation.
Interaction Monitoring	Formal mechanisms for monitoring interactions, such as telephone/email monitoring.
Decision Analysis	Formal mechanisms for analysing decisions for biases. See Chapter 9 for examples.
Pre/Post Authorization	Requiring transactions to be independently authorized.
Reinforcement	Structuring decision-making to 'reinforce' preferred behaviours and minimize biases.
Mystery Shopper	Testing interactions with specially trained 'mystery shoppers' or equivalent testers.

TABLE 5.1   *continued*

Risk treatment	Actions/Rationale
Rewards	
Reward for Risk Management	Providing rewards, both financial and other recognition, for expertise in identifying, assessing and treating People Risks.
Reward for Training	Providing rewards for completion of training and education.
Reward for Behaviour	Providing rewards for displaying 'good' behaviours.
Formal Behaviour Review	Undertaking formal reviews of past behaviour as part of performance reviews.
Soft Performance	Rewarding 'soft' performance, such as interpersonal behaviour, in reward reviews.
Minimizing Conflicts of Interest	Aligning rewards to minimize conflicts of interest, for example removing volume-based remuneration.
Propensity for Risk	
Education and Training	Informing individuals of specific People Risks and periodically reinforcing that knowledge through dedicated training material.
Testing	Formal scenario-based testing of individuals' understanding of People Risks.
Recruitment	Undertaking formal behavioural and personality analyses during recruitment process.
Risk Propensity Analysis	Analysing an individual's 'propensity' for risk-taking.
Risk Self-Assessment	Requiring staff to analyse their own risk-taking behaviour and biases.
Personalized Code of Conduct	Requiring individuals to develop a 'personalized' code of conduct based on standard template(s) (see Chapter 10).
Counselling	Provision of independent counselling support for individuals to discuss personal behavioural issues.
Register of Interests	Requiring maintenance of formal statements of interests by staff in a formal register.

Such scrutiny in itself will dissuade some individuals from misbehaviour by increasing the *perceived danger* of getting caught. The same is true of 'mystery shoppers', who are trained external parties given the job of testing the 'system' by turning up and attempting a transaction and recording their interactions.

In addition to generic treatments, however, specific treatments will be necessary to handle People Risks that are specific to particular individuals/roles. In the example in Table 5.2, some sample treatments to address the risk of bribery for the role of the senior manager in the Procurement department are suggested, as shown in Figure 5.8.

TABLE 5.2   Specific People Risk treatments – examples

Risk treatment	Action/Rationale
Incidents and Losses	
Bribery Case Studies	Require individuals to prepare a 'case study' for publicized cases of 'bribery', to present the case study to staff, colleagues and executives and to recommend changes to working practices that would minimize the possibility of the same events occurring in the firm.
*Record **Bribery** Incidents*	Require staff to record incidents of approaches by external or internal individuals that are not within formal Interaction Guidelines.
Perceived Danger	
Interaction Guidelines	Require management to develop a formal set of guidelines for conducting interactions, in particular identifying limitations as regards receipt of gifts and entertainments. Such guidelines to be reviewed annually.
Escalation Processes	Identify specific rules for escalating possible bribery within, and external to, the firm.
Authorization	Require all external contracts to be formally and independently reviewed, such as by Legal, Risk and/or Audit departments.
Rewards	
Reward for Risk Management	Reward individuals for developing specific anti-bribery risk treatments before a new supplier is used by the firm.
Reward for Behaviour	Reward individuals for displaying 'good' behaviour in dealing with possible opportunities for bribery when negotiating with suppliers.
*Reward for **Bribery** Training*	Providing rewards for completion of training and education specific to bribery.
Propensity for Risk	
Risk Self-Assessment	Requiring staff to analyse their own attitude to bribery, in particular to identify concrete situations and actions in bribery situations.
Personalized Code of Conduct	In an individual's 'personalized' code of conduct include specific rules covering bribery situation.

Note that rationale for the development of a *Personalized Code of Conduct* is developed further in Chapter 10.

5.8 Escalation of People Risks

It is not sufficient to work with an individual, however senior, to develop a sense of understanding of the risks that they face in their job, here specifically interactions with other people, and to encourage the taking of personal responsibility to address those risks. Because, unfortunately, not everyone will understand the risks involved there must be mechanisms for escalating concerns – outside of the normal chain of command. To be effective, such escalation processes must be independent of the regular organizational hierarchy. In effect this means that for every interaction that is identified as giving rise to risk, there must be an independent escalation channel that is known and communicated to *everyone* involved in the interaction.

Figure 5.9 shows an example of a hypothetical individual, such as a salesperson or marketer whose primary external interactions are with customers and competitors. The main internal interactions[18] are shown as being with executives and control functions. Situations will inevitably arise where an interaction goes wrong or is not working as designed such as, for example, a customer complaining about sales practices or services, or an individual being bullied by management or colleagues. If these issues are not resolved satisfactorily between the individuals concerned there is a need to escalate the issue to someone else who can mediate and, if that doesn't work, take action.

In Figure 5.9 the *escalating* actions are shown as thick bars with a telephone (although other communication mechanisms such as letters and email would also be used). The people/groups who attend to the escalation are shown within grey boxes that may straddle the firm and the external environment to indicate that they are at least partially independent of the firm.

5.8.1 *Handling complaints*

Customers have complaints – sometimes justified, sometimes not. After a sale is made, customers are usually provided with information as to how they may lodge complaints which can range from product failures to inappropriate sales pressure. This is shown on the left of Figure 5.9, where a customer first complains to the designated escalation channel (eg 1–800 number) and if the issue cannot be addressed immediately it is escalated to an internal function for follow-up. The PPI scandal, described in Chapter 4, is an illustration of how NOT to handle customer complaints.[19] For many years, customer complaints about PPI products were forwarded to general banking complaints desks but were generally ignored. By not monitoring and detecting trends in such complaints, the major UK banks were caught flat-footed when customer advocacy groups and the media brought PPI issues to light. The scandal has been very expensive for UK banks because they have been forced to set up dedicated resolution units that have been given targets for resolving problems and are monitored closely by regulators. A major lesson from the PPI scandal is that

FIGURE 5.9 Escalation Map for an individual – example

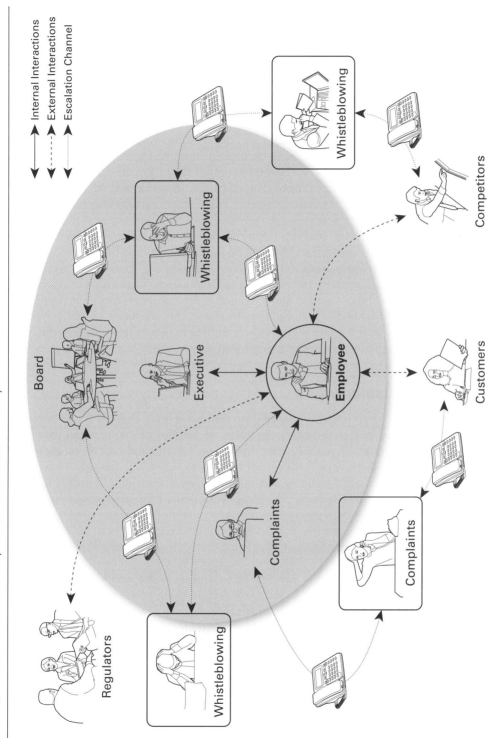

Internal Interactions
External Interactions
Escalation Channel

Whistleblowing

Whistleblowing

Competitors

Board

Executive

Employee

Customers

Complaints

Complaints

Regulators

Whistleblowing

customer complaint/escalation channels are very important mechanisms for monitoring trends not only in product faults but also in emerging People Risks.

Also shown in the figure is an escalation channel for competitors, which at first glance may appear unusual. But in several cases of rogue trading, for example, firms were actually warned by competitors about potential problems within their operations but had no mechanism for escalating competitors' concerns to the board and senior management. If competitors think that something is wrong and worth raising with a firm, then there probably is something very wrong indeed. The worst thing that can be done is to ignore warnings without investigating them first.

In some industries, regulators have become so concerned with the lack of response by industry players to customers' complaints that they have taken over the role of frontline complaints handlers, publishing statistics to 'name and shame' offending companies. For example, the new Consumer Financial Protection Bureau (CFPB)[20] in the United States, which was set up in the wake of the GFC, has created a new online 'open complaints process' and is publishing statistics and making available a database of complaints, naming and shaming financial institutions. In another industry, the Australian Telecommunication Industry Ombudsman[21] provides a service for helping to resolve issues with the provision of telephone services and it too publishes details of complaints, naming and shaming telecoms providers. The approach appears to work as, in 2013, complaints to Australian telephone service providers were the lowest in five years because the complaints departments in the providers improved, prompted no doubt by adverse publicity.

5.8.2 *Whistleblowing*

In business, the most often-referenced internal escalation channel is the 'whistleblowing' hot line. In fact, following the ENRON and WorldCom scandals described in Chapter 4, the US Sarbanes-Oxley legislation[22] mandated that firms create an independent whistleblowing function, which allows individual concerns to be escalated to the board and executive. But whistleblowing remains a sensitive issue in many firms. Like many risk issues, the identification of a whistleblowing event is seen somehow as a deficiency in management or as a failure of corporate culture. This, of course, is an immature attitude as whistleblowing is one of the best, if not *the* best, means of detecting wrongdoing that is being covered up within a firm. It helps to make the invisible visible.

However, whistleblowing is not a panacea and there are well-known problems, not least complaints raised maliciously, but despite those problems it addresses two important risk management issues. Whistleblowing acts as a deterrent on misbehaviour, because it increases the *perceived danger* in taking a particular course of action. But if operated properly, with an effective 'no retribution' policy, whistleblowing supports individuals in taking personal responsibility for their actions in highlighting something going wrong, increasing their *propensity for risk*. Without a robust and well-used whistleblowing system, a firm will be subject to more, rather than less, People Risk.

5.9 Appetite for People Risk

Before an individual can take a decision or make a complaint about others' actions, the limitations of an individual's behaviour must be articulated, as clearly as possible. Such articulation must come from the very top of the organization, ie the board and senior executives. An extremely important task that must be done then, by the board and senior management is, as ISO 31000 states, to 'ensure alignment of risk management objectives with the objectives and strategies of the organization'. A key part of this alignment is for the board to develop a statement of the firm's *Risk Appetite* or the 'amount and type of risk that an organization is willing to pursue or retain'. This is a clear statement of what risks the firm will take and the limits on those risks, and importantly what risks the firm will *not* take. Such a statement, in effect, will control the 'amount and type' of risk that different businesses throughout the firm will be allowed to take. It should be noted that having articulated such an appetite there will be a need for controls at the decision-making level to ensure that the Risk Appetite is not exceeded and processes in place to ensure that excesses and breaches are correctly rectified.

It is important to articulate a Risk Appetite at the outset, otherwise it will be difficult to:

● compare one risk against others;

● monitor risks effectively, because all risks will appear equally important; and

● allocate resources to address the most critical risks.

Again, it is beyond the scope of this book to discuss the fine details of developing a Risk Appetite across all of the dimensions that a firm will need to execute its strategies, not least because it is still an emerging discipline. However, using the COSO framework, Larry Rittenberg and Frank Martens have written a good guide[23] as to the steps that are necessary to develop a workable Risk Appetite. It should be noted, however, that at the time of writing this book there are few examples of actual best practice that have been published in this area.

For example, assume that the board and senior management of a retailer (such as Tesco) is developing the People Risk part of their overall Risk Appetite. Table 5.3 shows an *example* of the articulation of such an appetite for a hypothetical retailer. It should be noted that Rittenberg and Martens distinguish between statements of Risk Appetite as high-level aspirational statements and 'Risk Tolerances', which quantify these appetite statements. While not strictly necessary, their model is used to demonstrate the cascading of Risk Appetite/Tolerance statements.

The examples of Risk Appetite Statements and Tolerances above give a flavour of what is required to articulate the limits on any risk-taking and in this case for People Risk. For example, it makes the invisible and trite (eg 'thou shalt not steal') into a visible set of rules and operating limits. A statement of Risk Appetite, with associated Tolerances, also allows the cascading of risk limits to different business lines. For example, an accounting division will have limits on 'shrinkage' that are effectively zero and would not be addressed explicitly. On the other hand, there may be differences between a division that handles low-value confectionary in large stores and one that sells high-value white goods primarily over the internet. The key is that the

TABLE 5.3   People Risk Appetite – example for a hypothetical retailer

Risk Appetite Statements	Risk Tolerances
People Risks	*Note Examples Only*
Bribery: The firm has NO appetite for bribery of suppliers, public officials or other parties.	1 All gifts and entertainment by suppliers to staff must be recorded in the agreed system within seven days. Failure to do so will result in in penalties including dismissal. 2 All gifts and entertainment by suppliers to staff that exceed $500 in value must be approved beforehand if possible and always afterwards. 3 No gifts (other than budgeted entertainment) must be provided to government officials.
Conflicts of Interest: The firm has a LOW risk appetite for conflicts of interest regarding purchasing from close or related family members.	1 Employees must recuse (disqualify) themselves from decisions concerning related entities, failure to do so will result in penalties including dismissal. 2 Staff may not accept goods or services from a supplier who was previously an employee of the company within the last 12 months.
Shrinkage: The firm has a LOW appetite for 'shrinkage' (lost, stolen or spoilt stock) consistent with ensuring the availability of items for customers.	1 Overall Shrinkage from Supplier to Customer should not exceed 1.4%. 2 Shrinkage due to employee theft should not exceed 0.4%. 3 Shrinkage due to shoplifting should not exceed 0.8%. 4 Product unavailability due to shrinkage should be less than 0.5% of orders.
Hiring: The firm has a LOW appetite for hiring inexperienced executives but a high appetite for hiring inexperienced junior staff.	1 All managers above the level of... must have (or intend to acquire) the professional qualifications for their role as defined by HR. 2 Aside from security checks, temporary employees need only the qualifications and experience described in the job description. 3 Exception to these rules are permitted for certain prescribed circumstances (eg diversity) provided permission is sought before hiring.

Risk Tolerances are adjusted depending on the business line characteristics but are monitored both at the business line and overall firm level.

In this chapter, we have developed a framework, based upon the IS31000 standard, and provided practical examples and tools for considering and managing People Risks. Practical tools, such as People Mapping, Risk Self-Assessment and People Risk Treatment models were introduced. The remainder of this book will cover some important further aspects of People Risk Management. Chapter 6 will discuss aspects of People Risk in the *Boardroom* and Chapter 7 will discuss the thorny issue of *Culture*. Chapter 8 will discuss *Roles and Responsibilities*, Chapter 9 will discuss how *Decision-making* may be improved and Chapter 10 will discuss *Individual Responsibility*.

Notes

1 See COSO (2004) *Enterprise risk management: integrated framework*, Committee of Sponsoring Organizations, www.coso.org

2 See OCEG (2004) *OCEG Capability Model*, Open Compliance and Ethics Group, www.oceg.org

3 The International Standards Organization (ISO) agrees standards such as *ISO 31000:2009* that are then published by national standards bodies, see www.iso.org

4 It should be noted that Audit should provide an independent view on the effectiveness of the risk management processes and department.

5 See Coleman (2001).

6 See Blunden and Thirlwell (2010).

7 See Chapter 4, Rogue Traders. Also see the AIB case and the role of John Rusnak is described in the so-called Ludwig Report: Ludwig, E (2002) *Report to the Board of Directors of Allied Irish Banks, plc ... concerning currency trading losses*, Promontory Financial Group, published by AIB plc, 12 March, www.aib.ie

8 See McConnell, P (2013) Systemic Operational Risk:The LIBOR manipulation scandal, *Journal of Operational Risk*, 8 (3), pp 1–41.

9 Not shown are other interactions, such as those between the firm and its regulators, such as the LIBOR committee of the British Bankers Association (BBA).

10 See the LIBOR case study in Chapter 4 for detailed references.

11 A Chinese Wall is an 'information barrier' that is implemented to prevent exchanges of information between groups in an organization that could cause conflicts of interest. For example, between groups that trade and those that sell products. While some of the walls may be physical, such as separating groups in different buildings, many rely on individuals managing their own interactions.

12 See Financial Conduct Authority (2013) *Treating Customers Fairly*, Financial Conduct Authority, London, www.fca.org.uk

13 See Financial Conduct Authority (2013) *FCA Risk Outlook 2013*, Financial Conduct Authority, London, www.fca.org.uk

14 The concept of *People Maps* was introduced and developed in McConnell (2013).

15 See the Washington Mutual case in Chapter 4 and the role of Ronald Cathcart in Permanent Subcommittee On Investigations (2011).

16 See Blunden and Thirlwell (2010) for a description of *Risk Self-Assessment* in the context of Operational Risk Management.

17 Such measures are designed to bring the issues to forefront of an individual's thinking as described in Chapter 3.

18 Note that there will be other interactions, in particular with colleagues. These are not shown because the diagram is already complex but would be included in real life.

19 See McConnell, P and Blacker, K (2012) Systemic operational risk: the UK payment protection insurance scandal, *Journal of Operational Risk*, 7 (1) Spring, pp 1–60.

20 See the role of Consumer Financial Protect Bureau at http://www.consumerfinance.gov/

21 See 'About Us' in Australian Telecommunications Industry Ombudsman, www.tio.com.au

22 See history and provisions of the *Sarbanes Oxley Act* in the Wikipedia article of the same name.

23 See Rittenberg, L and Frank Martens, F (2012) *Understanding and communicating risk appetite*, COSO, www.coso.org. See also Hillson and Murray-Webster (2012).

People Risk
in the boardroom

06

> *To set aside one's prejudices, one's present needs, and one's own self-interest in making a decision as a director for a company is an intellectual exercise that takes constant practice. In short, intellectual honesty is a journey and not a destination.*
>
> **MERVYN KING, CHAIRMAN: KING REPORT – SOUTH AFRICA**

KEY MESSAGES

- Board effectiveness: it's not just a matter of ticking boxes.

- Conflict in the boardroom can be a double-edged sword, but when a board is truly committed to the success of the organization, nothing should be left unsaid.

- Having an effective board structure in place does not mean having an effective board in place.

- It is human nature to listen to all the arguments, form a view on what is going on and then fail to notice or dismiss evidence that challenges that picture. It is also dangerous when a group of people does this.

- Polite questioning by the (non-executives) is not good enough. The pendulum needs to swing towards a more forensic and inquisitive approach which provides effective challenge on key decisions.

This chapter is concerned with People Risk in one part of an organization, namely the boardroom, where, as we pointed out in a number of the case studies in Chapter 4, bad decisions can lead to catastrophic outcomes for a business. The following quote[1] from the UK Financial Services Regulator (FSA) serves to illustrate how board directors can be lulled into a false sense of security about how well they *think* they are governing the business when in reality they are moving towards the edge of a precipice:

> The review team concluded that there were substantive failures of board effectiveness at Royal Bank of Scotland, even if there were no formal failures of the governance process... The review team was able to identify little significant disagreement on major issues during the review period in a board containing tough and experienced individuals with successful track records. Clearly constant disagreement would be debilitating for a board, but some divergence from consensus would not be unhealthy.

The reader is invited to note that as a result of the 'substantive failures of board effectiveness' noted above, the bank had to be bailed out by the UK taxpayer to the tune of £45bn (US $70bn), and five years later in 2013,[2] the UK Government still retained its original 82 per cent stake in the RBS Group. Prior to the bailout, the Group, which also had a very large insurance business, was the second-largest bank in the UK and Europe (fifth in stock market value) and the fifth largest in the world by market capitalization.[3]

The stark implications of the words from the FSA review should have reverberated around all boardrooms because there is a clear message that has gone largely unnoticed or has been ignored in the corporate world. That message is: 'ticking the boxes' to make sure you are compliant with good corporate governance practices isn't really the main issue for a board – the key is how the board members interact and work together effectively.

In addition, it raises further questions about boards and the way that they operate, for example:

- How many other boards are out there ready to make poor decisions due to substantive failures of board effectiveness?
- What are the warning signs that indicate that a board is heading towards substantive failures of effectiveness?
- How do you assess whether there is an appropriate level of 'healthy scepticism' and 'respectful uncertainty' within the boardroom environment?
- How do board members recognize when an important decision needs challenging or supporting?
- What are the factors at play that inhibit board members, particularly non-executives, from really probing into a matter they may feel uncomfortable about?
- To what extent are counter arguments concerning an important decision put before the board before the final decision is taken?
- How confident are board members that their specialist advisors, who provide advice on key decisions, are themselves able to question, probe, challenge and effectively assist the decision-making process?

- Do sufficient board members have the ability to spot, and the willingness to avert, a fellow board member's unproductive or unhealthy ambitions for him/herself or the business?

We shall explore some of the above questions in this chapter and leave the reader to assess whether the words of the FSA review team are relevant to his/her organization. Our concern is with People Risk and how the board works together to ensure that the strengths and weaknesses of the personalities involved create an environment that mitigates against the possibility of substantive board failures happening. It is not an easy task when attitudes and behaviours are at play and power struggles and personal agendas become more important than doing what is best for the company.

Incidents like the Royal Bank of Scotland and others such as Enron, WorldCom, Lehman Brothers and Tesco, all of which were discussed in Chapter 4, have thrown the spotlight on what is going on in the boardroom to try to prevent these types of risk events happening. Given that the board itself consists of a team of people working together and making decisions, People Risk as we have defined it must exist within the boardroom environment, and yet how many of such risks can be readily found in the corporate risk registers of organizations?

6.1 Board governance and maturity

Maturity models have become more prevalent in the business world and a number have sprung up in various areas of business, including risk management.[4] They represent a good starting point for a board to take stock of where the area of the business they are evaluating sits on a scale which, in simple terms, varies from immature to mature. More importantly, the maturity models can provide guidance on how an organization can move up the scale should it wish to do so.

Figure 6.1 illustrates the main components of a governance high-performance model developed by Professors Geoffrey Kiel and Gavin Nicholson.[5] This model has in turn been used to develop a system of assessing the maturity of a board by two Australian consultants, James Beck and Mark Watson,[6] who have worked in the governance area for many years. Assessing the 'maturity' is based on a ranking scale of one to five, described as Baseline (1), Developing (2), Consistent (3), Continuous Learning (4) and Leading Practice (5). Each of the Board Roles (there are 10 in total) together with the Board Intellectual Capital (Competencies, Behaviours and Structures) are then assessed against pre-determined criteria to give a ranking of between one and five. Note that one of the Board Roles is concerned with decision-making, which is very much at the heart of People Risk. If we take the Board Role of risk management as an example, an organization would be assessed as 'Baseline' if it had little in the way of risk management processes, no formal risk committee, no formal risk reporting, no monitoring of risk and so on. At the other end of the scale, 'Leading Practice', an organization would have a formal and documented risk management process, ongoing risk management training, risk as a regular item on the board agenda, rewards for good risk management and so on. The rankings in between would have increasing levels of standard risk management practices and would provide an organization with a pathway to moving up the rankings.

FIGURE 6.1   Components of a governance high-performance model
(from Beck and Watson)

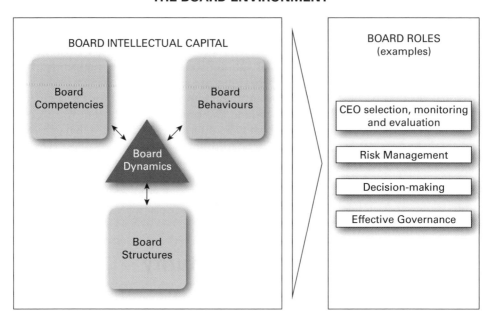

THE BOARD ENVIRONMENT

Perhaps the most interesting part of the model is the triangle labelled Board Dynamics which seeks to look at the interplay between the skills and behaviours of the board relative to the governance structures and procedures that are in place. This is fine as far as it goes but, as was implied by the FSA review team at the Royal Bank of Scotland, there appeared to be nothing wrong with either the board competencies or the board structures. The issue lay in the board behaviours, specifically the personalities in the boardroom and the way that they interacted *when in a group environment*. More importantly, this interplay operates at both a conscious and a subconscious level, ie a psychodynamic level, and it is, therefore, much deeper than is illustrated in the model. The model is without doubt a useful evaluation tool for boards but it should be heavily weighted towards evaluating board behaviours if a board is to be considered leading practice, ie there should be the right people in place as well as the right processes. Additionally, using the model to evaluate a board takes a snapshot at a moment in time, whereas the psychodynamic elements are at play all the time and can vary from board meeting to board meeting depending upon such factors as which board members are present, the subject matter being discussed and the types of decisions being made.

So, whilst board evaluations and best practice board processes are important elements in helping boards to work effectively, the greatest risk to a board's success or failure is embedded in the collective and individual behaviours of its members.

This is a view supported by others who have studied board effectiveness. Dr Oliver Marnet,[7] who has researched extensively governance in the boardroom, argues that board decision-making is negatively affected by behavioural factors including conflicts of interest, emotional attachments, anchored attitudes, implicit 'no-go' areas and unwarranted reliance on prior experience. Clearly, boards cannot be continuously self-evaluating to see if they have the right group of people to be effective but awareness of the potential risk (rather than just ignoring it) would be a good first step. Whilst the kinds of situations discussed in the case studies in this book can never be totally prevented, they can be mitigated if action is focused on the risks that really matter: those that focus on people rather than processes and particularly the people in the boardroom.

6.2 Boardroom dynamics

> We continuously refresh our board membership to ensure that it retains the right dynamics

This quote[8] from an official spokesperson was issued shortly after Standard Chartered was given a US $340m fine for breaches of US sanctions in its dealings with Iran. It is a pity that the spokesman did not go on to say exactly what he or she meant by 'retains the right dynamics' and what is meant by the word 'continuously'. Changing board members is easy to understand but ensuring that the board retains the right dynamics is not quite as straightforward although it clearly gives the impression that some members of the board are removed because they are creating the wrong dynamics. The most welcome point in this short statement is that Standard Chartered appears to recognize the importance of having the right dynamics (whatever they may be) in place.

What do we mean by boardroom dynamics? We believe that boardroom dynamics can be characterized as the interplay amongst the directors both within and outside the boardroom environment. It is important to recognize that these interactions can, and do, take place in formal as well as informal surroundings, thus making for a complex series of interactions that will influence the way directors think about an issue. Boardroom dynamics can thus have both a positive as well as a negative influence on the way that directors behave, particularly when important decisions are being made. They can help educate directors and influence biases that they may have about a particular subject matter or individual. These biases are of particular importance at the time the board has to make a decision which could have a major impact upon the business, such as whether to acquire or merge with another firm, whether to close or sell a business, whether to relocate production facilities overseas or whether to outsource part of the business to a third party.

One aspect of boardroom dynamics that can have both a negative and positive effect is conflict and how it manifests itself in boardroom discussions and behaviours.[9] Conflict can be typically seen in two forms: conflict about the matter in hand and conflict relating to the person.[10] The former demonstrates a difference of opinion about a course of action that a business might wish to pursue such as launching a new product, developing a new IT system or changing the design of the brand or brands. The latter is much more personal in nature and concerns the emotions and feelings that a board member may have about another board member's intentions, aspirations, attitudes or behaviours. Comments such as 'Are you supporting what we are trying to do?' or 'You never seem to see anybody else's point of view' serve to illustrate the point being made. Note that comments relating to the person are quite often said outside the boardroom environment for fear of offending the person in question.

Opposing views about a particular course of action should be encouraged as they can serve to illustrate that somebody is concerned about the business and they don't want it to come to any harm. The views expressed should be listened to carefully and the person's concerns addressed albeit that it is never easy to address opinions about something that might happen in the future – but this is where risk management comes into play as unforeseen events should be identified, evaluated and mitigating put actions in place. Take, for example, redesigning the company brand, which can cause heated debates in the boardroom between the marketers (we need to do this to keep the brand fresh and vibrant) and the accountants (what return will we get from the money that is spent?). This is, of course, where judgement comes into play and directors have to align themselves with one or the other point of view. However, once the final decision has been made, cabinet responsibility, the notion that all parties involved in making the decision should support it, should take over, with all sides supporting that decision. Whilst cabinet responsibility sounds fine in theory, there is evidence to suggest that it may equally encourage Groupthink as illustrated in Chapter 4 with cases such as Washington Mutual and Royal Bank of Scotland.

Conflicts that are personal in nature can be much more difficult to address. Personal conflicts may involve strongly held views about an individual's behaviour and will be influenced by the biases and prejudices that we all hold based on our view of the world, our experience and how *we think* people should behave. As the saying goes, 'One man's terrorist is another man's freedom fighter'. There is no right or wrong way of dealing with these situations, particularly if such views are expressed in a boardroom meeting where tensions and emotions can be running high. The Chairperson plays a crucial role here in making sure that such tensions and emotions are diffused and resolved and, where necessary, such criticisms can be taken out of the boardroom and addressed in private. All board members have to accept personal responsibility for what happens in conflictual situations and we discuss this further in Chapter 10.

Governance Matters[11] is a website set up to help serve New York's communities better and provides non-profit leaders with the governance resources needed to strengthen their boards. It provides a step-by-step approach to mitigating conflict risk in the boardroom which can be summarized in five steps. The approach is aimed at all board members but would be of most relevance to the Chairperson:

1 test your own understanding of what is happening;
2 determine the nature of the conflict;

3 when there are real differences of opinion, consider:

   a clearly defining the issue;

   b identifying a mediator;

   c building commitment to try and resolve the issue.

4 when people's actions are creating the conflict, consider:

   a establishing and reinforcing (board) meeting arrangements;

   b holding each other accountable;

   c if all else fails, removal from the board.

5 when the structure is the problem, consider:

   a removing any conflicting loyalties;

   b redefining the scope of work of committees that overstep the mark.

The behavioural aspect of boardroom dynamics has to be seen in the context in which board members operate. For example, despite the fact that the board should be as one when it comes to making decisions and overseeing the business, there can be an inherent tension amongst the board members as in the case of the Anglo-Saxon board structure with executives and non-executive directors. It is the executives that are responsible for producing the reports and papers that are presented to the board for review and critiquing by the non-executives. On the one hand, the non-executives are there to challenge, question and generally make sure the executives are doing their job effectively, whilst on the other hand they should be supportive and respectful of the views, ideas and proposals being put forward. Given that board members should be there to act in the best interests of the shareholders[12] you might expect that this single 'we're all trying to achieve the same goal' focus would make it easy, but when behaviours start to manifest themselves, it can become a difficult balancing act. Only one view can prevail and that may not be to the liking of everybody in the boardroom.

The behavioural aspects of what goes on outside the boardroom also create risks. Taking up a cause behind the scenes instead of in the boardroom can create tensions which can be difficult to diffuse, especially when the cause in question involves a different agenda to what has been discussed/agreed by the board. This situation is exacerbated when the cabals created as a result of this run along the lines of executive versus non-executive directors – it becomes the classic 'us versus them' syndrome. The natural diffuser of this situation, the Chairperson, may find him- or herself in a difficult position but ultimately he or she may have to come down on one side in order to put a stop to these antics as they create an unhealthy environment in which the board has to operate. In addressing this issue the Chairperson has to recognize that there may be genuine differences (of opinion) which need resolving. No easy task, of course, but the guiding principle should be what is best for the company.

There is no definitive checklist of things to look at in order to ensure that the risks inherent in boardroom dynamics are being mitigated, but Box 6.1 lists a few pointers that should be of help in considering this issue:

Box 6.1   Boardroom dynamics: some considerations

- Being a good director is about both the behaviours demonstrated by the individual and the competences that the individual has acquired.

- The Chairperson has a key role to play in managing the board dynamics and should periodically talk to the rest of the board about how he or she sees the situation and gain feedback on whether their view is correct. This should be done by the Chairperson setting aside time to meet with the directors on a one-to-one basis.

- The CEO should engage constructively with the board by ensuring that the executive team is actively encouraged to speak when they have a different view on a matter being discussed. Likewise, non-executive directors should meet with the executives outside the boardroom to discuss 'how things are going'. This does, however, need to be done with some sensitivity to ensure that the dynamics between the CEO and the executives are not undermined.

- Retired CEO's don't necessarily make good non-executive directors, since they are used to being in control and this attitude can sometimes prevail when in a non-executive position. This is a key point which should be addressed by the Chairperson at interview stage to ensure that the new recruit will be able to switch mind-sets to that of a non-executive.

- Non-executives should endeavour to see whether the direct reports of the executive board members perceive conflicts in the boardroom. This can be a good pointer to something being amiss or about to go amiss, even if there aren't any issues within the company and the business results are sound.

- How much intragroup *trust* is there between the directors, particularly the executive and non-executive? Good directors should be trustworthy of their peers but will continually seek to verify that the trust is being earned.

- Do board members receive peer feedback about their behaviours? One simple tool is to seek answers to the three questions: 'What should the director carry on doing? What should the director stop doing? What should the director start doing?'

- All directors should champion board decisions, even if they disagree with the course of action being taken. This can be done in staff meetings and briefings, internal committee meetings, informal meetings and so on.

- Bad behaviour by a director in the boardroom is not difficult to spot and is likely to be driven by emotional immaturity and lack of self-awareness of the individual concerned, or overconfidence and hubris. The rest of the board must, however, remember to first ask themselves whether the point(s) being made is valid.

Ongoing poor boardroom dynamics is, therefore, a key risk for a business and needs careful monitoring to ensure positions do not become entrenched and an environment of distrust and suspicion does not become the norm. Various ways of mitigating this risk are suggested by the UK Institute of Directors[13] which focused on the role of the Senior Independent Director (SID), who is seen as providing support for the Chairperson and being a sounding board on board issues (such as boardroom dynamics). The UK-based Financial Reporting Council (FRC)[14] also discusses the role of the SID and provides examples of when the SID could intervene in order to maintain board and company stability:

- there is a dispute between the Chairperson and CEO;
- shareholders or non-executive directors have expressed concerns that are not being addressed by the Chairperson or CEO;
- the strategy being followed by the Chairperson and CEO is not supported by the entire board;
- the relationship between the Chairperson and CEO is particularly close, and decisions are being made without the approval of the full board; or
- succession planning is being ignored.

One example of a board undergoing a period of stress where the SID could have potentially helped out, is the Co-op case study discussed in Chapter 4. Paul Myners was appointed as the Senior Independent Director in December 2013 and his first task was to look at the governance arrangements in the group and what could be done to improve them. He resigned his post just four months later in April 2014 amid concerns that his proposals were going to be resisted by those who did not want to see the sorts of changes he was recommending. However, in his report,[15] issued in May 2014, he was scathing about the lack of governance within the Co-op group. A number of his recommendations focused on improving people skills and board dynamics thus:

- The inescapable conclusion of [this review's] analysis is that the present governance architecture and allocation of responsibilities is not fit for purpose. It places individuals who do not possess the requisite skills and experience into positions where their lack of understanding prevents them from exercising the necessary oversight of the Executive.
- The stark evidence is that there has only been a façade of control, and the individuals exercising it have been drawn from an excessively narrow pool of entrenched incumbents on the regional boards of the Group.
- This deeply flawed system of elected member representation has consistently produced governors without the necessary qualifications and experience to provide effective board leadership and to monitor, challenge and provide direction to management.

The bad experience of one SID, however, does not necessarily mean that the SID role cannot be influential in resolving board problems and we would support the FRC guidance as being an effective risk mitigation tool to help manage boardroom dynamics.

6.3 The role of the Chairperson

The Chairperson acts as the first line of defence in ensuring that People Risk (within the boardroom) is being managed effectively. It is he or she who determines the red lines that the others should not cross when it comes to acceptable behaviours both inside and outside the boardroom when discussing board issues. It is not an easy job because of the interplay of personalities alluded to above and Chairpersons may fall into the trap of becoming complacent about people issues simply because they have been around for a long time and nothing serious has happened. But this is a backward-looking approach and is turning a blind eye to what might happen in the future.

In 2000, Dr John Roberts from Cambridge University interviewed a number of Chairpersons of large businesses.[16] His detailed report discusses many aspects of becoming a company Chairperson and how challenging the role can be once an individual has been selected to lead the board (typically the non-executive role) or lead the company (typically the executive role). Every business is different with different people and personalities (on the board), different objectives and different challenges. For businesses that are running smoothly and providing healthy returns to shareholders with good solid reputations, the challenges for the Chairperson will be different compared to businesses that have major concerns, whether they be financial, reputational, people and so on. Some businesses may transition from being bad to good with the same Chairperson in situ, whilst others may find the journey is reversed, leading to huge pressure being put on the Chairperson and/or CEO to resign.

One very important point that Roberts established was how every company and every board are unique and that the Chairperson has to mould their role to the character and demands of the company and the web of relationships that exist at the top of the organization. Fundamental to achieving this is the role that the Chairperson plays in building what Roberts describes as a complementary board, ie a board in which the non-executives complement the executives and where the Chairperson and the CEO show mutual respect for each other's position. By building a complementary board, the Chairperson is building a more effective board as it is reducing the inherent risks alluded to by Roberts. Box 6.2 sets out a number of inherent risks in establishing a complementary board.

Box 6.2   Risks in establishing a complementary Board

- Failing to set the ground rules as to how the relationship should work, for example, no conversation between the Chairperson and a member of the executive team should ever be confidential from the CEO or the CRO/control functions.

- The Chairperson fails to give the CEO absolute confidence that he or she has no aspirations to hold executive power and a power struggle results.

- The Chairperson (or CEO) regularly oversteps their boundaries of authority.

- Lack of mutual respect, and with it trust, between the Chairperson and CEO (and other board members).

- The Chairperson and the CEO develop a 'club of two' and run the organization with little recourse to other board members.

- Non-executives are only concerned with the business when they attend board meetings and are not engaged enough with what is going on.

- The Chairperson fails to get everybody to speak during a debate or impresses his view on a situation at the outset.

- Failing to have the balance of skill sets needed to oversee and run the organization, including NEDs with analytical skills and the ability to get to the heart of a matter very quickly. [17]

These risks are most apparent in the early stages of a new Chairperson/CEO relationship when both parties are 'testing the water', particularly if one of them is new to the business. When a complementary board is in place, the Chairperson will recognize that board members are not competing to be right about an issue but are collaborating to test what is the right way forward for the business. Whilst risk is unavoidable in a complex set of relationships, in the context of a boardroom environment, where critical decisions are being made about the business, it is incumbent upon the Chairperson to proactively use *all* the talent and experience within the boardroom to help inform the decisions being made.

MWM Consulting, a board advisory and search firm that acts for a number of the largest companies in the world, undertook a study of board effectiveness during 2012.[18] The qualitative research it conducted consisted of a series of interviews with 70 experienced UK board directors followed by a series of follow-up events with a further 45 directors. The results of this research point to the Chairperson as the single biggest determinant of board effectiveness and six factors are singled out that contribute to being what they describe as a great Chairperson. These can be used as a guide during the recruitment process, and subsequently the appraisal process, to make sure that the business increases the likelihood of getting the right Chairperson and then makes sure he or she is performing well:

1 The Right Motivations – they need to be focused on promoting the success of the company and on looking after the interests of all the stakeholders.

2 Commitment and Engagement – they need to be intelligently and meaningfully engaged in the business without overstepping into executive responsibilities.

3 EQ (emotional intelligence) as well as IQ – they need to demonstrate a balance of leadership skills by not being overly dominant on the one hand and being intellectually sound on the other.

4 Optimizing board composition – they need to build the right board with the right blend of skills and personalities.

5 The right agenda with the right rhythm – they need to ensure the right balance is struck between performance and conformance (governance) issues.

6 Effective board management – they need to encourage contributions from all in the boardroom and have a disciplined but not dogmatic approach to chairing meetings.

At this point we would sound a note of caution on what might constitute a great Chairperson. This is because the Chairpersons of a number of the financial institutions that suffered catastrophic failures during the Global Financial Crisis (see case studies in Chapter 4 for examples) were being lauded as heroes by the press and politicians but were then subsequently castigated as fools when the full effect of the crisis became apparent. If, however, a Chairperson is seen to tick the six factors above, then this should go some way to mitigating People Risk issues in the boardroom as well as establishing a board culture which will guide the unspoken rules that are used in making decisions about the business.

From a character point of view, Roberts points out that this role is not for alpha males[19] who, if left unchallenged, will tend to dominate meetings and drive through their own agenda. In some cases where firm leadership is required, this approach may work fine but first and foremost, the Chairperson is there to encourage debate and hear others' views before expressing his/her own view on the matter in hand.

6.4 The role of the CEO

Whilst the role of the Chairperson may not be for alpha males, the role of the CEO may be more suited to this type of individual.[20] On the one hand, the CEO must be driven and confident in what they are doing but on the other, they must take the board and the people in the organization with them down the strategic path that the board has agreed. New CEOs in particular have to establish their credibility early on and must maintain the full confidence of all the board members who were instrumental in selecting them in the first instance. There can never be any room for complacency on the CEO's part.

The CEO must work tirelessly and constructively with the board. He or she will form his or her own impressions about individual board members just as they will form their own impressions about him or her. He or she will know who can normally be relied upon for constructive advice on how the board operates and those who are resistant to change. It is all about building effective personal relationships and mutual respect as well as recognizing, and for the CEO exploiting, the technical skills of the other board members. MWM Consulting summed it up by way of four lessons for the CEO. These four points could help to mitigate against people risks in the boardroom and provide for a more constructive decision-making environment:

1 The CEO needs to embrace the board – the board is, or at least should be, a valuable source of expertise and experience for the CEO to tap into and should not be seen as nuisance to be managed.

2 The CEO should be a role model who creates open and constructive dialogue – whilst the Chairperson can play his or her part, the CEO must encourage and legitimize challenge, welcome input and listen to arguments without defensiveness.[21]

3 The CEO must encourage engagement outside of board meetings – informal contact between non-executive directors and senior executives across the business should be easy and unrehearsed. The non-executive directors need, however, to be mindful of any filtering of information that the senior executives may apply when they are being provided with information about what is going on around the organization.

4 If the CEO has the wrong attitude, it must be addressed by the Chairperson – ultimately, wrong behaviour on the part of the CEO should lead to his or her removal, although in practice this is easy to say but difficult to do, particularly when the business is seen as performing well and the incumbent CEO has some support from other board members.

Professor Jean-Francois Manzoni from Insead Business School has studied difficult relationships in business for many years[22] and he provides a good example of how a new CEO did not work, highlighting how the reasons why a board selected a new CEO can often be the very same reasons why they fall out with them (see Box 6.3).

Box 6.3   The case of the Nike CEO

The Sports Manufacturer Nike was founded by Phil Knight and in 2004 he appointed outsider Bill Perez to be the CEO whilst he moved into the Chairman's role. The aim was to bring some rigorous controls to a company known for its entrepreneurial, creative culture that focused on the consumer. But a year later Perez stepped down after the board concluded that he did not understand Nike's creative mind-set, and he was replaced by a veteran insider. Knight and the rest of the board began to suspect that Perez might be a poor fit when he brought in consultants to review operations and tried to reduce the number of meetings. Perez, on the other hand, came to view Knight as 'unable to let go' and 'unreceptive to outside ideas'. Perez sought to forge ahead with the changes he had been recruited to introduce so that he could show performance improvements. But the board did not give him credit for these improvements and communication between the two sides became uneasy and distant. As Perez sensed the growing mistrust, he found it increasingly hard to remain open to the feedback he was receiving, though not always explicitly. Once the board had lost confidence in the CEO, they started to exert control and it soon became very difficult for Perez to put a foot right. So, the reasons why the board had selected Perez in the first place became the excuses for why he had to go.

The recruitment of a new CEO or indeed the elevation of the CEO to the Chairman position are always risks to a business and in this case the risk manifested itself because the initial actions of the board (to bring in more business control) were seen to be forcing unwarranted cultural changes. There is an important message for board members coming out of this incident and that is to recognize the inevitable cultural changes that will occur when any new CEO is brought into the organization. On top of this, however, when the board is the driving force behind the cultural changes, as was the case with Nike, the decision process should include a thorough analysis of the potential unintended consequences of making such significant changes. It is clear that Nike wanted to do the right thing by improving the control environment but bringing in a new CEO is not the only way to do that. The incumbent CEO together with the board could have accepted personal responsibility for making this happen and used experienced mentors to help bring about the changes.

Even in boardrooms where the human dynamics and interactions between the participants are good, conflict is inevitable from time to time. Where a conflict involves challenging the CEO's position on a particular issue, it becomes a real test for the CEO to see how he or she reacts and responds to what is being said. The CEO's response will likely depend upon who is doing the challenging, whether there is enough information to make a decision, how much expertise they have in the particular area, whether their comments are based on fact or opinion, the strategic importance of what is being said and, without wishing to sound trite, whether the CEO is having a good or a bad day. Clearly the other directors have to be satisfied that they have all the information, have asked all the questions they wanted to ask and generally feel confident about the position that they are taking when they disagree with a proposal from the CEO.

The CEO is, therefore, both part of the problem and part of the solution when it comes to managing People Risk (in the boardroom), particularly when it comes to making major decisions, and some of the case studies in Chapter 4 attest to this. A successful CEO may indirectly dismiss challenge because he or she is, or has in the past, been successful. This was the case with RBS, which was discussed in Chapter 4. Fred Goodwin, who was CEO at the time, acquired National Westminster bank and successfully integrated it into the business.[23] An overly powerful CEO who has been given a long leash of responsibility may, either inadvertently or deliberately, create a climate of blame and fear that can become debilitating. A politically motivated CEO may create unhealthy tensions and embittered relationships that can divert attention away from doing what is best for the business. A consensus-seeking CEO may lack courage and conviction which can result in poor leadership and poor performance.

6.5 The warning signs

Warning signs are very useful in alerting people to things that might be about to go wrong and are often described in the risk management literature as Key Risk Indicators, much the same way an organization may have key performance indicators to measure how well the business is performing. Trends in such indicators are a most useful way to detect that something needs to be done to correct a situation that will get worse if nothing happens.

Warning signs that something may be amiss in the boardroom are not just confined to the softer side of people issues and behaviours, they may equally manifest themselves in the so-called hard factors such as the metrics associated with financial performance. Whilst metrics are of use in identifying things that may be going wrong, they may not get to the root cause of the problem. For example, poor financial results are as a result of the actions (or inactions) and decisions of people throughout the business. Equally, good financial performance can result from bad sales practices, as was evident in the UK Payment Protection Insurance scandal described in Chapter 4.

As we have illustrated in earlier parts of this chapter the behaviour of the CEO and/or the Chairperson can give pointers towards things going wrong. boards can be tolerant of poor performance if the other directors judge that getting rid of their colleague(s) will in itself cause problems both internally and externally: as the saying goes, 'Better the devil you know than the one you don't'. This can lead to dysfunction in the boardroom as sides are taken between those in favour of removal (of the director) and those against it, which then becomes a power struggle that only one side can win. In the meantime, directors can find themselves expending far too much time on coping with the conflicts and politics that persist whilst the board remains divided, and this can be a draining experience as well as being a distraction from achieving the business plans.

In an ideal world, when such a situation exists, the honourable thing would be for the director(s) in question to acknowledge their poor performance, adjust their behaviour or even leave, but sadly it is rare to find people behaving like this unless they are put under a huge amount of pressure and have little choice but to resign. It is never going to be easy for even the most self-aware of board directors to willingly step down, if only because of the reputational impact it may have on them by admitting that they are not good enough or are maybe just plain 'fed up'. Much will depend on how the departure plays out and the extent to which reputations remain intact.

In order to provide a framework for establishing possible warning signs for People Risk issues, we have used the model of organizational disasters[24] developed by the late Professor Barry Turner who we introduced in Chapter 2. Turner was very clear in his analysis that disasters, other than those arising from natural forces, are not created overnight. Man-made disasters creep up on you and are caused by an individual or group of individuals together with the unwitting assistance offered by access to the resources of large organizations, and time. He described the two main stages before the disaster strikes as the failure of initial beliefs and norms and the incubation period, and within these there are features or warning signs that can be used to spot the looming disaster. In Table 6.1 we have used this element of the

TABLE 6.1 Disaster warning signs and People Risk issues

Stage of development	Features/warning signs	Examples of People Risk issues
1. Initial beliefs and norms	a) Failure to comply with existing regulations	• Clash of cultures and values across the organization • Board does not fully understand the business(es) it is managing • Board has little empathy with the values of the business • Board considers it knows better than the regulators
2. Incubation period	a) Rigidities of beliefs and perceptions – ingrained culture	• Myopic thinking • Failure to challenge
	b) Decoy phenomena – management distracted by other problems	• Other problems seen as more important and take priority • Board attention diverted and action taken on the wrong things
	c) Disregard of complaints from outsiders – clear warnings from outside the business	• Board ignores the complaints and concerns • Board knows its business better than outsiders
	d) Information difficulties and noise – internal messages ignored or not reported	• Board incompetence and arrogance • Board communication and reporting seen as adequate • Culture of only telling the board 'good news stories'
	e) The involvement of strangers – the influence of external people	• Board too reliant on advisors • Board ridicules the comments being made by the outsiders
	f) Failure to comply with regulations – seen as discredited or out of date	• Regulations are seen as a hindrance to business rather than a control
	g) Minimizing of emergent danger	• Board does not notice or misunderstands the events due to reluctance to accept that something bad might happen • Board underestimates the scale of the problem • Board does not accept that a crisis is looming • Blame culture grows

Turner model to identify possible People Risk issues that would support the warning signs and indicate that all may not be well.

This table could be extended to include actions that could be taken to mitigate the People Risks highlighted. For example, with initial beliefs and norms, culture/values audits may be undertaken together with board effectiveness reviews to counter the issues raised. The table also serves to reinforce a number of the points that we have made in this chapter about People Risk issues and the possible consequences if they are ignored. We shall return to the issues around culture and values in Chapter 7, and discuss what may be done to address them.

6.6 Monitoring board behaviour

We believe that there are certain aspects of a board's collective attitudes and behaviours that would benefit from ongoing assessment by the directors with the results of this assessment being made explicit to board members by way of a Board Behaviours Map. This map would highlight the key behavioural characteristics that the board wish to monitor and look at how the assessment has moved over a period of time. The assessment itself would be done by each individual board member every board meeting (say end of quarter) to provide trends related to the characteristics. The results can then be aggregated to provide a summary of what the directors as a whole think, and provide evidence of how effective the board is from a behavioural point of view. An example of such an aggregated map for 10 directors is shown in Table 6.2.

We have selected a number of behavioural characteristics as shown, and for each one a question, or series of questions, should be asked to guide the director on how he or she views the assessment at the time of completing the review. If we take Groupthink as an example the questions could be:

> Groupthink – to what extent do you think we aim, above all else, to have conformity and harmony in the decisions that we make? Are we in danger of discounting views either from internal or external sources that do not conform to our way of thinking on a certain matter? Can you point to any examples of where this may have occurred recently? Do we make sure there are counter views put forward when the CEO-sponsored projects are put forward for approval?

The aim is to test the director's understanding of how he or she perceives a particular characteristic using examples wherever possible. This will build up into providing a picture of how the whole board views that characteristic and whether that view is held consistently amongst the directors. A brief descriptor for each of the other characteristics is provided below:

- Challenge – an assessment of the rigorousness of the debates that happen in the boardroom and whether everybody expresses their views.
- Support – an assessment of the extent to which proposals are actively supported both within and outside the boardroom.
- Complacency – an assessment of whether the success of the company is tending towards creating an atmosphere of 'we can do no wrong'.

TABLE 6.2   Example of Board Behaviours Map

Behavioural Characteristic	Assessment Apr 2014			Assessment Jan 2014			Assessment Oct 2013			Comments
	R	A	G	R	A	G	R	A	G	R = Red (Major Issues) A = Amber (Some issues) G = Green (No issues)
Groupthink		1	9			10			10	Monitor
Challenge			10			10			10	
Support			10			10			10	
Complacency		5	5		4	6		3	7	Business has been doing well but we need to be on our guard
Overconfidence		2	8		3	7		2	8	Current acquisition targets, are they a stretch for us?
Trust			10			10			10	
Personal agendas		1	9			10			10	
Collaboration		2	8		3	7		5	5	Has improved due to chairman's input
Understanding the business	3	2	5	1	4	5	1	4	5	We're getting worse at getting out and truly understanding the issues
Values			10			10			10	

- Overconfidence – an assessment of whether the directors' decision-making is being driven by too much confidence in the ability of the board to deliver based largely on the personal experiences of board members.
- Trust – an assessment of the extent to which board members consider they are able to rely on others and the experience that they bring to the boardroom table.
- Personal agendas – an assessment of whether directors are making decisions based on personal interests rather than the best interests of the business.

- Collaboration – an assessment of the extent to which board members, executives and non-executives, work together on matters delegated by the board.
- Understanding the business – an assessment of the extent to which board members, most particularly the non-executives, are engaged with what is going on in the business and meet with the senior management and other staff on a regular basis.
- Values – an assessment of whether the board actively lives the values of the business and promulgates them throughout the company.

In the example above, the director has a choice of three assessments (based on the traffic light system) to use for each of the characteristics:

- Red – I see major issues with this characteristic and we need an action plan to address the matter.
- Orange – I see some issues with this characteristic and we need to monitor to make sure the situation does not deteriorate.
- Green – I see no issues with this characteristic.

Finally, comments can be added to document to give the reasons why scores may have moved either negatively or positively.

One question that arises is whether the directors are sufficiently independent to be able to objectively make an unbiased assessment so that the results are meaningful and reliable. This is a valid criticism and can be countered by having an external expert attend a board meeting, monitor proceedings and challenge the results of the assessment. An alternative approach could be to have an external expert review the minutes and analyse the results of the board Behaviours Map independently in order to provide an unbiased assessment of what took place.

Such a map provides the board and, in particular, the Chairperson with a reference point on how the board as a group sees themselves behaving. Clearly, the behavioural characteristics shown here are not set in tablets of stone and can be adapted by boards to suit the context and the environment in which they operate. In addition to the board, regulators who have to inspect businesses may find this type of behavioural map useful in assessing how well the directors perceive themselves to be performing.

6.7 What are the main People Risks in the boardroom?

We have defined People Risk in the organizational context as being the risk of loss due to actions as well as non-actions of people. The non-actions element is important at board level because of the nature of the decisions (or actions) that the board has to take. Take, for example, the strategy of the company. Some of the board's key roles are signing off the company strategy, endorsing the goals that have been set, having plans in place to achieve those goals and establishing an effective monitoring programme. Achieving goals does not happen without the company taking risks, which leads to the question of how much risk the board should be prepared to take in order to achieve the business goals. This is not an easy question to answer because it depends upon a number of factors including the growth stage of the company, the growth stage of the business in which the company operates, the economic cycle and the collective attitude of the board towards taking risks. In this environment, one inaction that the board may be guilty of is not taking enough risk. The effects of this can be dramatic as is evidenced by the decline of the Blackberry smartphone, a case we discussed in Chapter 4. The reader may recall that the board of Blackberry decided that the Apple iPhone would not catch on when it was introduced in 2007 since it posed a real challenge to its users (customers). As a result, the board decided not to take any action to counteract the threat until it was too late. This is an important point for a board to remember, particularly, as was the case with Blackberry, when a business has been successful, results are strong and the future looks rosy. It is very easy for complacency to set in and for board members to be blind to the gathering storm clouds (the Invisible Gorilla syndrome we discussed in Chapter 1).

Box 6.4 provides some pointers towards the main people risks that should be found in the boardroom risk register:

Box 6.4   People Risks in the boardroom

(NB. Like the assessment of all risks, those below represent a list of gross risks without any mitigating actions attached. We would expect mitigating actions in place to reduce the assessment – probability and impact – thus leading to a net risk which would be judged as either acceptable or otherwise):

- failure to have an effective challenge process;

- overconfidence in decision-making;

- too much Groupthink in decision-making;

- failure to agree on the key risks in the organization;

- too much focus on recruiting new board members with the right competences rather than the right attitude;

- balance of board members (skills and attitudes) is not conducive to good boardroom dynamics and a healthy working environment;

- board members fail to speak up when they have a genuine concern;

- failure to have at least one constructive devil's advocate (this does not have to be the same person as there is a danger of alienation if it is);

- a Chairperson who fails to create effective boardroom dynamics;

- overly domineering and overly ambitious Chairperson or CEO;

- inadequate succession planning for the Chairperson and Executive roles;

- board collectively focuses too much on process rather than the substance of the discussion;

- decision-making is dominated by the CEO or the CEO and those who support him/her;

- failure of board members to live up to the values that they expect throughout the organization;

- sub-cultures within the organization are at odds with the organizational culture that the board desires;

- failure (by the Chairperson) to act when board dynamics are clearly not working.

6.8 Managing People Risk in the boardroom

Improving People Risk Management in the boardroom is as much about the right recruitment (particularly with the positions of Chairperson and CEO) as it is about making the right decisions. As we have illustrated earlier in this chapter, the human dynamics that operate both at a conscious and subconscious level are more important to having a successful board than ticking the governance process boxes. Achieving, and subsequently maintaining, the right boardroom dynamics begins with the recruitment of people with the right attitude and behaviours, people who want to join the board because they fundamentally care about the company, people who share the same corporate values and people who also have the requisite skills.

We have not touched on issues of gender in this section albeit that there are increasing calls for more women in the boardroom. This is not say that we do not recognize that women can and do have a valuable part to play in providing balance in the boardroom. For us, the issue is about having the right people, irrespective of their gender, in the right posts, who collectively will oversee the running of the firm for the benefit of all its stakeholders and, in doing so, help to mitigate against people risks in the boardroom. Clearly, our description of the typical CEO being an alpha male applies equally to women as it does to men.

There is no one right way of managing People Risk in the boardroom. The risk management process can be simplified into identification, evaluation and mitigation and there is no reason why those who have a direct (the board) or indirect (the Assurance functions) influence over People Risk cannot use this process to help improve the management of People Risk. Our experience suggests that the Assurance functions can find this a difficult area to deal with because it focuses on the risks of people and their personalities, and not just people but senior (or very senior) people in the organization. For example, providing evidence (rather than opinions) to assess whether the Chairperson is creating effective boardroom dynamics is not the easiest of things to do, so it goes without saying that tact, diplomacy and professionalism are required when working in this area. Clearly, external input can be used to help give a balanced view.

The Assurance functions, most notably Internal Audit and Risk Management, should have a role to play in providing assurance to the board that it is managing its own people risks. Both functions have similar roles in making sure the business is managing risk effectively with a particular focus on the key risks across the organization. The first step would be to ensure that the area of people risk is identified in the risk/audit universe and then, having established its significance – which we would argue is high because of the potential impact that board decisions can have on the business – audit and risk work can be planned accordingly. The process of reviewing the risk work that is carried out by the board could be done with external help to ensure that the right experience is available to assess what is a difficult and sensitive area.

In addition to the Board Behaviours Map described earlier in this chapter, there are other practical steps that can be taken to help manage People Risk in the boardroom:

1 All board members should be subject to specific personality tests[25] as a basis for ensuring a good cultural/behavioural fit as well as a rigorous interview process for new board members aimed at cross-checking personality traits.[26]

2 After every board meeting, there should be a quick 'temperature test' taken to see how directors felt about the board meeting: questions such as, what was the one good thing about the board meeting? What was the one bad thing? Did you feel you contributed enough? Do you have any concerns you did not express? This can be done privately or by way of a simple short questionnaire completed before the board member leaves the meeting.

3 There should be a clearly laid out policy concerning the length of tenure for directors. Whilst it may seem counter-intuitive to change directors when all is well, it should be a consideration when the director's contract is up for renewal.

4 The board should consider undertaking a regular *Values Audit* to ensure that the values of the business are in line with the values of individual directors. We shall return to this topic in Chapter 7.

5 Executive board directors should be encouraged to sit on the board of another business in a non-executive capacity to better empathize with the non-executive director role.

6 People Risk within the boardroom could be a standing item on the agenda so that directors have the opportunity to air their views and have them recorded in the minutes.

7 External reviews of board performance should be undertaken so that board members gain experience of how other boards/businesses operate.

8 The SID role recommended in the Financial Reporting Council guidance should include a specific responsibility for managing risk issues, and people risk issues in particular, within the boardroom, ie the guardian of the boardroom risk register.

9 More radically, we would call for board directors to be licensed and a professional body to be set up for non-executive directors to help drive up standards and behaviour.[27]

We will leave the final word of this chapter to Professor Roger Steare, Professor of Organizational Ethics at City University, writing in the Institute of Directors report on Business Risk.[28] Steare co-authored a submission to the UK Financial Reporting Council when a review was being undertaken of its UK Corporate Governance Code. The submission was seeking to address the character, judgement and behaviour of directors and boards:

> Character, judgement and behaviour are connected stages in a process. Character, or integrity, is the sum total of all our moral values and informs the behaviour of trusted adults. Good collective judgements and decisions are made when we consider not only legal rules and obligations (which should be regarded as the 'letter' of the law), but also how our values (the 'spirit' of the law) help us to decide fair and reasonable outcomes for all stakeholders. We must also acknowledge that this process will vary according to the situational context faced by boards. As a consequence, it is critically important not only that the behaviours of organizations are better understood, but that there are processes in place to monitor the environments in which they operate, particularly to identify those situations when rational human behaviour is most challenged.

We conclude that if processes are put in place to monitor the environments in which boards operate then the chances of another Royal Bank of Scotland type disaster happening again will be reduced.

This chapter has looked at people risk issues within the boardroom and how the interactions between board directors and the resultant board dynamics play a critical role in influencing the decisions that are made. Whilst good governance processes are necessary they do not on their own guarantee that mistakes will never be made. The board has a crucial role to play in managing People Risk not only within the boardroom itself but more broadly across the company. Much of this will come down to the organizational *culture* that is created by the board and we will look at this more closely in Chapter 7.

Notes

1 See Financial Services Authority (2012) *Failure of the Royal Bank of Scotland* and Chapter 4 for further references.

2 The RBS holding is held by UK Financial Investments Limited, which is 100 per cent owned by the UK Government (HM Treasury). Further information about the RBS and other holdings can be found at http://www.ukfi.co.uk/

3 See the claim by the Scottish Financial Enterprise, an industry body, at http://www.sfe.org.uk/Royal-Bank-of-Scotland-Group.aspx

4 See, for example, Hillson, D (2014) *Towards a Risk Maturity Model*, http://risk-doctor.com/pdf-files/rmm-mar97.pdf

5 See Nicholson, G and Kiel, G (2004) A framework for diagnosing board effectiveness, *Corporate Governance: An International Review*, **12** (4), pp 442–60.

6 See Beck and Watson (2011) Transforming board evaluations: the board maturity model, *Keeping Good Companies*, **63** (10), Nov 2011 pp 586–92.

7 See Marnet, O (2010) *Bias in the boardroom: effects of bias on the quality of decision-making*, Exeter University Business School, https://ore.exeter.ac.uk

8 See the Governance section of the 2012 Standard Chartered Annual Accounts at http://reports.standardchartered.com/

9 See Nicholson, G and Kiel, G (2004).

10 Simon, T and Peterson, R (2000) Task conflict and relationship conflict in top management teams: The pivotal role of intragroup trust, *Journal of Applied Psychology*, **85** (1), pp 102–11.

11 See Governance Matters (2010) *When disagreements get ugly: conflict in the boardroom*, Governance Matters, New York, www.governancematters.org

12 It is recognized that there are many other forms of company legal arrangements which may not involve shareholders. The point being made, however, is that the directors should have a common goal for the business: creating value for the stakeholders.

13 See Institute of Directors (2013) *Role of the Senior Independent Director*, Institute of Directors, London, www.iod.com

14 See Financial Reporting Council (2011).

15 See Myners, P (2014) *The Co-operative Group: Report of the Independent Governance Review*, www.co-operative.coop

16 See Roberts, J (2000) *On becoming chairman: building the complementary board, report prepared for Saxton Bampfylde Hever plc*, The Judge Institute of Management Studies, University of Cambridge, www.saxbam.com

17 We recognize that there is an inherent conflict of interest for the CEO who has to operate both as an executive (responsible for running the business) and a board member (overseeing the business) but this could be resolved by the Senior Independent Director who can act as an (independent) sounding board to make sure that such conflicts do not influence the CEO's decision-making on board matters.

18 See MWM Consulting (undated) *The behavioural drivers of board effectiveness: a practitioner's perspective*, MWM Consulting, London, www.mwmconsulting.com

19 In the animal kingdom the alpha male is seen as the dominant male in the pack. As a generalization, the alpha male is likely to have biases which manifest themselves particularly in overconfidence and be prone to using more System 1 (intuitive rather than reflective) thinking, as described by Kahneman (2011).

20 This statement is, of course, a generalization and some of the cases discussed in Chapter 4 demonstrate how alpha males are not always suited to being CEOs.

21 This did not, for example, appear to have happened with the Royal Bank of Scotland, Blackberry and Tesco cases discussed in Chapter 4.

22 See Manzoni, J F (2012) *The dysfunctional dynamics behind boardroom conflicts*, Pictet Report – Insead on boards, Winter, www.insead.edu

23 See Martin (2013).

24 See Turner (1976).

25 There are a range of personality tests that are used including numerical and verbal reasoning exercises, behavioural assessments, role plays and work-based case studies. Due diligence prior to the appointment of a director should not just be limited to these tests, however, and should be supplemented with background checks (medical, financial, criminal), reviews of social media sites as well as the normal rigorous interview process.

26 The disgraced chairman of the Co-operative Group (see Chapter 4), Paul Flowers, illustrates why personality tests should not be used in isolation as it was reported that he was given the job because he did well in such tests. See *Financial Times* (2014) Psychometric tests led Co-op Bank to make Paul Flowers chairman, 28 January, www.ft.com

27 A Non-Executive Director Association was set up in the UK in 2006 and whilst still embryonic, is a step in the right direction – see http://www.nedaglobal.com/

28 See Institute of Directors (2012) *Business Risk: a practical guide for board members*, Institute of Directors, London, www.iod.com

The influence of organizational culture

07

The most important question human beings can ask themselves is whether the world is a friendly or unfriendly place, for their answer to that question determines whether they spend their life building bridges or building walls. ALBERT EINSTEIN

KEY MESSAGES

- The mismatch of corporate values and personal values is perhaps the most pervasive problem facing companies today.

- If directors in the boardroom fail to set the right tone and ensure appropriate oversight, business becomes more of a game of chance.

- Organizational culture is a reflection of the personalities of those who lead and manage the business.

- A good risk culture will involve the organization maintaining a sense of vulnerability.

- Human nature is both part of the problem and part of the solution to embedding a risk culture.

- Trust is a value that can bind the people in the organization together, but it should never be taken for granted.

There are numerous books, articles and papers available on organizational culture and it is not our purpose in this chapter to discuss and analyse every aspect of culture and how it may impact on the management of People Risk. Rather, we intend to focus on those aspects that are important in helping to influence the softer side of risk management, ie the way that individuals behave in the workplace on a day-to-day basis and, as a result, how their actions or inactions may result in loss to the firm. We have seen in Chapter 3 the various biases that people exhibit in day-to-day organizational and social settings, and these behavioural traits are just one of the influences on corporate culture. But let's begin with a short vignette that highlights how culture influences behaviour and vice versa.

Imagine you are the CEO of a large multinational corporate and it is appraisal time. It's been a busy year and the business has had to cope with a large number of projects which have been necessary to help secure the future development plans of the organization. Amongst these are a number of e-commerce projects, all of which were due to be implemented in different parts of the business during the year. You decide to review a couple of the appraisals for two of the project managers, one of whom had implemented the system on time, while the other hadn't. Your selection criteria was based purely on project implementation (yes or no) without at this stage considering costings, impact upon the business, project outcomes or system performance. Box 7.1 provides you with the text of how each of the project managers sums up their performance:[1]

Box 7.1   The case of the two project managers

The Risk Taker

'Well, I know that we had to cut a few corners on the way to making this project a great success but if you were in my shoes you would have done exactly the same. Let's not forget, we managed to implement the new e-commerce system in just 12 months and nobody believed we could do it. A few customers may not return as we continue to iron out the remaining bugs but the fact that turnover is rising proves it was the right thing to do. I realize that the paperwork is behind and the press picked up on the teething problems we initially had but let's not forget that the team were working seven days a week for the best part of six months to get this system up and running. Despite the problems, I know the company will be pleased with the admittedly lower than expected profit we're now generating and I'm looking forward to a significant bonus.'

The Risk Manager

'Whilst I appreciate that we are six months behind schedule with our implementation of the e-commerce system, we need to see this in context and look at the bigger picture. The most recent survey of the project team illustrated how highly motivated the staff are, with all of the training schedules fully met and the project documentation being marked as excellent by the Quality Assurance team. This demonstrates great commitment on their part and will help to mitigate against problems when we eventually go live. Most importantly, we are fully compliant with the recently introduced corporate guidelines on home/work/lifestyle balance and are the first project team across the whole group to achieve this. Despite our being behind schedule, I know the company will be pleased with all the hard work and effort we have put in and I'm looking forward to a significant bonus.'

So, what would drive the two project managers to display completely different behaviours in the same organization? Certainly, the project objectives that each were set (which may have been conflicting). Or maybe they were being influenced by their interpretation of the culture of the business and how things get done in the organization or their part of the organization? As CEO, and the person who can have most influence the culture, you have to ask yourself whether you would prefer to have Risk Takers or Risk Managers running projects.[2] Who do you think deserves a bonus?

This is, of course, a hypothetical example to illustrate a point and the reality in most organizations is unlikely to be as black and white as this situation. As regards the question of who deserves a bonus, there is no right or wrong answer and our purpose was to use this example to illustrate how culture can influence People Risk across an organization.

7.1 Culture in context

When it comes to risk management, *Corporate Culture* matters. In fact, it matters a lot and this is an important message for frontline managers to understand. It matters because if culture is not actively managed, it can create a climate in which risks, and people risks in particular, can emerge and grow until they manifest themselves in the events and consequences discussed in the case studies in Chapter 4. There are numerous examples of where the word 'culture' has been used as a reason why a major disaster has happened. For example, in Box 7.2 we provide a brief vignette on the Columbia Space Shuttle Disaster and the impact of culture on the events that took place.[3]

Box 7.2   The Columbia Space Shuttle Disaster

On 1 February 2003, space shuttle Columbia broke up as it returned to Earth killing all seven astronauts on board. The Columbia Accident Investigation Board (CAIB) determined that a large piece of foam fell from the shuttle's external tank and fatally breached the spacecraft's wing. The piece of foam became dislodged when the flight took off but the degree of damage was not considered serious enough to warrant any further intervention. This problem with foam had been known for years, and the National Aeronautics and Space Administration (NASA) came under intense scrutiny in the US Congress and in the media for allowing the situation to continue.

The CAIB investigated the disaster over a seven-month period and produced a detailed report which pointed out that several factors of the NASA culture, which were detrimental to safety, had a direct impact on the failure of the Columbia Space Shuttle in 2003:

- reliance on past success as a substitute for sound engineering practices;

- organizational barriers that prevented effective communication of critical safety information and stifled professional differences of opinion;

- lack of integrated management across programme elements;

- the evolution of an informal chain of command and decision-making processes that operated outside the organization's rules.

It would appear that over a period of time the people in NASA had shifted the 'safety culture' norms, allowing bad practices to creep in and undermine the efforts of decision-makers who thought they were doing what was right for the Space Shuttle Program.

Sending a complex and large man-made object into space is, however, inherently risky and it is perhaps hard to imagine how anybody who worked for NASA could not put safety, or more generally managing safety risk, as their number one priority. But the report points out several factors at play at the time that were having a negative effect on the culture within NASA. These included:

- Organizations with strong safety cultures generally acknowledge that a leader's best response to unanimous consent is to play devil's advocate and encourage an exhaustive debate. The Mission Management Team leaders failed to seek out such minority opinions.

- Organizations that deal with high-risk operations must always have a healthy fear of failure – operations must be proved safe, rather than the other way around. NASA inverted this burden of proof.

- The Shuttle Program's complex structure erected barriers to effective communication and its safety culture shifted such that hard questions about risk were not being asked.

- The detection of the dangers posed by foam (a leakage of foam was the technical cause of the accident) was impeded by 'blind spots' in NASA's safety culture.

- Whilst NASA emphasizes safety, its training programmes are not robust and methods of learning from past failures are informal.

- The intellectual curiosity and scepticism that a solid safety culture requires were almost entirely absent. Shuttle managers did not embrace safety-conscious attitudes. Instead, their attitudes were shaped and reinforced by an organization that, in this instance, was incapable of stepping back and gauging its biases. Bureaucracy and process trumped thoroughness and reason.

The reader will note how the human aspects of risk, including biases and blind spots, were cited as being part of the problem of not having a strong safety culture.

There are many technical aspects that were part of the causes of the Space Shuttle Disaster. The root cause, however, goes further back than just the technical issues, which in any event can be traced back to individuals doing something wrong (People Risk). The real issue at NASA was organizational culture, and in particular safety culture and how the pendulum of accepted norms and beliefs had been allowed to swing from good to bad.

So where is the starting point for sowing the seeds and nurturing and growing a good organizational culture in the corporate petri dish? Professor Mervyn King, who chaired the King Committee on corporate governance in South Africa, made the point[4] that it was alright to talk about the 'tone at the top' of the organization (driving culture), but the key thing was to listen to the 'tune in the middle'. There can be no doubt that the culture of an organization is influenced by factors outside of the business such as regulation, the industry in which the business operates and the competitive environment, but the response to these influences is determined, first and foremost, in the boardroom. The board has a crucial role in determining not only culture but also the values that drive it. But it doesn't end there. Indeed, how the board 'walk the talk' and ensure that the cultural characteristics they expect are translated into 'playing the same tune' by the senior management, who in turn should be listening to 'the song on the shop floor', are critical elements in engraining the desired culture throughout the business.

Like risk, culture is a complex topic. Intangible in nature, it can be a difficult concept to grasp and an equally difficult thing to talk about with any degree of certainty or accuracy when relating it to a particular organization. The raw material of organizational culture includes the attitudes and beliefs (of the people), the norms and policies, the way that things get done, the 'taken for granted' assumptions (of the people) and the social and business practices. It is influenced heavily by the values of the individuals in the organization who, by their actions or inactions, provide a window into the organizational culture through which the outside world can peer and assess what makes the business tick. Ultimately, as the evidence from previous risk management incidents demonstrates, it influences the way that people behave both positively and negatively.

A number of models of organizational culture have been developed that provide organizations with tools with which they can analyse and interpret their own cultural characteristics as a basis for making changes to where they are now and where they would like to be in the future. Based on comprehensive research into corporate effectiveness, Professors Kim Cameron and Robert Quinn[5] developed a *Competing Values Framework* which synthesizes corporate differences in two main dimensions: (i) stability versus flexibility – does the organization prefer stability and control over flexibility and individuality in the way that it operates?; and (ii) internal versus external focus – is the organization inward- or outward-looking in its focus? They went further and identified four main cultural types based on the dimensions identified thus:

1 **Hierarchy – Do Things Right** (Internal Focus versus Stability)
    An organization that values stability and control, formalized structures and rules and internal efficiency, with a focus on the organization itself, and often exemplified as a 'bureaucratic' culture. In banking terms, this might be typified by credit card operations or a mortgage-processing unit.

2 **Clan – Do Things Together** (Internal Focus versus Flexibility)
    An organization that values collaboration, participation and teamwork, with a focus on individuals, and often exemplified as a 'family' culture. In banking terms, this might be typified by a merchant banking group or an audit, compliance or risk management function.

3 **Market – Do Things Fast** (External Focus versus Stability)
    An organization that values competition, market share and profitability, with a focus on transactions with external parties, and often exemplified as a 'results-oriented' culture. In banking terms, this might be typified by trading units and sales functions.

4 **Adhocracy – Do Things First** (External Focus versus First)
    An organization that values innovation, risk-taking and creativity, with a focus on creating new products for external parties, and often exemplified as an 'entrepreneurial' culture. In banking terms, this might be typified by a Mergers and Acquisitions (M&A) group.

It should be noted that these dimensions are not absolutes but are a spectrum and within one part of the organization there may be different sub-cultures, some of which may be quite different from the organizational culture being driven down from the board. For example, a trading and sales group will be primarily 'market focused' but may include high-volume Foreign Exchange market making (with an emphasis on control and efficiency) and specialist derivatives units (with an emphasis on creativity and new products). These sub-cultures would, therefore, espouse different cultural values and norms and there is an inherent danger that the areas involved may develop an 'ivory tower' approach and become marginalized and seen as 'different from the rest of us'. In addition the organization is at risk if the culture espoused by a board is not the actual culture in the firm. 'What we say is not what we do' will create mixed messages for staff about how they should behave. As a result, culture needs to be 'espoused' by management through, for example, consistency of actions, treating people fairly, rewarding appropriate behaviour and codes of conduct that support the desired culture.

The organizational culture types described by Cameron and Quinn, together with the sub-cultures within them, are likely to contain different degrees of inherent People Risk. The hierarchical 'Do Things Right' culture will drive behaviours in people to conform or suffer the consequences if they don't. The adhocracy, 'Do Things First' culture encourages people to step outside the boundaries and perform actions that may cause losses. Both of these behaviours, however, represent intentional acts and are being driven by the culture rather than being impeded by it. Running across all the cultural types are the unintentional or deliberate acts of individuals that may cause harm to the company. In other words, no one culture can, on its own, prevent People Risk events from happening.

For example, the final report of the Banking Standards Review[6] headed by Sir Richard Lambert calls upon UK banks and building societies to create a new organization which will have as its objective 'to contribute to a continuous improvement in the behaviour and competence of banks and building societies doing business in the UK'. It would be responsible for 'setting standards of good practice' which would include, inter alia, establishing procedures for 'whistleblowing protocols' or 'the approach to retail sales incentives'. The clear aim is to influence the culture of banking operations by setting out what good behaviour looks like and establishing metrics that will enable firms in the sector to be able to benchmark themselves against their peers. One particular aspect of Lambert's consultation paper, which goes to the heart of People Risk, is ethics/conduct and the report envisages the new organization will help to 'identify and encourage good practice in learning, development and leadership, with a particular focus on behaviour and ethics'. Lambert recognizes that there will be challenges to be overcome in setting up this body (which will be funded by the banks themselves) but he sees it as an important step to winning back public trust and confidence in an industry which has been rocked by a series of scandals, a number of which we have illustrated in Chapter 4.

Ethical conduct and the way it is influenced by culture was at the heart of the Woolf Committee report[7] which looked at BAE systems (see Chapter 4.5.11). The report was produced in 2008 after a series of damaging allegations were made against the company and its conduct and reputation came under close scrutiny. The report lists 23 recommendations which describe how BAE could 'embed a more open and transparent culture' through 'strengthening its policies and procedures in key areas of ethical risk'. Whilst these recommendations are focused on BAE, we believe that they provide a useful checklist for other organizations to use to assess their own approach to culture, conduct and ethics. Two of the recommendations that particularly address People Risk issues are:

- The company should develop formal processes to ensure business decisions are only taken following an explicit consideration of ethical and reputational risks. Where such risks are identified, the process should ensure any decision to proceed is taken at the appropriate level, and should include ratification by the board.

- A well-resourced training programme, in which every person in the company participates, should be undertaken as part of the implementation of the global code and revised and repeated at regular intervals. Specific training modules should also be developed for senior executives and business unit leaders. Systems for monitoring these programmes should be developed so that they are able to provide the necessary assurance to the CRC (Corporate Responsibility Committee) as to their effectiveness.

7.2 Understanding risk culture

Risk culture is a subset of organizational culture to the extent that it focuses on one area of the business operations. In this sense it is no different from safety culture, cost-cutting culture, sales culture or governance culture. However, the implementation of an appropriate risk culture, or any other sub-culture, depends on having the right organizational culture in the first place and many of the drivers of having a good risk culture, such as board commitment, will equally apply to organizational culture.[8]

There are a number of definitions that describe what is meant by a *Risk Culture*. Here are two of them:

1 David Millar, COO of PRMIA (The Professional Risk Managers International Association).[9]

A risk culture is the sum of the individual and corporate values, attitudes, competencies and behaviours that determine commitment to and style of risk management:

● it includes both risk and the response to risk, ie mitigation tactics;
● it requires clear lines of responsibility, segregation of duties and effective internal reporting;
● it requires high standards of ethical behaviour at all levels;
● although a framework of formal, written policies and procedures is critical, it needs to be reinforced through a strong control culture;
● it is the responsibility of both the board and senior management.

2 The Institute of International Finance (IIF).[10]

The norms and traditions of behaviour of individuals and of groups within an organization that determine the way in which they identify, understand, discuss, and act on the risks the organization confronts and the risks it takes.

Unsurprisingly, there are features common to both of them and, as can be seen, there is a link back to organizational culture with use of the word 'behaviours'. The PRMIA definition also contains an important component of the Risk Management Framework when it talks about response to risk and having a strong control culture in place. This is touched on by the IIF with the words 'act on the risks' but given that controls are an important risk mitigation tactic, the PRMIA definition looks to better articulate what we mean by risk culture.

One element of risk culture that is not mentioned relates to the reaction of the business when things go wrong, as inevitably they will at some stage. This is, of course, People Risk in action. So how should the business react when a person causes a loss or harm to the company? The answer: it depends. Clearly, where the intent was deliberate and the consequences large then punitive action will undoubtedly be taken. But in the case of mistakes caused by human error the action may well be different. The oft quoted 'no blame' culture may well be used at this point although we are of the opinion that this mantra serves no useful purpose because it is too black and white and no blame is very unlikely to mean no blame on every single occasion. Better to use the words 'fair culture' or 'just culture' which recognizes that people are fallible and do make mistakes. As an example of this, it is common in the airline industry for pilots and other staff to log mistakes that are made, knowing that they will not be punished.[11] The mistakes are used to inform and change training programmes.

What are the things that make a good risk culture, ie a culture that helps *all* staff to understand the importance of risk within the organization? In short, many things, some of which we illustrate in Box 7.3.

Box 7.3   What makes a good risk culture?

- A committed board and senior management who recognize that risk management is a core competence of the business and not something that is delegated to the risk manager(s).

- A board that is not complacent about things going wrong and maintains a sense of vulnerability. This is a particularly important concept because it requires the board to recognize the risk of complacency setting in when things are going right.[12]

- A recognition that risk management is not just a regulatory requirement but an essential element to achieving business success.

- No witch hunts when things go wrong or when people whistleblow, ie the matter is treated 'fairly and justly'.

- A challenge process about risk management matters that is actively encouraged.

- Clear risk policies, processes, responsibilities and so on, ie all the hard factors of risk management are in place.

- Appropriate HR practices that recognize good risk management practices and address bad ones.

- A good 'risk radar' that is constantly monitoring the internal and external environment for things that could go wrong.

- Shared values vis-à-vis risk management (we shall return to the subject of values later in this chapter).

All of these factors will help to inculcate the importance of risk management across the organization, which in turn will drive behaviours aimed to mitigate People Risk. These behaviours can be reinforced at *all* levels in the organization by taking active steps to ensure that people understand the part they have to play in managing risk. This is no more so than when it comes to individuals making decisions, even mundane ones, where risk is an important element that *always* needs to be considered. Just as marketing is everybody's business, so too is risk management. Here are some of the things that you would expect the people across the organization to know whether it be members of staff, senior management or the board:

- their own risk responsibilities (as spelled out in the Job Description or Personalized Code of Conduct, see Chapter 10);
- how they report risk events (and what happens to them when they've been reported);
- how not managing risk in their job can impact upon the business;
- how a risk may be mitigated using controls or other mitigants such as transferring the risk through insurance;
- what a control is (we discuss this further in Chapter 8);
- the organization's Risk Policy;
- the organization's Risk Appetite and tolerance for risk;
- how to champion risk management throughout the business.

Some organizations may, of course, require staff to have awareness of the risk policy and risk appetite and our point here is merely to provide the reader with what we would see as minimum requirements.

Having a good risk culture in place will not prevent People Risk events from occurring – all it can hope to do is reduce their likelihood (to as close to zero as possible). This raises the question as to what is going to cause an event to take place and is there anything further that can be done to prevent it? We are, of course, discussing people, their fallibilities, their foibles and those 'hard to control things' that influence the way they behave at certain times. We all have bad days, we all miss things, we all avoid things, we all fear things, we are after all human. The best we can hope to do is to recognize that mistakes are more likely to be made when individuals (or groups of individuals):

- are overworked or underworked;
- are tired;
- are stressed;
- are overconfident or underconfident;
- are forgetful;
- are complacent;
- are in the wrong job;
- have been promoted above their level of competence;
- have problems at home;
- have different priorities (to doing their work).

And doubtless there are many more that can be added to the list.

In looking at risk culture, we must not lose sight of the risk-taking side of risk management. Businesses must take risks to grow. The future is uncertain: launching a new product may be a great success or it may be a great failure, and whilst steps can be taken to reduce the likelihood of failure, it can never be eliminated. Organizations that have an external focus as illustrated in the Competing Values Framework model[13] will have a greater propensity to take risks than those whose focus is internal. It is worth noting, however, that risk-taking has to go hand in hand with risk managing. For example, power plants have to take huge risks to deliver the appropriate service but they equally have to manage risks in extraordinary detail to minimize the likelihood of something bad happening.

Fear of risk-taking can be particularly debilitating in organizations especially if you are a person who likes to take risks but find yourself working in a Hierarchical culture. Equally, if you are the risk-averse type you may struggle to work in an Adhocracy culture where risk-taking is positively welcomed and encouraged. Figure 7.1 illustrates how we all have an appetite for taking risks whether we are very risk-averse or very risk-seeking. Our appetite is influenced by, amongst other things, the type of job we have to do, the environment in which we work, the nature and scale of decisions that we have to make, the state of mind we are in at the time and our biases. This is not to say that we are permanently fixed at one point on the continuum and the circumstances described in the previous sentence may cause us to become more adventurous or more risk-averse when faced with a risky decision. We have mentioned the Royal Bank of Scotland case study on a number of occasions and we consider that its former CEO Fred Goodwin demonstrated both ends of the spectrum. On the one hand he was involved with the minutiae of detail within the bank, whilst on the other he was pushing hard on the ABN AMRO acquisition with little regard to thorough due diligence.[14]

FIGURE 7.1   The continuum of risk-taking

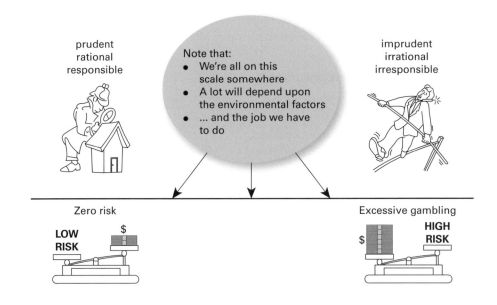

Within very large businesses, the organizational appetite for risk-taking can be sub-stituted with a departmental appetite. Thus, in Assurance functions for example, you would expect to see a low tolerance for risk-taking matched by people who are equally control-tolerant. By the very nature of what they do, bank trading operations will have exactly the opposite profile. Auditing a trading desk is never going to be an easy task for the internal auditor and his/her low tolerance for risk! The challenge for the board and senior management is to manage these inherent tensions by sup-porting the need for effective controls and ensuring risk management frameworks are in place *at all times* in the trading business. As we illustrated in Chapter 4, rogue traders, together with the invisible factors that make up the culture of the organization, can create havoc, cause huge losses and even bring a company down if their actions are not properly checked.

Whilst aligning risk appetites in this way creates an environment in which indi-viduals will feel comfortable, it must be noted that this type of utopian organization is unlikely to be found in practice. Indeed, every organization is likely to benefit from having individuals who lean towards being Risk Takers/Risk Managers when it comes to risk management. Why? Imagine the organization is a car and the accelerator pedal represents the business moving forward and taking risks whilst the brake pedal represents the business holding back and managing risks. If you are going to drive the car well, you need both pedals to work and people to operate them. Try driving a car without a brake pedal and you will appreciate why Risk Managers are important!

So, where should the development of a risk culture fit into the priorities of the business and, in particular, the board? 'Culture eats strategy for breakfast.' This quote, attributed to management guru Peter Drucker,[15] can be interpreted, in the context of managing risk, as putting the characters, judgements and behaviours of people first and the processes that they have to follow second. In this context 'people' includes not just individuals acting on their own but the social groups, such as the board, that exist in the workplace. Get the (risk) culture right, make sure it stays right and the business will improve its chances of achieving its strategy and creating value for its stakeholders.

7.3 Embedding a risk culture

Our brief tour into the conceptual world of culture and risk culture has focused on analysing the various facets that make up the cultural characteristics of an organiza-tion. As human beings, we like to analyse things, especially things that have gone wrong (risk events), as it satisfies our curiosity to understand (and maybe apportion blame) as a precursor for making sure those things don't happen again. Whilst hind-sight may be an exact science, foresight certainly isn't. In fact, the application of hindsight requires an element of foresight because as the saying goes, 'past performance is not necessarily a guide to the future'. Witness the rogue trader incidents over the last 20 years: Barings, Allied Irish Bank, National Australia Bank, Société Générale and JPMorgan. The common characteristics were that they were all headlined as rogue trader events, they were all in the public domain, they all had large financial losses, they all had opportunities to be prevented and they were all committed by the actions of people 'not doing what they should have been doing'. There were the usual cries of, 'we mustn't let this happen again' coming from a wide range of people who had an interest in the crises. But as history has proven these are empty words and we are sure that it will continue to happen, particularly to those banks who do not remain vigilant and accept that they will always be vulnerable to rogue traders. There is no such thing as a risk-free environment, especially when that environment contains people.

Whilst no two incidents will ever be exactly the same (for example, the National Australia Bank involved collusion between employees) these rogue trader events indicate that we are not good at learning 'with the benefit of hindsight'. This is a theme taken up by Professor Brian Toft and Simon Reynolds, who in their book[16] *Learning from Disasters* provide scores of examples of incidents with isomorphic qualities.[17] In failing to recognize the isomorphic qualities possessed by two or more events we are missing an opportunity to prevent or at least minimize the risk of another similar incident occurring. Box 7.4 provides an example of incidents with isomorphic qualities that had loss of life consequences.

Box 7.4   Nightclub disasters

On 27 January 2013 at 2.00am in Santa Maria, Rio Grande do Sul, Brazil a fire swept through the Kiss Night Club killing 242 people and injuring 168 others. The fire started when the band Gurizada Fandangueira ignited a pyrotechnic device (similar to a signalling flare) whilst performing on stage. The flare ignited the highly flammable acoustic foam in the ceiling causing panic amongst the audience. The high death toll was also attributed to the lack of emergency exits and the fact that the number of people inside exceeded the maximum capacity (by hundreds). The two nightclub owners and two members of the band were subsequently charged with manslaughter. This incident is tragic enough on its own but when a review of other nightclub fires is undertaken with similar causes, it highlights how unnecessary these deaths were:

a The Station nightclub fire (2003), West Warwick, Rhode Island, United States – 100 people killed when a pyrotechnic device was set off.

b The Republica Cromanon nightclub fire (2004), Buenos Aires, Brazil – 194 people killed when a pyrotechnic device was set off. Four of the six emergency exit doors were chained shut.

c Lame Horse nightclub fire (2009), Perm, Russia – 150 people killed when a pyrotechnic device was set off. Emergency exits were reported as not being adequately lit.

We can only hope that there is now a blanket ban on the use of pyrotechnic devices in nightclubs across the world (learning from hindsight) and that nightclubs ensure that they look at the other risks which might cause a fire to break out (foresight).

The reader may wish to speculate on the extent to which businesses such as nightclubs have adequate risk management systems and an appropriate risk culture in place but the point that these and other tragic incidents highlight is that embedding such a culture (the soft side of risk management) and processes (the hard side of risk management) will take time, effort and commitment from the top of the organization. If the organization has a learning disability and fails to explore potential new sources of risk (or return for that matter) from the experience of others then it will remain constantly exposed to threats, particularly those caused by people. This is, of course, a good argument for having regulation in place to help drive the right behaviours.

Embedding a risk culture means risk becoming a sixth sense in people's minds. Risk management becomes second nature and a normal and natural thing to do. People understand risk, they perceive the dangers of what they might do and they act accordingly. Their 'sixth sense' compass kicks in when faced with a risky decision and they just *know* what is best for their organization. We will return to this subject more in Chapters 9 and 10 when we discuss Personalized Codes of Conduct and decision-making.

Aside from learning from others' mistakes, there are other practical steps that can help to embed a risk culture across the organization and influence people's behaviour. We have listed these in Box 7.5 structured by:

Corporate Governance: steps that relate to the overall governance of the organization.

Risk Governance: steps that relate specifically to the management of risk across the organization.

Risk Process: steps that relate to the identification, evaluation and mitigation of risk across the organization.

Box 7.5   Embedding a risk culture: practical steps

Corporate Governance

- Recruitment – recruitment criteria should seek to establish how people react in risky situations relative to the job that they have to do. For example, questions could be asked about how the person would deal with a situation where a colleague has left their computer password in easy view of their desk.

- Accountability – make people accountable for the risks they take and the risks they manage. This can be done by including such accountabilities in individual job descriptions and in performance appraisals.

- Decision-making – all major decisions should have a risk/reward profile presented to help inform the decision. A checklist approach to making sure all the relevant criteria have been included can be used with the risk section picking up the range of risks relevant to the company and the business sector in which it operates.

- Trust – make sure employees are motivated by trust rather than being driven by fear and check to establish that this is the way that they feel about the company through (ongoing) staff surveys.

Risk Governance

- Champion(s) – make sure that the organization has a risk management expert on the board who, with the rest of the board members, will help champion the need for risk management around the organization.

- Training – doing the right thing when it comes to risk involves training people in knowing what the right thing to do is. The trainers should be a mixture of external people, who can bring in the outside view, and internal people who know how the organization works. The training should cover the basic principles of risk management, reporting risk incidents and case studies on good and bad risk management.

- Maturity – there are a number of risk maturity models around that assess how mature an organization is vis-à-vis risk management. These can be used to identify weak spots and improve risk management.

- Behaviours – be very clear about the actions and behaviours that are off limits when it comes to risks, for example, no taking short cuts when it comes to prescribed processes.

Risk Process

- Communication – excellent and open communication around the business about risk-related matters. This is particularly important in the context of risk incidents where staff should be actively encouraged to report anything that happens.

- Controls – make sure people understand the nature and purpose of controls and when a preventative control has worked to stop a major event happening, why not celebrate? This can be achieved as part of the training programme mentioned above.

A good risk culture can act both as a precondition for managing People Risk and as an oversight mechanism for monitoring risks that may be incubating. Embedding such a culture takes time and effort starting with the board and then moving to others down the line, ie the tone at the top drives the tune in the middle which creates the song on the shop floor.

7.4 Values

Our previous discussions in this chapter have used the word 'values' without giving any clear indication of what it means in either the personal or organizational context. In his book, *Liberating the Corporate Soul*, Richard Barrett[18] described values as being the 'rules for living'. He goes on to say that they are 'deeply held beliefs that a certain way of being or a certain outcome is preferable to another. Values are externally demonstrated through behaviours.' Values thus apply at an individual level, a group level, a company level and even at a national (country) level. Core values at the individual level can work through the chain to be company/national values and where such values are shared between the individual and the company/nation, the individual is likely to feel more contented working in the company they are in and living in the country where they live. This is illustrated in Figure 7.2 which we have developed to illustrate with a sample of values and how they may overlap.

Sharing values in this way is seen as an essential building block of creating *Trust* throughout the organization (and for that matter the nation).

'Values' has become an important word in the corporate lexicon over the last few years and it is now considered normal practice for companies to publicly espouse 'what they stand for' as a way of demonstrating commitment to being a good corporate citizen. Box 7.6 illustrates three examples of *Corporate Value Statements* that can be found on the internet.[19] The organizations in question were chosen to represent two large multinational businesses and a small national organization and are from different parts of the world.

FIGURE 7.2   The sharing of values

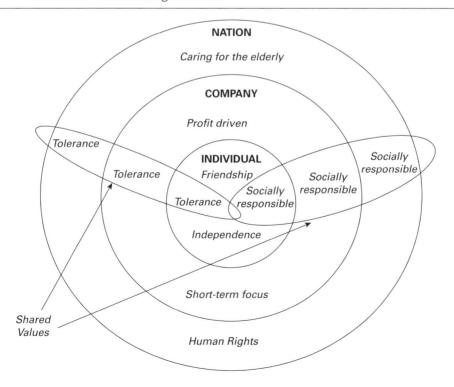

Box 7.6 Examples of Corporate Value Statements

Johnson Controls (a US globally diversified technology and industrial business). Values have strengthened our organization, shaped our culture and guided behaviour on the job for more than 125 years. These values support our 10-Year Marker, a set of strategic guideposts for operating our businesses to achieve long-term success. We expect the company's values to be followed at all times across Johnson Controls:

- Integrity
- Customer Satisfaction
- Employee Engagement
- Innovation
- Sustainability

(NB. A brief description of each of the values is provided)

Bosch (a German global supplier of technology and services) has always been a value-driven company. Many of our values can be traced back to our founder Robert Bosch, while other values have changed or have arisen over the decades. Now we have put our guiding values in writing. Our values reflect the manner in which we run our business and our professional ethics in dealing with our business partners, investors, employees and society:

- Future and Result Focus
- Initiative and Determination
- Openness and Trust
- Fairness
- Reliability, Credibility and Legality
- Cultural Diversity

(NB. A brief description of each of the values is provided)

Quitline (a New Zealand charity dedicated to help New Zealanders quit smoking): we are committed to making a positive difference by living our values:

- Client focus
- Excellence
- Trust
- Support
- Communication

(NB. A brief description of each of the values is provided)

These three examples highlight a number of points about these Value Statements:

1 values are inextricably linked to, and influence, culture and behaviour;
2 values may change over time;
3 companies can use the same value statements irrespective of the nature and size of the business and where in the world they operate;
4 values provide the corporate glue which binds the people in the organization together;
5 the people in the organization are expected to live up to the values at all times when working in the corporate environment.

Whilst these organizations were selected to show the commonality that exists in value statements and to illustrate the five points above, other organizations could equally have been used. The point that we are illustrating is that values are now made explicit and are meant to characterize how the organization, or more precisely the people within the organization, will behave.

The last point in our list, that of people living up to the values at all times, is particularly interesting and, whilst it is overtly stated by two of the organizations, we believe that all organizations would expect their people to embrace the shared values quoted in their values statements. The question arises as to whether this expectation is monitored to ensure there remains a close correlation between the personal values of the individual and the values of the company. Barrett[20] noted that the mismatch of corporate values and personal values is perhaps the most pervasive problem facing companies today. This mismatch is a risk in any organization and deserves to be included in the organizational risk register and monitored accordingly.

As is evident from the examples in Box 7.6, the words used to describe the values represent underlying concepts, each of which is further explained so that what is meant by the concept is clear. For example, Bosch has a value of fairness which is described as, 'we view mutual fairness as a condition of our corporate success when dealing with each other and with our business partners'. Defining fairness by using the word fairness may not be particularly helpful but it nonetheless indicates that Bosch see fairness as something they *expect* their employees to practice both internally and externally. At a personal level our values are those things that are important to us at a particular moment in time so that as we grow older and wiser our values may change, as do the things that matter and make us feel contented. So particular values will start to appear on the horizon as we move forward on life's pathway and we decide whether they are important to us or not. A good example would be financial stability, which tends to be seen as a more important value as we grow older. Whilst some of our values may change or shift in priority, other values remain fixed. Barrett refers to these as our *Core Values*. They are often established early in our lives and may always remain important to us. They can also be important in binding people who may have other differing values. Take, for example, the inter-generational gap and the 'rules for living' between a teenager and a senior citizen. As a generalization, the former will have a different outlook on life to the latter and this may be reflected in the way they behave in an organizational environment. If, however, both sides have 'respect' and 'trust' as core values, these can help to bring older and younger generations together even if they have otherwise different values.

Another important aspect of values is that they can be either positive or potentially limiting. Potentially limiting values usually have a negative physical or emotional effect on our lives. Examples of potentially limiting values include: blame, crime/violence, hierarchy, inequality and unemployment. The use of the word 'potentially' is important here because not everybody will see crime/violence as limiting if that is their chosen profession!

Are there any practical steps that organizations can take to help instil their core values into the hearts and minds of their people? Aside from undertaking a values audit, Andrew Forrest, together with three other researchers from Cass Business School in London identified a number of factors to help embed values within an organization.[21] Their work[22] was carried out in 2011 and involved surveying organizations that encompassed over a quarter of a million volunteers in the Charities sector. Whilst limited to this sector, the results could equally apply to any business. Here is what they had to say:

> Looking right across all the data this survey produced, there is no one model that fits every organization. But there are some clear messages as illustrated below (the words in italics are quotes from survey participants):

> ● When producing a list of values, consult widely – not just with employees or the board but also with volunteers and beneficiaries.
> *'Take time to identify them clearly, but then do not tinker.'*

> ● Use simple, memorable language that points clearly to taking action in day-to-day work (the reader may note that the values highlighted in Box 7.6 are not expressed in this way nor are they stated as outcomes).
> *'State them as outcomes.'*

> ● The way in which values are used may vary from one team to another within your organization. They should be kept fresh through regular conversations.
> *'Share the good stories that show what a difference your values make.'*

> ● Most charities use regular 1:1s within a performance management system as a method of checking on the values' implementation. Some charities bring them into a competency framework.
> *'The values maximize the ability to empower individuals.'*

> ● Use values to re-energize your people.
> *'I do not think we could have survived the past few years without having had these in place... The attitude that we have now, rather than that of even five years ago has seen us through.'*

> ● Some organizations find it useful to consider both the internal and external impact of values.
> *'We have externally published values that communicate our core beliefs. We also have cultural values that describe the behaviours we want to exhibit.'*

> ● Do not 'police' the values too closely.
> *'There's been five years of spreading the values gently, so everyone's not necessarily living them, but conversations about the values have led to improvement and adopted behaviours.'*

> ● The Senior Management Team[23] must not only help to create the values but must be seen as role models for them.
> *'Authentic and genuine commitment from the Senior Management Team.'*

Values are an important element in the People Risk equation. A person who does not share the same personal values as the organization's core values is likely to be a greater risk than one who does and in terms of managing People Risk, it would suggest that managing such people is where the focus should lie. Of course, it would be better all round if such people were working in an organization where their respective values were closely aligned but that may not always be possible. In a similar vein, organizational values may not always be right (see for example the Enron case in Chapter 4) and we believe employees have a duty of personal responsibility to challenge this (we shall return to this subject in Chapter 10).

Another area to monitor is where the predominant values in sub-cultures are at odds with the core values of the organization. Large multinational organizations, for example, need to be cognizant of this in countries where bribes and corruption are seen as the normal way of doing business.

7.5 Trust

One value that is deeply embedded in organizational culture and is an important ingredient of People Risk is *Trust*. We discussed trust in the first chapter of this book and highlighted how we believe that it is important to try and recognize the possibility that there are individuals in the organization who we may trust but who may equally not be doing what they are supposed to be doing. The old adage, 'In God we trust, everyone else we audit' applies to this situation.

Trust is not only a value in itself, but a sense of trust is created by having shared values throughout the organization. Trust breeds trust.[24] Trust is very much a personal thing that describes how people relate to one another and, in an organizational context, the extent to which they are prepared to work together, share information and discuss matters pertaining to the business. It is partly driven by emotions (I like this person so I trust him) and partly by logic (this person has given me what I asked for, when I asked for it and, therefore, I can trust him to do it again). The more you like the person and the more they do things that you like, the greater your propensity to trust them. It is a judgement call that may turn out to be wrong, of course, if that person lets you down. So trust has to be earned, and it can quickly disappear, leading to distrust and a souring of relationships.

Further evidence of the importance of trust in a cultural context can be found by the use of so-called 'trust indexes' which are designed to assess how much trust employees have in their employers. Robert Levering, co-author of the *100 Best Companies to Work for in America*,[25] has developed one such index and the survey he uses is divided into five dimensions, all of which are themselves values – *credibility, respect, fairness, pride and camaraderie*. Figure 7.3 illustrates the linkages that Levering developed.

The diagram illustrates how an employee's *trust* with Management is built around the three core values of *credibility, fairness and respect*. In turn, building this relationship assists the employee in building relationships with other colleagues in the organization (developing a feeling of *camaraderie*) and a relationship with the job that they do (developing a feeling of *pride* in the work that they do). This model of

FIGURE 7.3 The five dimensions of trust (from Levering)

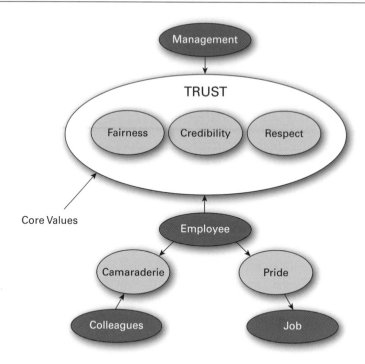

trust serves to illustrate how it is an essential element for building teams and team-work across the organization – the feeling of camaraderie becomes pervasive and binds people together in working for the company and one another. Conversely a lack of trust implies issues with the five dimensions: for example, mutual respect and credibility may diminish if the organization is not seen as treating its employees or customers fairly. This can be debilitating and cause people to focus on doing things that are neither productive nor useful. If you know or feel you're not trusted you may hide mistakes, not ask for help, hold grudges or lack confidence: all elements that can contribute to People Risk.

Such breakdowns in trust at the industry level can have a ripple effect across many organizations, even if some organizations have done nothing wrong. Across the world, for example, trust in bankers generally reached a low point following the Global Financial Crisis and confidence in banking has remained at a low level ever since, following a series of scandals, some of which are described in Chapter 4. For example, a Gallup poll taken in the United States in November 2011 found that only 15 per cent of people had confidence in the US banking system.[26] Similarly, in its evidence to the UK Parliamentary Commission on Banking Standards, Barclays Bank[27] admits a 'crisis of trust' in banking following the Global Financial Crisis:

> Some commentators have suggested that, as well as contributing to this trust deficit, market instability, misselling, and other failings are symptoms of fundamental weaknesses in the standards, values, and culture of banking. This is a serious suggestion that must give the banking industry pause. It is important that the industry acknowledges and repairs areas where flaws in the norms and standards to which the industry operates have been exposed.

Note how the 'trust deficit' is linked back to the values and culture of banking. We would argue that this is because the espoused values did not match the observed values. Whilst this is an example from the banking industry the principles will apply to other business sectors.

7.6 Example of risk culture and values in action – managing Health and Safety

We have argued that organizational culture contains a number of sub-cultures and one particularly important sub-culture is in the area of Health and Safety (at work). Health and Safety is important in any organization because the possible impact of inadequate management of Health and Safety risk can be injury to people or at worst loss of life. Additionally, it can have a significant effect on the reputation of the business concerned. This is more so in the case of organizations that work in hazardous industries or where members of the public are put at risk merely because of the service they are using, for example, swimming pools.

Professor Scott Geller[28] has spent many years looking at how behaviour-based psychology can be used to improve Health and Safety, and he developed a simple model to describe three domains that need continuous management attention and focus in order for an effective culture to exist. The three domains are:

1 **Person**... covering... knowledge, skills, abilities, intelligence, motives and personality.
2 **Environment**... relating to... equipment, tools, machines, housekeeping, temperature, engineering standards, operating procedures.
3 **Behaviour**... looking at... complying, coaching, recognizing, communicating, demonstrating, actively caring.

The three domains link by looking at the *person* and their *behaviour* in the *environment* within which they have to operate. The three domains are dynamic and interactive with a change in one affecting another. For example, a person who has not been adequately trained may behave incorrectly and cause a problem in the workplace environment.

Within the Health and Safety culture model described by Geller a number of cultural characteristics should be present to illustrate that an effective culture is in place:

- everyone feels responsible for safety and does something about it on daily basis;
- people go beyond the call of duty to identify unsafe conditions and at-risk behaviours, and they intervene to correct them;
- safe work practices are supported intermittently with rewarding feedback from both peers and managers;
- people 'actively care' continuously for the safety of themselves and others;
- safety is not considered a priority that can be conveniently shifted depending on the demands of the situation; rather, safety is considered a value linked with every priority of a given situation.

Note how safety is seen as a value across the organization and, as such, should be 'shared' by all concerned.

Box 7.7 provides an example of an organization[29] that has improved its health and safety culture over a three-year period driven by the arrival of a new CEO. The reader will note how the action taken links back to the points made by Geller; for example, people were made to 'actively care' by making everybody a Health and Safety champion.

Box 7.7   Healthy Leisure: improving the management of Health and Safety risk

Healthy Leisure (HL) is a small company that runs a portfolio of leisure facilities located in southern England. The portfolio includes swimming pools, gyms, community centres, various sports halls and a boating lake. It operates these facilities on behalf of the local authority and exists as a social enterprise (not for profit) to serve the communities in which it operates. HL employs around 300 people, consisting of a mixture of full-time, part-time and casual members of staff. Visitor numbers exceed 1 million per annum.

In August 2010 a new CEO was appointed who was given a number of objectives by the board which included, inter alia, a focus on improving income generation/profitability and implementing cultural changes to create a more satisfied and motivated workforce. The board was also keen to make sure that the profile of Health and Safety was raised and that a culture of 'engagement' in Health and Safety matters permeated throughout the organization. The manifestation of this would be improving compliance scores in the various independent health and safety audits that are carried out by industry experts on a quarterly basis.

As evidence of the improvements that were made, the overall compliance score improved from 61 per cent to 91 per cent between August 2010 and August 2013.

So what did the CEO do to make this happen? In his own words, 'We didn't change the people, we set clear expectations that they were all responsible for Health and Safety. A number of specific actions were taken, all of which were designed to improve the Health and Safety culture':

- Structural changes were made to move away from a silo-based structure (different sub-cultures) to a functional-based structure (one company culture).

- Board commitment and engagement was reinforced (a board member attends the quarterly Health and Safety meetings, Health and Safety risk has been elevated on the corporate risk register).

- Staff were briefed on what the business was aiming to achieve with Health and Safety and their role in getting there.

- Staff were trained and more actively engaged in being responsible for Health and Safety.

- Nobody was designated the Health and Safety 'expert' officer, instead 300 people became Health and Safety champions.

- Health and Safety became an enabler for doing business and not a blocker, ie improvements to Health and Safety were actively welcomed because they provided additional peace of mind.

- An external Health and Safety practitioner was brought in to regularly challenge and support the business on Health and Safety matters.

- Health and Safety external auditors/inspectors were not seen as the enemy but were actively engaged to encourage a culture of continuous improvement.

- A culture of no blame/no surprises was promulgated throughout the organization.

- The business was used by the Health and Safety external auditors as a case study when something had gone wrong to illustrate the response and how it was put right.[30]

HL continues to enjoy excellent Health and Safety scores and in the Autumn of 2013 both their flagship leisure centres were awarded an 'Excellent' award by Quest, the UK quality scheme for Sport and Leisure, placing it in the top 5 per cent of leisure centres in the UK. This result was influenced by the significant improvements noted in the Health and Safety culture of the business.

The quote by Albert Einstein at the beginning of this chapter focuses on the world being a 'friendly or unfriendly place'. We would like the reader to think about Einstein's quote in the context of their own organization and ask themselves whether it is a friendly or unfriendly place. Do people build bridges or do people build walls? Do you, the reader, build bridges or build walls? Do people group together to build bridges or build walls? How many walls or bridges are there in your organization? How long have they been there? Reflecting on your answers to these questions will help you to better understand whether your organization has a culture of shared values where people work together and take risks to grow the business, and manage risks to protect the business.

This chapter has illustrated the importance of *Organizational Culture* to the effective management of risk and people risk in particular. Culture is often cited in media reports when things go wrong in an organization even though it can be a hard concept to pin down. Values are a principal driver of culture, particularly risk culture. In an ideal world values would be shared throughout the organization and everybody would feel a sense of fulfilment or job satisfaction. But when reality kicks in, the best we can hope for is a close match when it comes to sharing core values whilst recognizing that there will be some outliers. We shall now turn our attention to roles and responsibilities and Chapter 8 will examine in more detail how everybody has a part to play in improving the management of People Risk.

Notes

1 The case is based on the work of Professor Michael Mainelli – see Mainelli, M (2003) *The Consequences of Choice*, European Business Forum on Managing Risk (in association with Marsh Insurance Broking and Risk Management).

2 This question is loaded in the sense that the simple answer would be to look at the risk appetite that is set by the board as this will be a pointer to whether the organization prefers to be risk averse or risk adventurous. However, for the purposes of this example risk appetite has not (yet) been set.

3 The full CAIB report can be found at NASA (2003) *Columbia Accident Investigation Report*, at http://www.nasa.gov/

4 See International Federation of Accountants (2014) *Profile: Mervyn King: Governance is King!* www.ifac.org

5 See Quinn and Cameron (2011).

6 See Banking Standards Review (2014) May, www.bankingstandardsreview.org.uk

7 See Woolf (2008) *Ethical business conduct in BAE Systems plc: the way forward*, May, www.baesystems.com

8 For a fuller discussion of risk culture within financial organizations, see Power, M, Ashby, S and Tomasson, P (2014) *Risk culture in financial organizations*, www.lse.ac.uk

9 See Millar, D (2007) *Developments in Risk Management*, Presentation given in Hyderabad, 9 October. The presentation can be found online at www.powershow.com

10 See Institute of International Finance (2012) *Governance for strengthened risk management*, October, www.iif.com

11 See Chapter 10 and, for example, see rules on Air Proximity at *UK Airprox Board*, http://www.airproxboard.org.uk/

12 There is an old Malay proverb which sums this concept up nicely: 'Just because the water is calm, don't mean there aren't any crocodiles'.

13 See Quinn and Cameron (2011).

14 See Martin (2013).

15 See *Huffington Post* (2013) It's the Culture Stupid, Eduardo Braun Blog, 25 July, www.huffingtonpost.com

16 See Toft and Reynolds (1994).

17 Isomorphic in this context means incidents that have similar qualities.

18 See Barrett (1998).

19 The organizations in question were found via a Google search and were chosen to represent two large multinational businesses and a small national organization and are from different parts of the world.

20 See Barrett (1998).

21 There is no mention as to whether embedding the values was measured in any form and whether one factor was any better than another. This could be done, for example, by a staff survey after the event to see if and why people remember the values of the organization.

22 See Forrest, A, Lawson, I, Chaput de Saintonge, L and Smith, M (2012) *To practise what we preach: An exploratory survey of values in charities*, Cass Business School, London, www.cass.city.ac.uk

23 The Senior Management Team is not defined but we would argue this should include the board of directors as they too should be role models.

24 Trust may not always be a positive thing as was evidence by the LIBOR scandal where the manipulators trusted one another.

25 See Levering and Moskowitz (1993).

26 See *Gallup Business Journal* (2012) What matters most to banking customers, 26 January, http://businessjournal.gallup.com/

27 See Barclays (2012) *Written evidence: submission from Barclays (S001)*, Parliamentary Commission on Banking Standards, London, September, www.parliament.uk/bankingstandards

28 See Geller (2001).

29 Healthy Leisure is based on a real company case study undertaken by one of the authors.

30 The approach to managing Health and Safety risk mimics the approach to the broader management of risk across the organization. As might be expected for such an organization the risk appetite is very low in recognition of the potential high impact (loss of life) that could occur with a Health and Safety event.

Roles and responsibilities

08

I violated the Noah rule: predicting rain doesn't count; building arks does. WARREN BUFFETT

KEY MESSAGES

- It's a worrying thought, but there is a good chance that your employees (and customers and suppliers) are putting your firm in danger by their actions.

- Everyone has a responsibility to be scanning for new problems and maintaining an attitude of constant curiosity.

- The best organizations expect people to make mistakes and systems to fail in ways that may not have been thought of.

- You won't find too many bad people in business but you will find those who are a bad fit.

- Good People Risk Management starts at the front door with an effective and robust recruitment process.

- The leader of the HR function must be fully engaged in the risk management process and not just be seen as a passive bystander.

As we demonstrated in Chapter 4, risky behaviour can happen in any business, large or small, public or private sector, local, national and especially international. There are no boundaries when it comes to people affecting your organization through their actions or inactions. Equally, the consequences of these actions or inactions can be devastating in terms of the losses they may bring to the company.

Take, for example, the case of France Telecom,[1] which suffered a series of 35 employee suicides between 2008 and 2009. The telecom operator's former CEO, Didier Lombard, was subsequently placed under formal investigation for psychological harassment and, at the time of writing, is awaiting trial following his arrest in June 2012. Box 8.1 provides an extract of the case from the website France 24.

Box 8.1   The case of France Telecom

Didier Lombard was CEO of France Telecom, which provides mobile and internet services through the Orange brand, during a sweeping restructuring period between 2008 and 2009 in which some 35 employees took their lives. In his five years at the helm, the number of France-based employees was reduced from 130,000 to around 100,000. The company has some 180,000 employees worldwide.

'Copycat suicide culture'

Didier has denied that his strategy as head of the international operator was responsible for the suicides, the number of which, he maintained, was no higher than the national average. Lombard is quoted in *Le Monde*, a French newspaper, as saying that 'The [restructuring] plans put in place by France Telecom were never intended to hurt the employees. On the contrary, the plans were destined to save the company and its workforce.

'I am conscious of the fact that the company's upheaval may have caused problems [for some employees],' he wrote, 'but I absolutely reject that these plans, which were vital to France Telecom's survival, were the direct cause of these human tragedies.'

In 2009 Lombard shocked France by claiming that there was a 'mode de suicide' – a 'copycat suicide culture' – at France Telecom.

Unions representing the company's staff maintained that specific policies, including forced moves and impossible performance targets, were put in place specifically to crush morale and force employees to quit.

'People were put under unbearable pressure'

'This was the biggest redundancy plan at a French company in decades,' said Sebastien Crozier, head of the CFE-CGC union at France Telecom. 'People were put under unbearable pressure. Thousands were forced to move geographically or to take on new job functions. They couldn't take it.'

'The whole strategy was to reduce the number of employees,' he added. 'It was an organized and planned method to make employees' lives difficult so that they would resign.'

Many of the workers who took their own lives directly blamed the pressure of the restructuring, and in 2010 a government report on the suicides written by labour inspectors concluded that the company had ignored advice from doctors about the effect these policies had on staff morale and on employees' mental health.

The court hearing was the first time that a CEO of a multinational company has been brought before French magistrates for psychological harassment. Crozier welcomed the development and said it was 'important for all the staff and the families. Since Lombard has left the company the number of suicides has dropped by two thirds and we need to ask why the rate was three times higher when he was CEO.'

We are not making any judgements about whether Didier Lombard is guilty or otherwise in presenting this case as the legal process will have to run its course before the outcome is known. Our point is to illustrate what *could* happen as a result of the actions of, in this case, the board (a group of individuals) as a precursor to what we will discuss in this chapter: whose job is it to make sure that these types of (people) risks are being managed within the organization? In this particular case, the main People Risk related to the action by the board to implement a restructuring programme and the biases that came into play when the decision was made.

Whilst we do not have the details about what information was available to the board when the restructuring decision was made, the labour inspector's government report cited above (which was apparently seen by the press agency Reuters[2]) appears to imply that the board was ignoring warning signs from medical experts about the consequences of what might happen. Ignoring warning signs from outsiders is a point that we have covered before with the work of Professor Barry Turner and his review of 'man-made disasters'.[3] The re-structuring plan was not only seeking to reduce headcount but also to move an estimated 10,000 people into different roles and the report states that this would have had a 'pathological effect' on staff morale.

The unions who instigated the report were very clear that what was happening was caused by the board's decision but were they involved prior to the decision being made? And, if so, what was their position at the time? It seems unlikely, given the scale of what was being proposed, that they would not have had a say in the proposal, but could they have foreseen the tragic events that eventually unfolded? Were they too ignored and if so, why?

Another question that arises is the extent to which a full risk assessment of the potential outcome of accepting the decision was done and then presented to the board. From the company's point of view, it is clear that the main benefit would have been a quantifiable, significant reduction in costs but if, as is suggested, the board were made aware that this would have come at the expense of the staff being totally demoralized, what, if any, risk treatment actions were put in place to mitigate this?

Further questions arise about this case, such as:

● Did any of the board directors raise concerns about the magnitude of the restructuring and the speed of implementation, and if so how were their concerns addressed?

- Given the circumstances, did the board have it on its radar to watch for the potential effect on staff when the decision had been taken?
- Did any of those who committed suicide have any other underlying problems?
- Are the circumstances peculiar to the business environment in France?

The full facts of this case will doubtless emerge when it goes to court. Given, however, the circumstances of the case and the fact that restructuring programmes are commonplace in the business world, it would suggest that boards who are considering changes that will affect large numbers of people in this way should carefully assess whether the events at France Telecom could happen in their business and consider whether there may be a resulting 'pathological effect' on staff morale.

8.1 The Three Lines of Defence model

The 'Three Lines of Defence' model has become widely used to describe how risk management should be organized within a business, particularly within the financial services industry.[4] The three lines of defence are in place to prevent risks from manifesting themselves and consist of:

1 First line: Business Operations/Line Management.
2 Second line: Risk and Compliance Functions.
3 Third line: Audit Functions.

The theory is that the first line of defence acts as the main barrier to preventing risks from impacting upon the business with the second line supporting the first line by providing oversight on what the first line is doing and providing subject matter expertise on specific risk areas. The third line is a further oversight function providing assurance that the first two lines are working effectively.

In practice, each line of defence will have weaknesses through which risks will be able to pass. If we think of each of the lines of defence as being like a piece of Swiss Cheese,[5] the holes represent the points of weakness where the defences will be breached. The causes of these holes can be many and varied and include lapses in control, mistakes, poor supervision, human misconduct and so on. As we have demonstrated in Chapter 4, there will always be holes because we live in a world where those who build and operate the lines of defence, people, are, and always will be, fallible. The model is illustrated in Figure 8.1.

Despite being used as a business model the Three Lines of Defence model has clearly not been working effectively, as the case studies we highlighted in Chapter 4 attest to. In fact, the model falls short in a number of areas, most noticeably in the number of lines of defence being restricted to three. When thinking about risk management, and People Risk Management in particular, we believe that the model should be extended to six lines together with a 'gatekeeper' role being provided by the Human Resources department. We illustrate this model in Figure 8.2.

FIGURE 8.1   The Three Lines of Defence model (from Reason 1990)

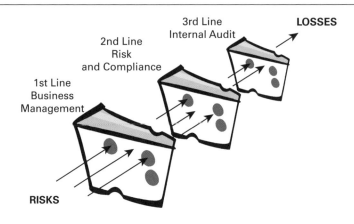

FIGURE 8.2   The Six Lines of Defence model

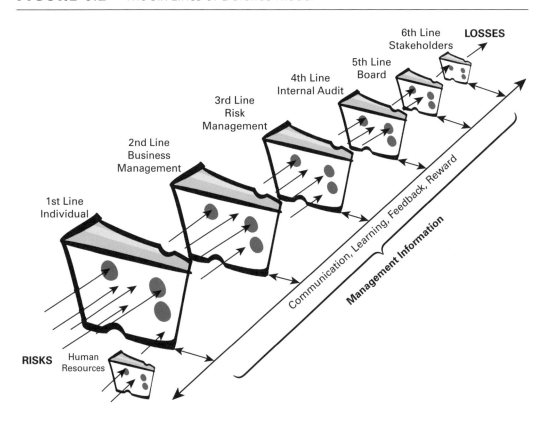

The six lines represent an extension of the three lines model with three important additions:

- Individual Responsibility (Line One) – we believe that the first line of defence in any risk situation lies with the individual carrying out his/her job in a diligent and thorough way. This is a theme we have touched on earlier in this book and we will explore this further in Chapters 9 and 10.
- Board (Line Five) – as we have illustrated in Chapter 6 the board plays a crucial role in the management of People Risk. In practice, the whole board oversees the operations of the lines of defence as each of them provides assurance to the board that the controls in place to mitigate risks are present and working effectively. In some (People Risk) cases, however, the board may be the first line of defence, for example, the recruitment process for a new CEO. Included within the board would be the Board Risk Committee to whom this oversight role may be delegated.
- Stakeholders (Line Six) – stakeholders include shareholders, customers, suppliers, the media and industry regulators. Stakeholders are typically external to the business and as such they can only be seen as a form of long stop to identifying and plugging holes in the Swiss Cheese. An example of shareholders acting in this way can be found within the IT industry where the CEO of Yahoo eventually resigned after one of the institutional shareholders found that he did not have the degree he purported to have on his CV.[6] Regulators can also take a proactive role in supervising business and some sectors, such as the financial services sectors, are being subjected to tighter external review. This has been driven by the Global Financial Crisis with regulators taking a much more intensive and intrusive approach.[7] This approach will mean an emphasis on preventing risks crystallizing in the first place.

The model also illustrates how the information flows between the various lines and how this can be co-ordinated by the Human Resources (HR) function who should act as guardians of the model, making sure that it is working effectively and taking action to improve the efficacy of the model itself. This could include, for example, working with the fourth line (Internal Audit) on training in controls where a particular vulnerability has been highlighted. As we illustrate in the model, HR plays an important role in ensuring that communication, learning, feedback and (where appropriate) reward mechanisms are in place and working. For example, where an incident occurs on the frontline there should be a mechanism in place to report (communication) this to the other lines with recommendations on how to prevent a recurrence (learning). Management information to support how well the lines are working (feedback), or not as the case may be, should be collated by HR and reports provided to the board. In the revised model, lines two (Business Line Management), three (Risk Management) and four (Internal Audit) represent the original model.

The Six Lines of Defence model thus gives us a starting point to look at roles and responsibilities vis-à-vis People Risk Management and, more importantly, the controls that should be in place. In this context, People Risk is no different from any other risk but the focus on managing People Risk needs to increase if risk management is to become more effective across the organization. In particular, we believe that the promotion of *individual responsibility*, as described in Chapter 10, and the embedding of this as a core value throughout the organization are critical to improving the mitigation of People Risk.

Managing People Risk is about managing behaviour throughout the organization. It involves a co-ordinated approach by the lines of defence so that the number of holes in the Swiss Cheese are reduced to as few as possible. In addition it requires explicit support from the HR function which should act as the guardian of all the people resources that exist in the organization. We recognize that co-ordinating the sixth line (stakeholders) is not an easy task and the best approach may be to consider it as a long stop or a final buffer which will operate autonomously and independent of the organization, ie the sixth line is not seen as part of the formal internal control system but provides an external perspective on how the organization is managing People Risk.

8.2 People Risk mitigation

We discussed the generic treatment or responses to People Risk based on John Adams' Risk Thermostat[8] in Chapter 2 and provided examples of actions that may be taken. Here, we will examine People Risk Mitigation more broadly and begin with what are frequently cited as the four T's of risk mitigation, which are generic to the mitigation of any risk and not just People Risk:

Treat – reduce the likelihood of the risk occurring, and the consequences if it does, by improving the internal control environment (for example, in the context of People Risk this could include training to address such areas as conflicts of interest and whistleblowing).

Tolerate – accept the risk (after detailed analysis) and then ensure ongoing monitoring of any risk that remains (for example, accepting that a new recruit may not have all the skills for the role but has enough to warrant hiring them).

Terminate – avoid the risk all together (for example, firing staff who break the rules through a zero tolerance policy).

Transfer – move the risk to a third party (for example, outsourcing certain functions although whilst responsibility can be transferred, accountability (for risk) cannot).

Treating the risk is by far the most widely used of the mitigation tactics and involves developing and maintaining an effective internal control environment. The COSO framework identified in Chapter 5 defines internal control as:

a process, effected by an entity's board of directors, management and other personnel, designed to provide 'reasonable assurance' regarding the achievement of objectives in the following categories:

- effectiveness and efficiency of operations;
- reliability of financial reporting;
- compliance with applicable laws and regulations;
- safeguarding of Assets.

Controls are, therefore, an important part of mitigating People Risk.

There are a number of different types of controls that are well established in the business world and various labels have been given to the most commonly used. For the purposes of this chapter, we have used the following three labels:

Directive Controls – these controls mitigate risks by establishing limits of authority within which people can operate (for example, authorization of expenditure limits).

Preventive Controls – these controls mitigate risks by stopping errors or deviations from required practice occurring in the first place (for example, training on how the system works or segregating the duties of people).

Detective Controls – these controls mitigate risks by identifying errors or mistakes that may have been made (for example, bank reconciliations).

Other control types that are often quoted include: corrective control (a control put in place when an error has occurred); management control (a type of detective control carried out by management to ensure that the basic preventative control is working); and automated control (a control carried out by a computerized system). Other risk treatments include such things as Business Continuity Planning that aim to reduce the consequences of a serious risk event.

In the context of our lines of defence, the second line (Business Management) will use all three types of control to mitigate risk, whilst the third and fourth lines (Risk Management and Internal Audit) are forms of detective control which make sure that the other controls and risk mitigants are working. In addition, Risk Management and Internal Audit will provide advice and guidance on all types of controls to the second and other lines.

8.3 Clarifying responsibilities in the lines of defence

In terms of responsibilities the lines of defence offer a basis against which we can assess people risks and identify controls and risk mitigants that should be in place in order to minimize the number of holes in the organization's Swiss Cheese. Some of the people risks that may find their way through the lines of defence have been analysed in Chapter 2 using a People Risk Triangle (see Figure 2.5) based on motivation, opportunity and rationalization. The various combinations were then shown in Table 2.4 together with an example of an actual consequence (or People Risk incident) that occurred. Fraud, for example, was an example of a specific motivation, an unintended opportunity and an individual rationalization.

If we take Fraud as our example, Table 8.1 provides examples of the types of control that could be in place for the Six Lines of Defence. For the purposes of this example, we have used 'Regulators' to illustrate the sixth line of defence.

We have not included the responses to a fraud incident, for example, conducting investigations after a fraud is discovered or dealing with the media in such circumstances, albeit that such responses are an important part of the overall system and

TABLE 8.1   Example: Fraud and the lines of defence

	Directive	Preventative	Detective
1st Line Individual	Being aware of the policies (including training) in relation to fraud and proactively reporting suspicious behaviour, transactions, incidents (both inside and outside the company) together with control weaknesses which could result in fraud. Maintaining a diligent attitude towards the possibility of fraud.		
2nd Line Business Management	• Developing a fraud awareness policy including consequences for those found committing fraud. • Developing a whistleblowing policy to enable fraud incidents to be reported. • Establishing limits of authority on expenditure.	• Creating a fraud awareness training programme for all staff. • Including fraud risk in the overall risk assessment process. • Developing operating procedures with clear segregation of duties. • Monitoring adherence to policies and procedures.	• Creating systems of reporting to identify potential fraud incidents. • Using external experts to sense check the systems for unidentified fraud risks.
3rd Line Risk Management	• Providing advice and guidance to Business Management in relation to the management of fraud. • Monitoring fraud trends and incidents outside the business.	• Participating in the fraud awareness training programme. • Participating in the fraud risk assessment process. • Assisting with developing fraud prevention controls. • Ensuring compliance with established fraud procedures and controls.	• Undertaking specific fraud audits. • Undertaking fraud risk self-assessment exercises and scenario analysis.

TABLE 8.1 *continued*

	Directive	Preventative	Detective
4th Line Internal Audit	Providing assurance that the above controls are adequate to control the risk of fraud and that the level of fraud risk is within the risk appetite set by the board. Undertaking specific fraud audits, monitoring employees in high (fraud) risk positions (lifestyles, habits, etc...), using audit software to detect fraud on a real-time basis.		
5th Line Board	Setting the fraud risk appetite and creating and embedding a control culture which seeks to counteract incidences of fraud. Monitoring risk reports, setting key risk fraud indicators, commissioning fraud audits, challenging assurance functions to 'find' fraud.		
6th Line Regulators	Monitoring fraud trends in the industry and alerting businesses on new threats, collecting/aggregating/disseminating data on fraud across the industry, organizing seminars/briefings on fraud.		

will help to prevent future occurrences of fraud. Our focus here is on fraud prevention and getting *people* to do the right things to stop fraud happening. Our analysis also presupposes that organizations are prepared to recognize that they may well be subject to fraud in the first place, rather than ignore it as a potential risk. The reader may wish to note the work done in the 1980s by the security firm Pinkerton that concluded that 30 per cent of the population will not only steal if an opportunity exists, but will actively create an opportunity to do so.[9] Another 40 per cent will take the opportunity if they're convinced they won't get caught. And only 30 per cent will not steal at all. We will leave the reader to draw his/her own conclusions as to the probability of fraud risk in their own firm.

Returning to our process, a framework of controls and responsibilities can be built up for all the People Risk exposures within the organization and we have provided a further example in relation to misselling – Table 2.4 identifies this as an ambiguous motivation, an unintended opportunity and a collective rationalization – in Table 8.2. For the purposes of this example, we have again used Regulators to illustrate the sixth line of defence.

The reader will note that in these two examples a pattern of general controls and risk mitigants is beginning to emerge, with specific items related to the People Risk area in question. These examples do not provide all the detail of what is required, because 'developing operating procedures with clear segregation of duties' can be further analysed into specific controls that are relevant to the business operation and the processes employed.

At this point we could argue that if all of these controls (and others that we may not have included) are put in place we have gone some way to filling the holes in the

TABLE 8.2   Example: Misselling and the lines of defence

	Directive	Preventative	Detective
1st Line Individual	Being aware of the policies in relation to customers and how they should treated. Pointing out training deficiencies, where appropriate, alerting management to emerging issues with sales techniques and reward systems.		
2nd Line Business Management	• Developing a policy on treating customers fairly including consequences for those found misselling. • Developing a whistleblowing policy to enable whistleblowing incidents to be reported. • In conjunction with HR, designing a pay and reward policy that does not encourage misselling.	• Creating a training programme on product sales that warns of the consequences of misselling. • Including misselling risk in the overall risk assessment process. • Developing operating procedures with clear management responsibilities for picking up misselling activities. • Monitoring adherence to policies and procedures.	• Creating an MI system of reporting to identify potential misselling incidents. • Using external experts to sense check the systems for the potential for misselling.
3rd Line Risk Management	• Providing advice and guidance to the 1st and 2nd Lines in relation to misselling. • Monitoring misselling trends and incidents outside the business.	• Participating in the training programme on product sales. • Participating in the misselling risk assessment process. • Assisting with developing misselling prevention controls. • Ensuring compliance with established procedures and controls.	• Undertaking specific audits to look for instances of misselling.

TABLE 8.2 *continued*

	Directive	Preventative	Detective
4th Line Internal Audit	Providing assurance that the above controls are adequate to control the risk of misselling and that the level of misselling risk is within the risk appetite set by the board. Undertaking specific audits of sales practices and remuneration structures including face-to-face interviews with frontline staff.		
5th Line Board	Setting the misselling risk appetite and creating and embedding a control culture that seeks to counteract incidences of misselling. Monitoring risk reports and challenging MI reports that purport to illustrate that customers are being treated fairly.		
6th Line Regulators	Monitoring product sales and profitability trends across the industry. Identifying potential novel and new risks in relation to treating customers fairly/misselling. Developing systemic and firm-wide key risk indicators for early warning of potential misselling, including contacting customers directly.		

lines of defence and the management of the organization can sleep at night knowing that the risk has all but disappeared. The perfect risk-free world does not, however, exist because the lines of defence model has a fundamental weakness in it: people. For the lines of defence to work effectively requires, amongst many other things, people to do their jobs effectively, not to make any mistakes, not to take any short cuts, not to deviate from laid down procedures, not to have any lapses of concentration and not to be pressurized into doing something wrong either by a colleague or a customer. The human dimension to risk management comes into play at this point and we cannot take it as read that people will always behave the way that we want them to when they are doing their jobs. The other important point with the lines of defence model is that, first and foremost, the best place to plug the holes is in the first line: it may already be too late if the risk has leaked through and is picked up as an issue in subsequent lines. The issue of *individual responsibility* and the first line of defence is a subject which we consider warrants a detailed look on its own and we will return to this in Chapter 10.

So the question is, what more can organizations do to make sure that all employees (including board members) are diligently carrying out their roles and responsibilities day in day out, whenever they are in a work environment? There is no one single answer to this difficult question because we are all different and we will respond differently to the stimuli used to influence us to take our roles and responsibilities seriously. A good starting point to try and answer this question is to look at organizations that do appear to have people who carry out their work diligently and where the holes in the Swiss Cheese have been, if not entirely plugged, then reduced to a size where very little in the way of risk will filter through. One example of such an organizational type is what is referred to as a High Reliability Organization (HRO).

8.4 High Reliability Organizations

In their book,[10] *Managing the Unexpected: Resilient performance in an age of uncertainty,* authors Kathleen Sutcliffe and Karl Weick discuss HROs and why such organizations have developed ways of doing things and styles of learning that enable them to manage the unexpected better than other organizations. They cite, for example, organizations such as emergency rooms in hospitals, flight operations of aircraft carriers and firefighting units as models to follow. The context in which these organizations operate is clearly important in that the consequences of getting something wrong can be catastrophic and potentially lead to loss of life but the principles by which these organizations operate reveal a number of patterns that are of use in both managing People Risk and ensuring that all employees are doing what they are supposed to be doing, ie understand their roles and responsibilities. According to Sutcliffe and Weick, an HRO organization can be characterized as one which:

- makes consistently good decisions;
- has high quality and reliable operations (hence the name HRO).

These are as a result of:

- performing almost error-free operations;
- doing it consistently and over a long period of time.

HROs are not just limited to organizations where consequences may be loss of life. An example in the financial services sector would be SWIFT, which provides highly reliable banking transmission services.[11]

Sutcliffe and Weick go on to discuss the five principles under which HROs operate that drive them to be successful, and contrast this with what happens in LROs (Low Reliability Organizations). Table 8.3 highlights the results of this analysis.

TABLE 8.3   The principles of HROs and LROs

LROs	HROs
• Focus on success	• Preoccupation with failure
• Underdeveloped cognitive infrastructure	• Resists over-simplification
• Focus on efficiency	• Sensitivity to operations
• Inefficient learning	• Commitment to resilience
• Lack of diversity (focused conformity)	• Deference to expertise
• Information and communications filtering	
• Reject early warning signs of quality degradations	
• Conduct briefings and persuade no one	

The principles that drive HROs provide a pointer to both the behaviours that are expected in the organization (culture) and the roles and responsibilities of the people (making the culture work). As we have discussed in Chapters 6 and 7 the culture of an organization will generally be driven down from the boardroom so in the case of HROs the five principles provide a clear picture of what the directors must be doing: they must live and breathe these principles, so they are seen as part of the values they expect everybody to subscribe to. Failure to do this is a big People Risk.

The five principles can be turned into specific action points giving advice on how they are made to work in practice as can be seen in the following examples:

- **Preoccupation with failure:**
  - ensure lapses or near misses are seen as information about the health of the system;
  - establish protocols for reporting failures;
  - extract lessons learned particularly in relation to near misses;
  - avoid drift into complacency when few failures are being reported;
  - ensure that Executive management and the board are never buffered from bad news.

- **Resists over-simplification:**
  - ensure that people take nothing for granted;
  - develop more complete pictures of process and information flows considering all the different nuances (particularly the points where things may go wrong);
  - position people so that they see as much of the business as possible and how it interacts with the outside world;
  - ensure there are people who take a different point of view than the established norm of working (this is a point that we develop further in Chapter 9).

- **Sensitivity to operations:**
  - develop an alertness mentality to when something may be going wrong (this relates to situational awareness as discussed in Chapter 3);
  - ensure that people are familiar with operations other than their own;
  - encourage people to network internally and actively look for problems;
  - develop warning signs of impending failures and actively seek out loopholes;

- **Commitment to resilience:**
  - build people's competences;
  - use informal in addition to formal contacts for problem-solving;
  - encourage the development of novel solutions for averting or containing errors;
  - have protocols in place for detecting, containing and recovering from errors.

- Deference to expertise:
  - train people to know the points of expertise to use, particularly in relation to decision-making;
  - promote the message that the company values expertise and experience over hierarchical rank;
  - migrate decision-making to experts at all levels when sign-off required;
  - audit information flows relevant to the matter in hand to make sure that there are no blockages and experts are aware.

We can then use this analysis to provide pointers towards the responsibilities for the lines of defence. Tables 8.4 and 8.5 provide further detail on the responsibilities for the second line, Business Management, in relation to the first principle, preoccupation with failure and the second principle, resist over-simplification.

Further analysis can be undertaken with the other three principles to provide a grid of responsibilities for Business Management. As we have indicated earlier, Risk Management and Internal Audit (third and fourth lines) would then provide support to the second line together with assurance that all is working as intended.

This type of analysis thus provides an opportunity to assign specific roles and responsibilities (job descriptions) to people across the organization which can be supplemented with expected behaviours (such as Personalized Codes of Conduct – see Chapter 10) to provide a route map for people to follow. HROs work well because people have bought into the principles of their role and focus on making things happen in line with what is expected. This in turn drives their behaviours and sets the culture within which the business will operate.

8.5 The crucial role of Human Resources (HR)

In our analysis of the Six Lines of Defence model, we proposed that HR should act as gatekeepers. HR should take a proactive and visible approach to raising the awareness of People Risk, particularly at boardroom level, and play a leadership role in ensuring that the organizational values are being supported throughout the business. It should be seen by the other lines of defence as the focal point when behavioural matters arise with an employee, providing support, guidance and expertise to help get the matter resolved. It cannot manage People Risk on its own but it can, and it should, be working closely with the Chief Risk Officer and his/her team, actively and constantly monitoring People Risk and the root causes which drive people to perform actions that could end up harming the business.

HR are the owners of the most important process in the organization; the recruitment, selection, training and rewarding of people. We discussed the initial hiring process in Chapter 2 and have expanded upon this to provide a typical 'recruitment and investment in people' process as shown in Figure 8.3.

As with all processes, however, there are risks (including people risks) in the execution of the steps and these risks need to be managed effectively if the holes in the Swiss Cheese are to be minimized. As an example of what one organization does

TABLE 8.4 HRO principle: Preoccupation with failure and Business
Management (2nd line) responsibilities

Principle: Preoccupation with failure	
Action points	**Business Management (2nd Line) responsibilities**
1. Ensure lapses or near misses are seen as information about the health of the system.	1 Train staff on what constitutes a lapse/near miss and their role in reporting all lapses without exception. 2 Regular communications with staff to remind them to report lapses/near misses. 3 Maintain register of lapses/near misses grading them, for example, using a traffic light system to highlight severity.
2. Establish protocols for reporting failures.	1 Reward staff (1st line) for reporting lapses and near misses. 2 Ensure staff review the register of lapses/near misses so that they know what went wrong and why.
3. Extract lessons learnt particularly in relation to near misses.	1 Undertake root cause analysis on reported events. 2 Publicize lessons learnt to all staff. 3 Ensure staff review and comment upon the events so they know what went wrong, why it went wrong and contribute to the learning process.
4. Avoid drift into complacency when few failures are being reported.	1 Survey selected members of staff to see if there are any potential problems brewing. 2 Engage Risk Management and Internal Audit (3rd and 4th lines) to undertake specific reviews and provide assurance that nothing is being missed.
5. Ensure that executive management and the board are never buffered from bad news.	1 Develop trigger system for reporting when a lapse/near miss occurs related to the severity of the event. 2 Produce reports and management information on lapses/near misses for each board meeting. 3 Actively seek out trends in lapses/near misses.

TABLE 8.5   HRO principle: Resists over-simplification and Business Management (2nd line) responsibilities

Principle: Resist over-simplification	
Action points	**Business Management (2nd Line) responsibilities**
1. Ensure that people take nothing for granted.	**1** Conduct exercises supported by training to proactively get people to think the unexpected: document the results.
	2 Undertake regular emergency drill training to avoid complacency setting in.
2. Develop more complete pictures of process and information flows considering all the different nuances (particularly the points where things may go wrong).	**1** Focus process and people mapping on the weak parts of the system and document what happens when things might go wrong (the exceptions to the rule).
	2 Undertake independent review of process and information flows.
	3 Complete walk-throughs of process and people maps using data with known issues to ensure that they are picked up.
3. Position people so that they see as much as the business as possible and how it interacts with the outside world.	**1** Develop a programme of staff rotation.
	2 Ensure exercise training includes people from across the organization not just the area affected.
	3 Use outsiders to provide training in what is happening externally.
	4 Monitor risk events in other companies in the industry.
4. Ensure there are people who take a different point of view than the established norm of working.	**1** Select people with different backgrounds and analytical skills to be part of the team.
	2 Use outside expertise when looking at establish norms of working.

to minimize these risks, Box 8.2 illustrates extracts from the Human Resources Risk Management Statement of the UK's National Gallery.[12] We have selected this to demonstrate how one organization manages their people-related risks, and the reader will note the linkages into the recruitment process shown in Figure 8.3. For example, 'staff are selected on merit' and 'unfair discrimination is avoided' would be part of the 'select the right people' activity.

FIGURE 8.3   The recruitment and investment in people process

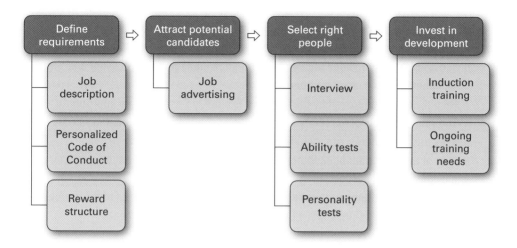

Box 8.2   Extracts from the National Gallery's Human Resources Risk Management Statement

Introduction

The Gallery's ability to serve its public depends on the calibre of staff and their effective management. The Gallery aims to ensure that:

- staff are selected on merit... and have access to the necessary training;
- unfair discrimination is avoided;
- a positive and constructive climate of relations with staff, staff representatives and unions is fostered;
- pay and related systems make due payments on time without fraud.

Risks

The risks of failing to comply with policies and procedures outlined here include:

- fraud;
- poor performance leading to failure to achieve organizational objectives;
- poor staff relations resulting in industrial action and business disruption;
- financial loss arising from grievances and disputes with staff;
- failure to comply with relevant legislation;
- reputational damage arising from any of the above.

Policies and procedures

Within the HR Department, there is a set of technical notes and instructions on key separate activities for day-to-day guidance, to help anyone covering for another's absence, and to train new members of staff. Key policies and procedures, and advice and support provided include: performance management... bullying and harassment, and grievance matters.

HR policies are approved by the Gallery's Executive Committee as appropriate.

The relevant parts of the terms and conditions of employment, and appropriate policies and procedures, are included in a Staff Handbook and... the relevant section of the Staff Handbook forms part of each individual's contract of employment.

The Gallery maintains a Negotiating Committee for the negotiation of the annual pay settlement and a Consultative Committee for other matters.

Responsibilities

The HR Department is responsible for the development of policies and practices... and together with the Gallery's managers, works to ensure their effective implementation.

The HR Department is responsible for developing and maintaining appropriate terms and conditions of employment.

Managers are responsible, working with HR, for the proper implementation of policies and procedures within their areas. They are responsible for the selection of staff... and for ensuring that staff members are making their best possible contribution to the work of the Gallery.

The risks noted are only a subset of the plethora of risks that can be better managed by having (effective) HR policies and procedures. Other risks that will be handled by the second line, Business Management, include high absenteeism, high staff turnover, skill shortages, excessive or insufficient remuneration, lack of succession planning and poor talent management. The National Gallery statement describes much of what HR departments (and frontline managers) should be doing in managing (HR) risks and people risks in particular. The statement is supported by, inter alia, the National Gallery's whistleblowing policy. HR is very much at the frontline of managing People Risk as it can significantly influence the people who join the organization, whether they be junior clerical staff or senior board directors, and assess whether they demonstrate the right behaviours and have the right competencies. In addition, we would expect that the management of the risks that appear to be at the root cause of the France Telecom incident we highlighted at the beginning of this chapter should have been heavily influenced by HR (but were not).

One simple technique the authors have seen used to assess the competencies of potential new recruits is to ask the interviewee a series of questions in relation to the required competencies and record them on (say) a flipchart. Having listed the competencies, which can be found in the job description, the interviewee is then asked to assess his/her own strengths and weaknesses in relation to the competencies. Table 8.6 shows an example of a risk manager position together with what some of the responses might look like.

TABLE 8.6   Risk Manager competence recruitment self-assessment

Competence	Strengths	Weaknesses
1. Analytical ability	* Trained as an accountant * Prepare monthly detailed risk management reports	
2. Knowledge of the risk management process	* Five years in the risk management field	* Limited to a banking environment
3. Training staff in risk awareness	* Delivered several conference presentations	* No direct experience of staff training
Etc........		

This technique of requesting candidates to self-assess their competencies can then be extended to include behaviours, and specifically those that are expected in the Personalized Code of Conduct that we will explore in Chapter 10, to provide a complete picture of how the interviewee sees *themself* in relation to the job they are expected to perform. This self-analysis can be revealing (if only to see how self-aware an individual is) and would supplement any ability/personality tests. The assessment can be concluded by asking the interviewee to reflect on the analysis they have provided and to ask them why they think a person with the characteristics they have outlined is suitable for the job!

Recruiting the right person for the job is only the first step in good People Risk Management (PRM). All this good work can be undone if that person is then subsequently managed badly once he/she is working in the organization. For example, if some of the interactions we illustrated in the people maps in Chapter 5 result in poor working relationships, lack of training opportunities or lack of recognition for good performance then this can cause the new employee to become disillusioned and to start to seek alternative employment.

8.6 Human Resources Risk Management

Human Resources Risk Management (HRRM), or the management of risks pertaining to the HR department, was the subject of research[13] by three South Africa academics, Marius Meyer, Gert Roodt and Michael Robbins, who looked specifically at how governing people risks can improve business performance. They assert that it is essential that a company's risk management plan includes People Risks and that a comprehensive analysis of an organization's People Risks is required, one that transcends the current narrow focus on 'safety in high-risk environments'. They include in their People Risks things like company culture, talent shortages and retention, incompetence, employee performance, unethical behaviour, low morale, grievances and disputes, excessive absenteeism, employee wellness, sabotage, workplace violence as well as non-compliance with industry and other regulations and laws. HR practitioners, they conclude, (and we would agree) must use their unique knowledge, skills and experience to help managers tackle these risks throughout the organization. They cite a number of actions that HR managers could use and these are listed in Table 8.7, together with a note of which of the lines of defence would benefit (and be strengthened) from these actions and comments on how the action would help.

TABLE 8.7   HR actions and the lines of defence

Action	Line(s) of defence affected	Comments
Developing an HR risk appetite and adopting suitable reward policies that encourage employees to manage risks.	Individual.	These are a form of directive control which would help establish boundaries for employees when it comes to taking risks.
Contributing to risk management training.	Individual, Business Management, Board.	Supporting Risk Management in the provision of training to others could include a specific focus on People Risk.
Ensuring the organization's risk management policy covers people risks.	Risk Management, Board.	Another directive control which HR should be able to influence in the area of People Risk.
Deciding on risk tolerance levels for the likes of strikes, absenteeism, employee turnover rates and remuneration.	Individual, Board.	These tolerance levels would be signed off by the board and apply across the firm to all employees.
Establishing systems to monitor people risks and ensure they remain within the tolerances set.	Business Management, Risk Management, Board.	The provision of management information (output from the systems) is an important detective control and would support the reporting done by Business and Risk Management to the board.

TABLE 8.7   *continued*

Action	Line(s) of defence affected	Comments
Providing input into the Risk Management reports that go to the Risk Committee/Board.	Business Management, Risk Management, Board.	As per the previous point.
Supporting the Risk Management strategy of the business.	Risk Management, Board.	Involvement from HR would ensure that the strategy addresses people risk issues.
Supporting managers in the management of People Risks.	Business Management.	Acting as a sounding board and being seen as the people risk 'expert'.
Compiling an ethics risk profile (how ethical do we want to be?).	Individual, Business Management, Risk Management, Board.	This is a form of directive control which would help establish boundaries for employees when it comes to ethical matters.
Conducting employee satisfaction surveys to unearth potential people risk issues.	Business Management, Risk Management, Board.	Surveys can be useful ways of determining people risk trends and finding issues that may not surface via the usual communication channels.
Using novel and progressive HR practices to reduce People Risks.	Individual, Business Management, Risk Management, Internal Audit, Board.	One example, which we develop further in Chapter 10, is the use of Personalized Codes of Conduct.
Championing the management of People Risks by demonstrating how their effective management leads to improved performance of staff.	Business Management.	As guardians of the model HR should be at the forefront of publicizing the benefits of People Risk Management across the firm.
Proactively providing advice to Risk Management and Internal Audit on the effectiveness of internal controls in relation to People Risk.	Risk Management, Internal Audit.	This is similar to the supporting role they play with Business Management in being the experts on People Risk matters.

Human Resources Risk Management and the effect it has on mitigating People Risk should never be underestimated in any organization. There is a lot that can be done and there is a lot that should be done, and the challenge for the HR department is to first of all recognize this and then to tirelessly work to keep People Risk at the top of the organization's risk management agenda. To do this HR must raise their game in terms of their own understanding of risks and develop effective working relationships with all the lines of defence in relation to management of risks in general and people risks in particular.

8.7 The Assurance functions

The Assurance functions are represented by the third and fourth lines of defence and their principal role is to both support and challenge the second line, in particular the HR department, in managing (people) risk. The functions themselves should aim, wherever possible, to act independently of the second line, Business Management, although this in practice can be difficult because of the inherent tensions that can exist when the second line is, for example, looking for advice from the third/fourth lines because they have the expertise to help resolve a particular issue. An example might be approaching Internal Audit for advice on improving controls in the recruitment process, which Internal Audit would subsequently be asked to provide assurance on. The Internal Audit purist would argue that there is an inherent conflict of interest in this situation and that management should look to others for advice, but we believe that a pragmatic view should prevail and that Internal Audit should provide guidance to their colleagues on how best to improve the situation. Any subsequent assurance on the control environment could be provided by a third party, such as the external auditors.

The third and fourth lines could, however, structure their work, and thus discharge their responsibilities by evaluating the management of People Risk against a proven framework to establish what gaps there might be and how those gaps might be filled.

By doing this, they maintain a degree of independence from the second line and provide an assessment based on something that is known to work. One such model that could be used is the European Foundation of Quality Management (EFQM) Excellence Model,[14] which is a self-assessment framework for measuring the strengths and areas for improvement of an organization across all of its activities. The term 'excellence' is used because the *model* focuses on what an organization does, or could do, to provide an 'excellent' service or product to its customers, service users or stakeholders. The model is non-prescriptive and does not involve strictly following a set of rules or standards, but provides a broad and coherent set of assumptions about what is required for a good organization and its management.[15]

Figure 8.4 shows the model adapted to provide a framework for managing People Risk.

The five boxes marked as 'Enablers' highlight what the organization needs to have in terms of capabilities to make People Risk Management work. The two boxes marked as 'Results' highlight what the organization needs to have to ensure that the

FIGURE 8.4 EFQM model adapted for the management of People Risk

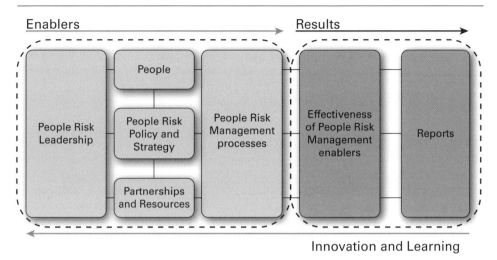

Innovation and Learning

enablers are working in practice. The Innovation and Learning arrow indicates the feedback loop that arises from the Results to improve the Enablers, ie it represents a continuous learning process.

Looking further at each of the boxes, we can build up a picture of the expected components of each box, as shown in Table 8.8 overleaf.

The components we have described are high level and further analysis can be undertaken to provide a detailed framework against which the third (Risk Management) and fourth (Internal Audit) lines can benchmark People Risk Management in their organization. Work could be allocated between the two lines so as to optimize the use of resources.

In looking at the work involved, the People Risk Leadership, People and Partnerships and Resources components are likely to cause the most difficulty, as they require a measure of subjective judgement and assessment of the soft factors we have alluded to previously in this book. But this is the one element of People Risk that cannot be ignored if a complete picture of how People Risk is being managed is to be established.

The more traditional roles of Risk Management and Internal Audit in looking at processes and controls can work to a point when assessing People Risk but the analysis of behaviour that would be required when looking at leadership, people and partnerships is always likely to be a constraint for the average internal auditor/ compliance officer/risk manager unless they are prepared to 'defer to expertise' and use the services of outside experts. Budget constraints as well as a reluctance on the part of the assurance people to stray into this more difficult territory are likely to hinder their ability in this area but that is not to say that it should be totally ignored.

Box 8.3, overleaf, provides some pointers/questions that both Risk Management and Internal Audit, working with Business Management, might consider when delving into this area.

TABLE 8.8   People Risk components of the EFQM model

Enablers	Components
1. People Risk Leadership	The board and senior management lead from the front on People Risk matters and the HR function, together with Risk Management, is at the forefront of embedding People Risk across the organization.
2. People	People are being managed effectively and support the People Risk culture.
3. People Risk Policy and Strategy	Documented polices and strategies in relation to People Risk are in place and reviewed on a regular basis.
4. Partnerships and Resources	Effective partnerships exist both inside and outside the organization to optimize the management of People Risk.
5. People Risk Management Processes	People Risk Management Processes are in place that both support the Risk Management Processes and provide control over People Risks.
Results	
6. Effectiveness of People Risk Management Enablers	The Risk Management Enablers are working across the whole organization.
7. Reports	Reports are produced on the outcomes of People Risk Management activities.

Box 8.3   Risk Management/Internal Audit considerations for the behavioural aspects of risk management

- Consider a person's ability to do the job in relation to the risks that they have to take in carrying out their responsibilities. This could take the form of reviewing a risk self-assessment carried out by the person.

- How much value are you adding to your organization if you avoid these risks altogether? Think about this in the context of what went wrong with the examples we have cited in Chapter 4 and ask what more the Assurance functions should have been doing?

- Do you think that inadequate or poor management might be a problem in your organization? Where is the hard evidence to support this? Have you discussed your concern with anybody at board level?

- Do behavioural People Risk incidents in other organizations stimulate your management and you into learning from those experiences in relation to your own organization?

- Is knowledge about incidents involving behavioural People Risk captured and shared within your organization? How is the information used and by whom?

- Is there a 'culture' of management actions, involving potential risk, being challenged by other people in the organization? If not, why not?

- How do people learn to ask the right questions when faced with a risky situation in their day-to-day jobs?

- How do people in your organization recognize a risky situation? Can you test them to see if they really do recognize risky situations and how they would respond?

- How do people perceive their own risk tolerances within the risk tolerances of the organization? Do they know the risk tolerances of the organization? Do they understand what the tolerances mean in relation to their day-to-day jobs?

- How well (if at all) are People Risk issues picked up by your organizational procedures for risk management? How well are they analysed and behavioural factors, amongst others, picked out as being the problem?

- How much emphasis do you place on reviewing the HR function where some of the practices and procedures that directly influence behaviours (and thus the amount of People Risk in the organization) emanate?

- How good are your streetwise instincts for sensing when people (at any level) are putting the organization at risk? Rule of thumb, the weaker your streetwise instincts, the more help you are likely to need.

- How does your organization identify competent people and encourage them to stay? Conversely, how does your organization deal with incompetent people?

- Does your organization use any form of psychometric testing to evaluate somebody's risk-taking profile? What action is taken as a result of the testing?

- How does your organization maintain people's 'alertness' to risk?

- How is risky behaviour discouraged?

- What systems are in place to look at team behaviour within the organization?

Above all, remember that *being an effective Assurance function takes courage*.

Finally, as we have alluded to in Chapter 7, the way people behave has a cause – for example, time pressures, inexperience, inadequate supervision – and it is looking for those causes that can further help to mitigate people risk in the organization.

8.8 Auditing corporate culture

In Chapter 7 we discussed culture, risk culture and the importance of values in driving the culture throughout the organization. In terms of responsibilities, audits of culture and values should not necessarily be left to Internal Audit as they are of primary interest to the board who, as we have seen earlier, are the key to ensuring that the values and culture permeate throughout the organization. Audits of this nature would typically consist of surveys of staff with specific questions designed to establish whether the required values/cultural characteristics are what people perceive in practice. This exercise could be done as part of an annual staff satisfaction survey in which employees complete a questionnaire about many aspects of the business from support for personal training and development through to attitudes towards corporate social responsibility.

Auditing corporate culture is growing in importance, driven by the constant media attention when a failing in an organization is quoted as 'having a bad/poor/ inappropriate culture'. It is never going to be a simple job to audit culture if only because larger organizations will inevitably have sub-cultures within them that may have different characteristics from the predominant organizational culture. Once the audit has been concluded and the results are known, the next difficult step is working out what can be done to shift the culture if that is what is required. As an example of the potential difficulty in doing this, the reader will recall we analysed in Chapter 4 the PPI scandal that took place in the UK, and how all the major banks were severely criticized for misselling insurance products to customers. Culture was mentioned as a factor for allowing this to happen and the banks responded by (supposedly) putting a stop to such practices and retraining staff to 'treat customers fairly'. And yet in December 2013 Lloyds Banking group, who were among the banks involved in the PPI scandal, were fined £28 million for misselling protection products to their customers.[16] The misselling took place *after* the PPI scandal and was driven by an inappropriate sales bonus structure that lead to a culture of 'incentives and threats' permeating down to the sales staff in the bank branches. As is evidenced by this incident, cultural changes can be difficult to implement throughout larger organizations.

In their publication *Governance for Strengthened Risk Management*, the Institute of International Finance looked at assessing risk culture by using risk culture surveys.[17] The idea behind such surveys is to get staff to speak freely about their understanding of the organization's risk culture and how it affects their jobs. By doing this, organizations can better understand attitudes to risk and identify gaps and potential problems. The approach taken is to present a series of statements, based on both organizational and individual factors, and ask staff to rate them on a scale of one to five. Sample questions to illustrate the areas being probed are shown in Table 8.9.

TABLE 8.9 Example of risk culture survey questions

Organizational Factors (sample questions)
Communication – this section looks to see if communications are clear, effective and set clear expectations.
Q1. Is there a clear and coherent strategy for managing risks in the business? Q2. Does the firm's leadership set clear expectations for risk behaviour? Q3. Do policies and procedures support effective risk management?
Resources – this section focuses on whether the organization provides adequate resources and training on risk.
Q1. Does the organizational structure allow staff to manage risk? Q2. Are there clear guidelines for risk reporting and escalation? Q3. Is risk management training effective for the employee's role?
Incentives – this section looks at the extent to which staff are provided with feedback and are rewarded for encouraging appropriate risk behaviour.
Q1. Are employees rewarded for adherence to risk behaviour? Q2. Are employees held accountable for non-compliance to risk policies/procedures? Q3. Are there meaningful consequences for not adhering to risk policies/procedures?
Individual Factors (sample questions)
Competencies – this section is aimed at assessing whether staff understand the risk skills required to do their job.
Q1. Do colleagues have the right skill set for effective risk management? Q2. Does the organization learn from past mistakes? Q3. Are the employees' required skills and competences clear?
Application – this section focuses on whether compliance with risk policies is actively encouraged within the organization.
Q1. Does management encourage compliance with risk policies and procedures? Q2. Is risk given sufficient weight and value in decision-making? Q3. Is sharing of information about risk processes encouraged?
Motivation – this section is aimed at testing whether staff understand the benefits of appropriate risk behaviour and if they are comfortable with challenge mechanisms.
Q1. Is the employee committed to the long term sustainability of the organization? Q2. Is it important to the employee that the business operates ethically? Q3. Is it clear to the employee how risk policies reduce risk to the firm?

Guidance on how Internal Audit should approach the audit of culture can be found in Dr Jim Roth's book, *Best Practices: Evaluating the corporate culture*.[18] This research report was commissioned by the US Institute of Internal Auditors (IIA) and it delves into creative and innovative practices implemented by exemplary (US) organizations to ensure 'soft controls' are working effectively. Roth goes on to describe the subjective and intangible nature of soft controls and how auditing them is neither simple nor black and white. He lists a number of examples of soft controls, such as tone at the top, morale, trust, empowerment, leadership, employee motivation, integrity and even notes shared values as being a soft control in need of auditing.

He goes on to identify five principles used by what he terms progressive organizations to evaluate soft controls. These are highlighted in Box 8.4.

Box 8.4   Five principles for evaluating soft controls

1 Ask 'constructively challenging' questions of management and 'confirming' questions of employees.

2 Identify and obtain management's agreement on the criteria for evaluation and what will constitute legitimate audit evidence.

3 Get 'hard' evidence about the results of the soft control when possible.

4 Focus on the underlying management process.

5 Develop and report results in partnership with those accountable. Use appropriate (perhaps informal) means of reporting.

Because soft controls are highly subjective, evaluating them objectively can be quite a challenge. Internal auditors must provide persuasive evidence indicating soft control weaknesses if they are to demonstrate real value to management. The 19 successful organizations cited in Roth's research said that their top management and audit committees value soft control auditing more than traditional audit work. This should speak volumes to those at the top of organizations, particularly Chief Internal Auditors, especially those who might think of 'soft' as being synonymous with 'unimportant' or 'unnecessary'. We believe that the Internal Audit profession needs to recognize the importance of soft controls and people risks and that the focus of internal audit work should be in these areas. As we demonstrated in Chapter 4, it is in these areas that the greatest risks to the future success of the firm will be found.

8.9 Values audit

One approach to undertaking a values audit is described by Richard Barrett in his book, *Liberating the Corporate Soul*.[19] In summary, the audit involves assessing the relationship between (a) the values of the individuals who work in the organization, (b) the perceived values of the organization and (c) the ideal values of the organization as suggested by the individuals participating. Each of the participants, who can range from a small team of people, such as the board, to everybody in the organization, is asked to select a set of ten values (from a list) which they believe fit those related to (a), (b) and (c). The results are then aggregated and compared to reveal the mis-matches that exist and to provide the organization with the opportunity to formulate action plans to reshape the values.

Auditing values in this way provides a detailed analysis at a particular moment in time but living those values on a day-to-day basis is the responsibility of everybody in the organization. This would suggest that the desired values should be published and, as we highlighted in Chapter 7, many organizations do just that with 'our values' statements. Actually living those values, however, means going beyond these 'words on paper'. This is a point that we will pick up in Chapter 10 when we look at the Duke University Health System.

Warren Buffet's quote at the beginning of this chapter illustrates the importance of having contingency plans in place if a People Risk issue was to manifest itself in an organization. His quote alludes to weather risk, an external event that can and does have a devastating impact on people and businesses. But, as we have illustrated in Chapter 4, so too can inadequately controlled People Risks. The holes in the organizational Swiss Cheese can never be completely plugged and 'building arks' as a contingency may sometimes be the only option available to the business when a risk finds its way through the Six Lines of Defence.

In this chapter we have focused on the Six Lines of Defence model to illustrate roles and responsibilities in relation to risk and specifically People Risk. Whilst the model itself is not perfect in preventing risks filtering through and impacting upon the organization, it does provide an organization with a framework and illustrates how an improved joined-up approach (from the various lines) is better than a fragmented one. Just as everybody can be a source of risk, everybody has a responsibility for managing risk, starting with the individual and an acceptance of personal responsibility. This is a topic we will come back to in Chapter 10 but we now move on to the next chapter which explores decision-making both at the individual and group level.

Notes

1 See *France24* (2012) Ex-France Telecom CEO probed over 35 suicides, 6 July, http://www.france24.com

2 See *Reuters* (2012) Ex-France Telecom CEO investigated over suicides, 4 July, http://www.reuters.com

3 See Turner (1976).

4 See Internal Audit e-bulletin (2008) *Three Lines of Defence*, Published by ACCA UK Internal Audit e-Bulletin, http://www.accaglobal.com/

5 See Reason (1990).

6 See *Yahoo Finance* (2014) Yahoo CEO Thompson Resigns, 24 June, http://finance.yahoo.com/ for further information.

7 As an example, the UK Financial Conduct Authority now produces a Retail Conduct Risk Outlook which seeks to highlight where the regulatory focus will be over the coming 12 months – see http://www.fca.org.uk/your-fca/documents/fca-risk-outlook-2013

8 See Adams (1995).

9 See *Harvard Business Review* (2012) Five house rules for managing risky behaviour, James Lam Blog, 13 June, http://blogs.hbr.org/

10 See Sutcliffe and Weick (2007).

11 SWIFT is an organization that provides secure electronic funds transfer services for international banks. For further information, see http://www.swift.com/

12 The UK National Gallery houses the national collection of Western European painting from the 13th to the 19th centuries.

13 See Meyer, M, Roodt, G and Robbins, M (2011) Human resources risk management: Governing people risks for improved performance, *South African Journal of Human Resource Management*, **9** (1), Art. 366.

14 Further information about the EFQM model can be found at http://www.efqm.org/

15 See Meyer *et al* (2011) who developed the idea for Human Resources Risk Management.

16 See Financial Conduct Authority (2013) *FCA fines Lloyds Banking Group firms a total of £28,038,800 for serious sales incentive failings*, 11 December, www.fca.org.uk

17 The IIF survey is not the only point of reference for auditing risk culture. The UK-based Institute of Risk Management has produced guidance for practitioners on risk culture (see http://www.financialmutuals.org/files/files/Risk_Culture_WEB_VERSION.pdf)

18 See Roth (2010).

19 See Barrett (1998).

Improving decision-making

09

> *Making good decisions is a crucial skill at every level.*
>
> **PETER F DRUCKER**

KEY MESSAGES

- Subject to biases, of which we are often unaware, and overconfident in our abilities, people are not good at making decisions, thereby giving rise to People Risk.

- Encouraging individuals and groups to improve their decision-making skills and rewarding them for doing so is one of the keys to managing People Risk.

- Decision-making can be improved by the use of a well-thought-out process that recognizes that biases do exist and must be made as visible as possible at all stages of making a decision.

- Decision-making can be improved by the use of Decision Checklists at all levels of an organization, from board to frontline staff.

Chapters 6, 7 and 8 looked specifically at organizational issues, such as culture and organizational roles and responsibilities. The final two chapters, however, return to the theme of the individual and their responsibilities. This chapter looks specifically at how to improve individuals' decision-making so that fewer bad decisions will be made, while Chapter 10 looks at individual responsibilities as regards People Risk. The chapter returns to the theme of making the Invisible Visible – in this case, tools and techniques such as a suggested decision-making process for uncovering possible biases and pressures that cause people to make bad decisions.

9.1 Making the Invisible Visible

People Risks are both *Visible*, that is they can be seen or at least detected after the event, and *Invisible*, or not directly observable and very difficult to detect. Bullying and discrimination are examples of *visible* risks, evident to the bullies, the victims and some of the colleagues who witness the bullying behaviour. However, the failure of witnesses to do something about bullying and discrimination is an *invisible* risk.

The acceptance and subsequent institutionalizing of such behaviour can be very expensive to a firm if a victim or group of victims subsequently successfully sue the company as, for example, in the Merrill Lynch discrimination case.[1] In August 2013, a settlement of US $160 million was shared by some 1,400 brokers who had worked for Merrill. The brokers claimed that Merrill, a firm typical of Wall Street in being dominated by white males, had discriminated against non-white brokers by excluding them from teams that provided services to white clients, thereby stifling their career progression. Despite having agreed in the settlement of a prior lawsuit in the 1970s to make its workforce more diverse, Merrill Lynch had never actually met its own 'diversity goals'. In Merrill, covert (invisible) racial discrimination appeared to be embedded in the firm's culture, and was widely accepted and rarely questioned. Such People Risks can be extremely difficult to tackle because a firm's culture must adapt to cope with such risks, which are deeply ingrained and often invisible to the individuals involved.

Risky decisions are both visible and invisible at the same time in that the *outcomes* become apparent over time, sometimes too late. However, the rationale for taking a particular decision is often shrouded in mystery or at best subsequently justified with dubious arguments and rationalizations. In other words, the process for making decisions, while outwardly observable, is often obscure and not usually subjected to rigorous and independent analysis. In his book, *Ending the Management Illusion*, Hersh Shefrin discusses the difference between what he calls 'closed book' and 'open book' firms.[2] Looking specifically at financial decisions, Shefrin characterizes an 'open book' company as one where all the employees know the firm's real financial numbers and make their decisions based upon, and confident in, that knowledge. Furthermore, the employees in an 'open book' company (Southwest Airlines is an example given by Shefrin) understand the implications of numbers such as costs and revenues because they are sufficiently trained in financial literacy to comprehend the meaning and dynamics of such numbers. This does not mean that everyone has to be an expert in finance, investments or actuarial science but that they can at least ask sensible, if sometimes awkward, questions about financial topics. In the case of the Global Financial Crisis, inquiries found that, while prepared to accept the higher returns from investing in complex financial instruments such as CDOs, senior executives did not really understand them, and certainly did not fully comprehend the risks their firms were running. Even today, complex finance is a 'closed book' to many directors.[3]

In a 'closed book' company, financial numbers are kept close to managements' chests, often for bogus reasons of commercial confidentiality, and staff are not encouraged to be knowledgeable as to their meanings and implications. When decisions are being made in closed book companies, Shefrin points out that 'bias gremlins' creep in by introducing bias into the (incomplete) numbers and making the numbers appear to lie. He argues that *psychologically smart* companies adopt open book principles, empowering staff to make decisions on the best information available and, specifically, to detect and eliminate bias gremlins. Improving financial literacy, particularly of consumers, has become a focus of new regulators created as a result of the GFC, such as the US Consumer Financial Protection Bureau (CFPB) and the UK Money Advice Service.[4] And as a result, employers and employees, especially in the financial services industry, will be forced to raise their game as these regulators demand more transparency about financial transactions.

While it may seem 'pie in the sky' to move towards improving financial, and in this context risk literacy, it must be remembered that the concepts underlying the Health and Safety (H&S) revolution[5] in business are less than 50 years old. Today, Health and Safety is embedded in the thinking of many people in many industries and people in risky industries, such as construction and energy, now think 'safety first and all of the time'. There is no easy way to change an ingrained mind-set, but experience with H&S in key industries shows that it can be done. The unpalatable alternative is to keep stumbling forward into even more disasters and blaming others for our own failures of vision.

If 'open book' or 'psychologically smart' companies make better decisions, why would firms not want to move that way? Shefrin argues that again conflicts of interest and biases get in the way. In closed book companies, 'information is power' and there are some middle-level managers who:

> serve as information channels between upper management and line workers. And for this reason, middle managers worry that excessive information-sharing will make their functions redundant.

In other words, there is a conflict of interest for some executives between helping the company to maximize the achievement of its objectives and their personal wealth.

In proposing psychologically smart companies, Shefrin is making the *invisible* (closed book) *visible* (open book). But such an approach is not restricted to financial information. It could just as easily be applied to other critical information, such as that used to make strategic decisions. In the case of Lehman Brothers, for example, key information was withheld from directors, not as a matter of deliberate policy, but important information was not tendered unless it was specifically asked for. In the Lehman situation, the board of directors had no alternate way of knowing the information that was required, which illustrates People Risk at the board level as described in Chapter 6. If certain information had been provided, such as the failure of other companies to succeed in similar ventures, then the non-technical directors may have raised reasonable objections to key aspects of the Lehman strategy and may possibly have averted a catastrophe.[6] But, of course, that is all history as there is no evidence that the Lehman directors would have acted any differently with better information. Nonetheless the objective of an effective People Risk Management framework must be to increase transparency and visibility of decision-making at all levels in the organization, including the board.

9.2 Improving individual decision-making

9.2.1 Human decision-making

Good decision-making is a skill. But humans are not born with the full set of skills needed to make good decisions, other than the natural 'flight or fight' choices that have meant, for example, that our ancestors chose to flee more often than fight predators, which is why we happen to be here today. Humans have developed over millennia the capability, which appears to be unique in the animal world, to make complex, considered decisions in our System 2 brain as described by Daniel Kahneman.[7] But, as described in Chapter 3, we also have an impetuous Systems 1 brain that means that, when making decisions, people are a curious mix of the thoughtful and thoughtless, responsible and reckless, and open and secretive.

People did not evolve to make business decisions (as opposed to day-to-day life ones), and until recently such decision-making was the purview of only a select few in society.[8] Nor are we generally taught 'decision-making' in school. We tend to learn it 'on the job' and thus we are subjected to biases already in the existing environment. Outside of our jobs, we learn by games (called 'scenarios' in business schools) or through case studies where decisions, usually ones that have gone wrong, are analysed. Our natural optimism and confirmation biases will convince us that we would never have made the mistakes that the people in those case studies made. Our alternative decisions will, of course, always remain perfect because, unlike real-world decisions, they will never get tested.[9] The thorny question of how business decision-makers should be educated has been raised by the respected business academic, Professor Henry Mintzberg[10] in his book, *Managers not MBAs*. In short, Mintzberg is strongly critical of traditional MBA programmes as, to paraphrase, they teach neither business nor administration and reinforce arrogance rather than teach humility in the face of uncertain realities.[11]

Our brains are not equipped to make perfect business decisions every time, so making that a goal for decision-making would be naive. However, managers can take practical steps to improve their own and others' decision-making and to detect bad decisions. But why would we want to be better decision-makers ourselves and why would we try to persuade others to do likewise? It is the premise of this book that bad decisions can cause sometimes disastrous losses. Chapter 4 gives only some of the many examples available of bad decision-making and other chapters give some reasons why some of these bad decisions were made. We do not claim that, in the same situations, we personally would have made better decisions, but we do contend that if the decision-makers in those cases had been better at making decisions, in particular countering some of their own biases, at least some of the losses and disasters would have been lessened, if not completely averted.

9.2.2 Individual versus group decision-making

This chapter is about decision-making but it is focused on individuals making (important) decisions in a business context. It is not about how people should make decisions in their private lives, which is a different set of discussions around ethics and personal freedoms. We do, however, believe that it is highly unlikely (but not impossible) that someone who is unethical in their private life will behave completely differently in business situations. In their excellent book, *Obstacles to Ethical Decision-making*,[12] Patricia Werhane and her colleagues tackle the thorny issue of personal ethics, which has engaged the attention of philosophers for centuries. They conclude that although ethical decision-making is very hard (not least because of the human tendency towards self-deception[13]), there is nevertheless hope that decision-making in business can be viewed as not a contest between 'ethics' and 'profits', in other words, 'what *should* be done' as against 'what *can* be done'. They illustrate this false dichotomy with a case study of a subsidiary of Bayer, the large German chemical company, which, when faced with an entrenched mind-set of using child labour in India, rather than continue the practice, developed innovative solutions that created a situation where, through incentives and education, peasant farmers embraced the notion that sending their children to school would be beneficial for everyone in the longer term. For Bayer, it was not a question or 'either/or' but instead 'both'. Werhane calls this 'moral imagination' and argues that what is needed is:

> A sound decision model, a strong dose of self-awareness, consciousness of our fallibilities, and a well-developed moral imagination.

We agree with these arguments and suggestions and will address them below in the narrower context of business decision-making. But we do not address the issue from a philosophical perspective that focuses on 'what an individual should do' but one that considers the more negative viewpoint of 'how can we stop individuals making (particularly) bad decisions?' In other words, we are not making value judgements other than on the quality, or otherwise, of the decision-making process.

In business few decisions are made by a lone individual, although the myth persists of high-powered CEOs doing just that. In business, decisions, and certainly important decisions, are generally made collectively, if only for the reason that the resources needed to implement any meaningful decision will come from multiple business units/divisions within a firm. In other words, there must be some sort of consensus about how a decision will impact various stakeholders, otherwise a decision may fail because of lack of commitment. Before proceeding it should be noted that very many, probably the vast majority of, day-to-day decisions appear to be made by line managers and staff working alone. However, these decisions are generally *pre-programmed* and repetitive in that they are taken within a set of policies, procedures and controls that have been developed *collectively* beforehand. In practice, a certain amount of licence to 'change the programme' is afforded to managers and staff in order to handle situations where the programme doesn't work. It is where such reactive changes grow and are adopted piecemeal that 'rules' become obsolete and dangers arise.

So what is the role of *individual* responsibility in *collective* decision-making? It is all too easy to hide within, and behind, collective terms such as the team, group, division or firm. In practice, it is very difficult to go against the general consensus of such collectives, because as Janis[14] points out, one of the defining characteristics of Groupthink is 'direct pressure on dissenters', ie groups freeze out non-conformists.[15] While such pressure may be seen as 'bullying' and in some cases, such as those of Enron and Washington Mutual described in Chapter 4, it certainly was, the pressure is often subtle and invisible. In recent research into pressures on individuals to behave unethically, Veronica Bohns[16] and her colleagues at the University of Waterloo found that people generally underestimate how much influence they have over others, even when encouraging decisions that are clearly unethical. The researchers found that even the mildest of pressure can influence people to do the wrong thing. These findings mean that individuals can be influenced by subtle factors, such as the body language and tone of voice of someone they respect, as much as the arguments being advanced. The desire to conform is part of the human make-up. Many thinkers, including Janis and Werhane, suggest that the role of the 'leader' is to promote diversity of thinking, like a Philosopher King sitting above, and remote from, discussions. While such objectivity is indeed desirable, even with the best will in the world such fine intentions can be undermined not only by the leader's behaviour but also by the way in which questions and decisions are framed.

We argue that the role of the individual decision-maker in the real world of collective decision-making is to *take each decision seriously* and to *think critically*. This means, as far as possible, ensuring that each decision is made: (a) following a sound process; (b) with an awareness of one's own biases and fallibility; (c) with respect for others; and (d) with a commitment to raising issues that are producing personal concerns. We recognize that in the real world this is much easier to say than do and that in order to promote critical thinking there is a need for disciplined decision-making processes, such as that described in section 9.3.

It should be noted that this process (or the decision model as described by Patricia Werhane) is *NOT* a replacement for the existing decision-making processes used in a firm (as each firm will almost certainly have one or more processes for making decisions) but as an addition to these models. Existing decision-making processes in firms deal reasonably well with *visible* factors, such as the financial inputs and outputs and the plans produced. What they do not do so well is deal with the *invisible*, especially the non-financial personal and group biases.

9.3 Decision-making process

Figure 9.1 shows three phases of a suggested decision-making model:

1 *Pre-decision*: the activities involved in preparing for a decision;

2 *Decision*: the activities involved in making a decision; and

3 *Post-decision*: the activities undertaken after a decision is made.

Note this is *not* considering the plan arising from the decision but a post-hoc analysis of the *quality* of the decision that was made.

The three phases shown in the diagram reinforce one another in that information considered, and importantly documented, in the first phase (Pre-decision) is used in the second (Decision) to drive the analysis of the decision and in the third (Post-decision) to review the actual decision-making process. In particular, the Post-decision phase is best seen as a learning opportunity rather than, for example, a formal audit of the decision. As shown in the diagram, however, there will be some decisions that are found to be unsatisfactory (for example, incomplete process or

FIGURE 9.1   Three phases of decision-making

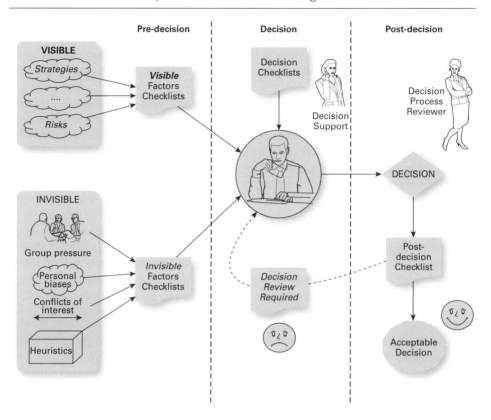

unacceptable pressure on participants) and should be returned for review by the original decision-maker(s) before they can be actioned.[17] If some measure of 'quality in decision-making' is also used in performance reviews, then there will be positive/ negative feedback for participants in the decision-making process.

In addition to the decision-maker (shown singly in the diagram but in most cases of important decisions usually a part of a group of 'decision participants') two other key roles are shown:

1 *Decision Support*: analysts trained in providing technical support and advice for making decisions. For example, in addition to providing decision tools, such as 'decision trees', these analysts would also collate checklists and maintain an 'issues/concerns register' and a 'risk register' during the decision-making process.

2 *Decision Process Reviewer*: an analyst trained in analysing and reviewing decisions. Such an individual could be a senior Decision Support Analyst and/or a senior individual in the firm who is trained in decision analysis. A reviewer may also, when required, call upon other expertise, such as Project Management experts to evaluate not the 'plan' but rather whether the 'plan' was constructed within a considered and comprehensive process.

Obviously the relative time and effort allocated to each of these three phases, will depend on: (a) the importance of the decision; (b) the 'routine-ness' of the decision;

and (c) the breadth of the impact, in that the greater the number of 'stakeholders' impacted the more time and effort is required to make a decision. *Not all decisions will require a full-blown process.* Some decisions, such as for example hiring temporary staff, which are routine, relatively unimportant and with minimal impact, will not require a complete process (although such decisions should be documented thoroughly for later review if required). However, some decisions, such as major projects or new corporate strategies, would, and should, require a detailed and comprehensive process. The level of detail for any particular decision should depend on the *predetermined* 'Risk Appetite' of the board and management as described in Chapter 5.

Some decisions are routine but important, such as, for example, the take-off of a jumbo jet. Pilots, flight engineers and air-traffic controllers spend much more time in pre-flight checks (*Pre-decision*), than they do in taking off (*Decision*) because by the time pilots throttle the engines to accelerate down the runway they need to be pretty sure that everything has been checked out. And when they are in the air, climbing to their flying altitude, there is a further set of post-take-off checks (*Post-decision*) to ensure that the take-off has been successful. If the take-off has experienced a problem, such as an undercarriage failing to retract, the plane will typically circle while a diagnosis takes place, often requiring that pre-flight checks be re-run or re-evaluated, before determining the next action. Much of the checking for a jumbo jet take-off uses pre-prepared checklists that are run through by the pilots/flight engineers with each step being checked by at least two individuals. These, of course, are the *visible* factors being checked.

Less obvious are the factors that are *invisible*, such as the mental state of the pilots and engineers. Before entering the cockpit, pilots are required to assess their own health for each flight using a suggested checklist for invisible factors with the mnemonic IMSAFE:[18] Illness; Medication; Stress; Alcohol; Fatigue; and Eating. Of course, as humans, pilots may deceive themselves into thinking that they are 'fit to fly' when they are not, but such a checklist follows the principles of counteracting behavioural biases by reminding/nudging pilots of their individual responsibilities *before they fly*. What if decision-makers were to give a moment's consideration as to whether they are mentally and physically equipped to make a 'good' decision before they start? For example, have they read the material fully in preparation for a decision? While there may a loss of face, delaying a decision until people are 'fit to decide' may even avert a disaster.

Some decisions, such as strategy and product development are non-routine, important and will likely have a serious impact on a range of stakeholders. In such decisions, the importance of invisible factors is amplified, as is the importance of the Pre-decision process.

9.3.1 Pre-decision phase

A business decision must have a *purpose* for being taken, such as a problem that has to be solved or a transaction that has to be completed. Otherwise, the decision is merely capricious. But surprisingly the real purpose for a particular decision is often not stated clearly, being assumed in the decision that is actually taken, giving rise to *confirmation bias*. The case of the takeover of ABN AMRO by RBS, described in Chapter 4, is one where the purpose was not only unclear at the outset but also changed as the decision was being taken.[19] At the beginning there was no problem to be solved, as the board had agreed to go forward with an organic rather than an acquisition strategy. However, an opportunity emerged to acquire the Dutch bank. During the prolonged take-over battle, however, the 'purpose' changed to one where 'beating Barclays' became the main driver of the board's thinking. The lack of clarity of its purpose and its detailed objectives was one of the reasons why the takeover was a financial disaster, with RBS paying far too much for the bank and consequently having to be acquired itself by the UK taxpayer.

It may sound obvious, but the first step in any Pre-decision Checklist must be to ask the question, 'What is the purpose for this decision?' and then to gain general agreement that the answer arrived at makes sense for the firm. At this point, when personal investment in any particular answer is not yet strong, constructive criticism may not only head off a potential disaster but also help to hone the rationale for taking a particular decision, making it more likely to be successful. Table 9.1 shows an example of a Pre-decision Checklist for invisible factors, such as possible biases. Documenting the answers for such a checklist will, in fact, create a semi-formal 'terms of reference', against which the final decision can be checked. It should also be noted that the debates and answers to the challenges raised in the checklist would be documented in a fashion that would support a Post-decision Review, so that those involved will be aware that the quality of their decision-making will be under scrutiny.

At first glance it may seem that there are a lot of questions to be answered before a decision can even start to be considered, but there are also a lot of very important questions asked in a pilot's take-off checklist. In fact, all of these questions are, or should be, addressed in any reasonably structured decision process and they are usually answered either explicitly (visible) or implicitly (invisible). The danger of not addressing key questions up front is that they will be addressed further into the decision process and possibly incorrect assumptions will be made, resulting in a bad decision.

An example of this is the case of the JPMorgan Whale,[20] discussed briefly in Chapter 4. In that case, the purpose of a decision to reduce overall risk was very clearly articulated by the board and senior management. However, what was not articulated were the constraints, such as acceptable costs, nor were possible risks addressed. This resulted in decision-makers making assumptions about costs and risks that were at odds with the original purpose of the board and in doing so they made a disastrous decision.

In developing a Pre-decision Checklist for a particular decision, the importance of the 'possible challenges' in Table 9.1 should not be underestimated as these will prompt or 'nudge' individuals to consider questions that they would never have thought of and to raise any concerns that they may have. It is in the interest of everyone, except potentially those who have conflicts of interest, to encourage openness at this stage as the costs and risks of dissent later in the process will be lessened. Do it Once, and Do it Right! And, of course, the situation may arise that, after due consideration of the Pre-decision Checklists, it may be decided not to proceed because, for example, the purpose is not well defined.

Note that one of the questions in this checklist is 'who has been assigned the role of devil's advocate?' In order to minimize Groupthink, Janis[21] recommends that for every major decision someone is designated to ask 'hard questions' and to make a nuisance of themselves. In considering the obstacles to making ethical decisions,

TABLE 9.1   Pre-decision Checklist – possible biases and challenges

Questions	Possible biases	Possible challenges
What is the purpose of this decision? Has the purpose been 'framed' properly? Who will sign off on the purpose?	Overconfidence, Groupthink, Framing, Anchoring, Loss Aversion, Confirmation bias, Sunk Cost Fallacy, Status Quo bias, Planning Fallacy.	Why is this purpose important? What if the decision was not made? What if the purpose was re-stated in a different way? What if we did the opposite? What if we did nothing? Are we doing this because others are doing it? Why do we believe that we will do better than others in achieving this purpose?
Why is this decision being taken at this time?	Availability, Groupthink, Action bias.	Why the hurry? Why should we be 'first movers' in this decision? Are 'deadlines' real or manufactured?
Who is proposing the decision? Who is taking the decision? Who should be taking the decision? Who will be impacted by the decision? Who will sign off on any decision? Who will review the decision process for quality? Who has been assigned the role of 'devil's advocate'?	Groupthink, Conflicts of Interest, 'Halo' effect, Attentional, Availability.	Are the owners of the decision clearly identified? Have all 'stakeholders' been identified? Have any stakeholders been excluded, deliberately or otherwise? Who is likely to support/oppose the decision? Who are the 'squeaky wheels'?
How much time, effort and resources have been allocated to the decision?	Action Bias, Availability, Planning Fallacy.	Is there a project plan for the decision process? Are the time, effort and resources adequate for making the decision?

TABLE 9.1   *continued*

Questions	Possible biases	Possible challenges
What are the conflicts of interest?	Self-serving bias, Blind Spots	Who benefits if the purpose is achieved? Who benefits if the purpose is NOT achieved?
What are the assumptions being made?	Anchoring, Availability, Confirmation.	Have all assumptions been recognized? Have hidden assumptions been articulated?
What is the preferred decision?	Confirmation bias, Status Quo, Blind Spots, Availability, Sunk Costs.	Has a decision already been made? Is an alternative 'too hard work'? Are there good reasons why the decision has not already been taken?
What is specifically included in the decision? What is specifically excluded from the decision?	Availability, Attentional, Groupthink.	Why has something been included/excluded? If something was included/ excluded, would the purpose change?
What information is essential to making this decision? What information is available to make this decision? What information is not available to make this decision?	Availability, Attentional, Confirmation bias.	What do we need to know to make this decision? How much will it cost to acquire the necessary information? What are the risks in not acquiring the information?
What internal expertise is needed to make this decision? What external expertise is needed to make this decision?	Groupthink, Availability, Halo Effect.	Where is the best expertise for analysing this decision? What are the reasons (eg costs/ opposition) for not involving the necessary expertise?
What constraints (eg timing, costs) are there in taking the decision?	Availability, Groupthink, Blind Spots.	Are constraints real or manufactured? What if we had unlimited resources, eg time and money?

TABLE 9.1   *continued*

Questions	Possible biases	Possible challenges
What are the potential impacts of any decision? What are the acceptable impacts of any decision? What are the unacceptable impacts of any decision?	Confirmation bias, Sunk Cost Fallacy, Planning Fallacy.	What is 'worst case' scenario? Have we asked stakeholders how they would be impacted, or made assumptions instead? What if we ended up on the front page of the newspapers?
What risks are there in the decision? What is the 'appetite' for risk?	Availability, Groupthink, Blind Spots, Planning Fallacy, Illusion of Control.	Have we considered possible risks? Have we clearly articulated a 'risk appetite' for this decision? Who analysed the risks, were they independent? Have we looked outside for similar ventures?
What are the criteria for a 'good' decision in this case? How have the criteria been established/prioritized?	Availability, Blind Spots, Planning Fallacy.	What would trigger a re-think? What are the desired outputs? What is the range of desired results? What if the decision was 'bad', see Pre-Mortem?
Decision Ranking (1-9) Routineness (1-9) Importance (1-9) Impact (1-9)	Each individual would assess the decision checklist according to pre-defined criteria.	Average and range of responses. Plus *anonymous* reasons.

Patricia Werhane and her colleagues describe the situation where Colin Marshal, a former CEO of British Airways, created the official role of 'Corporate Fool'[22] and put a senior manager into the role. The purpose of this self-perceived 'court jester' was not only to 'draw attention to things that are going wrong' but to become a means, or lightning rod, to encourage critical thinking and dissent by others:

> When things go wrong employees usually have a good idea of how to fix them. You need to create a state in which they've got the courage to do something. You want to build organizations where everyone sees provocation as one of their essential roles.

In management mythology, chairs of boards and CEOs are supposed to somehow sit as objective 'judges' analysing competing views on a particular decision/strategy before leading 'their people' to a common decision. This, of course, ignores human nature as Chairpersons and CEOs are as prone to behavioural biases as the rest of us and often have an interest in a particular course of action, if only because it vindicates prior decisions, ie there is a *confirmation bias*. There is nothing wrong with a leader having a particular viewpoint, provided that he/she is prepared to let other competing perspectives be heard. Ideally, there should be no need for a devil's advocate in a decision process because, in theory, everyone would have the right, and responsibility, to speak up. Human nature being what it is, however, individuals will be reluctant to do so, and, as in flight cockpits, well-designed checklists provide a platform for junior staff to raise concerns and ask uncomfortable questions. Likewise, checklists provide a mechanism for proposers of a particular decision to pre-empt concerns by addressing possible challenges ahead of time, rather than being in the invidious position of having to 'defend the indefensible' later on. The advantages of using checklists as decision-making tools are explained later after the Decision phase itself is described.

9.3.2 Decision phase

The classic process for making a decision, developed by Herbert Simon and others in the1960s, is a sequence of:

1 defining a 'problem': note this is already covered by the *purpose* described in the Pre-decision Checklist;

2 developing the *options* (possible solutions) for achieving the *purpose* of the decision (ie solving the problem);

3 collecting the *information* required to *analyse* the options;

4 *analysing* each *option* by comparing it against the predefined purpose;

5 *selecting* between *options*, ie taking a decision, which may in fact involve a combination of several options. At this stage an outline plan will usually be developed.

In real life, however, the decision-making process is rarely that simple and, as shown by Henry Mintzberg,[23] most decision-making in business is messy in that the process of analysing options may turn up new options that have to be analysed or may even rule out all options, necessitating a rethink of the original purpose. It is this iterative nature of real-life decision-making that creates risk, because individuals, however diligent, take shortcuts and make unwarranted assumptions in their haste to come to a decision and to be seen as decisive (ie action bias). Table 9.2 shows an example of a Decision Checklist, using Simon's decision phases, which describes possible challenges that may be raised during the decision-making process to counteract possible biases. Again it should be noted that the debates and answers to the questions raised in this checklist would be considered and scored by Decision Participants and documented in a fashion that would support Post-decision Review.

TABLE 9.2 Decision Checklist – questions and possible challenges

Decision phase	Possible challenges
DEVELOPING OPTIONS	
What options are already on the table?	Why have some options been selected? Who benefits from the options already selected? Why have these pre-selected options not been accepted in the past?
Who is proposing each option?	Who benefits from a particular option?
What options have already been excluded?	Why have some options already been rejected? Who benefits from the options already rejected?
What is the process of developing options?	Who will be involved in developing options?
What are the criteria for selecting an option for analysis?	Are criteria clearly identified? Who will sign off on the options to be analysed?
DOCUMENTING OPTIONS	
What is the purpose of each option?	Has the purpose of each option been clearly identified and agreed? Have the options been framed properly?
COLLECTING INFORMATION	
For each option, what information is necessary to perform analysis for this decision?	Have information sources been identified? Has the information been acquired or must it be purchased/ created?
What information will be used?	Has each source of information been verified for *relevance, completeness and accuracy*? Have data quality checks been carried out? Have data capture processes been verified? If existing information sources are used, has their data quality been checked? Has the information used been extracted and stored securely for later analysis and review? Have standard statistics been produced for sense-checking?
ANALYSING OPTIONS	
For each option, what is the plan for analysis?	Does a plan for analysis of each option exist? Are appropriate tools being used to address the agreed criteria for a good decision
For each option, what assumptions and constraints will be used	Has each assumption been articulated, justified and documented? Are the constraints documented and credible?
How will each option be analysed?	What are the results of each option analysis? Has sensitivity analysis been performed?
For each option, how will risks be identified and analysed?	Has independent risk analysis been performed? Is there a risk register?
How will unknowns and uncertainties be identified and analysed?	Are the uncertainties recorded, eg in a risk register. Has a sensitivity analysis of uncertainties been undertaken?

TABLE 9.2   *continued*

Decision phase	Possible challenges
SELECTING OPTIONS	
What is the process of selecting between options that have been analysed?	Is there a description of the selection process and has it been followed? Has each option been analysed to the same standard? Have the same assumptions been used in analysing each option? Have the same uncertainties been analysed in all options?
What is the preferred option(s)?	Have options been compared objectively and to the same criteria? Have challenges (for and against) been given equal weight?
What is the decision?	Does the decision follow the logic of the selection? Is there a *formal* decision with *conclusions* clearly specified? Have the *impacts* been clearly identified?
What is the agreed plan?	Has a comprehensive plan been developed, reviewed and internally agreed? Has a realistic budget been identified, reviewed and internally agreed? Have the risks of implementation been identified, documented and addressed?
What is the Risk Mitigation Plan?	Has the mitigation for each important risk been identified, agreed and action planned, including integration into budget? Have Key Risk Indicators (KRIs) been identified?
What are the unknowns and uncertainties?	Have the unknowns and uncertainties been documented and monitoring actions agreed? Has the need for further information been identified?
What is the sign-off process?	Has the decision process been documented fully? Who will sign off the decision? Who will review the decision?
Assessment of Decision Quality (1–9)	Average and range of assessments. Plus anonymous comments.

9.3.3 Decision phase – tools and techniques

There are many books on how decisions *should* be made (known as 'normative decision-making') with descriptions of many tools and techniques for considering decisions. In fact, there is an emerging international standard (ISO 31010)[24] which describes such tools, including (as a sample of many):

- Decision Tree Analysis: a mechanism for ordering and ranking options (as a tree) and assigning weights to each branch to arrive at the 'best option'.

- Multi-Criteria Decision Analysis (MCDA): a more sophisticated mechanism for ordering and ranking options against multiple rather than a single criteria.
- Brainstorming: a mechanism for encouraging a group of individuals to 'envisage' possible outcomes and risks.
- Discounted Cash Flow (DCF): a mechanism for comparing the financial impacts of various options by using standardized assumptions about prevailing interest rates.
- HAZOP (Hazard and Operability study): a structured technique for identifying risks; and so on.

Such tools are invaluable in trying to come to an objective decision because their purpose is to provide a template into which information can be loaded and (at least semi-) objective results can be determined. But in general such tools deal with *Visible* factors, such as projected cash flows and losses. It is not the purpose of this book to suggest which tools should be used for analysis of visible factors, only that there should be a conscious choice of tools for a particular decision within a particular industry. We are interested here in tools that will bring to the fore *Invisible* factors, which can then be used in conjunction with more conventional decision tools.

One such tool is the *Pre-mortem*. As noted throughout this book, people tend to be optimistic, preferring to see the upside of any decision rather than its risks. The concept of a pre-mortem has been developed to help counteract over-optimistic assessments.[25] A pre-mortem is a post-mortem that takes place before death rather than afterwards, but does not answer the question 'what did cause death', rather 'what could have caused death'? In other words, it is a risk analysis tool. A pre-mortem is usually conducted as a brainstorming exercise after a decision has been made in which a facilitator develops a scenario where the decision being considered has not just gone wrong but has gone horribly wrong. Each individual in the brain-storming group is then given time to come up with a long list of reasons for why the decision could have gone so wrong. These reasons are then revealed, discussed, consolidated and analysed. While noting that a pre-mortem is not a panacea, Daniel Kahneman considers its main virtue is that, like a devil's advocate, it legitimizes doubts and 'encourages even supporters of the decision to search for possible threats that they had not considered earlier'. As a pre-mortem is specifically designed to 'think the unthinkable' it is more likely to make unpalatable risks more visible.

Daniel Kahneman and his late colleague, Amos Tversky, identified a type of 'pervasive optimistic bias', which they termed the *Planning Fallacy*,[26] in which decision-makers develop forecasts and plans that are close to a 'best case scenario' but are at odds with similar situations elsewhere. This is a form of arrogance that results from a conceit that the decision-makers know better than their counterparts in other firms. Bent Flyvbjerg,[27] a Danish transportation planning expert, argues that the major source of error in forecasting is the 'prevalent tendency to underweight or ignore distributional information' and his solution, called 'reference class forecasting' is to develop databases of the outcomes of similar projects. By looking at the 'distribution' of the outcomes of similar decisions, the optimism of decision-makers will be somewhat tempered. In writing on 'strategic risks', Adrian Slywotzky[28] makes the same point by providing statistics on failure rates on 'typical' business projects, such as the well-known 70 per cent failure rate for large IT projects. Slywotzky points out that 'when you overestimate the odds [of success], you underestimate the investment needed to win'. In other words, you almost guarantee failure. Even when such databases are not available, the basic question that individual decision-makers should ask is 'why do we think that we are better than [others] who have failed at the same thing?' The objective is to force decision-makers to search for disconfirming information at the outset. The answers, like a pre-mortem, will help to bring *invisible overconfidence* to the fore.

Simulation is a well-developed technique for unveiling the *range of outcomes* of a particular decision option being analysed.[29] The technique uses the power of computers to run millions of possible scenarios varying the underlying assumptions in each scenario. For example, in considering the introduction of a new product the range of profits from a varying mix of assumptions about costs, pricing and market share can be determined. Simulation is already widely used in industries such as energy exploration as part of their toolkit for analysing *visible* factors, especially where there is a great deal of uncertainty involved in estimating various factors. It can also be used for unearthing *invisible* factors using so-called 'sensitivity analysis'. As part of their standard set of outputs, simulation software packages not only provide the average and range of results but also importantly the sensitivity of the results to underlying assumptions. For example, the profitability of a new product will be highly sensitive to factors such as market share and price. By discussing how assumptions about such factors have been arrived at, then biases such as overconfidence and confirmation can be unearthed.

What are the roles and responsibilities of the individual in such analysis? The checklists, tools and techniques described here are designed to bring to the fore the biases and (sometimes unwarranted) assumptions that everyone brings with them to considering every problem. The responsibility of the individual in making decisions then is not to be defensive but to admit that they may have biases and to be open to, and to look for, opportunities to question their own understanding of a particular situation. It's not wrong to be wrong, but it is wrong to believe that you can never be wrong.

9.3.4 Post-decision phase

The purpose of the Post-decision phase is *NOT* to second guess or re-make a decision but to assess a particular decision for *quality*. In particular, did the decision-makers follow a good process and as far as possible identify and try to counteract any individual and group biases? Nor is such a review considering the outcomes of a decision but ideally would be conducted immediately after a decision was made and before any plans are signed off for implementation. The review can be seen as a last chance to catch any problems with the decision before resources are expended and to identify any unresolved concerns.

Table 9.3 shows an example of a Post-decision Checklist that describes 'possible tests' of good decision-making with assessments and an overall assessment as to whether a formal Decision Review is required. Note the assessments here are examples from a range of 1 to 9, but other measures of decision quality could be used.

TABLE 9.3   Post-decision Checklist – decision quality

Questions	Possible tests (examples)	Assessment
Did the decision-makers follow a good decision-making process?	Was the documentation adequate? Was sufficient time given to raise and address concerns? Was there an Action bias?	1= Minimal process. ..... 9 = Comprehensive well-documented process.
Has the purpose of the decision been identified properly?	Did the purpose change during the decision process?	1 = Purpose unclear. ..... 9 = Clear well-documented purpose.
Was participation in decision-making adequate?	Was there evidence of bullying or Groupthink? Was there evidence of 'passivity'? Was there evidence of 'denial' among participants?	1 = Lack of challenge. ..... 9 = Decision challenged and concerns resolved satisfactorily.
Were decision-makers and stakeholders involved?	Was there sufficient challenge or was the decision a 'fait accompli'? Were there any attempts to close down discussion prematurely?	1 = Lack of involvement. ..... 9 = All decision-makers and stakeholders involved.
Were conflicts of interest identified and addressed?	Did individual participants identify their own and others' conflicts of interest?	1 = No conflicts identified. ..... 9 = Conflicts clearly identified and addressed.
Were assumptions, and constraints identified and addressed?	Were assumptions, and constraints fully documented?	1 = No assumptions, and Constraints identified. ..... 9 = Assumptions and constraints clearly identified and addressed.

TABLE 9.3   *continued*

Questions	Possible tests (examples)	Assessment
Was information collected and analysed properly as to relevance, completeness and accuracy?	Were sufficient reasons given for each source of information used? Was each source of information analysed for relevance, completeness and accuracy? Did the decision-makers search for disconfirming information?	1 = No rigorous analysis of information quality. ..... 9 = All information collected and analysed.
Was internal and external expertise sought and listened to?	Was the rationale documented for seeking the expertise used? Did the decision-makers incorporate the advice of external experts?	1 = No expertise sought. ..... 9 = Relevant expertise sought and opinions used.
Were the interests of non-participant stakeholders considered?	Did the decision-makers seek to engage non-participants? Were the concerns of non-participants taken into account?	1 = Non participants ignored. ..... 9 = Concerns of non-participants sought and considered.
Were the full range of options considered in the decision?	Was there comprehensive documentation on each option? Were the arguments for discarding certain options credible? Was there evidence of 'Confirmation bias'?	1 = Options not considered ..... 9 = All options analysed methodically and objectively.
Were the full range of risks considered in the decision?	Was there a formal Risk Management process and did it complete properly? Were risks assessed properly? Have risks been reviewed by Risk Management professionals?	1 = Risks not considered. ..... 9 = Risks identified and assessed methodically.

TABLE 9.3   *continued*

Questions	Possible tests (examples)	Assessment
Were unknowns and uncertainties adequately documented?	Have uncertainties and unknowns been identified? Has the rationale for not resolving uncertainties been given and is it credible? Have processes for monitoring uncertainties been proposed?	1 = No analysis of uncertainties. ..... 9 = All uncertainties identified and monitoring initiated.
Was there a formal decision?	Was a formal decision agreed with outstanding issues recorded?	1 = No formal decision. ..... 9 = Formal decision documented and agreed with outstanding issues highlighted.
Have plans been developed and agreed?	Have the plans been documented in sufficient detail? Have the plans been reviewed by external experts?	1 = No agreed plans. ..... 9 = Detailed plans produced and reviewed.
Have concerns been addressed?	Have documented concerns been addressed to the satisfaction of those who raised them?	1 = Concerns ignored or overridden. ..... 9 = Concerns addressed.
Assessment of Decision Quality (1–9)	Decision Reviewer(s) and participants would review decision.	Average and range of assessments. Plus *anonymous* assessments.
Review Required?	**Yes/No**	Reasons for decision-maker review.

In this model of decision-making, Post-decision analysis would be conducted by an independent, skilled Decision Process Reviewer, whose role would be to consider the *documentation* provided by the decision-makers to support the decision. The documentation provided to the reviewer would not only include formal reports and analyses but also meeting notes (including in the case of board decisions, official board minutes) and detailed reports/artefacts used to support analysis (such as spreadsheets). Individuals involved in the decision-making process would also be asked to complete the Post-decision Checklist(s), anonymously if preferred, with annotation as to their reasons for a particular viewpoint. The Decision Process Reviewer would take the reasons proffered by decision-makers, and in particular dissenters, into account when assessing the quality of a decision that was made and requesting a Decision Review by decision-makers, if required.

It is likely that a Post-decision Review would not be a one-off exercise but somewhat iterative as it is possible, even probable, that further documentation would be requested to back up parts of the decision process that were not adequately documented. In such cases, the overall assessment of the decision 'quality' would reflect the lack of comprehensive documentation. Note here we do not discuss the issue of measuring 'decision quality' as we believe this should be determined by management as part of setting up a comprehensive decision process. As noted elsewhere, the action of developing such assessment (and subsequent reward) criteria would provide a valuable learning opportunity for management and HR experts to tailor the concept to the unique situation of their firms. The danger, as with any assessment scheme of course, is that it may be 'gamed' by individuals to their benefit.

9.3.5 Decision process – output

The output from any decision-making process would normally be a formal *Decision* that is ready for sign-off/approval by the board and/or management. Like the 'lines of defence' described in Chapter 8, the approvers would act as yet another check on the decision made and the quality of the process used to make that decision. But by considering carefully the *invisible* pressures at each stage of the decision process and by documenting them, ie making the decision *visible*, approvers can be assured that a sound decision process had been followed.

It is highly probable that when significant decisions are made, some information will be unknown, and there will be some degree of uncertainty, or risk. Provided that the unknowns are documented, management can put in place the monitoring and information-gathering processes to make the unknown better understood, ie to reduce risk.

To some, following a formal decision-making process, such as that described here, will seem overkill, and to others it will appear to be merely a 'tick in the box' exercise. In some situations this may indeed be the case, but a formal process with challenges, pauses, reflection and cross-checks is more likely to identify concerns that may lead to serious problems than an overconfident decision-maker relying on their instinct. *Just Do It* is an appealing advertising slogan but the athletes that front such advertisements have not arrived at the pinnacle of their chosen fields by 'just doing it'; they have put in years of disciplined hard work beforehand. The athletes only make it look easy because of the effort and thought that they have already put in. Decision-making too needs hard work – 'just doing it' is a recipe for disaster.

9.4 Checklists and decision-making

9.4.1 Use of checklists

In his best-selling book *The Checklist Manifesto*, the American surgeon and academic, Professor Atul Gawande[30] describes how he became a convert to, and vocal advocate of, the use of seemingly simple checklists in medicine, precisely because they are proven to save lives by picking up mistakes. In his book *Risk Savvy*, the noted psychologist and behavioural scientist Gerd Gigerenzer[31] discusses the growing (but still insufficient) use of checklists in medicine, citing examples where fatality rates were dramatically reduced by the use of simple checklists. With humans, sometimes the simplest solution is indeed the most effective. If highly-educated, skilled, senior medical personnel are prepared to go through tedious checklist drills why should managers in other disciplines not be prepared to do the same?

Checklists have a bad reputation in business, and are generally seen as enforcing control and stifling creativity. But, as practical experience and research studies in aviation and medicine have demonstrated, checklists save lives.[32] So why could checklists not be used to prevent losses in business? Box 9.1 shows an example of how the disciplined use of checklists helped to save lives.

Box 9.1   Example of the use of aviation checklists

Professor Atul Gawande, a vocal proponent of checklists in medicine, uses the example of the forced ditching of US Airways Flight 1549 into the Hudson River in New York, in January 2009, after a catastrophic and unprecedented 'dual bird strike' had destroyed both engines of the plane. While the pilot, Captain Chesley B. Sullenberger III, has been rightly lionized for his skill in saving all of the passengers, both Captain 'Sully' and Professor Gawande credit the disciplined use of emergency checklists and the professional expertise of all of the crew, especially the co-pilot, for the successful ditching and subsequent rescue. Despite the fact that the pilot and co-pilot (who incidentally had not flown together before) had never, in their long careers, been in a plane accident, their training had taught them that this was not the time to panic or to experiment.

On the contrary, the crew coolly worked their way through a number of checklists that helped them keep the plane in the air until it was belly-flopped into the river near to rescue craft. In this case, checklists were used to quickly eliminate fruitless possibilities, reducing the many alternatives to a few practical options, which the training and skill of the crew allowed them to take advantage of. Here, we may think of checklists as 'windscreen wipers' for decisions, increasing visibility.

Gerd Gigerenzer discussed the same incident and noted that the pilots just did not have time to complete all of the necessary checklists, but used their skill and intuition to select the most important ones, in this case those checklists concerned with evacuation safety. The pilots also used rules of thumb, or heuristics, to gauge the severity of their unfolding situation – a fine example of 'situational awareness'.

But, as Professor Gawande admits, business managers shy away from checklists, seeing them as boring and useful only for clerical tasks. This is, of course, a sort of hubris, a behavioural bias that states that 'my job cannot be automated'. But such a bias misunderstands the key point about checklists in support of non-routine decisions. Checklists are not about telling a decision-maker what to do but to remind them *what not to do*. As shown throughout this book, human memory is fallible. We quickly forget or underestimate past mistakes and remember or overestimate triumphs, especially those that are recent, ie the *availability bias*. Professor Gawande also identifies another behavioural trait that is essential in good decision-making – discipline. Humans are not good at discipline, preferring instead instant gratification. But a checklist forces us to go through the necessary checks item by item in a disciplined manner because someone else is watching and doing the checks along with us. The gratification is the sense of relief that, at the completion of the checklist, the checkers did not bring anything untoward to mind.

Professor Gawande argues that the most successful checklists are those that are built up from an objective analysis of past failures and updated as new failures occur. They are not a control measure, restricting professional autonomy, but an 'aide-mémoire', that is designed to remind decision-makers of possible pit-falls. If a well-constructed checklist is followed in a disciplined manner, in 99 out of 100 or even 999/1000 times, the checks will reveal nothing. However, in the one case among many, the checks may throw up something that justifies the tedious checking effort when everything was OK. The final argument that Gawande demolishes is that checklists slow down decision-making. While that is true when a checklist is first introduced, Gawande found, in both medical and non-medical situations, such as investment management, that after a time the use of good checklists improves overall productivity because less time is wasted investigating fruitless options. Completing a checklist does not guarantee success, especially if decision-makers just 'tick the boxes' but if taken seriously and done by more than one person, it gives a level of comfort that at least all of the bases we already know about have been covered.

9.4.2 Checklists and individual responsibility

The language of business is *impersonal* and *collective*, with terms such as corporation, board, executive, division, management, staff, customers, regulator, shareholder, etc. This is deliberate because, to a large degree, the individuals in these groups are replaceable and interchangeable. But there is a paradox, in that while individuals in particular roles are indeed replaceable, on the other hand, when they are in their jobs they are very important even though, as shown throughout this book, they can give rise to considerable losses. Likewise, *responsibility* is diffuse and often collective, with terms such as 'the company has declared a profit', 'the board has agreed a strategy' or 'the firm has paid a fine'. The last term is interesting in that the wording should be reframed to something like 'the individual directors have agreed collectively that shareholders (collectively) should pay a fine'. These are real people making decisions that impact the wealth of real people but are hidden behind a cloak of collective anonymity.

In the face of collective pressures then individuals will find it hard to persist in raising their concerns unless there is a support structure that gives them the right *and the responsibility* to raise concerns. In extreme circumstances the whistleblowing processes described in Chapter 5 will provide a safeguard for those who feel that their concerns are not taken seriously, but the whistleblowing process cannot be used in the case of every decision. There would be chaos and paralysis if that was the situation. Firms that are interested in improving their decision-making performance, if only to avert disasters, must then put in place mechanisms for individuals' concerns to be raised and respectfully addressed.

In the industrial era, checklists in the form of inspectors with clipboards became an anathema to workers, as the inspectors were seen as policemen or informers. In the modern industrial era, however, Japanese working practices, such as Six Sigma[33] have given workers responsibility for checking and adjusting their own work and have revolutionized manufacturing, especially in the automotive industry. In the much admired Toyota Production System (TPS),[34] an individual worker is allowed/ encouraged to 'stop the production line' if they detect a problem, even though this may cause delays costing millions of Yen. Jidoka, as it is called in Japanese, recognizes the reality that it is much less expensive to detect and correct a problem as early as possible than to let its effects spread throughout a system. Surely the same is true of a bad decision? In conventional business decision-making processes, there are so-called 'decision gates' at which there is a decision, usually collective, to 'Go/No Go'. Such gates are similar to the old industrial model of post-manufacture inspections, which are too late to prevent problems corrupting the production line. The traditional approach may catch some problems but in doing so much time and effort has already been wasted. It is, however, relatively easy to detect a manufacturing quality problem, but much more difficult to detect a bad decision, since much of the thinking leading up to the decision will be invisible.

In Japanese manufacturing, individuals do not shut production down on a whim, precisely because they have been given, or *empowered* with, the responsibility for closing down the line when they think fit, and they *take the decision seriously*. Nor do employees take such a decision without data; in fact they are constantly monitoring production line statistics to detect potential problems. As Hersh Shefrin argues, such an approach is *psychologically smart*, training people to understand data, empowering them to make sensible decisions based on that data and respecting them for taking hard decisions.

In the Decision Model shown in Figure 9.1, the 'data' are the checklists that provide individuals with prompts or 'nudges' as to what a 'good' decision should cover. By populating the checklists with questions and possible challenges, not only are people *allowed* to ask those questions but also those proposing a particular decision are prompted to address potentially embarrassing questions ahead of time. That is, the individual decision-makers think through the answers to questions that they possibly would never have raised themselves. Checklists may be boring and lend themselves to a 'tick in the box' response but critical thinking and review by multiple people during the decision process should help mitigate against such tedium.

Throughout this book, the dangers of *not* making decisions have been highlighted. This chapter has looked specifically at tools and techniques for improving decision-making. In particular a new decision-making process is developed which is designed to make visible the biases and pressures that may cause bad decisions to be made. In particular the increased use of Decision Checklists is promoted as a tool to improve good decision-making. While the use of checklists will not completely eliminate an individual's natural tendency not to get involved, the discipline of having to complete checklists will encourage individuals to at least answer positively rather than not taking part in discussions. If, in addition, *passivity* is seen as a trait that does not support others in their decision-making, that will be reflected in lower assessments of decision-making performance not only for the individual but also the group as a whole. The next chapter considers how individuals can be encouraged to take more *Personal Responsibility* for their decision-making.

Notes

1   See Weise, K (2013) Meet the broker who made Merrill pay for racial bias, *Bloomberg*, 4 December, www.bloomberg.com Note, this was the largest settlement in such cases at the time.
2   See Sherfin (2008).
3   The same logic is applicable outside of finance, of course. If more senior managers were literate about project management, for example understanding 'critical path analysis', and project managers were forced to provide more detail of the risks in their plans and their potential impacts, then it is probable fewer really bad projects would get off the ground.
4   The Money Advice Service is an independent body set up in the wake of the UK PPI scandal, and aims to help people manage their money through a free and impartial advice service. www.moneyadviceservice.org.uk
5   For a description of the evolution of Health and Safety legislation in the United States see the Wikipedia article *Occupational Safety and Health Act*.
6   This is another example of what is called the Planning Fallacy or the failure to look elsewhere for examples of success or failure.
7   See Kahneman (2011).
8   This does not diminish the day-to-day decisions made by ordinary people, such as when to plant a particular crop, but these were often pre-programmed using tools such as a 'farmer's almanac'.
9   This is also known as 'Monday Morning Quarterbacking'.
10 See Mintzberg (1978).
11 A discussion of such heresy is beyond this book other than to note that as holders of advanced Business Administration degrees and significant managerial experience, the authors have a lot of sympathy for Professor Mintzberg's point of view.

12 See Weharne *et al* (2103).

13 See Ariely (2013) and Heffernan (2011) for examples of self-deception and 'wilful blindness'.

14 See Janis (1971).

15 See Heffernan (2011).

16 See Bohns, V, Roghanizad, M and Xu, A (2013) Underestimating our influence over others' unethical behaviour and decisions, *Personality and Social Psychology Bulletin* XX(X) 1–15, published online at http://www.ncbi.nlm.nih.gov/pubmed/24327670

17 Care would have to be taken that this process does not result in 'paralysis by analysis'.

18 See for example Flight Fitness (undated) *The 'I'm Safe' Checklist* at http://www.leftseat.com/imsafe.htm which provides references to the FAA (Federal Aviation Authority) regulations in this area.

19 See Martin (2013) and Fraser (2014) for descriptions of the chaotic decisions made by the RBS board and management during the ABN AMRO takeover.

20 See McConnell, P (2014) Dissecting the JPMorgan whale: a post-mortem, *Journal of Operational Risk*, **9** (2), pp 1–42.

21 See Janis (1971).

22 In Economics, the more acceptable term, Contrarian Thinker, is often used for the same role.

23 See Mintzberg (1978).

24 *ISO 31010 Risk management – Risk assessment techniques* is a standard developed by ISO as a part of the ISO 31000 set of standards. At the time of writing it is currently under review. See www.iso.org

25 See Kahneman (2011).

26 For a description of the Planning Fallacy, see Kahneman (2011).

27 See Flyvbjerg *et al* (2003).

28 See Slywotsky (2007).

29 See Vose (2008).

30 See Gawande (2010).

31 See Gigerenzer (2014).

32 See Gawande (2010) and Gigerenzer (2014).

33 See Pande *et al* (2000) for a description of Six Sigma and its uses.

34 See Pande *et al* (2000) and article *Toyota Production System* in Wikipedia.

Personal responsibility

10

"Remember always that you not only have the right to be an individual, you have an obligation to be one. ELEANOR ROOSEVELT

KEY MESSAGES

- Persuading individuals, through carrots and sticks, to take personal responsibility for their conduct and decisions is key to effective People Risk Management.

- Corporate Codes of Conduct tend to be impersonal, legalistic and remote from the individual.

- Job Descriptions concentrate on 'what' individuals should do, not on 'how' to do it.

- To encourage personal responsibility, what is needed are *Personalized* Codes of Conduct that describe how individuals should behave in their specific jobs.

As noted in Chapter 1, following the Global Financial Crisis, a Special Commission of the UK Parliament[1] produced recommendations for *Changing Banking for Good*, in particular placing a new emphasis on 'making *individual responsibility* in banking a reality, especially at the most senior levels', because 'too many bankers, especially at the most senior levels, have operated in an environment with *insufficient personal responsibility*'. Among other recommendations, the Commission proposed 'new licencing and regulatory regimes aimed at identifying and enforcing *personal responsibilities* for senior executives'. We support these initiatives but we also argue that, as People Risk exists at all levels, the need for improved personal responsibility extends to all individuals in a firm, not just directors and senior executives. And it extends to firms other than banks. In industries such as aviation and medicine, the journey towards increasing individual personal responsibility has already started but it needs to begin in other industries also, especially those, such as banks and energy companies, that create significant risks for the general economy and the public.

However, changing the attitudes of people towards personal responsibility will be a huge endeavour that will take years and even then will only be partially successful. There is no 'silver bullet'! This chapter, however, suggests some mechanisms that can help firms to create an environment where individuals can take more personal responsibility for their decisions and subsequent actions. The logic of this is simple – if individuals take more personal responsibility for their decisions, there will be fewer thoughtless decisions made and hence there will be fewer *bad* decisions from which losses can occur. This does not, however, guarantee that bad decisions will never be made. This chapter looks at an area where individual responsibilities can be enhanced, in particular helping to improve individuals' conduct through *Personalized Codes of Conduct*. Corporate Codes of Conduct and Job Descriptions are worthy documents but are written from the perspective of the company rather than the individual. Such documents, which by necessity are legalistic, tend to be 'one size fits all' and thus are difficult for individuals to apply to solving the day-to-day ethical problems that they face. To affect individuals' behaviour and to encourage individuals to take personal responsibility for their actions, such documents must be tailored to the individual.

10.1 Codes of Conduct

10.1.1 Corporate Codes of Conduct

Codes of Conduct (sometimes called Codes of Ethics) have been a feature of corporate governance for many years. In the aftermath of the Enron and WorldCom failures described in Chapter 4, the US Government enacted the Sarbanes-Oxley Act[2] (Public Company Accounting Reform and Investor Protection Act). This so-called SOX Act requires companies that do business in the United States (not just US firms) to disclose annually whether the company has adopted a code of ethics for the company's major officers and, if not, to explain why not. In practice, this means that most major international companies are required to produce such a code. The SOX Act defined a 'code of ethics' as:

> Written standards that are reasonably necessary to deter wrongdoing and to promote:
>
> **1** honest and ethical conduct, including the ethical handling of actual or apparent conflicts of interest between personal and professional relationships;
>
> **2** full, fair, accurate, timely, and understandable disclosure in reports and documents that a company files with, or submits to, the Commission and in other public communications made by the company;
>
> **3** compliance with applicable governmental laws, rules and regulations;

4 the prompt internal reporting of code violations to an appropriate person or persons identified in the code; and

5 accountability for adherence to the code.

It should be noted at this point that Enron and WorldCom did have published codes of conduct before they failed, so it is not obvious what the SOX requirement would have achieved in those situations, other than to have the weight of law behind the codes for any transgressions.[3]

Examples of significant corporate codes of conduct or ethics[4] that have been developed since the GFC uncovered examples of individual and corporate misconduct, include:

- BP – 'Our Code: It's what we believe in';
- JPMorgan – 'Integrity It starts with you';
- Bank of America – 'Life's Better When We're Connected'; and
- Goldman Sachs – 'Our Shared Responsibility to Our Clients, Colleagues and Communities'.

Following the LIBOR manipulation scandal and an independent Board-commissioned review by a leading lawyer, Sir Anthony Salz,[5] Barclays embarked on a *multi-year* programme to develop a new Code of Conduct based upon the tag 'Tough Questions, Honest Answers'.

As would be expected from such large corporations, these new codes are impressive and motivational documents that embody the aspirations of the respective firms to live up to the highest ideals of conduct. For example, in a statement by Jamie Dimon, Chairman and CEO of JPMorgan Chase, the code states:

> The core concept behind our Code of Conduct is that no one at JPMorgan Chase should ever sacrifice his or her integrity, whether for personal gain or for a perceived benefit to the Company's business. Harm to our reputation affects the entire Company and is enduring. Any perceived ethical transgression, no matter how isolated or minor, can damage our Company.

The sentiment that 'any perceived ethical transgression, no matter how isolated or minor, can damage our Company' is based on the experience of having paid over US $20 billion dollars in fines and compensation for transgressions in several businesses in the years following the GFC.[6] This code is described as a document for *everyone* as 'we believe that all who work for, or on behalf of, JPMorgan Chase have a duty to demonstrate the highest standards of business conduct'. At this stage, a sceptic might mention bolting horses and closing stable doors but that might be overly distrustful as the intention, at least publicly, is to change the way that the people within JPMorgan conduct their business. But the devil is in the detail, specifically how to make such aspirational goals relevant to employees in their day-to-day work and how to measure their adherence to these goals?

The codes of conduct of major firms tend to be a mix of motivational and somewhat threatening sentiments. For example, the Bank of America code contains well-meaning sentences such as: 'Bank of America Corporation is committed to the highest standards of ethical and professional conduct' but at the same time warns that 'employees must not obtain or use intellectual property of others in violation of confidentiality obligations or by other improper means'. Bank of America is not alone. For example in BP's 'Our Code' there is the motivational statement from the CEO:

> To be a trusted company, year after year, we need to work to a consistent and higher set of standards and follow them in everything we do and say, every day, everywhere we work.
>
> [coupled with]
>
> NEVER... Conceal, or assist in the concealment of, the offering, giving or receiving of gifts and entertainment.

On the other hand, Goldman Sachs' code is distinctly motivational and somewhat self-congratulatory:

> The dedication of our people to the firm and the intense effort they give their jobs are greater than one finds in most other organizations. We think that this is an important part of our success.
>
> [but does have statements such as]
>
> We do not tolerate any type of discrimination prohibited by law, including harassment.

Table 10.1 is an analysis of the key Conduct Issues covered in these official codes of conduct. It should be noted that this table lists the issues that were highlighted in the respective codes, for example, with a dedicated section. It does *not* imply that other issues are not considered elsewhere by the company or are considered unimportant.

As can be seen, and as might be expected from leading firms, these codes cover roughly the same issues. However, the number of pages in these codes are very different, from 9 in that of Goldman Sachs to 112 in the case of BP. Of course, codes of conduct are only summaries of a whole range of policies and procedures that make up an official Employee Handbook or are expanded on internal websites. For example, BP's code does contain a lot of detail that is referred to, rather than expanded, in other codes such as that of Bank of America. Goldman Sachs' code is short but does refer to a separate document, the Business Principles,[7] which was created over three years by a specially convened Business Standards Committee, following large fines against the bank in the wake of the GFC. These Principles are largely motivational and aspirational such as 'Our assets are our people, capital and reputation' but also (albeit as the final principle) 'Integrity and honesty are at the heart of our business. We expect our people to maintain high ethical standards in everything they do, both in their work for the firm and in their personal lives'. Interestingly, the reference to integrity in 'personal lives' is somewhat more threatening than motivational, since 'integrity' outside of work is very subjective and difficult, if not impossible, for employers to police.

10.1.2 What should be in a Code of Conduct?

So what should a Code of Conduct contain? The codes of conduct summarized above (and others) raise interesting questions around 'Who is the code aimed at?' and 'How does the management of the firm know that their code is being read and understood, never mind adhered to?' Obviously, the answer to the first question must include employees as the primary target, but employees range from the lowest

TABLE 10.1   Contents of selected Codes of Conduct

Conduct Issue	BP	JP Morgan	Bank of America	Goldman Sachs
Internal				
Legal Compliance	Yes	Yes	Yes	Yes
Conflicts of Interest	Yes	Yes	Yes	Yes
Health and Safety	Yes	Yes	Yes	
Ethical Decision-making	Yes	Yes	Yes	Yes
Insider Trading	Yes	Yes	Yes	Yes
Diversity	Yes	Yes	Yes	Yes
Discrimination/Bullying	Yes	Yes	Yes	
Intellectual Property	Yes	Yes	Yes	
Use/Abuse of Assets	Yes	Yes	Yes	Yes
Use of Technology	Yes	Yes	Yes	
Whistleblowing/Non-Retaliation	Yes	Yes	Yes	Yes
Investor Information/Media	Yes	Yes	Yes	
Political Contributions	Yes	Yes	Yes	Yes
Alcohol and Drugs	Yes	Yes		
Customers				
Fairness		Yes	Yes	Yes
Information Protection	Yes	Yes	Yes	Yes
Suppliers				
Bribery	Yes	Yes	Yes	
Gifts and Entertainment	Yes	Yes	Yes	
Regulators				
Financial Reporting	Yes	Yes	Yes	Yes
Anti-Trust/Anti-Competition	Yes	Yes		Yes
Anti-Boycott	Yes	Yes		
Anti-Money Laundering	Yes	Yes	Yes	
Government Employees	Yes	Yes	Yes	
Other, eg Societal				
Corporate Social Responsibility		Yes	Yes	
Human Rights		Yes		
Environment	Yes	Yes	Yes	
Number of Pages in Code	112	52	20	9
Independent Monitoring	Ethics and Compliance	Code Specialist	Ethics and Compliance	External Party

level entrant to the Chairperson and all levels of staff and contractors in between. This begs the question, can a 'one size fits all' approach ever work, given the vast range of opportunities for misunderstanding and misconduct in a large international corporation? A single cover-all code is also dangerous, not least because one serious transgression by management, such as a regulatory fine or adverse publicity, will weaken the power of the code for many employees, because they perceive that management's talk is not being walked.

The second question is even more important. Just how does a firm know that their code is actually working? At JPMorgan for example, new employees are required to 'affirm' that they: (a) have read and understood the code before joining; (b) must complete training in the code shortly after joining; and (c) affirm their adherence periodically, 'usually annually'. Likewise, Bank of America requires employees to take training and to 'acknowledge' the code each year. While admirable, how does the firm know that after a time the affirmation does not become merely a 'tick in the box' exercise? Unless there is periodic and rigorous *testing* of employees on their understanding of the meaning and implications of a firm's code on a regular basis, such as the type of testing undertaken by pilots, firms will not know that their codes are effective.

The codes of conduct of these large firms are documents aimed at presenting the firm to its employees and other stakeholders, such as investors, as being *thoughtful* about a wide range of conduct and ethical issues. In other words, they are aspirational values that are espoused by the firm. However, as explained in Chapter 7, espoused values are not necessarily the same as the 'invisible assumptions' of the employees. Codes of conduct are important – not as manuals that drive day-to-day conduct (because even the most detailed are too high-level for that) but as route maps for driving corporate culture, as templates for developing personal responsibilities, and importantly, as a tool for managing People Risk.

The Open Compliance and Ethics Group (OCEG),[8] a not-for-profit group that aims to improve corporate governance standards, identifies what it calls the 'Code of Conduct Conundrum' in which firms spend considerable time and effort crafting codes of conduct but do not understand or measure what value such codes actually have. It is true that, after the Sarbanes Oxley Act, firms are legally required to have such a code and to regularly 'affirm' that the codes are effective, at least at senior management level. But beyond senior management is there any real traction of typical codes throughout firms? The OCEG believes *not* and answers the question 'what value do codes of conduct have?' with:

> Not much if the only reason we have one is to satisfy a legal requirement to do so. But quite a lot if we use it as the central hub of a well-thought-out and supported capability for driving corporate values and expectations for conduct into the fabric of the company culture and designing a code system that truly can be measured for effectiveness.

We agree with the OCEG but go further than their suggested solution of using technology to keep a corporate code relevant and up to date (in a legal sense) by distributing updates to all employees electronically. While agreeing that distributing updates to a corporate code is valuable, the key is to get individuals not merely to receive updates of the code but to really understand it by applying its principles to their individual situations on a day-to-day basis. The concept of a *Personalized Code of Conduct* is described below after discussing the concept of Personal Responsibilities.

10.2 Personal responsibilities

10.2.1 Individual responsibilities in Codes of Conduct

The codes of conduct described above are predominantly one-directional, articulating, with a list of dos and don'ts, what the company *expects of the employee*. But what precisely are individuals responsible for? BP's code talks about 'shared responsibility' for example for 'protecting people's health, safety, security and the environment' but does note that there is a need for 'personal responsibility for putting our code into practice'. Likewise, Goldman Sachs and Bank of America talk about 'shared' or 'our' responsibilities.

In the same vein, the JP Morgan code describes the 'shared' responsibility for 'preserving and building on the company's proud heritage'. And for each major section in its code it summarizes with personal 'Your Responsibilities'. The final responsibility in the summary section is significant – 'If something doesn't seem right, say something'. This statement is the licence given to an employee to question decisions and raise issues of concern but it is hidden in one sentence in 52 pages of sometimes necessarily legalistic prose. However, in concluding remarks, the code does reinforce the message of 'non-retaliation':

> Finally, remember that JPMorgan Chase doesn't tolerate retaliation against anyone who raises an issue or concern in good faith. If you seek advice, raise a concern or report suspected acts of misconduct, you are complying with our Code and helping to maintain an ethical JPMorgan Chase. Integrity – it starts with you.

But while this statement is designed to be motivational and is undoubtedly well-meaning, it does raise the problem of how does one question a decision 'in good faith'. The statement raises the bar on raising questions directly with managers or colleagues as opposed to so-called 'code specialists'. If an employee has to follow a separate process to question operational decisions, it is likely that this route will be reserved for exceptional matters that are normally handled by the firm's whistle-blowing processes. In short, while the code does provide more avenues for redress for staff who feel aggrieved or uncertain about specific decisions, it does not, in practice, promote the open and transparent exchange of ideas and information that would encourage staff to take personal responsibility for their own decisions and actions.

10.2.2 Codes of Conduct that stress individual responsibilities

As noted in earlier chapters, the aviation industry has, through sometimes bitter experience, worked to adopt an open, transparent, no-blame approach to the risks that pilots face when flying. The Aviators Model Code of Conduct (AMCC)[9] is a *set* of codes of conduct for the aviation industry developed by private companies, delivered free of charge to the industry and endorsed for training purposes by regulatory bodies such as the US Federal Aviation Administration (FAA). The FAA notes that training in the codes will 'advance flight safety by improving judgement, honing aeronautical decision-making skills, and encouraging an ethical approach to flying'. The AMCC for pilots begins with general statements of personal responsibilities, for example:

> Pilots should: a) make safety the highest priority;... d) recognize and manage risks effectively, and use sound principles of risk management; and... h) adhere to applicable laws and regulations.

The statements throughout the code then reinforce the personal nature of a pilot's responsibilities, for example in relation to passengers:

> Pilots should: a) maintain passenger safety first and then reasonable passenger comfort; b) manage risk and avoid unnecessary risk to passengers, to people and property on the surface, and to people in other aircraft...

For each of these responsibilities, the AMCC provides an explanation that reinforces the point, such as 'Pilots are responsible for the safety and comfort of their passengers'. The Pilot Code also gives practical advice such as 'Improve safety margins by planning and flying conservatively'. Through this code, which is reinforced by regular training and testing, the personal responsibilities *and priorities* of pilots are made very clear. In the UK, the Civil Aviation Authority (CAA) has taken a different approach[10] but clearly articulates what is expected of pilots, airlines, airport operators and so on. Of particular interest, the CAA encourages aircraft maintenance operators to develop a Maintenance Error Management System (MEMS) which encourages the recording and dissemination of human and system errors for learning and inspection purposes.

But as the case of the death of Mrs Elaine Bromiley, described in Chapter 4, illustrates it is not just the aviation industry that is taking individual responsibility seriously. Prompted by Mrs Bromiley's husband the UK National Health Service is working to incorporate 'Human Factors' into its day-to-day processes. For example, the NHS promotes the use of the 'World Health Organization Surgical Safety Checklist' which is a simple but proven mechanism of reducing errors in surgical operations.[11] Among the questions on this list, surgeon(s) are asked to confirm that everyone involved in the operation has introduced themselves to one another. This simple courtesy helps to build the respect that is essential as advice and help may be needed when difficult issues arise.

As an example of respect and individual responsibility, the approach of the Duke University Health System presents one model. Duke, a large health system in North Carolina, United States, with over 26,000 employees, has published a document called 'Living Our Values'[12] which describes its five principal values as being teamwork, integrity, diversity, excellence and safety. Taking 'teamwork', as an example, the individual employee (surgeon or clerk) asserts that they will, amongst other things:

- welcome the ideas and value the concerns of others;
- refrain from saying 'It's not my job'. If I'm unable to meet the request, I will find someone who can;

- keep people informed by making sure the patient, family, and each co-worker knows the patient's plan of care and explain delays;
- welcome new staff members by being supportive, offering help and setting an example;
- be positive, enjoy others, celebrate successes and share laughter.

In Duke's statement, the key behaviours that are expected of staff members include aspirations that individuals should, amongst other things:

- smile and make eye contact;
- wear ID badges facing forward;
- pick up trash and clean up spills;
- acknowledge outstanding service;
- take personal responsibility for patients and family requests.

While some of these statements may sound trite, in effect they constitute a *Personalized Code of Conduct* for individual employees. Of course, individuals will not always live up to these high-minded statements since, for example, it is difficult to always smile in life and death situations. However, the ground rules are laid down and persistent breaking of the rules can legitimately be picked up and remarked upon by colleagues and managers. In essence, such statements reinforce the need for respect between colleagues which is essential when dealing with difficult decisions and unforeseen events.

Industries other than aviation and medicine can also benefit from describing the personal responsibilities of their employees not in terms of the generic or shared but the specific – what this means to *ME*. Only by *internalizing* their responsibilities can staff engage in the questioning needed to identify risks to the firm. And only by openly admitting and recording mistakes and human errors can staff learn, from the reactions of senior management, what is acceptable and what not. At the highest level, a clear statement of the responsibilities of each director, rather than generic governance statements and committee charters, can assist in a better level of strategic decision-making. Some suggestions for achieving this degree of openness are presented below, after discussing the issue of Job Descriptions.

10.3 Job Descriptions

For most of us, when we are being recruited for, or start, a new job we are given a 'job description' that states what is expected of us. It is often an impressive document that typically contains sections about: the tasks that have to be done; the responsibilities in terms of outputs and staff managed; the qualifications, skills and experience required in the job; locations; conditions of employment; and sometimes personal qualities. These descriptions are typically heavy on 'what has to be done' but light on 'how to do it'. The example in Box 10.1 shows part of a job description that highlights the problems of specifying 'what' but not 'how'.

Box 10.1   Example of a Job Description for a lecturer

A template published by the HR department of a US university for a task description for the job of 'Lecturer' includes 'Supervise four Master's dissertation students; co-supervise two PhD students'.

For those familiar with such tasks, this part of the lecturer's role is, aside from reading drafts, almost 100 per cent personal interaction. The whole task is replete with potential People Risks such as plagiarism, bullying, discrimination, personal biases, unrealistic expectations, overconfidence, etc.

The US Council of Graduate Schools (CGS) reports[13] that some 50 per cent of all PhD students fail to complete their doctorate. As with many situations, the tendency is to blame the drop-out as if it was completely their fault. But it is becoming obvious that failures to complete research projects, like medical and aviation errors, are often a function of the system as much as the individual.

For example, finance is a large cause of drop-out in the United States but the two major causes of attrition are in fact people-related: (1) wrong student on the wrong research project and (2) insufficient support from the faculty. The drop-out of a promising student, who had the potential to complete, from a multi-year course is a huge waste of resources (time, talent and money).

The Job Description for a lecturer then should include the task to 'Supervise, etc' but should also include a discussion of how to approach the job, the personal interactions/behaviours and importantly the risks involved.

Little research has been done in this area, but it is likely that if some form of risk management principles were applied to the job of supervising a dissertation, fewer wrong people would be admitted and fewer would fail to complete because the risks would be discussed and managed *from the outset*.

As noted in Chapter 2, the hiring process is replete with People Risks, in some cases almost, like the lecturer in the example in Box 10.1, setting the successful candidate up to fail. So how to improve the process? Practically, it is just not possible to expand the traditional Job Description to include details of the complex interactions that a potential candidate, or existing job holder, might encounter. In other words, the Job Description has a specific purpose; to specify 'what' a role will entail. Therefore some other means of specifying 'how', and especially 'how not', is needed. Job descriptions are, by their nature, impersonal, describing an idealized perfect candidate, rather than a real-life, error-prone person with behavioural biases.

So, if not job descriptions, where do individuals, from frontline staff to chairman of the board, obtain information as to *how* they should conduct their day-to-day interactions with one another, customers, suppliers, regulators and other stakeholders?

10.4 Individual Interactions

As described in Chapter 5, a People Map that describes all an individual's '*interactions*' with others would provide a useful mechanism for demonstrating to individuals, their colleagues and executives what their individual responsibilities should cover. When a particular *interaction* is identified in a People Map, then the risks in that interaction can be identified and assessed and the personal responsibilities of the individual can then be clearly articulated. In effect, such a statement will provide a person-specific (mini) 'code of conduct' for each specific interaction, in which personal responsibilities can be clearly defined and more importantly permission given to question deviations from agreed interactions. Having an individual frame of reference, which can be subject to review and audit, will give people a much better chance of saying something when they should, rather than relying on remote and necessarily bland corporate codes of conduct. This, of course, will involve a lot of work and commitment by management but the benefit should be better, or at least more thoughtful, decision-making by individuals.

The People Maps in Chapter 5 are complicated, even though they are only relatively trivial examples. But that is because business itself is complex. There are countless person-to-person interactions every day in business, the vast majority of which work roughly as they are supposed to. Firms spend millions every year recruiting, training, rewarding and promoting their staff but spend very little on making sure that their interactions with other people are understood and managed properly going forward. There are some jobs that are solitary and lacking in much human interaction. A lighthouse keeper springs to mind but today even lighthouse keepers keep in continual radio contact with meteorologists and vessel captains. On the other hand, many jobs, such as salespeople and general managers, are largely about human interaction. In the modern knowledge economy, even when sitting at a computer terminal most of us interact electronically with multiple people every day, through email or telephone, to complete what we need to do.

At this stage, it should be noted that not all possible interactions will be formal and part of one's recognized job – some will occur in the normal course of business. For example, a salesperson may be approached by a supplier directly, rather than through the Procurement function, to recommend one of their products to a customer either as part of the company's product set or separately. There is clearly a conflict of interest, the response to which should be considered in advance. In this example, because there is no official interaction between the salesperson and the supplier, the employee, who would not normally be involved, would not have a template for this behaviour. However, for unsolicited interactions such as this one the employee, through training, would be encouraged to respectfully close down the conversation and then discuss the issue with his/her manager or a specialist in HR or ethics. Note, however, this is not sufficient and separate and distinct monitoring and escalation actions need to be developed, as described in Chapter 5.

10.5 Personalized Codes of Conduct

One of the prerequisites of improving the management of People Risk is not only to have people *take* personal responsibility for their decisions but also to *give* people responsibility for determining what they need to do. The traditional approach is for people to be provided with instructions about what they *should* do, in the form of a Corporate Code of Conduct and a Job Description. As discussed above these are usually elegant, well-written documents that are specifically designed to homogenize the actions of the whole firm. Individual situations and dilemmas are subsumed by a one-size-fits-all approach. However, these documents are often remote and difficult to apply in day-to-day work situations for those they are aimed at.

What if employees created their own code of conduct? That may sound like anarchy, but we already give many employees a degree of autonomy in other circumstances. For example, education and training are often individual choices and good employers support their employees in undertaking personalized training programmes. Some training is mandatory of course, but the rate at which training is undertaken is often determined by the individual concerned. In other words, the employee is given control of his/her personal development. What better way to understand a firm's code of conduct than to have an individual tailor it to his/her own day-to-day role?

10.5.1 Creating a Personalized Code of Conduct

So what would a Personalized Code of Conduct look like? Certainly *not* a blank sheet. Without training in ethics, few people would know where to start to create such a code. Obviously, an HR department would have templates and standard processes that would form the basis of any personalized code. It is suggested that the starting point should be the development of a personalized People Map which would begin with a set of questions, the most basic being 'Who do I interact with?', 'How often do I interact with them?' and 'How important are these people to my job?'

One can see, even at this early stage, that other more significant questions would be raised. For example, the initial reaction of most employees (and unfortunately the conceit of many managers) would be to assert that their most important interaction would be with their immediate bosses. On the contrary, from an organizational perspective, an employee's most important interactions would almost certainly be *external*, such as with customers or regulators. Discussing these questions raises the essential differences between interactions; in other words, how should an employee behave with different people? This, in turn, leads people to understand the boundaries and limitations of particular interactions and leads (maybe after prompting) to questions such as 'What if my boss were to ask me to do something that may be detrimental to my customers or my colleagues?'

Again the best way to explain is through an example. Table 10.2 shows a hypothetical Personalized Code of Conduct for the imaginary Head of Procurement used as an example in Chapter 5. Note the sample Code here is organized using the 'interactions' described in Chapter 5 (ie Internal, Customers, Suppliers and Regulators) but other types of structure could also be used. Note also the word *I* is used to make the code personal and relevant to the individual concerned.

TABLE 10.2   A Personalized Code of Conduct – hypothetical example

Example	Personal Code of Conduct
INTERNAL	
Bullying and Discrimination	*I* will not bully a colleague, customer or supplier or member of the public. *I* will not discriminate against a colleague, customer or supplier on the basis of sex, race, age... If *I* witness examples of bullying or discrimination in dealings with colleagues, customers or suppliers, *I* will: a) refer to *my own* and the company's code of conduct in discussing the event and *if not resolved immediately*; b) record it as a risk event in the People Risk database; c) if the behaviour continues, *I* will report it to the whistleblowing hotline. If *I* witness bullying or discrimination during the year, *I* will address it in annual reviews and seek guidance from managers as to further actions.
Bribery and Excessive Entertainment	*I* will not bribe nor accept a bribe especially in the form of excessive entertainment. *I* will maintain a personal log of all entertainment provided to me and gain pre/post approval for entertainment above my department's risk limit. If *I* witness examples of attempted bribery or excessive entertainment by colleagues, *I* will: a) refer to my own and the company's code of conduct in discussing the event with colleagues and *if not resolved immediately*; b) record it as a risk event in the People Risk database; c) if the behaviour continues, *I* will report it to the whistleblowing hotline. *I* will address excessive entertainment in annual reviews and seek guidance from managers as to further actions. In annual reviews, *I* will discuss and review my department's risk limits.
CUSTOMERS	
Unsolicited approach	Direct interactions with customers is *not* part of *my* role. If *I* am approached by a customer, *I* will respectfully direct them to the sales force and ensure that someone follows up on the approach/inquiry. *I* will inform the customer of the firm's complaints handling and whistleblowing protocols and give *my* own contact details.
Sales Support	Direct support of sales activities is *not* normally part of *my* role, but if requested by a sales colleague, *I* will clear this in advance on each occasion with *my* manager.

TABLE 10.2   *continued*

Example	Personal Code of Conduct
SUPPLIERS	
Preferred Supplier List	If *I* am approached by a supplier who is not on the Preferred Supplier List, *I* will respectfully direct them to the colleague who is in charge of the list; Except in rare circumstances, such as trade shows, *I* will *not* accept entertainment from suppliers who are not on the Preferred Supplier List. If *I* am approached by an authorized colleague requesting information about suppliers who are on the Preferred Supplier List, *I* will provide the information as accurately as possible, highlighting deficiencies in the information provided.
Invoices	*I* will countersign each invoice from a supplier, within my agreed authority limits. *I* will produce and countersign the monthly invoice analysis report. *I* will initiate analyses of invoice limit breaches, such as outstanding invoices, and countersign each limit breach. *I* will produce a monthly report of invoice trends and answer queries as to causes and implications of trends.
REGULATORS	
Unsolicited approach	Direct interactions with regulators is *not* part of *my* role. If *I* am approached by any regulator or government official (such as Tax authorities), *I* will respectfully direct them on all occasions to *my* manager. If, however, *I* am approached by police or other officials, such as Customs, *I* will contact the whistleblowing unit and when they respond, *I* will follow their directions. *I* will provide no information unless authorized to do so.

It is obvious that most individuals would have difficulty raising, never mind answering, questions about their conduct and ethics on their own. They would need the help of others, trained in elicitation, to work through the difficult process of raising and answering very tough questions, such as 'What should I do if my boss asks me to do something which I believe to be improper?' Such support would have to be given by HR and ethics experts (such as those termed as 'code specialists' by JPMorgan) ideally supported by local managers and supportive colleagues. Paradoxically, it is at the lowest level where it is most likely that a standard template rather than a blank sheet would form the basis of discussion, since junior staff would not yet have developed the skills needed to create such a document. Where a template is used, then it would be the role of HR specialists and local managers to take the time to ensure that: (a) a personalized code is indeed created; (b) the individual understands each personal responsibility, if necessary including specific questions and concerns of the individual to gain acceptance; and (c) a level of quality is maintained across the firm.

Group exercises in a training environment would also help employees to swap ideas and generate questions. For example, the major firms whose codes of conduct are described in section 10.1, require staff to undergo ethics training soon after they join and periodically after that. If one of the outputs from such training was a Personalized Code of Conduct that was subsequently kept up to date, this would be an indication that the employee had indeed learned the lessons well. On the other hand, if an employee shows difficulty in engaging in the debates necessary to understand their personal responsibilities this would give some indication of the individual risks involved. Furthermore, if the creation of a good Personalized Code of Conduct is tied to 'reward', such as remuneration and promotion, there would be an incentive for staff to participate wholeheartedly. To ensure quality and consistency, personalized codes would also have to be reviewed and rated (for performance purposes) by trained HR staff.

The example above begs the question, 'how far up the organization should such personalized codes be used?' The answer, unequivocally, is to the very top. In fact such tailored codes may be of most use where external scrutiny is most often missing, such as with the board and senior executives. Such codes would also be useful to regulators when reviewing board performance. The development of personalized codes will, in fact, help to address sensitive conflicts of interests at the most senior level, such as the 'dual' role of CEO and board director or the responsibilities of the Chief Risk Officer and the board Risk Management Committee (RMC). The development, and hopefully acceptance, of personalized codes of conduct by a manager will help him/her deal with questions from their subordinates on conduct and ethical issues. If used properly, the code(s) should form the basis of a constructive dialogue between colleagues on ethical issues.

While not downplaying the difficulties, the creation of a Personalized Code of Conduct by an individual, with support from HR professionals, is essentially a learning exercise that should result in personal ownership of the code itself. If approached methodically creating a code that is specific to and more importantly *owned by* an individual may not be in the 'too hard basket' after all.

10.5.2 Testing a Personalized Code of Conduct

As noted earlier, some corporate codes of conduct require that employees 'affirm' or 'acknowledge' the code on an annual basis. However, it is not obvious what such affirmation would achieve other than provide an opportunity to tell a lie about re-reading the code. As with pilots, some regime of regular testing is needed to reassure management and the individual that their code is meaningful to their day-to-day decisions.

One way to achieve such an insight is to include a discussion of the code and its practical application in an individual's performance appraisal. That might take the form of a specific example of, and a discussion on, how the code was used (or not used) in a real business situation during the appraisal period. On the other hand, it could take the form of a discussion of why and how the individual's own code was updated (or not), during the year, and/or a commitment and plan to revise the code as a result of business changes. A discussion of departmental risk limits and any excesses or 'near misses' that have occurred could demonstrate knowledge of an individual's understanding and commitment to behave responsibly. Yet another way to test understanding could be to discuss a real, or hypothetical, case that would draw out key lessons for personal conduct. It should be noted that such a testing regime should apply not only to employees but, equally importantly, to senior managers and board directors as part of their ongoing education and affirmation of the firm's overall Corporate Code of Conduct.

The concepts described in this chapter, such as the Personalized Code of Conduct, are novel and may be considered by some to be difficult to implement but it is obvious that, particularly after the Global Financial Crisis, the status quo cannot be sustained. The consequences of bad decision-making and the reluctance of key individuals to take personal responsibility for their actions have been shown to be destructive, not only in the financial industry. It is not enough merely to tell people what to do and hope that they understand and conform – individuals must be encouraged to apply the company's aspirations to their individual actions. In turn, although it might be sometimes uncomfortable, managers must be prepared to support individuals when questioning the firm's actions. An ethical, empowered workforce will be one of a company's defences against People Risk. Changes are needed, but what is not obvious is how to instigate the necessary changes. The final chapter first summarizes the lessons learned in earlier chapters and then discusses how People Risk Management may be made a reality.

Notes

1   See Parliamentary Commission on Banking Standards (2013).

2   See the history and provisions of the *Sarbanes Oxley Act* in the Wikipedia article of the same name.

3   Note, however, for accounting frauds such as WorldCom, the penalties in the SOX Act are severe, with a prison sentence of up to 20 years and/or a fine of US $5 million.

4   At the time of writing in mid-2014, the Codes of Conduct of the various corporations were available at their websites in various locations, ie www.bp.com, www.jpmorganchase.com, www.bankofamerica.com, www.goldmansachs.com. Note that over time these codes and their focuses change.

5   See Salz, A (2013) *Salz Review: An independent review of Barclays' business practices*, Barclays, www.barclays.com

6   See, for example, Slater (2013) Sins of past, present and future haunt banks, *Reuters*, 13 October, www.reuters.com

7   See *Business Code and Ethics* at www.goldmansachs.com

8   See *The Code of Conduct Conundrum* at www.oceg.org

9   See an example of the *Aviators Model Code of Conduct* at www.secureav.com

10 See *CAP 716: Aviation Maintenance Human Factors*, Civil Aviation Authority website, www.caa.co.uk

11 See *WHO Surgical Safety Checklist* at the NHS National Patient Safety Agency, www.npsa.nhs.uk. In 2012 the functions of the Agency were transferred to the NHS Commissioning Board Special Health Authority.

12 See *Living our Values*, published by the Duke University Health System Patient Experience Oversight Team, http://www.hr.duke.ed

13 See Cassuto, L (2013) Ph.D. attrition: how much is too much? *The Chronicle of Higher Education*, 13 June, www.chronicle.com

Conclusion

11

> *The great thing about fact-based decisions is that they overrule the hierarchy.* **JEFF BEZOS (CREATOR OF AMAZON.COM)**

11.1 Lessons learned

As we were writing this book late in 2013, even more examples of unacceptable People Risk were reported in the press, such as the manipulation of FX Benchmarks in the financial industry,[1] and the taxation scandals[2] facing Apple and other large international companies. We are not claiming that the messages in this book would have prevented such major abuses but rather that the book provides methods for detecting such unethical events in the future, hopefully before they become disastrous for shareholders and taxpayers.

This chapter summarizes the book in terms of some lessons learned and provides an insight into some of the legal and regulatory measures being developed to address People Risk. Unfortunately, we believe that these initiatives are being taken by individual regulatory bodies in a vacuum without a proper *framework* for guiding them. Finally we consider how business managers may start to convince themselves and their colleagues as to how to improve the management of People Risk.

There are a number of key themes that surfaced as the arguments in the book were developed and these have been repeated throughout. These themes bear summarizing because they are not commonly articulated, even though we argue they are extremely important in managing one of the greatest risks facing any firm – People Risk.

11.1.1 People and People Risk

Corporations often assert that 'their people are their greatest asset', and for many firms in the so-called 'knowledge economy' this is undoubtedly true, as their success is based on the talent they employ and nurture. However, what is less often articulated, because it is a taboo subject, is that a firm's 'people are often its greatest risk'. While one can see why such a recognition would be uncomfortable, a basic understanding of the relationship of *risk* and *reward* would dictate that without some risk there can be no reward. Every business activity involves some risk, so why would the rewards created by people not also create some risks?

People Risk is real. Just as a hurricane can destroy a factory, the actions or inactions of a few staff can drive a company to the wall. Chapter 4 described only some of the many possible examples of losses, some disastrous, that large firms incurred as a result of the actions and non-actions of people, ie People Risk. But, as Chapter 4 shows, People Risk is more than fraud and more than accidents caused by people who did not follow Health and Safety rules. People Risk comes from individuals and groups of individuals making *bad decisions*. However, People Risk is extremely difficult to measure and to manage, causing many managers to put it in the 'too-hard' basket. The first step in managing its potentially disastrous consequences is to recognize that People Risk exists and like any other risk *cannot* be ignored. As in the management of any problem, the first step is to recognize that there is a real problem and until that is accepted, further actions will be treating the symptoms rather than the root causes and hence will be a largely wasted effort.

People Risk is about the individual. Having made this first giant step of recognizing that people-related risk must not be ignored, then it must be recognized that People Risk is about the individual, and not about people in general, or in aggregate. People will, on average, behave well and do what they are supposed to do within their levels of skill and ability. So looking at a total population, such as all staff in a firm, will, through the law of large numbers, give fairly predictable and repeatable results. Because most people behave well they generally make sound if unspectacular decisions. It is the statistical outliers, however, where the greatest risks exist and it is difficult first to identify and then to manage those outliers (ie the individuals who give rise to the greatest People Risk). While superficially attractive, firing an outlier is rarely the answer, not only because employment law would probably forbid it, but also because the outlier has not done anything wrong, *yet*. Understanding *why* individuals deviate from expectations and what measures can be put in place to prevent this happening is critical to managing People Risk and potentially saving the firm.

People have blind spots. As humans, our brains are just not able to cope with all the information needed to process complex (even sometimes simple) decisions. To survive we take short-cuts, so-called *heuristics*, or we limit our *search* for information to a smaller subset that we can cope with. In most of our everyday situations, these short-cuts work (or at least work well enough) but in some instances our instincts let us down. Behavioural psychologists and neuroscientists have demonstrated that humans are subject to blind spots (so-called *inattentional blindness*) in that while concentrating on the task in hand, even experts can miss what is obvious. Chapter 3 described some of the theories of how these blind spots arise and Chapter 4 provided examples where blind spots caused spectacular losses.

People behave differently in different situations. People don't always behave in a consistent fashion, which does not mean that people are capricious (although some are), only that people will modify their thinking to the current situation and the current audience. Chapter 3 describes a number of situations where people *consistently* demonstrate what are called behavioural or cognitive biases. One 'bias' in particular, *Overconfidence*, can be dangerous. Humans are 'hard-wired' to be optimistic – we *like* to be upbeat and confident. While optimism is an admirable trait, as Chapter 4 shows, for example in the cases of Lehman Brothers and Royal Bank of Scotland, when confidence becomes overconfidence it can cause even the most experienced decision-makers to 'lose the plot' and make really bad decisions.

People behave differently in groups. While the saying 'two heads are better than one' is a good heuristic, it is not always true. Alone or in close company of others whom they respect, most people will be open and reasonably honest about their beliefs as regards a particular situation. They will be prepared to admit uncertainties, insecurities and shades of grey. But in a group of their peers and superiors, people tend to be less forthcoming, usually out of fear of being thought incompetent or weak. Valid objections will be stifled, especially if others express strong views, and there will be deference to the views of their superiors, and of bullies in the group. This gives rise to the very dangerous phenomenon of *Groupthink*, whereby a group comes to a decision based on achieving consensus rather than debating the benefits, disadvantages and importantly the risks inherent in a decision. The group's decision may be good, bad or even disastrous but is accepted by an individual for the reason that it is the *group's* view.

People change over time. As people grow older and (most times) wiser their behaviours change. The bright, fresh-faced enthusiastic associate or apprentice who joins a company after school or university will behave very differently as they mature and as their responsibilities grow. A personality test applied to a potential recruit will say very little about the behaviour of the same person many years on in their mid-career. In Chapter 2, the concept of White Collar Crime was discussed and experts, such as James Coleman,[3] have found that white collar criminals tend not to be the young and reckless; on the contrary they are typically well-established and trusted individuals who, at a later stage in their careers, face an opportunity to restore their flagging fortunes. As described in Chapter 4, this is the situation that several rogue traders got themselves into, first making a loss then covering it up by deception that they rationalize to themselves as being temporary and necessary to restore the status quo.

People are their own worst judges. Although reward is very important, people also go to work to experience personal satisfaction and the approval of others. People like and strive for praise but, on the other hand, tend to reject criticism, even when it may be justified. It is not surprising then that people often create an unrealistic picture of themselves and their abilities. And when someone is rewarded with pay rises and promotions then any unrealistic perception of their abilities will naturally be strengthened.[4] As described in Chapter 3, people deceive themselves, and they prefer things to be the way that they want them to be rather than how they really are. And often, humans rationalize the actions they take *after not before* they make a decision – this is a form of self-protection that allows people to move on and complete a course of action without constant regret. If the outcome is good (or 'good enough') they will take credit for their prescience in taking the action that they rationalized.

People's expectations of themselves and others' expectations of them are often unrealistic. Not only are people not good judges of their own abilities they often set wildly unrealistic expectations of what they can actually achieve. Nowhere is this more obvious than at the senior management and Chief Executive Officer level. CEOs are hired and are immediately expected to turn a company around or to continue to grow the company at the speed of their predecessors. But a moment's reflection would show that is not always realistic unless nothing has changed in the economy and competitive environment. When a firm puts someone in a role for which they are not (yet) fitted they are creating People Risk and the more senior the role the more risk is created. An example of this was illustrated in Chapter 4 by the collapse of the venerable Halifax/Bank of Scotland,[5] whose senior management was found to be lacking in the technical experience required to operate at that level.

People Risk is about the organization and its culture. Organizations, especially large ones, are a sort of primordial soup for evolving behaviours. If a particular behaviour is seen to be successful, it proliferates, whereas unsuccessful behaviours will diminish and probably die out. But, like evolution in nature, it is not always the best or most desirable behaviours that survive and grow within a large organization. It is the so-called *culture* of a firm that determines which behaviours will prosper and which will fade. Chapter 4 described examples of corporate cultures, such as with Enron, where bad behaviours proliferated, eventually resulting in the demise of the firms concerned. Chapter 7 illustrated the importance of organizational culture to the effective management of risk in general, and People Risk in particular. Culture is often cited in media reports when things go wrong in an organization even though it can be a hard concept to pin down. But people intuitively know what it means even though they might not be able to define it. Within large organizations, sub-cultures will exist, some of which may have very different characteristics from the organizational culture sought by the board.

A risk sub-culture affects and influences the way that individuals are expected to behave (and manage risk) when faced with risky situations. Having a good risk culture will not prevent people doing things they shouldn't do (we all make mistakes) but it will help to reduce the likelihood of errors and also encourage people to own up, knowing that they will be treated 'fairly'. At its best, a good *risk culture* will facilitate the reporting of risk events, drive the production of timely risk information and influence the way that risk management processes work. *Values* are a principal driver of culture, particularly risk culture. In an ideal world values would be shared throughout the organization and everybody would feel a sense of fulfilment or job satisfaction. But when reality kicks in, the best we can hope for is a close match when it comes to sharing core values whilst recognizing that there will be some outliers. *Trust* is a value that should never be underestimated. It is an essential value when it comes to People Risk Management because it creates bonds between people both inside and outside the organization. When trust disappears, it is a warning sign that people may start to behave differently towards others and the organization.

This book is heavily indebted to the work of behavioural psychologists, such as Daniel Kahneman, Dan Ariely and many of their co-workers who have demonstrated not only that they are great researchers but also have an abundant sense of fun.[6] Through really novel and entertaining experiments, they shine a light on our human foibles, and it turns out we are not as smart as we think we are. But this observation is not new. The ancients knew it, as Cicero wrote:

> The enemy is within the gates; it is with our own luxury, our own folly, our own criminality that we have to contend.

11.1.2 People and decision-making

However, in this book we are not discussing the full diversity of the human condition, only the biases and blind spots that *all* managers bring to their *business decision-making*. From the top of a corporation to the bottom there are innumerable decisions being made every day in all companies. Most of these decisions are mundane and pre-programmed within a firm's policies, procedures and computer systems. However, even the most routine decision such as selling a product to a customer is replete with risks. Some of these risks will be outside the control of the salesperson, such as a product that has been manufactured incorrectly. The *sales interaction* has risk nonetheless, such as the sales person overstating the capabilities of the product, which is misselling. This is just one example of the many bad decisions that are made each day in every firm that give rise to People Risk.

People sometimes make bad decisions. In business, all but the most trivial decisions are made with imperfect knowledge. If everything were known in advance, a computer rather than a person would be able to make important decisions. But good information is not always available and in many business situations, managers must be prepared to make a decision anyway. Making a decision without information is not stupid, but making a decision and not searching for additional information as the decision makes an impact is imprudent. Not changing a decision when new information appears and shows that the original choice to be flawed is downright stupid. But why do people keep going with a decision once it has been made? Because they fear being considered indecisive and weak-willed. Though easier said than done, admitting mistakes is a brave, rather than a stupid, action, although admitting the need for a rethink may be career-destroying if upper management is not equally mature. Chapter 4 provides examples of some bad decision-making that proved catastrophic to the firms involved.

No one in a firm is immune to bad decision-making. Bad decisions made at the bottom of a company hierarchy can have disastrous consequences, such as the hurried decisions by oil rig staff that caused the Gulf of Mexico oil spill, which cost BP billions. But as Professor Barry Turner,[7] a renowned expert in man-made disasters, contended, major disasters are incubated in large organizations because reality begins to diverge from the beliefs of managers and they become arrogant and distrustful of external advice – 'we know better how to run our own business'. And as Chapter 4 shows, in the case of Tesco, the higher a bad decision is made in a corporation, the more costly its consequences will be. Boards are therefore a source of People Risk because directors are human. Chapter 6 discussed how risks in the boardroom may be tackled. This is not just about looking at the negative aspects of risk, although it invariably focuses in this area. The board has to take risks to grow a business and the decisions it makes in this regard are likely to be better decisions if the focus is not just on process but also on the people involved. The behaviour of people working in groups making decisions can change for a variety of factors and because of this managing People Risk will always be work in progress and will need constant monitoring, particularly by the Chairperson. Perhaps the most important point to remember is that the board consists of a group of fallible human beings who are, or at least should be, operating collectively in a social/commercial environment making important decisions about the firm and its future. The outcome of their decisions may, at times, be wrong but the directors need to ensure that when they made a decision not only were they ticking the boxes to demonstrate good corporate governance from a process point of view but they were also making sure that their biases, prejudices, influences, behaviours and entrenched positions had been collectively challenged and documented.

Not all decisions that people make are equal – some decisions are riskier than others. The context in which people make decisions is important as not all decisions carry the same risks. A simple example of this is in banking, where a decision to lend money is being made. It is obvious that if the risks are equal the loan that makes the best return should be chosen, but rarely are all risks equal. So how does one choose between loans where one pays a higher return but also carries a higher risk? To do that one must look at the so-called 'risk-adjusted return', which attempts to compare risky apples with risky apples. Despite much research, however, calculating risk-adjusted returns remains an art rather than a science. If comparing risks is complex in the financial field, how much more difficult will it be where the outcomes cannot be measured in financial terms, such as with lives and reputation. In order to make decisions about risks it is necessary then to identify and (despite being difficult) attempt to measure, or at least rank, risks of different types. To make such a comparison in the commercial context, a firm's *Risk Appetite* for different types of risk needs to be clearly articulated by the board.[8] If this is not done, people will be making decisions without a so-called 'risk compass' and losses will inevitably occur, but the size will be indeterminate.

Individuals' goals are rarely aligned precisely with those of their firm. In economics, the mismatch between the goals of the owners of a company and its managers is known as the 'Principal Agent' problem and there is branch of economics called 'Agency Theory'[9] to address such *Conflicts of Interest*. Much of this theory deals with mechanisms, such as pay structures and profit sharing, that attempt to align the interests of the owners and management. But there is another conflict of interest that is less well understood, that of the mismatch between the goals of the individual employee and his/her employer. The pre-1960s model of a 'job for life' no longer holds except in parts of the traditional professions. Business schools and academics now describe the working life of the future as being a 'portfolio' of careers where people see their work not as an end in itself but as a means to an end, seeing their current employer as just one stop on their working journey.[10] This lack of attachment increases People Risk because the possibility of losing one's job no longer holds debilitating fear for many workers. This in turn means that the incentives of employers and employees need to be aligned in different ways, emphasizing the needs of the present rather than of the future. But this can be dangerous, as the Global Financial Crisis (GFC) showed. In the lead up to the GFC, some employees improved their own wealth at the expense of their employers by, mostly legally, taking advantage of the temporal mismatch between risk and return. For a whole new breed of financial products, such as the Payment Protection Insurance (PPI) products described in Chapter 4, sales bonuses were received up front whereas the risks appeared much later down the track.

11.1.3 Improving decision-making

If faulty decision-making is (at least) a large part of the problem, how does one improve decision-making? Managers in large organizations make hundreds of decisions each day – they pride themselves in being 'decision-making machines'. But are they any good at it? And how could an outsider, such as a shareholder or regulator, know if they are good or not? We don't test ourselves on our decision-making skills, instead we (wrongly) measure ourselves on the outcomes. If the outcomes are good we take the credit but if not we blame unforeseen circumstances or someone else for not implementing the decision correctly. As the old proverb says 'success has many fathers, but failure is an orphan'. A bad result becomes a blame game, where unfortunately the loudest or the most aggressive voice often wins. But what if we were able to identify potentially *bad decisions* before significant resources were committed? Chapters 9 and 10 looked at this problem and developed some novel suggestions for management action.

Persuading individuals to take personal responsibility for their decisions and actions is key to successfully managing People Risk. The collective nature of corporate decision-making creates a situation where, at the same time, everybody *but nobody* has responsibility. Merely dictating that individuals should act responsibly when making decisions may work for a time but, unless there is active and consistent support for individual decision-making, people will melt back into the crowd when key decisions are needed. In collective decision-making, the factors that result in a decision are *invisible*. These factors may only be apparent to those closest to the decision-makers and, even if recognized, may not be articulated. Ultimately, this will result in bad decisions being made because biases and conflicts of interest come to dominate those who wish to take good decision-making seriously. The *Decision Model*, described in Chapter 9, attempts to improve decision-making by describing a decision process with prompts and nudges as to the types of questions that individuals should ask before, during and after a decision is being made. In the model, formal decision-making is followed by a formal review of the *quality* of the decision that was taken. It is not suggested that such a comprehensive process would be needed for every decision, especially those that are pre-programmed within policies and procedures, but a more thoughtful and transparent process would be beneficial for complex risky decisions, such as new strategies, complex projects or the development of new products.

We freely admit that the suggested decision model is far removed from the gung-ho approach to decision-making that is apparent in many business situations, often masquerading as 'seizing the initiative' or 'being proactive'. In reality, such an approach is often little more than 'flying by the seat of their pants' and will inevitably lead to bad, even disastrous, decisions, as described in Chapter 4. We make no excuses for suggesting that better decisions would be made by a considered process of critical thinking rather than 'gut feeling'. As the founder of Amazon.com, Jeff Bezos said, 'the great thing about fact-based decisions is that they overrule the hierarchy' – in our terms, 'the better and more transparent the decision-making process, the less likely the decision will be bad'.

Not making a decision is making a decision. Decision-making is hard as it implies that real money and effort will be expended to implement the decision.

If the outcomes of a decision turn out to be good, the decision-maker will usually be applauded. If wrong, however, he/she/they will be castigated and prior caveats and conditions will be conveniently forgotten. It is therefore often much easier for an individual or a group of individuals to prevaricate and put off an important decision than to expose themselves to possible censure later. And it is relatively easy to justify such delays with excuses such as the need to collect more information or the need to concentrate on other priorities – so-called 'paralysis by analysis'. But not making a decision is in fact making a decision since time does not always resolve and may even increase uncertainties. Not making a decision when one is needed is risky, especially if repeated delays mean that an important risk drops off the radar. In the context of People Risk for example, delaying the censure of someone for bullying or inappropriate behaviour is implicitly condoning the aberrant behaviour until action is taken.

People and bad processes are a dangerous combination. All businesses operate through defined processes, most explicit, some implied by 'the way we do things around here'. When repetitive, business processes are often embedded in computer programs, allowing people to concentrate on the non-repetitive, interesting and creative decisions. However, unlike computers, people do not always follow the agreed processes exactly. There may often be good reasons for deviating from published rules, in that processes become outdated and people have to work their way around them. In his research, Barry Turner[11] found that failure to comply with outdated or discredited processes or regulations was a recurring warning sign of 'man-made' corporate disasters. Without a clear set of rules, people will not know precisely what they should do and hence, through ignorance, may do the wrong thing. Bad business processes create People Risk for those that use, or misuse, them.

Individuals need support to make good decisions. In order to begin to take personal responsibility for their decisions, employees have to be aware of what precisely is expected of them, as individuals, not as anonymous, interchangeable employees. In Chapter 10, we developed the concept of a *Personalized Code of Conduct* in which an individual is encouraged to create a code of conduct that is *specific to them* and the job they are doing. Such a personal code would expand and make specific the aspirations of a firm's Corporate Code of Conduct, and through rewarding the individual for creating, living and applying their own code would encourage individuals to take responsibility for the decisions that they make every day.

Individuals need support from higher levels of management to make good decisions. Both the CEO and the Human Resources (HR) department have critical roles to play in managing People Risk. HR, in particular, should be at the forefront of creating a People Risk mind set across the business. The leader of the HR function needs to maintain a constant dialogue with the Chief Risk Officer and be fully engaged in the risk management process and not just be seen as a passive bystander. The key HR processes, and particularly the recruitment one, help to set the 'tone from the top' about the type of people that the organization is looking for from a behavioural and attitudinal point of view. Chapter 8 suggested that organizations can learn from the principles applied in High Reliability Organizations (HRO), such as power plants and hospital emergency rooms, to help manage People Risk. These principles provide guidance on how to embed both the behaviours that are expected in the organization (culture) and the roles and responsibilities of the people (making the culture work). People risks can manifest themselves at any level in the organization and even the Assurance functions (Compliance, Audit and Risk) are a source of People Risk. If the Assurance functions are not doing the work that they are supposed to be doing or not doing it in an effective way, the holes in the so-called *Swiss Cheese* in the organization will be bigger than they need be.[12] The Assurance functions themselves need to embrace approaches to managing People Risk that are novel and step outside traditional methodologies, including the People Risk Maps we described in Chapter 5 and look at the more difficult areas of culture and values.

Making the Invisible Visible. When an executive receives a proposal from a manager or a board is required to agree a decision on a project put forward by senior management, how do they know that the process to arrive at the proposal has not been not subject to personal biases or conflicts of interest? In general, they don't! They must *trust* the person(s) putting forward the proposal. But why would they trust the people making the proposal? As Chapter 7 shows, experience has much to do with trust – if someone has a good record it gives a lot of comfort. If the proposal looks impressive and has been reviewed by other managers that also gives comfort. But even the best decision-makers make mistakes sometimes and an impressive fact-laden document may be based on assumptions that may be overstated or even wrong. The *visible* can be misleading. In this book, we reiterate the need to *make the invisible visible* and to bring some of the uncertainties, biases and conflicts of interest to the forefront when making a decision, especially a major one.

The main arguments against making decision-making more transparent are that, by doing so, decision-making will be slowed down and extra costs will be incurred. Decision-making will be slowed down and we argue *should be* slowed down but not so much that a decision is not made. In his book, *Thinking, Fast and Slow*, Daniel Kahneman describes[13] two *systems of thinking* – System 1, which is automatic and intuitive and System 2, which is controlled and analytic. Unfortunately, when we are observing others make decisions, and for that matter making them ourselves, we cannot observe which system contributed most to the result. What we believe to be a considered decision may in fact have been in haste, because of blind spots, biases or just plain over-work. We argue that the only way one can tell if biases or conflicts come into play is to address these issues explicitly in the decision-making process – to make the invisible visible. If that takes additional time, so be it! The worst that can happen is that the decision is found not to be biased and conflict-free, which is not only a comfort but also, because there is less uncertainty about the decision, it will be less risky. On the question of additional costs, the costs of making a bad decision, as shown in Chapter 4, will often far outweigh the additional effort needed to ensure that the decision is good in the first place.

11.2 Regulation of People Risk

11.2.1 *Failures of regulation*

Not only were the boards and executives of large firms criticized in major disasters, such as the Global Financial Crisis, the Gulf oil spill and the Fukushima nuclear meltdown, but also their industry regulators were severely castigated for not pre-venting the disasters.[14] These cases were not only failures of corporate decision-making but also failures of regulation. The UK Parliamentary Commission on Banking Standards in its report, 'Changing Banking for Good', described[15] banking regulation in the UK as a 'Potemkin façade'[16] with the 'the appearance of effective control and oversight without the reality.' In our terms, the UK banking regulators just did not do what they were supposed to do. In their response to the disasters, politicians, whose role in the failures of regulation has also been severely criticized, have created new regulatory structures, often without fully analysing the root causes of the disasters.[17]

Though the GFC has been identified by the Financial Crisis Inquiry Commission as being almost totally 'man-made', few men or women in the corporations respon-sible have been charged with criminal or even civil offences.[18] A full analysis of the reasons why more prosecutions have not taken place at the time of writing is beyond this book. However, we recognize that this is, at least partly, due to the fact that the 'wheels of justice grind exceedingly slow' and it takes time to fully consider and then enact the legal changes needed to reform any system of regulation.

Nonetheless there has been some movement as, for instance over time, the fines imposed on large banks have grown steadily as prosecutors have come to grips with legal strategies and tactics in prosecuting large corporations. For example, in mid-2014, the fines against Credit Suisse for helping American citizens to evade taxes totalled some US $2.6 billion and, in addition, US government prosecutors insisted that the Swiss bank plead guilty to a criminal conviction, making Credit Suisse the first major bank since the GFC to be forced to make such an admission.[19] Over time, fines for unacceptable conduct, particularly in the United States, have become larger and enforcement actions stronger.

To the layman, the fact that no board member or senior executive of the firms described in Chapter 4 has been indicted for their incompetence comes as a surprise. Anton Valukas, the diligent bankruptcy administrator for Lehman Brothers, points out two major reasons why it is, in practice, difficult to convict directors.[20] First, most large corporations are not one entity but are a sometimes-bewildering maze of companies operating in different jurisdictions with complex cross-holdings. In the case of Lehman, the overall holding company was incorporated in Delaware, United States, although the firm did minimal business in that state. It may have been that Delaware is known as a state with an extremely 'light touch' in regulation.[21] But there is another more serious impediment to putting in place sanctions – the so-called 'business judgement rule'. This rule, which is incorporated in most western jurisdictions, makes 'officers' of a corporation immune from liability for loss if they make their decisions in 'good faith'. As Valukas pointed out in the Lehman case, 'the proof necessary to defeat the business judgement rule and establish gross negligence is particularly high with respect to risk management and financial transactions'. In other words, provided that directors tick the formal boxes as regards receiving and approving decisions, it is difficult to prove *beyond doubt* that they did not act in good faith. So far politicians have not addressed this source of People Risk.

11.2.2 Recklessness in banking

The UK government has taken a different approach from its US counterparts. In its final report,[22] the Parliamentary Commission on Banking Standards made several far-reaching recommendations for the 'radical reform required to improve standards across the banking industry' and, in particular, argued that 'new criminal sanctions for recklessness will further sharpen directors' focus on their personal responsibilities and duties in respect of the firm'. The Commission recommended that the UK Government introduce 'a criminal offence for reckless misconduct by senior bank staff', which could result in a jail sentence of up to seven years. The UK Government accepted most of the recommendations[23] and, in mid-2014, was in the process of enacting those changes.

A law to penalize recklessness could have resulted in some bankers in HBOS and RBS being indicted, if not eventually convicted, for their reckless actions in managing their banks. Nonetheless, the proposed changes to UK law are narrow in that they only apply to the banking sector and even then only to so-called 'senior persons', such as the board and senior executives.[24] Despite that narrow focus it is hoped (by the government) that the potential for criminal liability for themselves will force directors to ensure that others lower in the hierarchy are also less reckless. Furthermore, other financial services, such as insurance, are not covered by the proposed legislation. In modern finance, the borders between banking and insurance are blurred: for example the PPI product described in Chapter 4 was a joint banking and insurance product. Insurance is also subject to People Risk. For example, in 2000, the UK insurance business Equitable Life collapsed[25] following its inability (due to insufficient reserving) to meet guaranteed annuity rate promises that it had made both to future and existing holders of its pension products. This collapse was a result of bad decision-making, in particular *overconfidence* and *illusion of control*.

11.2.3 Behaviour and regulation

Chapter 5 describes the creation of the Financial Conduct Authority (FCA) in the UK and the Consumer Financial Protection Bureau (CFPB) in the United States as banking regulators that focus on issues of 'conduct' towards customers. One example in particular is the FCA's so-called *Treating Customers Fairly* (TCF) initiative,[26] which was developed by the FCA's predecessor, the Financial Services Authority (FSA). Interestingly, the FCA has taken a *Behavioural Economics* perspective on its regulation of conduct. In his first speech outlining his 'vision' for the FCA, the new head Martin Wheatley explained[27] 'why the FCA is taking its first steps towards incorporating behavioural economics into the regulatory fold [and...] our economists are building an understanding of behavioural economics into how we assess markets; how we think about competition; how we develop and test potential solutions'. Furthermore, the first working paper published by the FCA was a fairly detailed outline of current thinking in the field, in particular that of Daniel Kahneman.[28]

In the United States, the new CFPB, which was set up in the wake of the GFC, has also introduced a focus on consumer behaviour and behavioural economics.[29] Other banking regulators, such as the German Deutsche Bundesbank,[30] have identified the potential usefulness of *Behavioural Finance* but have noted that the discipline is still in its infancy as regards regulation and 'further research is therefore necessary'.

11.2.4 Behaviour and the financial services industry

But it is not only regulators who have identified the need for improving conduct in the financial services industry. In 2011, the City Values Forum (CVF) was founded[31] in the City of London with a goal 'to embed the principles of trust and integrity in the financial and business services sector and to improve business cultures and behaviours'. Note that this goal is very much in line with the thinking and arguments in this book, although the CVF has an industry-wide as opposed to a firm-specific perspective.

The Forum provides a course in *Leading with Integrity* for financial services personnel working in the City of London and has developed 'toolkits' for boards: (1) a 'roadmap' to help directors to make 'an assessment of how mature the board's approach is to governing values', which is similar to the *Board Maturity Model*, described in Chapter 6; and (2) an 'agenda' for boards with 'some questions that boards can ask of themselves to help govern values', which is similar to the *Values Audit*. This book supports the approach and objectives of the Forum and provides detailed suggestions as to how their overall goal may be met.

However, at the time of writing, there is little evidence that this new focus on behaviour and conduct has as yet been turned into practical regulation or market 'best practice'. Like the boards and executives in the financial services industry, regulators too have to negotiate how to start the journey towards a new regulatory model.

11.3 Starting the journey

As Chapter 2 described, People Risk is a recognized *operational risk* but to date little has been done to try to manage these risks, despite the fact that as Chapter 4 shows, they can give rise to enormous losses and even the bankruptcy of a firm. But how to start on the journey towards a viable People Risk Management system in a large firm? While everyone in a firm would eventually be impacted there are three major groups who would have to be deeply involved in starting the journey: (1) the board; (2) the Chief Risk Officer; and (3) Human Resources.

11.3.1 The role of the board

As noted in Chapter 5, boards are required to create a so-called Enterprise Risk Management[32] systems. In terms of the ISO 31000 framework, the board needs to *Mandate and Commit* to managing risks within such a framework. The first steps then that a board must take then is to *Mandate* that *People Risk be taken seriously* and then the board (possibly through its Risk Management Committee) needs to *Commit* the necessary resources to developing a firm-wide People Risk Management Framework. This is not a trivial task and will be discussed below in terms of the role of the Chief Risk Officer (CRO).

But the board also needs to look inward at itself and its own workings. While it may seems trivial, a good first step for directors would be to read in more detail a number of the cases covered in Chapter 4, ideally those closest to their own industry, but the cases of Royal Bank of Scotland and Tesco are worth reading and considering – 'could it happen here'? If they conclude that such an event, even with less disastrous consequences, could *never* happen in their firm, they should be able to debate and point out why not. For those directors who concede that a similar event could happen, the next stage might be to consider what to do to reduce the likelihood of it happening on their watch. A next step would be consider the main sources of People Risk in the boardroom, specifically those outlined in Box 6.4 in Chapter 6, and consider whether any of those risks exist in their own boards. If any of these risks do exist, then some form of active risk management will be needed, so it is not a question of 'whether' but 'how much'?

Having decided that something must be done,[33] there are a number of practical actions that a board can take immediately and in parallel with the work of the CRO and HR:

1 *People Risk Management Framework*: specifically task the Chief Risk Officer with producing a comprehensive proposal for such a framework.[34]

2 *Pre-Mortem*: undertake a formal pre-mortem, as described in Chapter 9, on a recent major decision, identifying reasons why the decision could possibly fail. Identify those risks that were not considered fully at the time and, without blame, consider the reasons why the risks were not considered then.

3 *Post Mortem*: undertake an analysis of two recent decisions, one that succeeded and one that failed (or did not succeed fully) and identify the reasons why they succeeded or failed, from the perspective of the board – what did we do well, what could we have done better and what biases were obvious?

4 *Risk Appetite*: identify a first-cut appetite for people-related risk, as described in Chapter 5 – which risks are acceptable and which not?

5 *Boardroom Behaviour*: complete a Boardroom Behaviour Map for the last board meeting, as shown in Table 6.2 of Chapter 6, and discuss the implications for improving board effectiveness.

6 *Appoint a Devil's Advocate*: assign one of the (non-executive) directors to be a 'squeaky wheel' on each major decision.

7 *Values Audit*: initiate a formal 'values audit' of the board and senior management group as described in Chapter 8 as a baseline for monitoring future changes in corporate culture;

8 *Risk Culture Survey*: if not already in place, mandate that HR initiate a survey of attitudes to risk across the firm, and if such a survey already exists, add questions related to People Risk.

9 *Education*: initiate a programme of education in People Risk, in particular covering personal biases and conflicts of interest.

By moving ahead with these activities, the board will be in a better shape to evaluate the framework that is proposed by the Chief Risk Officer and Human Resources.

But one of the most important actions a board and senior executives can take is to change the discourse around (especially major) decisions. Chapter 3 identifies a number of *behavioural biases* that people have when making decisions and *rationalizations* that people provide for having made a decision. In particular, directors and senior executives should be on their guard when they detect:[35]

- *Overconfidence*: if excessive certainty in the outcomes is claimed, boards should ask questions such as, 'if this was so easy, why hasn't some else done it?' and 'just because it worked before (ie the 'halo effect') why should it work this time?'
- *Groupthink*: congruence of opinion on a proposal, which should raise questions such as 'didn't anyone have any reservations?'
- *Planning Fallacy*: not fully considering alternatives and experience elsewhere, which should raise questions such as 'has anyone else attempted this?' or 'if this is so new, why hasn't anyone else thought of it before?'
- *Action Bias*: an excessive need to 'Just Do It' which should raise questions such as 'why do we have to do this, now?', 'why do we have to be first?' and 'what if we didn't do this, now?'

Questions such as these are 'reinforcing' as once asked then people making subsequent proposals, aware of the directors' interests, would attempt to cover the questions, *ahead of time*. A more difficult discourse, however, is that of dealing with *rationalizations*, since decision-makers may not be aware that they have, in fact, rationalized a decision to themselves. In particular, directors and senior executives should be on their guard when they detect arguments of the following types:[36]

- *Ubiquity*: or 'everyone else is doing it'. Boards should ask questions such as, 'why should we follow, is this in fact going to drive down margins?' and 'do we understand the risks that other firms are experiencing?'
- *Economic Necessity*: or 'it is needed to survive', which should raise questions such as 'why don't our competitors have the same problems?' and 'what is the worst that can happen if we didn't do this?'
- *Victimless Crime*: or 'no one gets hurt', which should raise questions such as 'what would be the reaction if our actions got into the newspapers?' and 'if no one loses, who wins?'

Of course, as described in Chapter 6, directors should be asking such questions anyway, but an objective of this book is to provide a framework for asking such questions in a non-threating, constructive way. If people proposing a particular course of action know in advance which arguments will work and which won't then they will, or at least should, pre-empt the questioning by considering possible challenges in advance.

11.3.2 The role of the Chief Risk Officer

Risk Management professionals are experts in Risk but not in People. The Chief Risk Officer should be an expert in the firm's Risk Management Framework (RMF), whatever its form, so the overall process of integrating People Risk into the firm's existing framework should be at least familiar to him/her. The new problem, of course, is identifying what exactly is People Risk in the context of their firm? In order to address this problem, the CRO must first identify a team of staff in the current Risk Management Department (RMD) who will be charged with designing the RMF. In the process, they will become the first of the firm's People Risk experts. As a first step, some or all of these risk managers would be tasked with understanding the role of cognitive biases in decision-making, ie they will need to embark on a self-education programme.[37]

But such education is theoretical: what of the practical? In order to tackle People Risk across the firm, the CRO must open a dialogue with the head of the Human Resources department with the objective of creating and monitoring the agreed framework *together*. The best way to achieve this is to create a multi-disciplinary team tasked with creating and implementing the firm's People Risk Framework. The smooth working of this team will be critical to the success of the longer-term programme and thus will need the active support of both the board and the CEO. A People Risk 'champion' of sufficient seniority will also need to be identified to ensure success by working to overcome organizational barriers to open communication.

The CRO should be given the overall objective of developing the People Risk Framework, proposing it to the board and championing it with senior executives. To be successful, the senior management of the firm will have to be involved in thinking about the problem from an early stage, it is the risks related to their people after all that will have to be managed. In order to facilitate this, the CRO, in his/her communications and education role, will have to organize education sessions for senior management.[38]

11.3.3 *The role of Human Resources*

Human Resources professionals are experts in People but not in Risk. In order to create an effective People Risk Framework, HR will need to fulfil two roles: (1) as educators in HR principles and practice; and (2) as pupils in risk management. These are not trivial, part-time roles and hence, with the commitment of the board and support of the risk champion, the head of HR will need to take key staff from their existing roles and assign them to the multi-disciplinary framework development team. The staff will have to include experts in: Learning & Development (L&D), since much training and education will be needed, not only initially but more importantly in the longer term; Conduct, as personal conduct[39] will come under the microscope; Culture, as the firm's corporate culture will almost certainly have to be changed; Reward, as new reward systems will be needed to encourage better risk management; Recruitment, as processes for recruiting staff will need to be shifted; Whistleblowing, as new complaint and whistleblowing processes will have to be developed; Health and Safety, as integration of H&S into People Risk will be needed; and other issues particular to the firm, such as international People Risks.

The (long) list of actions listed for the board, the CRO and HR are of course only those needed to start the long journey of managing People Risk but they give a clue as to the size of the effort that will be involved. The costs will be significant but compared to the losses that might be averted should not be overly large. Not covered here are the ongoing activities of corporate and industry regulators which are moving, all too slowly, to address some of the problems that gave rise to the unacceptable losses described in Chapter 4. And it is that pressure more than cost that will dictate how firms will be required to act to manage People Risk in the medium term.

11.4 What will success look like?

Success in any form of risk management is hard to measure – how can one measure the impact of something that hasn't happened (yet)? Successful risk management is not measured by completely preventing losses (as this is an unachievable goal) but by reducing uncertainty through decreasing variability of outcomes. With good risk management, losses will still occur, but they should occur less frequently and with less severity and lessons (however painful) will be learned from each episode of loss.

Success in People Risk Management will be measured by 'better' decisions across the firm, from the board to the frontline. It will be on the business frontline, however, that changes to the firm's culture will be the last but probably the most important place to take effect. So success should become apparent in the boardroom and on the frontline in ways such as:

- steadily increasing use of formal decision-making tools, such as pre-mortems and checklists, across the firm, from the board outwards to the frontline;
- steadily increasing understanding of what constitutes 'better' decision-making;
- steadily increasing measures of board effectiveness;
- steadily increasing levels of training and education in 'better' decision-making;
- steadily increasing success in meeting objectives resulting from 'better' decisions;
- steadily decreasing frequency of complaints about the interaction between employees and customers;
- steadily increasing frequency of use of whistleblowing services;
- and others, specific to each firm.

Note that in order to monitor success, senior management will need to put in place and actively monitor Key Performance Indicators (KPIs) that drive improved decision-making. After reading this book, managers will be well aware that employees will almost certainly attempt to 'game' any measures put in place (as they do with other KPIs) and hence the design of the measures will be important. In particular, changes in KPIs should NOT be tied to an individual's remuneration but like Health and Safety should be a team, division and firm measure of success that uses behavioural reinforcement techniques to promote better decision-making.

11.5 The imperative for change

We are aware from (bitter) experience that change is hard and that change in any organization never goes to plan, as there are always unforeseen circumstances. So the question for a board when facing potential change is whether to take the initiative or whether to wait until change is forced upon them. Their answer to that question depends of course on the specific situation being faced. In the case of People Risk Management, the answer will depend on the Risk Appetite of the board – do directors know what risks they are running and if so are they happy running those risks on behalf of their shareholders? If the answer is genuinely yes, then a board can defer, at least until prodded by regulators or shareholder activists, otherwise the directors should consider at least starting the journey as described in this book.

Notes

1 See, for example, *Daily Telegraph* (2014) New York regulator demands documents from banks in Forex probe, 5 February, www.telegraph.co.uk

2 See, for example, *Reuters* (2014) EU investigates tax rulings on Apple, Starbucks, Fiat, 11 June, www.reuters.com

3 See Coleman (2001) for a description of White Collar Crime.

4 See Heffernan (2011) and Ariely (2013) for a description of 'how we lie to ourselves'.

5 See Perman (2013) and Chapter 4 for the failure of HBOS.

6 See Sutherland (2013) and Heffernan (2011) for descriptions of such experiments.

7 See Turner (1976).

8 See Hillson and Murray-Webster (2012) for a discussion of the concept of *Risk Appetite*.

9 See the Wikipedia article *Principal–agent problem*.

10 See for example *Forbes* (2013) Portfolio careers: is the latest work trend right for you? 27 February, www.forbes.com

11 See Turner (1976).

12 See Chapter 8 and Reason (1990) for a description of the concept of Swiss Cheese risks.

13 See Kahneman (2011.)

14 See for example self-criticism by the FSA of its role in the LIBOR scandal, Financial Services Authority (2013) *FSA publishes its Internal Audit Report on: review of the extent of awareness within the FSA of inappropriate LIBOR submissions*, 5 March, www.fsa.gov.uk

15 See Parliamentary Commission on Banking Standards (2013).

16 A Potemkin Village or Façade refers to the habit of Russian governors of creating false villages to impress visiting dignitaries. Such habits, however, persist until today – see for example *BBC News* (2013) G8 fake shop fronts make headlines, 13 May, www.bbc.com

17 At the same providing good examples of 'action bias'.

18 The notable exceptions are those firms such as WorldCom and Enron where directors and executives conspired to falsify accounting information.

19 See *Bloomberg* (2014) Credit Suisse plea sends warning to banks under scrutiny, 19 May, www.bloomberg.com

20 See Valukas (2010) for a detailed forensic analysis of the failure of Lehman Brothers.

21 In other words, the Lehman Board had chosen to 'arbitrage' its regulators to incorporate in a low regulation jurisdiction.

22 See Parliamentary Commission on Banking Standards (2013).

23 See HM Treasury (2013) *The Government's response to the Parliamentary Commission on Banking Standards*, HM Treasury, London, www.gov.uk

24 See McConnell (2014) Reckless endangerment: the failure of HBOS, *Journal of Risk Management in Financial Institutions*, 7 (2), pp 202–15.

25 For full details see the so-called Penrose Report archived at *BBC* (2004) The Penrose report in full, 8 March, www.bbc.com

26 See Financial Conduct Authority (2013) *Treating Customers Fairly*, www.fca.org.uk

27 See Wheatley, M (2012) *My Vision for the FCA*. Speech by Martin Wheatley at the British Bankers' Association, 25 January, Financial Services Authority, London, available at www.fca.gov.uk/

28 See Kahneman (2011).

29 See the description of the work of the CFPB's Office of Research at http://www.consumerfinance.gov/

30 See Deutsche Bundesbank (2011) *Investor behaviour in theory and practice*, Monthly Report, January, www.bundesbank.de

31 For more on the City Values Forum see www.cityvaluesforum.org.uk

32 Note some firms do not call their firm-wide risk systems an ERM and so People Risk must be integrated into whatever 'framework' they employ.

33 If a board decides that there is no People Risk in their firm, a consideration of possible *confirmation bias* might be in order.

34 As noted in Chapter 2, we recommend that this framework be located within the firm's overall approach to Operational Risk Management.

35 Many similar challenges are described in Chapter 9 in Table 9.1.

36 See Chapter 4, Table 4.3.

37 Staff could start by considering the biases and heuristics literature in the reference section of this book.

38 This implies creating a People Risk Education function, within the existing RMD, from the outset.

39 See Chapter 10 for a description of Personalized Codes of Conduct.

GLOSSARY OF TERMS AND ABBREVIATIONS

		Internet Address
ABN AMRO	A Dutch bank involved in a takeover by Royal Bank of Scotland (see Chapter 4)	
AIB	Allied Irish Bank (see Chapter 4 – Rogue Traders)	
AIC	Australian Institute of Criminology	**www.aic.gov.au**
AMCC	Aviators Model Code of Conduct (see Chapter 10)	**www.secureav.com**
AML	Anti-Money Laundering (see Chapter 4)	
Anglo	Anglo Irish Bank (see Chapter 4)	
APRA	Australian Prudential Regulation Authority	**www.apra.gov.au**
AUD$	Australian Dollar	
BAES	British Aerospace Engineering Systems (see Chapter 4)	
BBA	British Bankers Association (see Chapter 4 LIBOR)	
BBS	Britannia Building Society (see Chapter 4 Co-operative Bank)	
BCP	Business Continuity Planning	
BOS	Bank of Scotland (see HBOS)	
CAA	UK Civil Aviation Authority (see Chapter 10)	**www.caa.co.uk**
CAIB	Columbia Accident Investigation Board	
CDC	US Center for Disease Control (see Chapter 4)	
CDO	Collateralized Debt Obligation – a type of 'derivative' security	
CDS	Credit Default Swaps – a type of 'derivative' security based on the likelihood of a firm defaulting	
CEO	Chief Executive Officer	
CFO	Chief Financial Officer	
CFPB	Consumer Financial Protection Bureau (see Chapter 11)	**www.consumerfinance.org**
CFTC	US Commodity Futures Trading Commission (see Chapter 4)	**www.cftc.gov**

COSO	The Committee of Sponsoring Organizations of the Treadway Commission (see Chapter 2)	**www.coso.org**
CRC	Corporate Responsibility Committee	
CRO	Chief Risk Officer	
CV	Curriculum Vitae	
CVF	City Values Forum (see Chapter 11)	**www.cityvaluesforum.org.uk/**
Derivative	A financial instrument that is created based upon or 'derived' from another financial instrument, such as an Equity Option.	
DOJ	US Department of Justice (see Chapter 4)	
EFQM	European Foundation of Quality Management	
ERM	Enterprise Risk Management (see Chapter 2 COSO)	
FAA	US Federal Aviation Administration (see Chapter 11)	
FCA	Financial Conduct Authority – UK banking regulator	**www.fca.org.uk**
FDA	US Food and Drug Administration (see Chapter 4 – Eli Lilly)	**www.fda.gov**
fMRI	functional Magnetic Resonance Imaging	
FOMC	Federal Open Markets Committee, the rate-setting body of the US Federal Reserve Board (see Chapter 3)	
FRC	UK Financial Reporting Council (see Chapter 6)	**www.frc.org.uk**
FSA	Financial Services Authority – previous UK banking regulator	**www.fsa.org.uk**
GFC	Global Financial Crisis (see Chapter 4)	
GRC	Governance, Risk and Compliance (see Chapter 5)	
H&S	Health and Safety	
HBOS	Halifax/Bank of Scotland (see Chapter 4)	
HR	Human Resources	
HRO	High Reliability Organization (see Chapter 8)	
HRRM	Human Resources Risk Management (see Chapter 8)	
HSBC	Hong Kong and Shanghai Banking Corporation (see Chapter 4)	**www.hsbc.com**
HSE	UK Health and Safety Executive	**www.hse.org.uk**
IB	Inattentional Blindness	
ICB	The Independent Commission on Banking	
IIA	US Institute of Internal Auditors	**www.theiia.org**

IIF	The Institute of International Finance	
ING	Internationale Nederlanden Groep – a Dutch bank	
IOD	UK Institute of Directors (see Chapter 6)	**www.iod.com**
IP	Intellectual Property	
IRD	New Zealand Inland Revenue Department (see Chapter 4 NZ Tax Avoidance)	
IRHP	Interest Rate Hedging Products (see Chapter 4)	
ISO	International Standards Organization (see ISO 31000 in Chapter 5)	
IT	Information Technology	
LBG	Lloyds Banking Group (see Chapter 4 HBOS)	
LIBOR	London Inter-Bank Offering Rate (see Chapter 4)	
LRO	Low Reliability Organization (see Chapter 8)	
LSE	London Stock Exchange	
M&A	Mergers and Acquisitions	
MBS	Mortgage-Backed Security, a derivative based on mortgages	
MIS	Management Information Systems	
MRSP	Manufacturer's Suggested Retail Price	
NAB	National Australia Bank (see Chapter 4 – Rogue Trading)	
NASA	National Aeronautics and Space Administration	
NED	Non-Executive Director	
NHS	UK National Health Service (see Chapter 4)	
OCEG	Open Compliance and Ethics Group	**www.oceg.org**
OFT	UK Office of Fair Trading (see Chapter 4 PPI)	
ORM	Operational Risk Management	
ORX	Operational Riskdata eXchange Association (ORX)	**www.orx.org**
OTS	Office of Thrift Supervision, a US banking regulator, now merged with the Office of the Comptroller of the Currency	**www.occ.org**
PPI	Payment Protection Insurance (see Chapter 4)	
PRM	People Risk Management	
PRMIA	Professional Risk Managers International Association	**www.prmia.org**

PSI	Permanent Subcommittee on Investigations, US Senate investigation committee (see Chapter 4)	
RBS	Royal Bank of Scotland (see Chapter 4)	**www.rbs.com**
RMBS	Residential Mortgage Backed Security, a derivative based on residential mortgages	
RMC	Risk Management Committee of the Board	
RMD	Risk Management Department	
RMF	Risk Management Framework	
RSA	Risk Self-Assessment (see Chapter 5)	
S&L	Savings and Loan – a type of US bank (see Chapter 4)	
SFO	UK Serious Fraud Office (see Chapter 4)	
SIB	Systemically Important Banks (see Chapter 4)	
SIFI	Systemically Important Financial Institutions (see Chapter 4)	
SID	Senior Independent Director (see Chapter 6)	
SOX	Sarbanes-Oxley Act (see Chapter 10)	
SPE	Special Purpose Entity (see Chapter 4 – Enron)	
SSN	Social Security Number	
SWIFT	The Society for Worldwide Interbank Financial Telecommunication – an organization that is used to communicate highly sensitive information, such as payment details, between financial institutions	**www.swift.org**
TCF	Treating Customers Fairly	
TEPCO	Tokyo Electric Power Company (see Chapter 4 – Fukushima)	
TPS	Toyota Production System (see Chapter 9)	
UBS	Union Bank Switzerland	
WAMU	Washington Mutual a bank that collapsed in the GFC (see Chapter 4)	
WCC	White Collar Crime (see Chapter 2)	

REFERENCES

Adams, J (1995) *Risk*, UCL Press, London

Ariely, D (2008) *Predictably Irrational: The hidden forces that shape our decisions*, HarperCollins, London

Ariely, D (2013) *The (Honest) Truth about Dishonesty*, HarperCollins, London

Barrett, R (1998) *Liberating the Corporate Soul: Building a visionary organization*, Butterworth-Heinmann, Woburn

Blastland, M and Spiegelhalter, D (2013) *The Norm Chronicles: Stories and numbers about danger*, Profile Books, London

Blunden, T and Thirlwell, J (2010) *Mastering Operational Risk*, Pearson Education, Harlow

Carswell, S (2011) *Anglo Republic: Inside the bank that broke Ireland*, Penguin, London

Chabris, C and Simons, D (2010) *The Invisible Gorilla: And other ways our intuition deceives us*, HarperCollins, New York

Coates, J (2012) *The Hour Between Dog and Wolf: Risk-taking, gut feelings and the biology of boom and bust*, Fourth Estate, London

Coleman, J (2001) *The Criminal Elite: Understanding white collar crime*, 5th edition, Worth, New York

Fenton-O'Creevy, M, Nicholson, N, Soane, E and Willman, P (2007) *Traders, Risks, Decisions and Management in Financial Markets*, Oxford University Press, Oxford

Ferguson, C (2012) *Inside Job: The financiers who pulled off the heist of the century*, Oneworld Publications, London

Financial Crisis Inquiry Commission (2011) *Final report of the national commission on the causes of the financial and economic crisis in the United States*, Financial Crisis Inquiry Commission, Washington

Financial Reporting Council (2011) *Guidance on board effectiveness*, Financial Reporting Council, London

Fine, C (2007) *A Mind of Its Own: How your brain distorts and deceives*, Icon Books, London

Festinger, L (1957) *A Theory of Cognitive Dissonance*, Stanford University Press, Stanford

Flyvbjerg, B, Bruzelius, N and Rothengatter, W (2003) *Megaprojects and Risk: An anatomy of ambition*, Cambridge University Press, Cambridge

Fraser, I (2014) *Shredded: Inside RBS, the bank that broke Britain*, Birlinn, Edinburgh

Gawande, A (2010) *The Checklist Manifesto: How to get things right*, Profile Books, London

Geller, E (2001) *Working Safe*, CRC Press, Boca Raton

Gigerenzer, G (2008) *Gut Feelings: The intelligence of the unconscious*, Penguin, New York

Gigerenzer, G (2010) *Rationality for Mortals: How people cope with uncertainty*, (Evolution and Cognition Series), Oxford University Press, Oxford

Gigerenzer, G (2014) *Risk savvy: How to make good decisions*, Penguin, New York

Gleick, J (1992) *Genius: Richard Feynman and modern physics*, Abacus, London

Gray, D and Watt, P (2013) *Giving victims a voice: joint report into sexual allegations made against Jimmy Savile*, Metropolitan Police Service and National Society for the Prevention of Cruelty to Children, London

Grind, K (2013) *The Lost Bank: The story of Washington Mutual – The biggest bank failure in American history*, Simon and Schuster, New York

Hallinan, J (2009) *Errornomics: Why we make mistakes and what we can do to avoid them*, Ebury Press, London

Heffernan, M (2011) *Wilful Blindness: Why we ignore the obvious at our peril*, Simon and Schuster, London

Hillson, D and Murray-Webster, R (2012) *A Short Guide to Risk Appetite*, Gower Publishing, Farnham

Hilts, P (1996) *Smokescreen: The truth behind the tobacco industry cover-up*, Addison-Wesley, New York

Independent Commission on Banking (2011) *Final report – recommendations*, Independent Commission on Banking, London, September

Janis, I (1971) Groupthink: The desperate drive for consensus at any cost, in Shafritz, Ott and Jang (eds) *Classics of Organization Theory*, Wadsworth, Belmont

Kahneman, D, Slovic, P and Tversky, A (1982) *Judgment Under Uncertainty: Heuristics and biases*, Cambridge University Press, Cambridge

Kahneman, D (2011) *Thinking, Fast and Slow*, Allen Lane, London

Leeson, N and Whitley, E (1996) *Rogue Trader: How I brought down Barings Bank and shook the financial world*, Little Brown, London

Levering, R and Moskowitz, M (1993) *100 Best Companies to Work for in America*, Plume Books, New York

Lucey, B, Larkin, C and Gurdgiev, C (2012) *What if Ireland Defaults?* Orpen Press, Dublin

Martin, I (2013) *Making It Happen: Fred Goodwin, RBS and the men who blew up the British economy*, Simon and Schuster, London

McDonald, L and Robinson, P (2009) *A Colossal Failure of Common Sense: The incredible inside story of the collapse of Lehman Brothers*, Random House, New York

McLean, B and Elkind, P (2004) *The Smartest Guys in the Room: The amazing rise and scandalous fall of Enron*, Penguin, New York

Mintzberg, H (1978) *The Structuring of Organizations (Theory of Management Policy)*, Prentice Hall, New Jersey

Mintzberg, H (2005) *Managers Not MBAs: A hard look at the soft practice of managing and management development*, Berrett-Koehler Publishers, San Fransisco

Nyberg, P (2011) *Misjudging Risk: Causes of the systemic banking crisis in Ireland*, Ministry of Finance, Dublin

Parliamentary Commission on Banking Standards (2013) *Changing banking for good, Volumes I & II*, Parliamentary Commission on Banking Standards, published 4 June by authority of the House of Commons, London

Parliamentary Commission on Banking Standards (2013a) *An accident waiting to happen: The failure of HBOS, Vols I & II*, Parliamentary Commission on Banking Standards, published in April by authority of the House of Commons, London

Pande, P, Neuman, R and Cavanagh, R (2000) *The Six Sigma Way: How GE, Motorola, and other top companies are honing their performance*, McGraw-Hill, New York

Payne, B (2012) *White-Collar Crime: The essentials*, Sage, Los Angeles

Perman, R (2013) *Hubris: How HBOS wrecked the best bank in Britain*, Birlinn, Edinburgh

Permanent Subcommittee On Investigations (2011) *Wall Street and the financial crisis: anatomy of a financial collapse*, US Senate Permanent Subcommittee On Investigations, United States Senate, Washington

Permanent Subcommittee On Investigations (2012) *US vulnerabilities to money laundering, drugs, and terrorist financing: HSBC case history*, US Senate Permanent Subcommittee on Investigations, United States Senate, Washington

Permanent Subcommittee On Investigations (2013) *JPMorgan Chase whale trades: a case history of derivatives risks and abuses report and exhibits*, US Senate Permanent Subcommittee on Investigations, United States Senate, Washington

Perrow, C (1999) *Normal Accidents: Living with high-risk technologies*, Princeton University Press, Princeton

Quinn, R and Cameron, K (2011) *Diagnosing and Changing Organizational Culture: Based on the competing values framework*, John Wiley and Sons, San Francisco

Rawnsley, J (1995) *Going For Broke: Nick Leeson and the collapse Of Barings Bank*, HarperCollins, London

Reason, J (1990) *Human Error*, Cambridge University Press, Cambridge

Reason, J (2008) *The Human Contribution: Unsafe acts, accidents and heroic recoveries*, Ashgate, Farnham

Reinhart, C and Rogoff, K (2011) *This Time Is Different: Eight centuries of financial folly*, Princeton University Press, Princeton

Roth, J (2010) *Best Practices: Evaluating the corporate culture*, The Institute of Internal Auditors Research Foundation, Altamonte Springs

Schiller, R (2005) *Irrational Exuberance*, Princeton University Press, Princeton

Schiller, R (2008) *The Subprime Solution*, Princeton University Press, Princeton

Sharot, T (2011) *The Optimism Bias: Why we are wired to look on the bright side*, Pantheon Books, New York

Sherfin, H (2008) *Ending the Management Illusion: Eliminate the mental traps that threaten your organization's success*, McGraw Hill, New York

Slywotzky, A (2007) *The Upside: The 7 strategies for turning big threats into growth breakthroughs*, Crown Business, New York

Sutcliffe, K and Weick, K (2007) *Managing the Unexpected*: *Resilient performance in an age of uncertainty*, Jossey-Bass, San Francisco

Sutherland, S (2013) *Irrationality: The enemy within*, Pinter & Martin, London

Swartz, M and Watkins, S (2003) *Power Failure: The inside story of the collapse of Enron*, Doubleday, New York

Thaler, R and Sunstein, C (2008) *Nudge: Improving decisions about health, wealth, and happiness*, Harvard University Press, Harvard

Tibman, J (2009) *The Murder of Lehman Brothers*, Bricktower Press, New York

Toft, B and Reynolds, S (1994) *Learning from Disasters*, Butterworth-Heinmann, Oxford

Travis, C and Aronson, E (2008) *Mistakes Were Made (But Not by Me): Why we justify foolish beliefs, bad decisions, and hurtful acts*, Mariner Books, New York

Turner, B (1976) The organisational and interorganisational development of disasters, *Administrative Science Quarterly*, 21, pp 387–97

Valukas, A (2010) *In re Lehman Brothers Holdings Inc. – Report of Anton R Valukas – Bankruptcy Examiner*, United States Bankruptcy Court Southern District Of New York, New York

Vose, D (2008) *Risk Analysis: A quantitative guide*, John Wiley and Sons, Chichester

Werhane, P, Hartman, L, Archer, C, Englehardt, E and Pritchard, M (2013) *Obstacles to Ethical Decision-making: Mental models, Milgram and the problem of obedience*, Cambridge University Press, Cambridge

INDEX